WOUNDED INNOCENTS

WOUNDED INNOCENTS

The Real Victims of the War Against Child Abuse

RICHARD WEXLER

Prometheus Books
Buffalo, New York

31610166
DLC

4-21-95

98 97 96 95   7 6 5 4

Library of Congress Cataloging-in-Publication Data

Wexler, Richard, 1953–
    Wounded innocents: the real victims of the war against child abuse / Richard Wexler. — [Rev. ed.]
        p.   cm.
    Includes bibliographical references and index.
    ISBN 0-87975-936-4
    1. Child abuse—United States—Case studies. 2. Child abuse—United States—Prevention. 3. Foster home care—United States. 4. Abused children—Services for—United States. I. Title.
    HV6626.52W44   1995
    363.2'595554'0973—dc20   94-39970
                                                                     CIP

Printed in the United States of America on acid-free paper

FOR CELIA AND VALERIE
The family I want most to preserve.

Table of Contents

Acknowledgments

There are a great many people without whom this book would not be possible, but there is one to whom I owe a debt above all others. It is my wife, Celia Viggo Wexler, who insisted that I could write this book and inspired me to try. She helped me through every step of writing the proposal and finding a publisher—Prometheus Books was her idea. Celia took over most of the running of the household for a year—on top of her demanding job as Legislative Director of New York State Common Cause—so I could have the time to write this book while still earning a living.

And she did much more. Celia is an accomplished journalist, and she took the raw material of each chapter and lent her considerable skills to shaping it into the final product. Every chapter bears her imprint. I mention her first so the reader who proceeds no further will at least know this much. I owe her more than I can ever repay.

I am also grateful to the many people who relived the pain of their own encounters with the child savers in the hope that others would not have to suffer as they did. In particular I would like to thank the Humlens, the Gabriels, the Dickersons, the Meyers, the families I call the Bennetts and the Heaths, and the many people whose stories I did not have room to include in this volume. And in particular I would like to thank a former foster child I refer to as Anne Williamson. Many years ago, she opened my eyes to what foster care was all about and planted the seed that would one day grow into this book.

People who work with families in trouble never have enough time for their own work, yet scores of them gave generously of their time to help me with mine. Without their help neither this book, nor much of my previous work on this topic, would have been possible.

Although I am critical of press coverage of child abuse in general, there are many exceptions. In putting together a picture of system failure from around the nation, I have drawn on the outstanding work of Tom Charlier and Shirley Downing of the Memphis *Commercial Appeal,* Suzanne Daley of the *New York Times,* Henry Goldman and Dan Meyers of the *Philadelphia Inquirer,* Debbie Nathan, whose work has appeared in the *Village Voice,* Kent Pollock of the *Sacramento Bee,* Caroline Young of the *Seattle Post-Intelligencer,* Dan Zegart, formerly of the Newburgh, N.Y., *Evening News,* and many others.

This book had its genesis in work I have done as a reporter for more than thirteen years. I have been fortunate in having a number of employers who believed in trusting and supporting their employees, even when they wanted to explore new and unconventional territory. In particular, I would like to thank Virginia Bacheler, John Irving, Mary Anna Towler, and Jack Mitchell. And I would like to thank Erwin Knoll, editor of *The Progressive,* where my article "Invasion of the Child Savers" was published in 1985.

My literary agent, Kathi Paton, guided me through the process of creating a book proposal that would convince a publisher to take a risk on an unknown writer with an unfashionable point of view.

Several editors at Prometheus Books helped me shape the final product. In particular, I would like to thank Bob Basil for his guidance and, especially, his trust. Jeanne O'Day and Mary Beth Gehrman also gave the manuscript their close attention and made crucial improvements.

Wherever there is accomplishment there is somewhere a teacher who helped make it possible. The influence of many teachers is in this volume, among them, Steve Brown, Fred Friendly, Phyllis Garland and Dan Kramer.

And finally, a book about why families are so important would not be possible if not for my firsthand experience. For that, I thank my parents, Eugene and Evelyn Wexler, and my brother, Steve.

1

Overview

In the Los Angeles County suburb of El Monte, a little girl cried herself to sleep and nobody listened.

Jennifer Humlen had been bruised on her arms and legs. Some of her blonde hair had been pulled out. She was filthy. She was dehydrated. She had a fever. She had an ear infection.

Jennifer Humlen was sixteen months old.

Jennifer Humlen was a victim of child abuse. But she was not abused by her parents. Her condition was the result of three days of the best efforts of the state of California to "protect" her.

Jennifer's substitute "home" was the MacLaren Children's Center, the place of last resort for children Los Angeles County officials suspect are abused or neglected, when everyplace else is full.

The current director says the place has been refurbished in recent years, but when Jennifer Humlen was there, MacLaren Hall, as it is commonly called, was a cold, ugly building once used to house juvenile criminals.

Everything was harsh at MacLaren Hall. Children were forced to wear prison-style uniforms, they slept on steel-frame beds with sagging mattresses, and there were no curtains in the showers. Even the soap was harsh. "If we could just get someone on a continuing basis to give soap that wouldn't hurt the kids," said a volunteer who works with children at the center.

Jennifer Humlen shared MacLaren Hall with 250 to 300 other children from infants to teenagers. It was chronically overcrowded and understaffed. It was one of those places that eats up administrators. Eight of them came and went between 1976 and 1986. Every few years there's another scandal.

Children are overmedicated to keep them under control. Children are physically and sexually abused. An infant's death is covered up. Staff members hauled into court plead "no contest" to dealing drugs.[1]

At the very time Jennifer Humlen was confined to MacLaren Hall, the facility was under investigation. A Grand Jury report said there was evidence to support the allegations of abuse and drug trafficking. The report urged that children under two be removed from the center.

Jennifer was supposedly being protected from her mother, Elene Humlen.[2] Like about two million other Americans every year, Humlen had been accused of child abuse.[3] Like more than one million of them, Humlen had been *falsely* accused of child abuse. For the Humlen family it was a nightmare from which they will never fully recover. There are more than a million such nightmares in America every year.

Elene Humlen is a single mother of two. At the time she was accused, she had a good job as fleet sales manager for a car dealership and a strong support network at home, including her mother and lots of friends and neighbors. She is the sort of parent who will drive an hour through Southern California traffic for an appointment with the children's pediatrician, because the doctor an hour away is better than the ones whose offices are more convenient.

Elene Humlen was not accused of abusing Jennifer. The incident involved her son Christopher, then age nine.

On May 7, 1985, Elene Humlen let Chris go to class at Laurel Elementary School in Whittier with a bruise over his nose and right eye. That was her first mistake.

Two days earlier Chris and two friends had been playing catch with a tennis ball on the front lawn of the Humlen home on Danbrook Drive in Whittier. They had been using a "pitchback," an aluminum frame with a net designed to pitch the ball back at you. The bruise was caused when Chris tried to catch the ball and missed.

When he arrived at school his teacher was concerned about whether Chris should go to gym class. He asked the school nurse to take a look at him. Chris told the nurse what happened. He thought the nurse believed him. But school nurses are legally required to report any suspicion of child abuse to authorities. Although the suspicion is supposed to be "reasonable," mandated "reporters" are bombarded with material telling them to report just about anything.

The nurse did not call Elene Humlen to ask what had happened. Instead, she called the Los Angeles County Department of Children's Services. The department got in touch with the County Sheriff.

At 2:20 that afternoon, all the other children were dismissed for the day. Chris Humlen was told to wait. Laurel Elementary School is only two blocks from the Humlen home. Chris is a very reliable child, so when he was forty minutes late returning from school that day, his mother began to worry. Elene's younger sister, Jeannette, said she would walk over to the school and see what was going on.

"Go bye-bye? Go bye-bye?" It was Jennifer, asking to go with her aunt. "You can't just say 'bye-bye' to Jennifer," Elene Humlen says. So she let Jennifer go along. That was her second mistake.

At first, Jeannette barely noticed the sheriff's car outside the school. She was directed to the nurse's office, but as soon as she identified herself she was rushed out before she caught sight of Chris. Inside, a tearful Chris Humlen was under interrogation. He had already explained everything to his teacher, to the nurse, to the school principal, and to a caseworker. Now he was telling his story to two men wearing uniforms and carrying guns.

And, Chris Humlen would later recall, the men with the guns were calling him a liar.

"They just kept on saying, 'Chris, don't lie.' And they were very pushy. They said, 'Come on, tell me the truth! Tell me the truth!' " Chris said.

Later, the deputies would explain that they took custody of the children in part because Chris seemed nervous and didn't make eye contact with them when he was questioned.

Outside, Jeannette Humlen was becoming increasingly anxious. People kept giving her conflicting explanations of what was going on. Then the social worker came out and demanded to examine Jennifer. She and the deputies found no indication of abuse or neglect and no reason to suspect it. They took her away anyway.

Neither the sheriffs nor the caseworker drove the two blocks to the Humlen home to talk to Elene. Although Chris had given them the first names of the friends he was playing with when he was hurt, no one went to the neighborhood to question them. And no one talked to the Humlens' pediatrician, who would have vouched for what a good parent Elene Humlen is. Instead, Jennifer was grabbed from her aunt's arms. She and Chris were hustled into the sheriff's car and driven off. They clung to each other as they were driven from place to place. No one would tell them where they were going or if they would ever see their family again.

Jeannette was frantic. She begged the caseworker for an explanation. "No," she said as she walked out the door. "I have another appointment. Here's my card."

First the children were taken to a police station, then to La Mirada Community Hospital, where they were X-rayed from head to toe. Fortunately, neither child had ever broken a bone. They were examined by Dr. Eloisa Vega, who found no injuries to Jennifer and only the bruise over Chris's eye and nose. Later, Vega would testify that Chris's injury was entirely consistent with the story he had told—the one nobody would believe. Yet in her report, under the heading "Impression," Vega wrote: "suspected child abuse." This was not a medical judgment. Vega testified that she always writes "suspected child abuse" when law enforcement officers bring a child to the emergency room. Why? Because there must be some suspicion of child abuse. Why else would they be bringing the child in?

By now it was early evening. Chris and Jennifer were back in the sheriff's car, headed for a foster home. Chris remembers: "They said, 'Chris, this is where you're going to be living from now on.' I asked if I could stay with my sister. They said: 'No you can't, because this is all boys.' "

Chris would not let go of his sister. He wanted to protect her. "I was hugging her," he said.

The people responsible for the "protection" of Chris and Jennifer Humlen pulled them apart. Chris was escorted inside as his sister's screams pierced the night air. Then the child savers drove Jennifer Humlen to MacLaren Hall.

*   *   *

The war against child abuse has become a war against children.

Every year, we let hundreds of children die, force thousands more to live with strangers, and throw a million innocent families into chaos. We call this "child protection."

For most of this century Americans denied the existence of child abuse. Doctors even speculated that some children's bones might be exceptionally fragile, rather than accept what they were seeing.[4] "People don't want to admit it," says J. Lawrence Aber, professor of clinical psychology at Columbia University. "They deny it and deny it and deny it, and when it finally breaks through they can't stand the pain of it." As a result, says Aber, "we went from doing nothing to trying to do everything."[5]

This book is about what trying to do everything has done to children.

It is not the first time we have tried. More than a hundred years ago wealthy Americans organized Societies for the Prevention of Cruelty to Children. They were given enormous power to destroy families—and they wielded it freely, almost always at the expense of the poor and disfavored ethnic groups, especially recent immigrants. That's not how these people saw themselves, of course. They considered themselves "child savers"—and that is the name they proudly gave themselves.

The nineteenth-century child saving movement was fueled by horror stories about what some parents did to their children. Today, it is no different.

In 1973, Senator Walter Mondale held a series of hearings that led to the passage of the federal Child Abuse Prevention and Treatment Act, the law that established the framework for the child-protective system as we know it today. Mondale wrote that nothing he had seen in his time in the Senate was as horrifying "as the stories and photos of children, many of them infants, who had been whipped and beaten with razor straps; burned and mutilated by cigarettes and lighters; scalded by boiling water; bruised and battered by physical assaults and starved and neglected and malnourished."[6]

Mondale himself worried that the law that emerged from these hearings might be too broad and could hurt innocent families.[7] But any such doubts were forgotten in the hysteria surrounding demands to "crack down on child abuse."

Believing that only the most brutal parental conduct was affected— so obviously the law only affected *them* and not *us*—Americans eagerly surrendered their most fundamental liberties to the child savers.

We have turned almost everyone who deals with children in the course of his or her work into an informer, required to report any suspicion of any form of child maltreatment, and we have encouraged the general public to do the same. We have allowed such reports to be made anonymously, making the system a potent tool for harassment.

We allow untrained, inexperienced, sometimes incompetent workers to label parents as abusers and even to remove children from their homes entirely on their own authority.

We have drastically lowered the traditional burdens of proof and relaxed the standards of evidence used during the investigative process and in court.

We have effectively repealed the Fourth Amendment, which protects both parents *and children* against unreasonable searches and seizures.

We have severely eroded the Fourteenth Amendment, which guarantees parents *and children* that they will not be deprived of their liberty without due process of law.

And we have forgone even more fundamental rights.

After she botched the famous "mass molestation" case in Jordan, Minnesota, prosecutor Kathleen Morris declared herself "sick to death of things like the presumption of innocence."[8] She needn't worry. In the real world of American justice that presumption has always been difficult to maintain. In child abuse cases, it's dead.

A standard form letter is sent to parents by the Massachusetts Department of Social Services when it declares a case "substantiated" and lists the parent in a central registry. That letter includes the following explanation for the decision: "At least one person said you were responsible for the incident and there was no available information to *definitively indicate otherwise*" (emphasis added).[9]

A mistrial was declared in a Texas case after a juror admitted she voted for conviction even though she really believed the defendant was innocent. She had been afraid to vote not guilty because she didn't want to be labeled as someone who "condones child abuse."[10]

The world of the child savers seems like something created by Franz Kafka with an assist from Joseph Heller. Susan Gabriel, whose husband Clark was falsely accused of molesting his stepdaughter, recounts this dialogue with one caseworker:

> Caseworker: We know your husband is guilty, you've got to force him into admitting it.
> Gabriel: How do you know he's guilty?
> Caseworker: We know he's guilty because he says he's innocent. Guilty people always say they're innocent.
> Gabriel: What do innocent people say?
> Caseworker: We're not in the business of guilt or innocence, we're in the business of putting families back together.
> Gabriel: So why not do that with us?
> Caseworker: Because Clark won't admit his guilt.[11]

Even some of the people who work in the system are starting to have second thoughts. "If the level of intrusiveness perpetrated allegedly to protect children were attempted in any other field, we would be in court . . . we would be in jail, we would have the Supreme Court coming down with innumerable decisions against us," says Philip Leduc, a veteran Child Protective Services (CPS) supervisor in Northampton, Massachusetts.[12]

Adds Robert Moro, a CPS supervisor in Worcester, and vice president of the caseworkers' union in Massachusetts: "Maybe we're just too damn intrusive."[13]

Part of what is fueling skepticism about Child Protective Services is the realization that the system has grown so far beyond its original mandate that the kind of cases Mondale described represent no more than 3 percent of what child savers now investigate under the rubric "child abuse." Sexual abuse represents another 6 percent.[14] The rest range from cases of marginal child-rearing, which could benefit from a helping hand instead of a slap in the face, to cases that are totally false. Yet we have applied to all of these cases the reporting laws, the power to remove children from their parents at will, the low standards of proof, and all the rest of what is erroneously called a "child-protective" system.

Douglas Besharov, founding director of the National Center on Child Abuse and Neglect (NCCAN—an agency created by the Mondale law), writes that current laws "encourage would-be reporters to report *any* minor assault, *any* suggestion of sexual abuse, and *any* marginally inadequate child care, without regard to the real danger to the child—and without regard to the harmful consequences of an unfounded report" (emphasis in original).[15]

About 60 percent of these reports are simply false. Of the remainder, the vast majority are cases of "neglect." What is neglect?

In Ohio, it's when a child's "condition or environment is such as to warrant the state, in the interests of the child, in assuming his guardianship." In Illinois, it's failure to provide "the proper or necessary support . . . for a child's well-being." In Mississippi, it's when a child is "without proper care, custody, supervision, or support." In South Dakota, it's when the child's "environment is injurious to his welfare." Lest any South Dakota child saver still hesitate, the Legislature added that "this chapter shall be liberally construed in favor of the state."[16]

Patrick Murphy, Cook County (Illinois) Public Guardian and former head of the Juvenile Litigation office of the Legal Aid Society of Chicago, writes that "the [neglect] statute is one of those broad nets of legislation that catch every fish swimming through and allow the fisherman to pick which he wants to keep and which he wants to throw back. Social agencies proposed it and social agencies love it."[17]

What is neglect? Anything a child saver wants it to be.

And these are some of the things they want it to be.

The National Committee for Prevention of Child Abuse (NCPCA) spent more than $2.5 million in fiscal year 1988 (not including what state affiliates spent)[18] to tell us that parents are guilty of neglect if they give their children money to go to McDonald's for breakfast too often.[19] NCPCA also has some advice for detecting child abusers. If someone looks at a young girl and says "wait 'til she grows up," that "might indicate" that the adult is a child molester.[20] And then there's the California psychologist who says that if a child has a "fear of monsters" and laughs and imitates the sound of a playmate passing gas, the child may have been molested— by a Satanic cult.[21]

Joe Pickard has seen the system close up. Now a lawyer in private practice, he used to prosecute abuse and neglect cases for a county department of social services in Colorado. "I have a six-year-old son," says Pickard. "I won't live in another county where they don't know me. . . . Attorneys' children have been taken. It can happen to anybody."[22]

The results of all this are predictable. Parents have been deemed child abusers for not letting children watch television after 7:30 P.M., for being late to pick up children after school, and for a host of similar "offenses." But most of all, just as they did more than a century ago, child savers report parents to authorities, substantiate cases against them, and take away their children, solely because the families are poor.

The broad definitions of neglect used in most state statutes are virtually definitions of poverty. Children are taken away because the family doesn't have a place to live. Children are taken away because the food stamps have run out. Children are taken away because the family can't pay for heat.

In Chicago, a widower with a heart condition lost his children because he couldn't pay the electric bill. The caseworker accused him of "financial neglect."[23]

The system has grown so huge that one out of every thirty children nationwide is reported to Child Protective Services as allegedly abused or neglected every year. In California, it's one out of twenty. In Missouri, it's one out of seventeen. In San Francisco, it's one out of ten.[24]

Besharov argues that the present child-protective system is like a 911 emergency dispatch system "that cannot distinguish between life-threatening crimes and littering."[25]

At a legislative hearing, Kermit Wiltse, Professor Emeritus of social work at the University of California at Berkeley, summed up the system this way: "We have a monster on our hands."[26]

*   *   *

When Jeannette Humlen raced home from Chris's school, "she was so hysterical I couldn't find out what happened," Elene Humlen recalls. "I thought she'd had a car accident. All she could do was stand there and scream, 'They took the kids! They took the kids!' "

Then Elene spotted the social worker's business card in Jeannette's hand. But when she called she couldn't get through to her. Finally, "I just said, give me a supervisor, give me anyone, you've got my children!"

After what seemed like a lifetime on hold, a supervisor came on the line and told her the one thing she already knew: The Department of Children's Services (DCS) had Chris and Jennifer in custody.

"But why?" Elene asked.

"I'm not handling the case," the supervisor replied. "I can't discuss any allegations."

"Where are they?"

"I'm not handling it."

"Do I need a lawyer?"

"Absolutely not. If you didn't do anything wrong, there's nothing to worry about."

"I want my kids. I have to see them now. I have to talk to you. What can I do?"

"Relax. The kids are safe. Don't worry. Go out to dinner, have a good time."

The worker said the children would be returned if there was no problem. "I was halfway hoping the police would pull into the driveway any minute and drop them off," Elene said. "Part of me kept saying, 'They'll drop them off any minute and apologize.' "

Of course they didn't. Instead, it was the beginning of what Humlen calls "four days of hell.

"It was nothing but pacing, crying, calling anybody and everybody. You can't describe it. Where are the kids? What are they thinking? Jenny can't talk; how can anybody explain to her that we didn't dump her?"

Wisely ignoring the advice of the supervisor, Elene called several lawyers, looking for one who would see her right away. She finally found an attorney who at least was able to find out that Chris was in a foster home, Jennifer was in MacLaren Hall, and there would be a court hearing in three days.

The hearing was the first time Elene saw her son since he had been taken. Chris was brought into the courtroom only briefly, toward the end of the hearing. "He was very scared, very pale. He kept saying, 'I want my mommy.' We hung onto each other for dear life.

"The court was a zoo," Elene said. "The entire neighborhood showed up with me. I thought we would be able to speak."

But only the lawyers spoke. Through her lawyer, Elene offered to move out of her house and let her mother or her sister take care of the children. If that wasn't good enough, she offered, how about placing them with a friend or neighbor? But the lawyer representing the Department of Children's Services was adamant, and judges rarely overrule the child savers at these hearings.

By this time, Chris Humlen had an attorney of his own.[27] The attorney, Norman Kallen, had no doubt that the Humlen children belonged at home with their mother. The DCS "took things out of proportion and created an unnecessary problem," Kallen said. "It was a very unfortunate situation that could have been avoided had there been a more thorough investigation." Kallen said he argued forcefully for the children's return. Humlen recalls Kallen pointing to Chris and yelling at the judge: "Look at his face! Look at it!"

The judge refused to return the children, but granted motions by Kallen for another hearing the following week and—over DCS objections—allowed Elene one visit with each child.

Humlen headed immediately for MacLaren Hall, where she found Jennifer, bruised and feverish, "writhing and crying." When she demanded to know what happened, one of the staff said, "Maybe one of the other kids got to her." That's possible. Children from ages one to three all are housed together at MacLaren.[28]

Humlen did the only thing she could do. She screamed bloody murder until someone agreed to move Jennifer to the infirmary.

Humlen's lawyer tried to get Eloisa Vega, the emergency room doctor who had first examined Jennifer, to come out to MacLaren Hall and see what three days of state care had done to her. But Vega said she could only examine children brought to her in the hospital.

Meanwhile, Chris Humlen was returned from court to the foster home.

When part of his experience becomes too painful to talk about, Chris says, "It's hard to explain." Living in the foster home is one of the things Chris finds too "hard to explain."

But there is one thing he remembers vividly. Some of the other boys in the home were foster-care pros. And they had given Chris a warning: If you're not returned home after your first court hearing, you never go back.

*　　*　　*

Dear Ann Landers: Recently my wife and I took our two sons out to dinner. We returned home an hour after the boys' normal bedtime. When our youngest son refused to get ready for bed, he received an open-handed spanking on his trousered bottom. His yelling and mine must have attracted the well-meaning attention of a neighbor.

An hour later, when the kids were sound asleep, the police and a child-abuse investigator arrived and took control of our lives for the next three hours.

They tied up the services of social service, police, and medical personnel. It left our children fearful that they could be separated from us by some unknown agency. It also made them distrustful of law enforcement personnel . . .

Something must be done to help victims of child abuse, but reporting every incident of parental discipline because it is not in accord with one's personal outlook is not a cure.—Wrongly Accused in L.A.

Dear L.A.: Authorities have methods of distinguishing between parental discipline and abuse. . . . Apparently no charges were pressed. I'm glad to know the Los Angeles folks responded so. Four cheers for them!

The vast majority of Americans probably would give Ann Landers four cheers for her answer. How dare that family complain about a little inconvenience when children's lives are at stake?

That's certainly the bill of goods the child savers have sold to the American public. And it isn't just the average citizen who is buying.

No court of law would say that police have the right to enter a home at will and strip-search the occupants solely because an anonymous tipster accused those people of a crime, no matter how heinous. Yet a federal district court in Illinois says child-protective workers should have the right to strip-search children—who of course have been accused of no crime at all—on just such flimsy evidence. Judge John A. Nordberg wrote that "this court finds that the life of even one child is too great a price to pay" for requiring more evidence before stripping children.[29]

A speaker at a public hearing in Missouri was certainly speaking for most Americans when she said that the worst that can happen to families under the present system is that they will "feel a real infringement upon their privacy. . . . [But] adults can and must tolerate frustration, inconvenience, and even anger more easily than children can tolerate abuse or neglect."[30]

When the issue of child saving is debated at all, that's generally how the debate is framed. And the child savers have all the good applause lines. They are the defenders of "children's rights." They are "child focused." They tell us that "no child ever died of a social work evaluation." And, most often of all, they tell us we must "err on the side of the child."

Lip service is paid to a "delicate balance" between children's lives and some amorphous concept of family privacy, but even the people who say it don't seem to believe it. And no wonder. How can there be a "delicate balance" between the torture of an innocent child and a parent's "feeling" that his or her privacy has been infringed upon? If that were really what this issue was about, I wouldn't believe it either.

I am not in favor of "parents' rights." The problem with our present child protective system is not that it hurts parents, though of course it does. *The problem with our child-protective system is that it hurts children.*

It hurts children who have never been maltreated, by disrupting their families, invading their privacy, and jeopardizing the bond of trust that is essential for healthy parent-child relationships. This is potentially serious psychological harm. It should not be brushed aside the way Ann Landers brushed off "Wrongly Accused in L.A."

It hurts children who may, in fact, have been neglected, as well as those who have suffered no harm at all, by making it too easy to pull them from their homes and place them in the nation's chaotic system of foster care. Often that leaves them worse off than if the state had never "helped" them at all. Children have been taken from their parents because their housing is inadequate, because their home is dirty, or because they don't have enough food in the refrigerator. Children have been taken from their parents because a child-protective worker botched the simple arithmetic on a "risk assessment form." Children have been taken from their parents because the abuse allegation was reported at 4:30 P.M. on a Friday and the worker wanted to go home for the weekend before doing an investigation.

"They would have you believe that the system works so well that they only separate children when it's absolutely necessary," says Martin Guggenheim, former director of the family law clinic at New York University Law School. "That's bullshit. They separate children for petty reasons and for no reason all the time."[31]

Often children are separated not only from their parents but from their brothers and sisters as well. Once placed the children often spend months or years bouncing from home to home, losing all chance to form a loving or trusting relationship with anyone.

"Mommy, do you love me?" a former foster child remembers asking her foster mother when she was five years old. "Of course I *like* you," the foster mother replied. Said the former foster child: "I was old enough to know the difference."[32]

"Foster care is the garbage dump," says another woman who survived it. "That's what they do with kids when they don't know what else to do with them—throw 'em in foster care."[33]

In at least one state, the same child savers who remove children for the slightest infraction on the part of their parents maintain that *they* have no responsibility for those children whatsoever once they are taken away and placed in foster care.[34]

Perhaps worst of all, the system does terrible harm to the children who need help the most, those who have been severely abused.

False and trivial reports flood the system, cascading down upon untrained, inexperienced workers who already have far more than they can handle, stealing their time and attention from the children who really do need their intervention.

In New York State, calls surge into a child-protective "hotline" and are immediately forwarded, with little or no screening, to local offices for investigation. In New York City, many of those cases pile up in boxes on office floors because no one has time to investigate them.[35] In Illinois, caseworkers carry loads of sixty to one hundred cases each. Says one Illinois caseworker: "If she worked for our agency for two minutes, even Mother Teresa would be a bad worker."[36]

In Virginia, the demand that more and more cases be reported led to an increase of 12,000 investigations between 1980 and 1986. Yet the investigators found a total of 3,000 fewer cases of abuse or neglect.[37] The same thing happened in New York State between 1980 and 1985: the number of reports soared, but the number of substantiated cases actually dropped—from 26,000 to 22,300.[38]

In fact, at every stage of the child-protective process the system the child savers have created does the most harm to those who need the most help:

—When child savers bribe or badger children into telling them what they want to hear during an "investigation," that doesn't just hurt innocent families. It also makes it more likely that the guilty will go free.

—When children who don't really need to be in foster care flood the system, they take up places that should be reserved for those who really must be in substitute care. Severely maltreated children often are harder to place, so they are the ones most likely to become "nomad children" spending their days in offices and their nights wherever a bed can be found.

—When funds are drained from other services in order to do more investigations, it is the children who really need treatment who will wait months for it. And it is the children who really can't be returned to their parents who will wait years, maybe forever, for a placement in an adoptive home.

In recent years, even some people who work in the system, from frontline workers to state administrators, have begun to have second thoughts. Eli Newberger, M.D., director of family development studies at Children's Hospital Medical Center in Boston and a man with impeccable child saver credentials, has written that ". . . had professionals, like me, known then what we know now, we would never have urged on Congress, federal officials, and state legislators broadened concepts of child abuse as the basis for reporting legislation."[39]

In fact, some people did know "then."

At least one popular book on the subject bases its defense of child saving in part on the premises that: (1) There was no "backlash" against the child savers and the system they created until September 1984, when the first of the "mass molestation" cases went awry. (2) The backlash is created by and largely confined to the group Victims of Child Abuse Laws (VOCAL). (3) Concern about overintervention involves only the question of sexual abuse.[40]

This is wrong on all three counts. What the public takes to be the conventional wisdom about child abuse and neglect has been the subject of sharp debate within the professional community right from the start.

One of the leading scholars in the field, David Gil, questioned conventional explanations for child abuse in 1970.[41] Patrick Murphy condemned the neglect laws in 1974.[42] Michael Wald wrote a model law calling for a drastic reduction in the scope of coercive intervention in 1976.[43] Three of the leading scholars in child welfare, Joseph Goldstein, Albert J. Solnit, and the late Anna Freud condemned mandatory reporting laws and called for even more stringent limits on state power in 1979.[44] I had no difficulty producing a one-hour documentary questioning the present child-protective system for a local public television station in July 1984, more than two months before VOCAL was formed.

Trees have been falling in this forest for more than a decade. VOCAL and the mass molestation cases merely brought the press out to listen to the sound they make.

*   *   *

It was Saturday, May 11, one day after the first court hearing. One day after Elene Humlen had seen her sixteen-month-old daughter at MacLaren Hall.

Elene had just returned from a pawn shop in Hollywood. She needed money to pay her lawyer. On the drive home, she felt terribly weak. When she got back, "I couldn't get out of the car. Suddenly I felt I had to have water. I started throwing up."

Jeannette Humlen rushed her sister to the hospital. The diagnosis: nervous exhaustion and dehydration.

The next day was Mother's Day. Somebody saw a story on the local news that night. The local chapter of VOCAL was picketing the county courthouse about a case similar to Elene's. The group's president was attorney Allen McMahon. Elene's mother, Jean Sutorius, and Jeannette went to see McMahon and he agreed to take their case. It was a turning point.

Three days later, there was another hearing. Elene's doctor didn't want to let her out of the hospital, but of course Elene paid no attention. She left the hospital wearing a portable I.V., "but as soon as no one was looking, I ripped it out." Friends had to help Elene pace back and forth outside the courtroom before the hearing.

As the hearing began, the lawyer from the Department of Children's Services demanded that only the DCS side of the story be heard. That was standard operating procedure and, McMahon says, usually it still is. Generally it takes a third hearing before all sides are heard in full.

But Juvenile Court Commissioner Jewel Jones allowed the Humlens to tell their story as well.

Jones listened as Howard Gaddis, the boy who had thrown the tennis ball at the pitchback, described how Chris had been hurt. She listened as Chris's teacher talked about what a wonderful, well-behaved student he was. And finally, Jewel Jones did something that is extraordinary only in the context of the child-protective system. Pausing to emphasize each word, McMahon described the scene:

"She got down off the bench, took Chris's face in her hands—*and— looked—at—him!*"

Elene adds: "She asked Chris if he wanted to go home. Chris said yes and started to cry, and she said: 'don't worry, I'll handle it.'

"In the whole time," Elene said, Jones "was the only person who calmly sat down, asked questions, and made an opinion. She wanted to know the whole story." Elene recalls Jones telling off the DCS, including a vivid account of the times she had gotten black eyes during her own childhood. She said that had she the authority, she would dismiss all charges then and there. (In fact, they were dismissed just before a third scheduled hearing.) But Jones ordered the immediate return of Chris and Jennifer to their mother.

Although she had been too weak to walk unaided a short time earlier, when she heard the decision, Elene Humlen grabbed Chris and ran out of the courtroom to get Jennifer from MacLaren Hall. It was as if she felt that if she stopped for even a moment the judge might change her mind. Chris seemed to feel the same way. He insisted that all his clothes be picked up from his foster home immediately, as though if the clothes remained there, somehow it meant he might have to go back.

When the family arrived home, there was a celebration underway. There was a big "welcome home" banner, and friends and neighbors all over the house and the lawn. "I was supposed to go back to the hospital right away," Humlen said. "I made a point of not being found."

But Elene Humlen couldn't really join in the celebration. It was Jennifer. Just eight days before, she had been a bright, happy, outgoing toddler. Now she was curled up in a fetal position in a corner. Every time anyone so much as touched her, the little girl would scream.

*   *   *

Although the professional community has been divided, the child savers have dominated the popular debate. They have fed sensational stories to a compliant and superficial press eager to lap them up.

The typical story begins with a tale of unimaginable cruelty inflicted by barbaric parents against an innocent child. The reporter often immediately jumps from this account to a statement like: "Every year, there are two million cases of child abuse in the United States." In addition to confusing "reports" with "cases," such journalism naturally leads the public to assume that all two million "cases" are like the one with which the story began. If anyone was interested in explaining that things aren't that simple, the press wasn't interested in hearing about it. Contrary to popular belief, the six worst words a reporter can say to an editor are not, "It won't be ready by deadline." The six words most guaranteed to get a reporter in trouble are, "Actually, it's more complex than that."

Here is an issue with such clear-cut heroes and villains. And it's so easy to be on the side of the angels. Why spoil it? "It's fun for them," says Martin Guggenheim. "It's a clean, easy issue."[45] Another commentator has noted that child abuse is an issue that allows respectable newspapers to behave like tabloids.[46]

And, of course, it's a wonderful opportunity for expressions of what has been called "no-cost rectitude" by politicians.

A survey by the Child Welfare League of America found that of 236 bills introduced in 46 state legislatures, 67 dealt with making it easier to convict alleged abusers in court, 60 dealt with toughening reporting laws, 48 increased criminal penalties, and 36 involved so-called child abuse prevention curricula in schools. Only 25 bills even tried to deal with treating the problems that cause child abuse.[47]

But this hasn't stopped the press from swallowing what the politicians are spoon-feeding. Here's a wire service story that made it into a major newspaper:

> Responding to reports of increased deaths from shaken-baby syndrome, a lawmaker yesterday proposed legislation to crack down on child abuse and close legal loopholes.
> State Sen. John D. Fox (R-Montgomery) said he planned to introduce legislation that would increase penalties and classify more types of child abuse as criminal offenses.
> . . . [Said Fox:] "It's time to get tough with child abusers."[48]

This legislator is a Republican. But using abused children to score political points is a bipartisan endeavor.

One month after six-year-old Lisa Steinberg was killed by the man who had illegally "adopted" her, New York Governor Mario Cuomo went to the state's child abuse "hotline" in order to get his picture taken, encourage more people to flood a system that can't handle the complaints it gets now, and announce that the state would spend nearly $500,000 to hire more workers to take hotline calls.[49]

Less than two months later Cuomo put out his proposed budget. The hotline operators were there. But there was also a $2.6 million cut in "preventive services" designed to help keep families together, a $1.3 million cut in aid to counties to help place children in adoptive homes, and a cut in the state's Children and Family Trust Fund.[50] The legislature restored those cuts, but a few months later Cuomo vetoed a bill to provide emergency housing aid for poor families so their children would not be taken from them.[51]

The combination of cynicism and hysteria probably reached its height in Washington State in 1987. Seven months after a sensational abuse death, the state House of Representatives debated a bill intended to toughen penalties against parents who murder their children. House members knew there were errors in the bill that caused it to *weaken* those penalties in some cases. But they were so anxious to look like they were cracking down on child abuse that they passed the bill anyway—unanimously.[52]

The press, the politicians, and the child savers feed off each other. And the child savers continue to push for more of the same, unwilling to confront the consequences of what they have done already.

*   *   *

Nobody in the Humlen family emerged unscathed from the efforts of the state to "protect" the children.

Elene Humlen lost her job at the car dealership. "They wanted me out right away," she recalls. She's so far into debt she says she's stopped counting.

People who hear Humlen's story often tell her she should sue. But she can't sue most of the people who hurt her children, or the agencies they work for. The law gives them absolute immunity, no matter what they do. She is suing the sheriff's deputies who took her children away, but a lower court judge ruled that they have absolute immunity, too. The decision is being appealed.

Elene kept Chris out of school for a week while she worked up the courage to send him back. He brought a note with him from his lawyer. But word about the case had spread through the school. The other kids started teasing Chris, yelling "mom's an abuser, mom's an abuser." Chris got into his first school fight.

The school year was almost over by then, so Elene kept Chris home. The next year, she sent him to a different school. There he would follow his teacher around constantly. He said very little, he wouldn't play with the other children—and he wouldn't play ball anymore.

One day a child was hurt at a neighbor's house. As the ambulance came racing down the street, siren blaring, Chris dove under his bed. "He was sure they were coming for him again," Elene said.

Eventually, Chris rejoined his Little League team. When the team took a trip to Disneyland, Chris got lost. He waited hours for the coach to find him. He could have asked a security guard for help, but he was afraid of the men in uniform.

Jennifer was an early walker, but when she was brought home from MacLaren Hall, she refused to walk. She'd just "stay in that tight, curled up little ball." Anytime someone tried to pick her up, she would become hysterical. Finally she'd calm down, only to start again when she was put down.

"Maybe she figured I betrayed her," Elene said.

For a long time, Jennifer was terrified of water. Even the sound of running water scared her. Nobody knows why. And her eating habits changed. She wouldn't eat when anyone was looking. Instead she would wait until she thought no one could see, then grab some food and hide it. "She still does that," Elene said. "We find little nests in her bed. Maybe they didn't feed her right."

Elene knows she's become "terribly overprotective." More than four years after Chris was taken, she still accompanies him everywhere, even though "at thirteen, who wants your mother all over you?" And if ever Chris isn't exactly where he's supposed to be at exactly the time he promised, his mother panics.

Elene wanted therapy for herself and her children. "You want somebody so bad to talk to," she says. But she's afraid. Therapists are mandated reporters. "If I explain why I'm here [for counseling] they might think I did it and take them away again.

"It can never really be over, you know."

*   *   *

What happened to Elene Humlen and her family is a "horror story" only in the sense that it is horrible. Some victims of false allegations suffer less than the Humlens did, but some suffer much more.

In the name of "child protection," children have been beaten. In the name of "children's rights," children have been raped. In the name of "erring on the side of the child," children have been murdered—and yes, many of them died of social-work evaluations.

In the 1990s, America faces an invasion of latter-day child savers. They are destroying children in order to save them.

Child-welfare systems often contrive to shovel their failures into the criminal-justice system. Then they become the responsibility of people like Dennis Lepak, a probation officer in Contra Costa County, California. In 1988, Lepak told a congressional committee that his experiences with the system "profoundly changed the way I view agencies that have the responsibility for the care of children.

"A child without an effective family to protect his or her interests is at great peril; their safety and well-being depend on luck and whimsy. *No one* will value and protect another's child as they will their own. . . . The system in most cases is simply not capable of doing what is best for the child and often is directly responsible for furthering the abuse, neglect, and suffering of the child" (emphasis in original).[53]

*   *   *

Elene Humlen knew the question before I asked it. She hears it all the time.

After all she and her family went through, after all the charges against her were dropped, did any of the people she dealt with in the child-protective-services system—the school nurse who made the original report, the caseworker who took her children but had no time to explain, the sheriff's deputies who took the children first and asked questions later, the supervisor who would tell her nothing, the DCS attorney who demanded the children be kept in care, the people at MacLaren Hall—did anyone ever say, "I'm sorry"?

Of course not, Elene Humlen explained. "They're in the right, don't you know? They're the child savers."

2

Child Saving Then

Many of today's child savers trace the history of their cause back 116 years, to the famous story of eight-year-old Mary Ellen Wilson.[1] Mary Ellen had been repeatedly and brutally beaten, but nothing was done until, as the child savers tell it, the local Society for the Prevention of Cruelty to Animals (SPCA) intervened and sought protection for her as an animal.

In court, Mary Ellen testified that "Mamma has been in the habit of whipping and beating me almost every day. She used to whip me with a twisted whip, a raw hide. The whip always left a black and blue mark on my body. I have now the black and blue marks on my head which were made by mamma, and also a cut on the left side of my forehead which was made by a pair of scissors. She stuck me with the scissors and cut me. . . . I do not know for what I was whipped—mamma never said anything to me when she whipped me. . . . I have no recollection of having been kissed by anyone—have never been kissed by mamma. I have never been taken on my mamma's lap and caressed or petted."

The furor over this case led to the creation of more than two hundred Societies for the Prevention of Cruelty to Children and similar groups around the nation.

To this day, child savers point to the case of Mary Ellen as a prime example of what life for children would be like without them. The case teaches us, they say, that parents cannot be allowed to control their children like property and that massive intervention is essential to protect "children's rights."

But there is one part of the Mary Ellen story that the child savers neglect to mention: Mary Ellen was a foster child. The "mamma" who never kissed Mary Ellen was a foster mother.

Mary Ellen was placed in what now would be called foster care by the New York City Department of Charities, which then failed to monitor her care.[2] (The part about demanding that Mary Ellen be protected as an animal because there were no laws to protect children isn't true either.)[3]

The real lessons of the Mary Ellen story concern the inability of the state to be an effective parent, the risks of abuse in foster care, and the need to help parents—like Mary Ellen's real "mamma"—take care of their children.

In short, the lesson of Mary Ellen is the lesson every doctor is taught in medical school: First, do no harm.

But just as we keep learning the wrong lessons from sensational cases of child abuse today, so the wrong lessons were learned in 1874.

The history of child saving has a text and a subtext. The text, written by the child savers themselves, consists of their lessons from the Mary Ellen story: That children were alone and unprotected from cruel and unfeeling parents until the child savers came along and rescued them; that child saving is done solely "in the best interests of the child"; that removal from allegedly abusive or neglectful parents and placement in substitute care is always the happy ending to an unhappy story. The subtext tells a very different story. It is a story of some genuine concern for children, mixed with a great deal of racial and religious bigotry, fear and loathing of the poor, and enormous harm done to children in the name of helping them.

The underlying philosophy of nineteenth-century child saving still guides the operation of what we now call Child Protective Services. Every tenet of the nineteenth century child saving movement has its late twentieth-century counterpart. It may be dressed up in psychobabble, multiple regression analyses, and point biserial correlations, but underneath it's the same old child saving.

The Mary Ellen case ushered in a major era of child saving. It would not be the last, but it wasn't the first either.

Contrary to child saver mythology, parents were not free to do anything they wanted with children until the child savers came along. There are records of state intervention on behalf of abused children dating back to colonial times. It is fair to say, however, that in the case of children whom we would now define as abused, there was far less intervention than was needed to protect them.

Neglect, however, is a very different story. For nearly four hundred years, neglect has been a euphemism for poverty. And government always has maintained the right to massive intervention in the lives of the poor.

The English "poor laws" of 1601 gave local authorities the power to take away children of poor parents and indenture them to wealthier families.[4] The colonists brought this system with them to America, and it was used into the early nineteenth century.[5] Indenture was replaced by the poor house and then by the orphanage, but the term orphanage was a misnomer. Most of the "orphans" had at least one living parent, but that parent was too poor to care for his or her children.

"The importance of the poor-law mentality in relation to child mistreatment cannot be overemphasized," write Jeanne Giovannoni and Rosina Becerra in their book, *Defining Child Abuse.* "Forfeiture of children because of economic dependency, with no other manifest reason, remained a fact of American life until well into this century." Giovannoni and Becerra argue that specific laws against so-called "neglect" were invented only when it finally became unfashionable to overtly remove children from their parents because of poverty.

I believe that to this day, most of what the child savers label "neglect" is either caused by or confused with poverty and that poverty remains a major cause of "forfeiture of children."

Neglect has always been the top priority on the child savers' agenda. Cases like that of Mary Ellen were used the same way sensational cases of abuse are used now—as a false front to build up public sympathy for massive coercive intervention and to divert attention from the real business of child saving: the "rescue" of poor children from poor parents, parents deemed genetically inferior then, psychologically inferior now.

In the late nineteenth and early twentieth centuries, the targets were the children of poor immigrants, whose parents were both hated and feared. Thus, when Massachusetts officials were asked why they had so many poor people, they replied: "Because we have a larger proportion of foreigners from which they are made. . . . Aliens who have landed in this state and their children are lazy, ignorant, [and] prejudiced. . . ."[6]

Similarly, nineteenth-century penologist William Douglas Morrison declared that "it is notorious that peoples of the type of the Italians and Hungarians exhibit much less respect for human life than is to be found among the northern races." Although "contact with the humanizing influences of American civilization" helps somewhat, Morrison said, it's just not enough to make up for their inherent inferiority.[7]

Perhaps the finest recent history of child saving is Linda Gordon's *Heroes of Their Own Lives: The Politics and History of Family Violence.*[8] Gordon examined the records of one child saving agency, the Massachusetts Society for Prevention of Cruelty to Children, from 1890 to 1960. The excerpts provide a fascinating insight into the thinking behind child saving. Gordon writes:

The [MSPCC] agents hated the garlic and olive-oil smells of Italian cooking, and considered this food unhealthy, overstimulating, aphrodisiac. Their languages were so different, even when they spoke English, that there was little opportunity for clients to make their individual personalities known to agency workers.

The records abound with derogatory references, even when made with kind intent. One girl . . . was called "a romancer but not more so than the average foreign born child." Black women were described as "primitive," "limited" . . . "fairly good for a colored woman." White immigrants came in for similar abuse: e.g. "a typical low-grade Italian woman" [Others were called] "typical Puerto Ricans who loved fun, little work, and were dependent people."⁹

That last remark appears in a record from 1960.

Even the name commonly used to describe children who roamed the streets reflected this sort of prejudice. They were called "street Arabs."¹⁰

These sentiments were shared by Charles Loring Brace, founder of New York's Children's Aid Society (an organization that still exists) and arguably America's first child saver. Brace's writing is filled with contempt for the "stupid foreign criminal class," the "scum and refuse of ill-formed civilizations" who lacked the traditional American virtues of "cleanliness, independence, good order, and decency."

Here are some of Brace's choicest words about Catholics:

To all words of spiritual warning or help there came the chilling formalism of the ignorant Roman Catholic in reply, implying that certain outward acts made the soul right with its creator. The very inner ideas of our spiritual life of free love towards God, true repentance and trust in a Divine Redeemer seemed wanting in their minds. . . .

I certainly had no prejudice against the Romanists . . . but these poor people seemed stamped with the spiritual lifelessness of Romanism. . . .

The lowest poor in New York are not, I think, much cared for by the Romanist priesthood. . . . [O]ne can only sigh that the once powerful body has lost so much of the inspiration of Christ which once filled it.¹¹

Brace's bigotry was rooted in part in a firm belief in the genetic inferiority of poor foreigners. He believed that "gemmules" in the blood, passed down from generation to generation, produced licentious and criminal tendencies. But the gemmules could be overcome and "latent tendencies for good coming down from remote ancestors" could be awakened largely by massive doses of the correct—that is, Protestant—religion.¹²

This view was very much in the mainstream of nineteenth-century child saving.

"A large proportion of the unfortunate children that go to make up the great army of criminals are not born right," declared one "expert."

They "come into the world freighted down with evil propensities and vicious tendencies," said another. "The impress of criminal dispositions and pursuits is stamped upon every feature and movement of the body—the dress, the walk, the skin, the eye, the shape of the hands and feet, the size and contour of the skull, the voice, the hair; all reveal it. . . ."[13]

Until the 1920s court psychiatric units employed "eugenics researchers" to trace the family trees of defendants.[14]

Obviously, then, there was no point in trying to improve the lot of these inferiors by improving their standard of living. Don't bother improving wages and working conditions, argued Charles Henderson, President of the National Conference of Charities and Correction in 1899, because "the causes of defect are largely biological, deep in our relations to nature. A swift and superficial change in law or modes of employing labor would not touch those causes. They would remain as active as before."[15]

And "outdoor relief," as welfare was called, was "too easy to get and not shameful enough to receive."[16] Brace argued that if there absolutely must be "outdoor relief," at least let the child savers control it. Then, "the influence of the giver's character may sometimes elevate the debased nature of an unworthy dependent on charity."[17]

Of course, there were some poor people who could be saved. And the child savers saw their mission as figuring out which was which—by seeing if they lived up to the child savers' "moral standards."

Thus case records abounded with descriptions like "weakness of character," "vice," "children get no training in honesty and sobriety," "low moral standards," and "mentally and morally lax." Sex outside of marriage was in and of itself "moral neglect." So was a woman working outside the home. Child savers were early crusaders *against* day care even for the children of single women. The child savers opposed their working and opposed their getting welfare. They were supposed to find a husband or give up the children.[18] One commentator, Michael Katz, has suggested that the severity of the child savers attacks on the sexual morality of the poor may have had a "tinge of envy."[19]

There was also much more than a tinge of fear. Brace, for example, had traveled extensively in Europe and had been terrified by the revolutions of 1848. He warned that "some demagogue might arouse their passions and fuse all the elements for a Parisian scene of riot and blood."

In fundraising appeals to wealthy New Yorkers, he suggested that contributions to his child saving efforts were a good way to keep the lower orders in line. If poor children were not dispersed to the countryside and given just enough education to know their place, "they will perhaps be embittered at the wealth, the luxuries, they never share. Then let . . . society beware, when the outcast, vicious, reckless multitude of New York boys, swarming now in every foul alley and low street, come to know their power *and use it*" (emphasis in original).

Katz writes, "Stripped of rhetoric, the goals of much nineteenth-century reform can be reduced to a desire to lower property taxes and keep the streets safe."[20] The child savers saw their job as separating the worthy poor from the unworthy poor, and separating the unworthy poor from their children. They called this "scientific philanthropy."

Katz writes, "Reformers in the 1870s often argued that it was better to break up a poor family than to risk accustoming children to life on the dole. . . ." Another commentator notes that "the Protestant Ethic's equation of moral worth with market value made it imperative to divorce the welfare of the child from the welfare of families as a condition of aiding the child."[21] As Hastings Hart, Secretary of the Illinois Children's Home and Aid Society, put it in 1899: Dependent children should be "taken out of the slums and placed in clean homes, physically and morally."[22]

So it is not surprising that the first massive wave of child saving in America began not with the SPCCs and their professed concern with abuse, but with Charles Loring Brace and his system for dealing with what he called "the dangerous classes." It was called the "placing out system."

From 1854 through 1929, Brace and his people loaded 100,000 children aboard trains and sent them around the country, mostly to the west and south. When the train came to town, people who wanted to take the children would look them over at the station or in the local church.

The Catholic church and other critics charged that what Brace really was engaged in was wholesale kidnapping. In one instance, a Catholic who had lost his child to Brace when he was ill wanted to be reunited after he had recovered. The boy had been passed on to Brace by a group called the American Female Guardian Society. When the father began making inquiries, the Guardian Society rushed a letter of warning to the foster parents: "As we dread Catholic influence more than the bite of the rattlesnake . . . if you have become attached to the dear boy, save him from the power of the fell-destroyer, and the conscious, approving smile of your heavenly father will be your reward." The letter recommended that the foster parent hide the boy. A copy was sent to an official of Brace's group, who agreed with the recommendation.

Evidence of child stealing can be inferred from the records of Brace's Children's Aid Society itself.

Although the journeys organized by Children's Aid have been romanticized as "orphan trains," data from the society's records suggest that somewhere between 39 and 44 percent of the children on board had at least one parent living, and for most of this group both parents still were alive. When those for whom the status of the parents is unknown are excluded, the number with at least one living parent rises to nearly half.

Giovannoni and Becerra write that at a Conference of Charities in 1872, Thomas P. Norris, President of the Board of Commissioners for Kings County, [Brooklyn] New York, charged that "some children who had been temporarily committed to institutions had been sent west without the consent and sometimes even the knowledge of their parents. He further noted that the parents of many children who had been put in orphanages had been coerced into surrendering them to the control of private institutions."

Norris proposed a resolution "that children should not be taken out of the state without the consent of their natural or legal guardians. His was the only affirmative vote."[23]

The entreaties made to townspeople by Children's Aid when their trains came through also had a text and a subtext. The text was an appeal to Christian charity. The subtext was an offer of free labor. The society screened out sickly and retarded children. One contemporary critic said only the healthiest—hence the most useful as farmhands—were sent west.

At the ninth annual Conference of Charities in 1883, J. H. Mills of North Carolina charged that Children's Aid handed out children in his state to anyone who wanted them, no questions asked. "Their slaves [having been] set free, these men needing labor take these boys and treat them as slaves," Mills said.

But one need not rely solely on the historical record to know what Brace's "placing out" system was like. Because it persisted until 1929, some of the victims still are alive.

The five Panzer brothers were sent west in 1922. Sixty-seven years later, Harold Pánzer choked back tears when he told an NBC News reporter what it was like to be lined up and looked over by prospective "foster parents." "It's quite a shock, you know. You feel like you're on display. That brings back memories I have problems with."

"These fellas went and felt our muscles and so on and so forth and I didn't like that at all," said Harold's brother, Ed. "That was just like making a slave out of you." Ed's "parents" were among those who just wanted the cheap labor. He still remembers when "they gave me the god-awfullest beating I ever had."[24]

But Charles Loring Brace blinded himself to the abuses of his system. He insisted that any problems were only occasional aberrations. Older children couldn't possibly be used as slave labor, Brace said, because they were big enough to run away.

Brace's efforts aside, most "neglected" children were not placed in homes at all. They were forced into large, often horrible "orphanages," and parents were required to surrender all legal rights to them. In her history of dependent children in Illinois, Joan Gittens of the University of Chicago writes, "Some reformers, in fact, expressed the view that the mothers' unwillingness to give up their children was evidence of a lack of affection for their families."

Very few child savers noticed the conditions in these orphanages. Gittens writes about a 1920 inspection report on one Illinois orphanage:

> The children were underweight and overworked and the staff uninspired at best. "The children seem more like little scrubbing machines than human beings," the report noted in dismay. Their toys sat in spotless rows in the dormitories, obviously rarely handled. The children's illnesses went untreated because their working hours conflicted with the doctor's visiting hours, and work responsibilities came first.
>
> The snowy, highly polished floors one almost fears to step upon and this high degree of perfection becomes [sic] irritating to the observer when he realizes that it is the product of the hands and backs of little children.[25]

And this orphanage was by no means the worst. As late as 1915, 58 percent of the children admitted to one Western New York orphanage as infants died before age two. At about the same time, two hundred children were placed in institutions in Baltimore. Within a few months, 90 percent of them were dead.[26]

There were, however, some enlightened reformers. As early as 1849, for example, there were calls for education and job training as solutions to the problems of poor children and their families. But they were drowned out by the child savers, who said the solutions lay in religious training and "character building."[27]

Around the turn of the century, the two sides squared off over the first effort at what today would be called "preventive services." By that time, the failure of child saving had become apparent to enough people to lead to suggestions that the poor be given direct financial aid to keep their families together.

In 1913, the Massachusetts Commission on the Support of Dependent Minor Children found that of 754 cases investigated, 426 involved children removed for poverty alone.[28] A year later, a New York commission found that 2,716 children of 1,483 widows "are at present in institutions at public expense who were committed for destitution only; 933 children of 489 widows are at present in institutions because of illness of the mother, resulting often from overwork and overworry that might easily have been prevented."[29]

Because of such findings, small stipends, called mothers' or widows' pensions, were proposed. The first such law passed in 1911, and by 1919 forty-one states had some sort of mothers pension program.[30] The pensions had the support of "moral reformers and economic-efficiency buffs,

women's clubs and labor unions, middle-class do-gooders and relief recipients, New Freedom advocates, and New Nationalism partisans. . . ."
But not, of course, the child savers. They felt a threat both to what has
been called their "cult of scientific philanthropy" and to their jobs as sort-
ers, labelers, and overseers of the poor. They proclaimed, "Untrained relief
is poisonous to the poor,"[31] and they argued that families preserved by
these pensions should have been "broken up" when "the moral tone was
low."[32]

At first, the child savers were able to defeat mothers' pension proposals outright. As early as 1898 the New York State Legislature passed
a mothers' pension law that would have granted widows in New York
City an allowance equal to the state's cost for placing a child in an institution. But New York City, then as now, labored under the yoke of private
child saving agencies more than anyplace else in America. They pressured
the mayor to urge the governor to veto the bill, and he did.[33] Later, however, rather than defeat mothers' pensions outright, the child savers co-
opted them. By the time New York State passed its mothers' pension law
in 1913, it was amended to put the child savers themselves in charge of
deciding who was worthy of getting the money.[34]

Similarly, the original Illinois law was amended to exclude women
whose husbands had deserted them, women who were not American citizens, women whose husbands were in jail, and women who had illegitimate children.[35] In Pennsylvania, recipients had to be "worthy in every
way."[36] And in Connecticut, pensions were to be cut off "if there was
a record of intemperance, wastefulness or misconduct on the part of the
widow," or "where the home and the children are not kept clean and
orderly. . . ."[37] Some mothers' pension agencies decided that "use of to-
bacco and lack of church attendance were evidence of being an 'unfit'
mother. Families were forced to move from 'neighborhoods whose morality was questionable.' . . . The eviction of incapacitated husbands could
be ordered if they were deemed 'a menace to the physical and moral welfare of the mother or children.' " Family budgets were to include "no
extras" and "warm clothes, not fancy."[38]

This then was the tenor of the times when the Mary Ellen case arose
in 1874. The intense attention it got in the press led to creation of the
first Society for the Prevention of Cruelty to Children, in New York City.

Such societies were quickly established all over the United States. By
1906 there were 240 SPCCs or Humane Societies—which concerned themselves with cruelty to both children and animals—nationwide.[39] Often, they
were known to their victims simply and appropriately as "the Cruelty."[40]

The groups were given the same sort of broad powers to investigate families and seek the removal of their children as is given to Child Protective Services today—with remarkably similar results:

—When the broad power they had wasn't enough, they bent or broke the law. Gordon writes that when agents of the Massachusetts SPCC couldn't get into a home legally,

> they climbed in windows. They searched without warrants. Their case notes frequently revealed that they made their judgments first and looked for evidence later. . . .
>
> As one annual report put it delicately: "It is true we have taken risks on the margin of legal liability which seemed needful to rescue the child . . . but without cost to the society. . . . If 'indiscreet zeal' which is made such a bugbear occasionally leads us into mistakes, the public will condone the error . . . much more readily than they would approve the opposite fault of timidity or lukewarmness in cases of well-ascertained cruelty."[41]

In other words, they were "erring on the side of the child."

—To maintain public support, the societies deliberately misled the public concerning the nature of their work. For public consumption, they emphasized the most brutal cases of physical abuse they could find—sometimes complete with "before" and "after" pictures. But their caseload was overwhelmingly dominated by so-called neglect cases. In Pennsylvania, for example, only 12 percent of cases dealt with physical abuse.[42]

—The societies crusaded for laws to ban children from "immoral" professions, such as acting or from playing outside unsupervised—and did little or nothing about child labor.

—Even by their own broad standards, the societies generally found that a large proportion of the reports they received were false. Most years, at least 65 percent of cases investigated by the Massachusetts SPCC were ruled unfounded.[43]

—The large number of false reports was partly due to the realization in the urban ghettoes of big cities that "the Cruelty" could be a potent tool for harassment. "Poor children said to their immigrant parents, mothers-in-law said to mothers, feuding neighbors said to each other, 'Don't cross me or I'll report you to the Cruelty.' "

There was even a case from 1878 similar to that of Elene Humlen. Gordon writes: "When the *Boston Herald* reported that a boy playing in the street had been injured in the eye by something his companion had thrown [an MSPCC worker] wrote to the Superintendent of Boston City Hospital to find out how badly he was injured, collecting evidence to prosecute the parents for neglect."

Yesterday's child savers, like today's, insisted that they never removed children from their homes because of "poverty alone." But, as Gordon writes, "poverty was never alone. The characteristic signs of child neglect in this period—dirty clothing, soiled linen, lice and worms, crowded sleeping conditions, lack of attention and supervision, untreated infections and running sores, rickets and other malformations, truancy, malnutrition, overwork—were often the direct result of poverty."[44]

*   *   *

Another aspect of nineteenth-century child saving should not be overlooked, since it, too, has had enormous influence on child saving today. It is this belief: "We're only here to help you, therefore you have no rights." This was the philosophy that underlay the earliest laws calling for the incarceration of poor children. Since the jail was not called a jail but a school, and the purpose was not to punish but to "help," there was no need for the normal protections of due process of law.

The same philosophy underlay the creation of juvenile courts at the turn of the century. At the time, child savers considered this their greatest triumph. In the juvenile court, there was—and still is—a euphemism for everything. The defendant is a "respondent," the complaint is a "petition," the arraignment is a "hearing," and the sentence is a "disposition." As Patrick Murphy writes, "There was no need for lawyers, because there were no adversaries, inasmuch as the mutual aim of everyone involved was not to contest, object, or even seek the truth of the charges against the juvenile and/or his family, but simply to treat the juvenile and his family regardless of guilt."[45]

In the earliest years of the nation's first juvenile court, in Chicago, more than half the cases involved charges of "disorderly behavior," "immorality," "vagrancy," "truancy," or "incorrigibility." In fact, since they were "only here to help," juvenile courts were free to look beyond the original charge to any aspect of the character of the accused or his family. Judge Harvey Baker of the Boston Juvenile Court wrote that "a boy who comes to court for some such trifle as failing to wear his badge when selling papers may be held on probation for months because of difficulties at school; and a boy who comes in for playing ball on the street may . . . be committed to a reform school because he is found to have habits of loafing, stealing, or gambling which cannot be corrected outside."[46]

Indeed, since "we're only here to help," why bother with a charge at all? The child savers wanted control over "pre-delinquents." In 1907, Chicago's chief probation officer declared: "A child who today is simply neglected, may be dependent tomorrow, truant the next day, and delinquent the day after that."[47]

Of course, the kind of "help" children got was no better, and often worse, than the "help" meted out in the orphanages.

In his landmark study, *The Child Savers,* Anthony Platt writes that though the institutions often were called schools, "bookishness was an undesirable attribute and the lowest form of menial labor was rationalized as an educational experience." Thus, one institution "taught" cooking and waiting tables "to the colored boys." A leading child saver proudly described his "reformatory" to be "like a garrison of a thousand prisoner-soldiers . . . a conscript fortress . . . a convict community under martial law. . . . Every incipient disintegration was promptly checked and disinclination of individual prisoners to conform was overcome. . . ." He went on to refer to this process as "self-denial and productive personal exertion."

A Chicago reformatory contracted out the inmates for cheap labor or brought the work to be done into the school. And, again, most of the institutions were overcrowded, understaffed, unsanitary, short on food, and run by people prone to abuse the children in their care. One institution frequently embroiled in scandals was a "shelter" run directly by the New York Society for Prevention of Cruelty to Children.[48]

As early as 1870, one court saw through this sham. The Illinois Supreme Court overturned a law allowing the commitment to reform school of children who were found to be "destitute of proper parental care or growing up in mendicancy, ignorance, idleness, or vice"—definitions quite similar to many current neglect laws.[49] But the decision was gradually eroded in Illinois, and there were no comparable decisions elsewhere. It was not until nearly one hundred years later, in 1967, that the United States Supreme Court granted some children limited protections against their "protectors."

The case began on June 8, 1964, when Gerald Francis Gault, then age fifteen, of Gila County, Arizona, was taken into police custody on charges that he and another boy had made an obscene telephone call. One week later, the county juvenile court judge sentenced Gault to the State Industrial School until he turned twenty-one or until state authorities decided they wanted to release him. An adult committing the same crime would have faced a maximum penalty of two months in jail or a fifty-dollar fine.

Gault's parents received no notice that he had been taken into custody. They received no copy of the complaint against him. The complaint itself was the equivalent of a form letter, with nothing specific about what Gerald was alleged to have done. At the hearing, the woman who made the original complaint was not present. Witnesses were not sworn under oath and could not be cross-examined. Neither Gerald nor his parents were allowed a lawyer, and no transcript or recording of the hearing was made. No appeal was permitted. There also was no right to indictment by a grand jury, to a public trial, to a trial by jury, or to conviction based solely on proof beyond a reasonable doubt. The rationale for all this was that "the basic right of a juvenile is not to liberty, but to custody."

In a scathing decision, Justice Abe Fortas denounced the fraud of the juvenile court:

> It is of no constitutional consequence—and of limited practical meaning—that the institution to which he is committed is called an Industrial School. The fact of the matter is that, however euphemistic the title, a "receiving home" or an "industrial school" for juveniles is an institution of confinement. . . . Instead of a mother and father and sisters and brothers and friends and classmates, his world is peopled by guards, custodians, state employees, and "delinquents" confined with him for anything from waywardness to rape and homicide.
>
> Due process of law is the primary and indispensable foundation of individual freedom. It is the basic and essential term in the social compact which defines the rights of the individual and delimits the powers which the state may exercise. . . . Under our constitution, the condition of being a boy does not justify a kangaroo court.[50]

The Gault decision did not end the abuses of children in the juvenile justice system, but it did provide minimum safeguards for children accused of crimes or of so-called "status offenses"—things like truancy or running away or being ungovernable or otherwise "in need of supervision."

But the Gault decision did little to address standards concerning "abuse" and "neglect."

It was shortly after the Gault decision was handed down that the most recent wave of child saving reached full force, with vastly expanded definitions of what sort of misconduct must be reported to authorities and investigated by them. One commentator[51] has argued that there was a direct cause-and-effect relationship. With the door to the juvenile justice system closing, the child savers needed to find a new way to introduce their concept of coercive, controlling "help" into the lives of children.

The evidence for such a direct connection is thin, particularly since a first wave of expanded reporting laws preceded the Gault decision by up to five years. But one thing is clear: the philosophy of the child savers who created the disastrous juvenile justice system—we're only here to help you, so you have no rights—and the approach of today's child savers to abuse and neglect is identical.

After studying the attitudes of various groups of professionals and the general public toward abuse and neglect, Giovannoni and Becerra concluded that for social workers, "since the intervention itself is viewed as a means of helping, broadening of the scope of definition is a means of expanding the arena wherein the help can be given." Or as one prosecutor put it: "Law enforcement [officers] in their worst days view the criminal justice system [with its respect for the rights of the accused] as a necessary evil. . . . [Social workers] often see it as an *un*necessary evil."[52]

For example, in arguing in court for the right to strip search allegedly abused children virtually whenever they feel like it, the Illinois Department of Children and Family Services said the protection of the Fourth Amendment against unreasonable searches applies only to accused criminals who might lose their liberty. Children can be strip searched at virtually any time for almost any reason, DCFS argues, because it's being done to "help" them.[53]

Unfortunately, even though the system created by the child savers to handle abuse and neglect works no better than the one they created for juvenile justice, courts have largely accepted the child saver line on abuse and neglect cases. It may take another hundred years before abused and neglected children receive basic constitutional protection from their "saviors."

The child savers' creed was summed up by Oscar McCulloch at a charities conference in 1888: "First, we must close up official outdoor relief [welfare]. Second, we must check private and indiscriminate benevolence, or charity, falsely so-called. Third, we must get hold of the children."[54]

3

Child Saving Now

It takes strength to work in the steel mills of the midwest. James Norman had that strength. But James Norman had more than the strength to forge steel; he had the strength to forge a family.

Norman lived in Chicago. In a neighborhood where half the children dropped out, his oldest child, a son, graduated from high school, and his two daughters, Lynetta, now age thirteen, and Jamie, now age eleven, were doing well in school.

"No father had more pride in his children than James Norman," his lawyer, Diane Redleaf of the Children's Rights Project of the Legal Assistance Foundation of Chicago, wrote in an unpublished essay. "He [would beam when he spoke of] their A's and B's in school. . . . He preached to them about rights and respect and he set an example as a person who stood up for himself and maintained his dignity."

James Norman held his family together through great personal misfortune. He had to give up full-time work to care for his wife, before she succumbed to a long illness in 1987. Then Norman developed a heart condition, limiting his employment opportunities further. But he kept trying. He took whatever part-time jobs he could get and enrolled in courses in advanced auto mechanics at a vocational school.

For a while the family got by on his part-time earnings, social security survivor's benefits, and a small Aid to Families With Dependent Children grant. But eventually, the bills became too much. In the summer of 1988, the electricity to the Normans' small apartment was cut off.

Then the helping hand of Child Protective Services struck. As Redleaf puts it, the child savers "took a problem and created a tragedy."

On August 16, 1988, a caseworker from the Illinois Department of Children and Family Services (DCFS) visited the Norman home. According to her written report, the home was messy, with "clothes and papers all over the place." There were bugs in the refrigerator, and of course the food was spoiled since there was no electricity. But the worker's report acknowledged that the children "appeared to be very healthy."

The worker filled out a "risk assessment" form, and assigned numerical values to the answers. But she botched some simple addition and came up with a number indicating higher risk than actually existed.

There was nothing wrong in the Norman household that emergency financial assistance and a housekeeper couldn't have fixed. Yet no such help was offered. Instead, the children were immediately taken into custody and placed with their great-grandparents, who are in their late seventies. Redleaf says the worker called it "financial neglect." Although the mathematical errors on the form are obvious to anyone looking at it, the children were not returned. More than a year later, they still were in foster care.

The foster home was more than ten miles—and three bus rides—away from where Norman was living. At each end of the trip, he faced a one-mile walk. For a month, he was denied visits altogether. He was forced to undergo a psychiatric evaluation even though his children's removal had nothing to do with his mental health.

Instead of offering help, DCFS drew up a so-called "service plan," which required the agency to provide no services. James Norman, alone and unaided, was expected to get a job and a two-bedroom apartment. But Norman's heart condition had hospitalized him twice, and the agency wouldn't even give him money for transportation to job interviews, making employment almost impossible.

The efforts Norman already had made were held against him. DCFS said his part-time jobs and vocational education classes had kept him out of the home too much, so they accused him of "lack of supervision." But welfare was out of the question, too, because parents can get that only when they have custody of their children.

By late 1989, Norman said, his family was growing apart, the girls had become depressed, and he was emotionally drained. Norman became a plaintiff in a class action lawsuit against DCFS. A social-work expert hired by the plaintiffs testified that "I was ashamed when I read [Norman's file]. . . . No good social work standard would have pulled those children from this working class poor man. . . ."

By September 1989, Norman's lawyers had done what the DCFS was supposed to do—help him get disability benefits because of his heart condition. That allowed him finally to get a new apartment. He filed a court petition to get his children back. It was to have been heard on October 26. But the buses were running late, and by the time James Norman got to the courthouse the judge wouldn't call the case again.

The hearing was delayed until November 28. At about the same time, a federal court was getting ready to rule on the class action lawsuit. Either court might have reunited James Norman with his children. In the meantime, Norman's lawyers pleaded with DCFS to at least make it easier for him to visit his children. They refused. William Curtis, chief counsel for the DCFS, said he couldn't comment on the specific allegations brought by Norman or the other plaintiffs in the lawsuit. But he questioned whether it is "good social work to take a parent who hasn't exerted any effort to get housing or a job or whatever and make them more dependent on the state than they were before. Does that even make sense?"

Neither Curtis nor the taxpayers of Illinois will have to worry about James Norman becoming too "dependent" anymore. On November 16, 1989, twelve days before the rescheduled court hearing, James Norman died of a heart attack. He was thirty-eight.

In the last years of his life, James Norman had a weak heart. But it took the child savers to break it.[1]

*   *   *

Yesterday's child savers believed neglect was caused by genetically inferior parents who could be redeemed only by religion. Today's child savers believe neglect is caused by mentally ill parents who can be redeemed only by "counseling." Yesterday's child savers said the problem was in the "gemmules." Today's child savers say the problem is "apathy-futility syndrome." Yesterday's child savers demanded control over "predelinquents." Today's child savers say all abuse is part of a "continuum."

In 1898, the governor of New York vetoed a bill to provide pensions to poor mothers so they would not have to place their children in institutions. In 1989, the governor of New York vetoed a bill to provide poor parents with rent subsidies so they would not have to place their children in foster care.

In 1888, the child savers declared: "We must get hold of the children." In 1975, when a state government wanted private child saving agencies to sign a contract specifying their obligations, they replied: "You ought to give us the children and trust us."[2]

What child saving then and child saving now have in common is an unwillingness to face up to the most salient fact about the maltreatment of children. Although that maltreatment has multiple causes, cases like James Norman's show that one cause is predominant: The over-whelming majority of child abuse and neglect cases are clearly, obviously, directly, demonstrably, linked to poverty.

Not every case. Wiping out poverty would not wipe out child abuse. But simply ameliorating the worst conditions of poverty would go a long way toward dramatically reducing child abuse and neglect.

Study after study finds far more abuse and neglect in poor house-holds. According to the federal government's second Study of National Incidence and Prevalence of Child Abuse and Neglect (commonly called NIS-2), "Family income was found to have a profound effect on the inci-dence of abuse and neglect."[3]

The study compared families of four with incomes of over $15,000 to those earning less than that in 1986, using two definitions for child maltreatment. Under the narrower definition, physical abuse was three-and-a-half times more frequent among lower-income children, sexual abuse was five times more frequent, and emotional abuse was nearly four times more frequent. Emotional neglect was five times more frequent among the poor, and educational neglect was nearly eight times more frequent. Physical neglect was almost ten times more common in poor families.

When a broader definition of maltreatment was used, the gap between rich and poor widened. Under the broader definition, which included children "at risk" of maltreatment, poor children were five times more likely to be labeled physically abused and nearly twelve times more likely to be labeled physically neglected.[4]

The more broadly maltreatment is defined, the more likely poor families are to be mislabeled abusive or neglectful.

A 1976 study of a national cross-section of families by faculty at the Universities of New Hampshire and Rhode Island examined only physical abuse, where family income should have the least effect. That study still found that abuse was twice as likely to occur in families where the annual income was below the poverty line (then $5,999 per year for a family of four) than in families with incomes of over $20,000 per year.[5]

The reasons are rooted not in genetic inferiority or mental illness, but in common sense. Almost all researchers now link child abuse to stress. Simply getting through the day imposes stresses on poor parents that the rest of us can hardly imagine. They face the stress of stretching meager budgets so the food doesn't run out, the stress of keeping the rats away from their children in the middle of the night and keeping the children away from lead-based paint flaking off the walls, the stress of crime-filled neighborhoods, and, often, the stress of raising the family alone.

At the same time as they are facing more stress, they have fewer re-sources to cope with it. "They don't have the buffers to deal with [stressful] situations," says Lawrence Aber. "They can't get a baby-sitter when they've just had it and need a day out. Rich families have some fat to cushion the blow of added stress; with poor families you're cutting into the muscle of family life."[6]

"Sometimes it's the little things that can make a family break down," says Susan Carter, Executive Director of the National Association of Foster Care Reviewers, a group that represents citizen volunteers in twenty-six states who monitor the status of children in foster care. "One parent may be working and the car breaks down. That can send the family over the edge and lead to abuse and neglect that wouldn't happen if supports were in place."[7]

"Of course there are other reasons besides poverty for the playing out of abusive impulses," writes Elizabeth Elmer, associate professor of child psychiatry at the University of Pittsburgh, "but poverty has proved to be the fertile soil that incubates and nourishes a variety of social problems that might wither away in a more comfortable social class."[8]

The gap between rich and poor widens when neglect is considered. There are two reasons for this. First, certain types of neglect can happen only in poor families.

For example, one caseworker estimated that 90 percent of the families with whom she deals don't even have telephones.[9] Every time a single parent in such a family needs to make a telephone call, she[10] must go to a neighbor or perhaps a pay phone a block or two away. That means for every call she must dress up the children to go outside and take them with her. For every call, she must hang onto the children while she talks on the phone so they don't run out into the street. Or she may risk leaving the children at home for the few minutes it takes to make that call. She is now guilty of lack of supervision, a commonly alleged form of neglect.

Or let's say it's winter and the food has run out in the home of a woman with an eight-year-old child and an infant. The welfare check arrives and at last she can buy food. But the infant has a cold and the mother doesn't have warm clothes for her. If she takes the children with her, she is guilty of physical and medical neglect of the infant. If she leaves the children at home, she is guilty of lack of supervision.

The most tragic such cases are those that result from the very efforts of the poor to lift themselves out of poverty.

Florence Roberts, Family Law Director for Brooklyn Legal Services, tells of a client who actually called the New York State Child Maltreatment Hotline herself, in the hope that they might help her find a baby-sitter so she wouldn't have to leave her ten-year-old daughter alone while she worked. Instead, they took the woman's child away and placed her in foster care. It took a week for Roberts' agency to get the child back.[11]

Such cases are not unusual. According to guidelines issued by the New York State Department of Social Services, "school aged children (age six to twelve years) may not be ready for the responsibility of being on their own for even short periods of time."[12] If a parent thinks her twelve-year-old son can stay home alone after school while she works, but a child protective worker disagrees, the parent is guilty of neglect. Yet a 1983 Harris Poll estimated that in New York City alone there are 100,000 "latch-key children" between the ages of six and twelve.[13]

Given the breadth of the definition, it's not surprising that over one-fifth of the reports alleging child maltreatment in New York State in 1982 alleged lack of supervision.[14] And New York is not alone. In Illinois, more than a quarter of all child maltreatment reports in 1988 alleged lack of supervision—it was the largest single category.[15]

A study of a sample of such cases by the Child Welfare League of America found that the services needed most often to solve the problem were baby-sitting and day care. But what was most often offered by child-protective agencies was removal of the child into foster care, followed by "counseling or parent education."[16]

The second reason for the gap in neglect cases between rich and poor overlaps the first somewhat. Just as it was in the nineteenth century, poverty itself is confused with neglect. The poor are automatically "defined in" by the broad scope of the neglect laws. For example, Connecticut defines a neglected child as one who "is being permitted to live under conditions, circumstances or associations injurious to his well-being."[17] Is there any child living in a ghetto who could not be labeled neglected under a law like that if an agency felt like it?

In some cases, workers are trained to confuse poverty with neglect. Mary Case, M.D., Chief Medical Examiner in St. Charles County, Missouri, writes that when she trains child-protective workers in deciding whether to remove children from their parents, they are "advised by me to look closely in the homes of children who are possibly endangered or neglected. They are directed specifically to look at food supplies, hygienic conditions, presence of rodents, and utilities (water, lighting, heating)."[18] This is exactly the type of advice that encourages the destruction of families like James Norman's. Citing another case, the same lawsuit alleges that DCFS actually sabotaged a mother's repeated efforts to find decent housing on her own.

First her caseworker ordered her out of one apartment because it was allegedly too small. After she had moved into a larger place, the worker told the woman's landlord "about her history with DCFS" and that she had seven children living there. That same day, the landlord told her to get out. The child saver also told the mother's welfare worker that she was "mishandling her AFDC grant" and got the grant canceled.

Then DCFS threatened to remove the children because of lack of adequate housing.[19]

Any lawyer who works regularly with poor clients can cite similar cases.

Marlene Halpern, Family Law Coordinator for Community Action for Legal Services in New York City, recalls a case similar to James Norman's: This time the children were removed because their clothes were dirty, their home was dilapidated and lacked electricity, and one child's broken eyeglasses had not been replaced. In New York, Medicaid, the state's health insurance program for the poor, allows only one pair of eyeglasses per year.[20]

Among the most common causes of trumped up "neglect" charges is homelessness or poor housing conditions. This case is recounted by the Juvenile Law Center in Philadelphia:

> When the agency worker visited the home, she noted there was no hot water. The children were not in the home during that visit. They were staying with their grandmother precisely because of the hot water problem.
>
> Despite mother's representations that the whole family could stay with grandmother, the agency worker presented a voluntary placement agreement and told mom to sign it or she would come back with the police. Mother signed the [agreement] and the children remained in placement for five months without a court hearing prior to JLC being appointed. . . .
>
> JLC . . . discovered the grandmother owned a three bedroom home in which mother was living which was more than adequate for the children's return. Grandmother stated the family could stay as long as it wanted. JLC prepared [litigation and] the county agency agreed to return the children. [They] are thriving in their mother's care.[21]

On the New York City Borough of Staten Island, Katherine Cosentino and her one-year-old son Jesse twice lost places to live because of "no children" rules. Both times, she asked the city's child savers for help. Both times, they took her child away from her instead. The first time, they took the child the very day she showed up at the office of the person who was supposed to help her. The second time, she was offered a choice: place your son in foster care or go live on the streets.

During one of her weekly visits to Jesse's foster home, Cosentino noticed that Jesse was ill and had bruises on his body. Don't worry, her caseworker said, everything is fine. Two weeks later, Jesse was hospitalized with a 104 degree fever, infections in both ears, and an upper respiratory infection. His mother again saw bruises on his body. Nevertheless Jesse was returned to the same foster home. Cosentino finally persuaded her caseworker to intervene when she called the foster mother on the phone and the woman sounded drunk. Jesse was moved to another foster home.

In another New York City case, eight-year-old Angela Hernandez and her sister Lisette were taken from their mother Iris solely because she could not afford a decent place to house her family. Iris Hernandez begged city officials for help. Instead, they took away her children. Angela was sexually abused by her foster father.[22]

In still another New York City case, a legal-aid attorney called a family's caseworker and pleaded with him to offer housing instead of just foster care. The worker replied, "That's a joke."[23]

Then there's the case of Wendell Merchant, described by the Long Island newspaper, *Newsday*: Merchant never was accused of doing anything to his three children; on the contrary, he's considered an excellent parent. He was awarded custody after his ex-wife was accused of neglecting them—and after the children, ages nine, eight, and three, had already spent years in foster care.

But custody was conditioned on his finding adequate housing, and the low pay he gets working on a loading dock in Islip makes that almost impossible on Long Island. So the county spends one thousand dollars a month to keep the children in foster care. The children can see their father only on weekends. Every week they lug plastic garbage bags filled with their clothes back and forth between Merchant's tiny apartment and their foster home. "Friday is my best day," says Merchant's nine-year-old daughter. "That's the day my daddy comes to get me. . . . I'd rather stay here all the time."

"They say I can have my kids if I find housing, but there's nothing they can do to help me find housing," Merchant said. "If they gave me just half the money they're spending on foster care, I can make it."[24]

These cases are not aberrations. The New York City cases are part of a class-action lawsuit alleging that removal of children from their families because of homelessness or poor housing conditions is standard operating procedure. State Supreme Court Justice Elliott Wilk not only upheld the claims made by the plaintiffs in this suit, he questioned the veracity of the city's attempt to defend itself. "Some of the papers submitted in support of the city's position are, on their face, lacking in credibility," Wilk wrote. Wilk ordered an end to the practice of removing children because their parents lack a home. He ordered that services be provided instead. But the ruling is stayed while the city appeals.[25]

In Illinois, a class-action lawsuit alleges that the Department of Children and Family Services "routinely removes children from their parents due to homelessness or other conditions caused by poverty alone."[26]

And in California, homeless children were given emergency shelter only on condition that they be separated from their parents, until a successful lawsuit put an end to the practice. [27]

The abuses are not confined to big cities. In and around the small community of Newburgh, New York, a reporter for the local newspaper found four cases in which Child Protective Services tried to pressure poor women into having themselves sterilized. Sometimes the pressure succeeded. The women said no other contraceptive options were discussed. One woman alleged that Child Protective Services threatened to take away her children if she didn't have the operation. "[The worker] said if I was sterilized I could keep my kids," the woman said. In another instance, a caseworker allegedly pushed sterilization on a twenty-four-year-old woman over the objections of hospital personnel who said she was too young.[28]

Study after study has found that a large percentage of children are declared "neglected" and taken from parents who are guilty of nothing more than poverty in general and homelessness in particular.

One out of four "neglected" children in foster care in Newark were placed there solely because their families were homeless, according to a New Jersey study. It was an "underlying factor" in another 17 percent of cases.[29] A study of "boarder babies"—children who spend months in hospitals because of a shortage of foster homes—found that the biggest single factor causing their forced hospital stays was lack of housing. For 14 of 97 children studied, it was the only reason.[30]

Families struggling to keep their children out of foster care are stymied by two major problems: homelessness and low public assistance grants, according to two New York City studies.[31] Yet even the most minimal effort to get New York City's children out of foster care when only lack of housing is keeping them in has been sabotaged by the city's child savers.

In late 1988, over the objections of city officials, the state passed a law making parents eligible for a rent subsidy of up to $300 a month if housing was all that was still standing between them and their children in foster care. It was estimated that 1,000 New York City children were in this category. (A bill to expand the program to prevent placement due to lack of housing in the first place was the one vetoed by Governor Cuomo.) Yet after a full year of operation, the subsidies had been used for a grand total of thirty-three families. Why? Because few workers in the city's giant child saving bureaucracy were even told the program existed. Because city officials have refused to allow the program to be advertised at shelters for the homeless. Because the private agencies that place foster children in the city were required to deal with sixteen pages of forms and instructions every time they wanted to use the program. Since these agencies already have a strong financial incentive to keep children in foster care, this was more than enough reason for many of them not to bother.

In one case, a woman who needed a rent subsidy to get her grandchild out of foster care had to fight the system all the way to an administrative hearing. Four months after she won, she still hadn't received the help she needed. In the meantime, the child, a one-year-old girl, was moved to three different foster homes.[32] In the face of such resistance, the chief judge of New York's highest court, the Court of Appeals, has proposed legislation giving the state's family court judges authority to order provision of housing aid where only housing is preventing a child's return.[33]

Such resistance isn't really surprising. A lot of child savers don't see anything wrong with using the neglect law to remove children because of housing problems. Eli Newberger, M.D., and attorney Richard Bourne, both of Children's Hospital in Boston, write that even when the problem is no fault of the parents, "a court should be able to order temporary removal until safe housing is found. . . . Removal here is simply a stop-gap measure until the inadequacy of the community's provision of shelter is remedied."[34] In other words, as soon as society is ready to provide decent housing for all poor families, they can have their children back.

Charles Ewing, a professor of law at the State University of New York at Buffalo and a child psychologist, is frequently called to testify in cases where the state seeks to permanently terminate the rights of parents to their children. In all of those cases, Ewing says, he's never seen the state try to terminate the parental rights of "a self-sufficient family. It's always done to someone on AFDC."[35]

Increasing AFDC benefits alone, with no other help, would be enough to return 6,000 Los Angeles County foster children—20 percent of the total—to their homes, according to Pamela Mohr, Director of the Children's Rights Project at Public Counsel, a public-interest law firm that represents children in abuse and neglect cases.

Lawrence Aber estimates that more than half the cases agencies label as neglect are really poverty cases. Patrick Murphy puts the figure at 90 percent, and Martin Guggenheim of New York University says it's at least 95 percent. "It is incredibly rare to have a case of neglect that is *not* poverty-related," says Florence Roberts of Brooklyn Legal Services.[36]

Sometimes poor and desperate parents don't wait for the child savers to take their children. The *Orlando Sentinel* told the story of four-year-old Lisa and her two-and-a-half-year-old sister Amanda. Their mother loved the children too much to raise them without a home, so she finally gave them up. At first, it was only supposed to be temporary, until she could get a home:

> She had been back and forth with state agencies and was worried her children would eventually be taken away from her. She figured giving the kids up

for temporary custody was her best chance of keeping them.

Lisa and Amanda's mother visited them at the church day-care facility every day. By fall, she was talking to [church worker Bill] Carter about giving the girls up for adoption.

She believed that having a stable home life "was going to be better for them than anything she could ever give to them. She did love the girls. If she could give them up, they could be taken care of, sent to college," Carter said.

The girls were unusual in one respect: because they were blonde, blue-eyed, and healthy, they were easy to place in an adoptive home. Now,

They wear flouncy, little-girl dresses and proper shoes. They also sleep in real beds . . . [they] have had real Christmas and Easter celebrations. . . . They have started taking piano lessons.

The girls told [their adoptive parents] that their mother "had water in her eyes" when she said goodbye. The mother left a necklace—a chain with a big heart and two little ones—behind as a remembrance. She told Lisa to tell Amanda she loved her. And she left.

When the *Sentinel* reporter asked a representative of the state's child saving agency about such cases, she replied, "Sometimes the parents want to give up their kids too quickly. . . . It can become so easy for people to give their children away."[37]

This view is not unusual. Most child savers share the view of Anne Cohn, Executive Director of the National Committee for Prevention of Child Abuse. Says Cohn: "There are a tremendously large number of people in this country who have little or no money who do not neglect their children. When parents neglect their children and are of low income, it is not sufficient to say they are excused because they have no money."[38]

*   *   *

Despite the overwhelming evidence of the link between poverty and maltreatment of children, Cohn and her fellow child savers cling to another theory, one rooted in the nineteenth-century philosophy of child saving. This theory is commonly referred to as "the medical model." Just as nineteenth-century child savers believed parents were genetically inferior but salvageable through religion, the medical model maintains that all the causes of child abuse and neglect are within the parents.

The theory postulates that child abusers are sick, they have some sort of mental disorder, and to the extent they can be helped at all, they can be helped only through intensive therapy combined with "parent education."

The medical model is the foundation upon which the entire modern child-protective system has been built. It has become so much a part of that system that one leading child saver actually referred to separating children from their parents as a "parentectomy."[39]

That system is now more than twenty-five years old. The overwhelming mass of data we now have about who does and does not maltreat children, some of which I have cited above, makes clear that the premise on which it has been built is false. For a quarter of a century we have squandered vast amounts of time and money—and the lives of countless children— pretending that it was true.

Granted, the medical model is not entirely false. Some child abusers are mentally ill, just as some child abusers are wealthy. Almost nothing the child savers say is entirely false. But most of what they say is between 75 and 90 percent false, and the medical model is no exception.

After the surge of child saving in the late nineteenth century, concern about child abuse faded again. Its "rediscovery" was due first to the efforts of radiologists, who discovered unexplained injuries on children's X-rays, and then to pediatricians, who followed up on this evidence. The problem gained intense public attention in 1962, when Dr. C. Henry Kempe, a pediatrician, published an article on "The Battered Child Syndrome" in the *Journal of the American Medical Association.*

"The first people to identify a problem often shape how others will perceive it," writes Barbara Nelson, associate professor at the Hubert H. Humphrey Institute of Public Affairs, in her excellent scholarly study of public-policy agenda-setting, *Making an Issue of Child Abuse.*[40] In the modern era, child abuse was identified by radiologists and pediatricians, so it's not surprising that they viewed it as a medical problem. "Psychiatric factors are probably of prime importance in the pathogenesis of the disorder," Kempe wrote in his original article, "In most cases some defect of character structure is probably present. . . ."[41]

As a result, we created a child protective system designed, in the words of Richard Gelles, former director of the University of Rhode Island Family Violence Research Program, "to cure symptoms that in many cases do not exist."[42]

But why does the medical model persist in the face of so much evidence to the contrary? Probably because it has been enormously helpful and therapeutic—to child savers, to politicians, and to the general public. In short, to everyone except abused children. Among the benefits:

—It confers enormous prestige on the child savers. Rather than being glorified welfare workers trying to get a poor family's electricity turned on, the medical model transforms child savers into doctorlike experts on the cutting edge of "treating" a "syndrome." Malcolm Bush, vice president for development and research at Voices for Illinois Children, writes:

the recognition that the troubled family inhabits a context that is relevant to its problems suggests the possibility that the solution involves some humble tasks. . . . This possibility is at odds with professional status. Professional training is not necessary for humble tasks. . . .

Changing the psyche was a grand task, and while the elaboration of theories past their practical benefit would not help families in trouble, it would allow social workers to hold up their heads in the professional meeting and the academic seminar.[43]

Thus the decision to give James Norman a psychiatric evaluation instead of help with his utility bill.

The tendency to medicalize the problem of child abuse may say more about the psyches of child savers than allegedly abusive parents. When the tables are turned and social workers and other therapists are themselves the subject of psychological assessments, it turns out, according to social worker Eileen Anderson, that "individuals who choose therapy as their vocation score high in personal power motive" on a standard test of such things. Anderson writes:

After more than nine years as a professional therapist and counselor, I have concluded that many therapists are addicted to power. . . .

As alcoholics manipulate their world to hide their drinking, addicted therapists disguise their own drives for power. They do so by proclaiming a desire for service, responsibility, and the right to use their expertise. . . .

Legitimate environmental stresses . . . are ignored. A depressed client, hungry and unemployed, is susceptible to a trite but common therapeutic response: "The fact is that it's your attitude that's the problem." . . .

Too often, therapists who are hooked on power believe their behavior is altruistically motivated. Too often, clients accept this view.[44]

—The medical model is essential for the child savers to rationalize what they do to children. Bush argues that child savers must convince themselves that sick parents are the source of the problem in order to justify taking their children away despite the enormous emotional harm done by foster care itself: "Where the parents are at fault, there is the comparatively simple solution of removing the child from the home," Bush writes. "Where the problem is rooted in the environment, the worker has no such simple solution." In studying case records, Bush found that they "exhibit a distinct tendency to elide the practical nature of distress and seize on the smallest clues of psychological determinants as explanations."[45]

But the most important reason for the success of the medical model is its tremendous political appeal. Barbara Nelson writes that the medical model fits the quintessential American view of all social problems: they are "individually rooted, described as an illness, and solvable by occasional doses of therapeutic conversation."[46] If child abuse is an illness, then it can affect people *like* us—people we can identify with. Yet at the same time, since "we" are well and "they" are sick, whatever is done to "cure" it will be done only to them and not to us.

Even more important, the medical model means that *nothing that causes child abuse and neglect is our fault.* We can sympathize with the plight of abused children while taking no responsibility for it.

According to the medical model, it doesn't matter that we prefer to retain one of the lowest overall levels of taxation in the industrialized world even if that means thousands of homeless children sleep on the streets; it doesn't matter that we allow welfare benefits to fall below subsistence levels; it doesn't matter that poor children often are sentenced from birth to inferior health care and inferior education; it doesn't matter that minority families face discrimination in all walks of life. According to the medical model, none of that matters. According to the medical model, it's all something inside *them.*

That the medical model would be invoked to explain away the causes of child abuse is hardly surprising. The same model has been offered to explain away poverty itself. People are not homeless because there is anything wrong with the American economic system, it is argued; all those homeless people must be mentally ill—aren't they the ones who were let out of mental institutions? Never mind that the fastest growing group among the homeless is families, not deinstitutionalized mental patients; never mind that large numbers of homeless people appeared on the streets many years after most of the mentally ill were let out of institutions.[47] (And never mind that even the mentally ill should have a more humane place to live than an out-of-sight-out-of-mind human warehouse.)

David Gil, one of the nation's leading child abuse researchers and one of the first to question the medical model, writes: "Whenever problems which are actually rooted in societal dynamics are defined as individual pathology or shortcomings, their real sources are disguised, interventions are focused on individuals . . . and the social order is absolved by implication from guilt and responsibility and may continue to function unchallenged in accordance with established patterns."[48]

The medical model also goes comfortably with the currently fashionable stereotype of poverty itself. Just as "child abuse" conjures up images of brutally beaten children when it actually means much more, the word "poverty" is today likely to conjure up an image of an unemployed unmarried black junkie in an inner city mugging respectable citizens to support his or her habit. In fact, the "underclass" represents less than 4 percent of all impoverished Americans.[49] Only 9 percent of children from families living below the poverty line live in inner-city ghettoes. Nearly 30 percent live in rural America, and 28 percent live in the suburbs. Half of America's impoverished children live in two-parent households, and in 45 percent of those households, one of the two parents is working. And 44 percent of America's poor children are white.[50]

These are the families that are destroyed when child savers break up families because they are poor.

The appeal of the medical model to politicians is as obvious as the result was inevitable. Nelson writes that whenever politicians put child abuse on the public agenda, "the connection between poverty and maltreatment was purposely blurred. In fact, strenuous efforts were made to popularize abuse as a problem knowing no barriers of class, race, or culture. For some politicians, particularly [Senator Walter] Mondale, this was part of a conscious strategy to dissociate efforts against abuse from unpopular poverty programs. The purpose was to describe abuse as an all-American affliction, not one found solely among low income people. . . ."

Mondale sponsored the federal law that set the standards for the sweeping reporting laws and broad definitions of maltreatment that we have today. Nelson writes that to Mondale, "the real stumbling block to passing the legislation would occur if it were considered poverty legislation, or if the problem were defined as a deviance confined solely to the poor, rather than as a social blight which attacked all classes."

So when Mondale held hearings, he steered witnesses away from any other approach.[51]

The medical model was being pitched by the child savers and the politicians alike. It also fits the media's definition of a great story with clear heroes and villains. It's no wonder any other view was, and is, largely unheard.

The apotheosis of the medical model is seen in the work of Norman Polansky, now Professor Emeritus of social work at the University of Georgia. Polansky and three colleagues describe their studies of allegedly neglectful parents in Appalachia and the inner-city of Philadelphia in a book called *Damaged Parents: An Anatomy of Child Neglect.*[52]

Polansky and his colleagues are unusual only in their candor, for which they deserve credit. They represent not an aberration, but the mainstream of the modern child saving movement.

Three times in the course of the book, the authors take pains to praise Charles Loring Brace. That's appropriate. Right from the start, the book reveals subtle biases worthy of Brace himself. On page two, the United States is described as "the largest democracy man has ever known." That is, of course, wrong. The largest democracy man has ever known is India. But India is populated largely by people who are poor and nonwhite, so presumably they don't count.

At one point Polansky does acknowledge that "one would have to be recently arrived from Mars not to think that family income affects the likelihood of child neglect."[53] By that standard, the rest of the book is written in fluent Martian. For example:

> Our studies led us reluctantly to conclude that chronically neglectful mothers are very likely to be character disordered. . . . The disability resides in large part inside the mother. . . . To describe someone as character disordered is to acknowledge that she is also life-accident prone. Many of the external pressures she experiences are self-induced.

Damaged Parents refers almost solely to mothers; in this world fathers bear no responsibility for child-rearing.

Critiquing a study that found "neglectful" parents reporting that they lived in worse housing than other poor families, the authors write that "their negative attitudes, of course, could have derived from their own low morale or bitterness, rather than their surroundings." They call neglectful behavior part of "a pervasive style of life," and they say improving living conditions probably won't help, because "neglectful" parents "are among life's losers. Opportunity has a way of passing them by and vice versa."

Neglecting parents allegedly suffer from "apathy-futility syndrome," which is characterized by "a pervasive conviction that nothing is worth doing. The feeling of futility predominates, as in the schizoid personality. As one patient used to say: 'What's the use of eating supper, you'll only be hungry before breakfast.' " Apparently, it never occurred to the authors that this comment might have been the way an impoverished woman expressed the fact that she did not have enough to eat.

In part, the authors' problem is that their expertise, as they note, was "in personality theory," and they get in trouble when they venture beyond it. Thus, *Damaged Parents* concludes that if neglecting parents are impoverished, it must be because they can't manage money. After all, if AFDC benefits are the same for all families in a given community, yet neglecting parents are the "poorest of the poor," they must be misusing the money.

This ignores the reality of life on AFDC:

—An enormous amount depends on who your welfare worker is. A stickler will knock you off the rolls for the slightest infraction, like missing an appointment because your child was sick, and it can take months to get back on. Someone more sympathetic might bend the rules. A welfare mother who gets the wrong caseworker can indeed end up poorer than someone else who theoretically has the same benefits.

—Contrary to the common stereotype, per capita welfare benefits often go down as family size increases. A larger AFDC family easily can be poorer than a smaller one. Even when the benefits don't go down, it's harder for larger families to find housing. They are more likely to live in more difficult, overcrowded conditions. Similarly, the AFDC family that makes it to the top of the waiting list for a good public housing apartment will live better than a family with the same income stuck in a slum or a crime-infested high-rise.

Such housing conditions easily can affect health. A family living in an apartment with intermittent heat in the winter is likely to have more sick people in it, and that means both higher medical costs and increased difficulty taking care of the children. (Polansky says, however, that the parents in these cases have a "tendency toward psychosomatic illness due to an inability to resolve life's problems or express feelings verbally.")

Polansky and his colleagues also go wrong because of their contempt for their subjects. Not only are they "apathetic" "losers," they also have "infantile personalities"; they're "emergency-prone," "[emotionally] famished, demanding" people who make a worker "feel as if he were about to be sucked dry." If day care is offered, "some women will sabotage the child's attendance by inducing fearful reactions in the child. . . ." If a homemaker is offered, "some mothers will exploit their helplessness" to avoid doing the housework. Case histories include descriptions such as "a mousy looking, frightened young woman" or "services were sabotaged by her, as she has done before." An eight-year-old girl is "dangerously manipulative," and a long, contemptuous description of one family ends with "[the mother], at least, is currently wearing an IUD."

Having said all this, Polansky and his colleagues then lament how difficult it is to get these people to accept a child saver's offer of "help."

Polansky & Co. know the ideal solution for "neglectful" parents: shove them all into mental hospitals. "In a monitored environment, one need be far less cautious about high levels of anxiety that might result from confrontation used in uncovering brittle defenses; group influences can be more effectively and consistently marshaled; opportunities for acting out and exacerbating life crises to distract oneself from conflicts can be better restricted."

From this theoretical base comes the authors' masterstroke. A 99-question "Childhood Level of Living" scale that they suggest workers take into homes with them to determine if parents are neglecting their children. Parents score a point if they exhibit certain good qualities or don't exhibit certain bad qualities. It takes 88 out of 99 possible points to be considered a "good" parent. Any score under 63 indicates child neglect.

The CLL is an amazing amalgam of class bias and sex-role stereotyping with a dollop of religious discrimination thrown in. Measured by the CLL, Ward and June Cleaver are safe. The rest of us are in trouble.

Nearly half the items—42 out of 99—require the expenditure of discretionary income to score a point. You gain, for example, if "a planned overnight vacation trip has been taken by family"; if "child has been taken by parents to a carnival," "a children's movie," or "a spectator sport"; or if "there is an operating electric sweeper." You lose points if the "house is dilapidated," "the roof (or ceiling) leaks," "the living room doubles as a bedroom," or "clothing usually appears to be hand-me-downs." Other requirements may be particularly difficult for single parents to meet, such as: "the floors of the house appear to be swept each day" or "mother sometimes leaves child to insufficiently older siblings." (Once again, the father is not graded.)

On the CLL, a little sex-role stereotyping is good: "Mother expresses pride in daughter's femininity or son's masculinity." But too much is bad: "Mother mandates child's play according to sex (i.e., girls may only play with dolls)." An earlier version of the scale also included points for "mother expresses feeling that her job is the housework" and "mother mentions that child, if son, prefers to be with father; if daughter, prefers to be with mother." She lost a point if she believed her work was harder than the father's.[54]

Other items on the most recent checklist include: "a prayer is said before some meals," "the child says prayers at bedtime," and "child has been taken fishing." A mother loses a point if she "complains a lot about life" or "mentions that she cannot get the child to mind."

The authors report that "we have had numerous requests for copies of the scale since it was first published, mostly from colleagues in social work and public health."[55]

I have included the complete CLL (1981 edition) as an appendix. Readers are invited to test themselves.

The views expressed in *Damaged Parents* are very much part of the mainstream of child saving. In New York City, for example, it is almost impossible to read a newspaper article about child abuse without the obligatory quote from pediatrician Vincent Fontana, longtime chairman of the Mayor's Task Force on Child Abuse and Neglect, and Medical Director of the New York Foundling Hospital, a private, sectarian child saving agency. What kind of expert is this man? In his own writing, he has gone so far as to blame early twentieth-century child labor on parents. He writes, "Of course the abusers [in the factories] were not their natural parents; but the abuse could only have occurred because their parents permitted it and, at least by default, encouraged it."[56] Fontana goes on to suggest that, if we could get away with it, most of us would enjoy killing a baby or two.[57]

When child saver literature links abuse with poverty at all, it is generally included as a minor component and then only in the context of a sudden financial crisis—which probably was the parent's own fault anyway.

A publication from the Massachusetts Department of Social Services, for example, lists eight causes of child abuse, only two of which are related to income. In the case of one of those factors, "life crises," the pamphlet notes that "external stress can be a way of life for some abusive families. Some families are crisis-ridden. It is a life-style posture." In the second category, "lack of support services," the pamphlet suggests that plenty of help is available, but the parents just don't know how to ask for it.[58]

Another pamphlet, used by at least two states, asks, "Why do parents abuse their children?" and answers by listing immaturity, unrealistic expectations [of their children], unmet emotional needs, frequent crises, lack of parenting knowledge, social isolation, poor childhood experiences, and drug or alcohol problems. "Problems with money" is mentioned under "frequent crises."[59]

A leading advocate of the medical model is the National Committee for Prevention of Child Abuse. An NCPCA pamphlet about neglect reads like an abridged version of *Damaged Parents*. Indeed, it reads much like the writing of the nineteenth-century child savers. The pamphlet sends the following messages: Poverty is *never* the real cause of neglect.

> Whatever the causes of physical child neglect—and they are multiple—the heart of the problem is always an emotional lacking in the parents. . . .
> The community and the caseworkers see the parental behavior as the problem and they are, of course, right. . . . [A] process of re-education must begin. . . . This . . . re-education process . . . may take years.

Don't bother with concrete help; the parents will just screw it up anyway:

> The worker who helps a family move from substandard housing and acquire some much-needed furniture and who drives the children to a clinic for necessary medical care can be excused for baffled anger and weary frustration when the new living quarters become as dirty as the old and the children are nearly as neglected as they were before any effort was made. . . .

If a single mother who spends her days trying to find a job and battling the welfare bureaucracy, her weekends going to food banks to get enough for her children to eat, and her nights awake with the lights on to keep the rats away from her children concludes from all this that the world is not a friendly place, it's all in her head:

Neglecting parents, and in time their children, see themselves as victims. . . . They cannot see that their very failure to act precipitates the problems that afflict them . . . instead they feel that misfortunes are directed to them from a hostile and alien outside world.

Research from around the country that shows severely neglecting families can be helped with the right combination of "hard" services as well as therapy (see Chapter 10) should be ignored, and thousands of families should be destroyed:

> . . . no change is possible in severely neglecting families by any means now known. . . . Resources were, on the whole, useless because parents did not make use of them. . . . The solution in this group has to be permanent removal of the children, termination of parental rights, and adoption.[60]

Two other elements of the medical model deserve mention, since each is crucial to justifying the massive coercive intervention into family life that the child savers favor. The first is the "continuum theory." This theory presumes that all acts of physical discipline are part of a continuum that begins with spanking and ends with murder. It is based on this theory that child savers argue that the massive, coercive intervention of the state is required in even the most minor cases because, without such intervention, they inevitably will get worse. It is the child savers' attempt to maintain a system analogous to the juvenile justice system before the Gault decision.

"We must conspire against language which describes physical punishment as something other than what it is," says James Garbarino of the Erickson Institute for Advanced Study in Child Development. "Assault is what it is. Let's not call it discipline, spanking, a good licking."[61]

"One of the single most important determinants of child abuse is the willingness of adults to inflict corporal punishment upon children in the name of discipline" writes Edward Zigler, a professor of psychology and director of the Bush Center in Child Development and Social Policy at Yale University.[62]

And what happens after spanking becomes abuse? Why, the abuse gets worse, of course.

According to the President of the National Committee for Prevention of Child Abuse, Frederick Green, M.D., "The progression of child abuse and neglect often follows a pattern similar to many diseases. The initial symptoms or consequences may appear quite superficial or result only in mild discomfort. Eventually, however, these symptoms can, if not treated, mushroom into permanently disabling or fatal conditions. Intervening after a child has suffered is simply too late. . . ."[63]

Another NCPCA official writes that "reports involving apparent minor physical maltreatment or failure to provide adequate care can and do escalate with serious, even fatal consequences for children."[64]

The head of a California child savers group goes even further, declaring that every report phoned in to a child-protective-services hotline must be true: "I really believe that when a case is being reported, something is going on, but what we're looking at is a continuum."[65]

And Richard Bourne, one of the child savers who advocates taking away children when the parents live in bad housing, flatly declares that "without appropriate intervention minor injuries are likely to increase in severity over time."[66]

The problem here should be obvious. Another study by the Universities of New Hampshire and Rhode Island found that 88 percent of parents spank their children.[67] If the continuum theory is correct—that is, if spanking leads to minor abuse and minor abuse leads to major abuse and major abuse leads to death—then roughly 88 percent of the children in America should be dead by now.

In fact, as the former NCCAN director Douglas Besharov has written, minor incidents simply "do not signal future maltreatment. Almost all parents have physically or verbally lashed out at their children during times of unusual stress; all parents have at least some moments when they neglect to meet the needs of their children." Based on data from the first National Incidence Study (NIS-1), Besharov estimates that fewer than one in five "minor assaults or other examples of poor child care will ever grow into anything resembling child abuse or neglect."[68]

But that still leaves the question of what to do about that one case in five. Since we cannot predict which one out of five it will be, the child saving answer is to intervene coercively in virtually all families, just as their nineteenth-century counterparts sought to get at "predelinquents."

But that would mean that thousands more families whose problems were relatively minor—or nonexistent—would be vulnerable to traumatic investigations, stigmatizing labels, and, often, wrongful removal of children. What is needed for such families is, first, the basics that alleviate the stress of poverty—like a telephone—and, second, easy access to voluntary help.

The continuum theory carries with it another, more subtle danger. To the extent that child-protective workers get any kind of training at all, the continuum theory, and particularly the equating of corporal punishment with abuse, is one of the things they are taught. Risk-assessment checklists used by some workers to decide whether a child should be removed from the home sometimes include the use of any corporal punishment at all as a "risk factor" to be counted against the parent.[69] The continuum theory also emphasizes that any parent can become an abuser. Zigler writes: "The continuum approach forces parents to come to terms with their own potential abusiveness."[70]

All this reinforces the presumption of guilt that underlies much child-protective work. CPS workers, who often are not parents themselves, learn values of acceptable child-rearing that are fundamentally different from those practiced in almost every home. And they learn to treat every parent as suspect.

Peter Strubel trained child-protective workers in Colorado until he quit in anger over the needless removal of children from their homes. Part of the problem, he says, was the attitude that "everybody is a potential abuser, everybody is capable of abusing, which is a pretty damn narrow and negative way of looking at parenthood."[71]

The other key element of the medical model is the "cycle theory." Readers may be surprised to learn this is only a theory, since it has been so widely accepted as fact by the press and public. It has even made it into some introductory psychology textbooks.[72] The theory postulates that almost all abused children will grow up to abuse their own children (unless, of course, the child savers can stop them). Thus, an NCPCA newspaper ad featuring a huge picture of a crying child carries this headline: "Help Destroy a Family Tradition." The text states that "child abuse is almost as American as apple pie. In many cases it's a family tradition in which helpless parents inflict beatings, neglect, emotional strain or sexual abuse on their helpless children. Abused children grow up learning abuse as a way of life. When they become parents, they pass that learning on to their children."[73]

This view has become all-pervasive. An otherwise excellent newspaper series states that patterns of abuse and neglect "are handed down, generation after generation, almost as if they are hereditary."[74] The executive director of New York's Council of Family and Child Caring Agencies states flat out that "most people who were abused will abuse their children."[75]

Neglect is said to be transmitted from generation to generation in much the same way. According to a publication from the American Humane Association, a group with an outlook similar to NCPCA's, "It is safe to assume . . . that when neglected children become parents, they are predisposed to neglect their own children."[76]

It's easy to see why the cycle theory would catch on. If child abuse is a cycle, it is obviously a mental health problem that can be solved only by lots and lots of "counseling" to "break the cycle of abuse." It dovetails perfectly with the medical model and allows poverty to be ignored. It justifies intervening before any problem is apparent and staying involved for a long, long time, because the problem is so "deeply ingrained."[77]

Unlike much of what the child savers say, the cycle theory is based at least in part on common sense. Almost everything I know about being a good husband and father I learned from the way my parents treated me and each other. (The rest I learned from my wife.) When, at age two, my daughter saw a woman on Sesame Street comfort Kermit the Frog, she said, "That's Kermit's mommy." She had already learned from experience what mommies do. So certainly it stands to reason that the child who is constantly hit or belittled may learn that that is the normal way to treat a child.

But it is equally plausible that such children will successfully resolve never to treat their children the way they were treated. And that appears to be the more common outcome. For it turns out that the cycle theory is just another child saver myth. This myth grew out of studies that looked only at abusive parents. Those studies found that most of those parents were in fact abused as children. But the researchers went for years without looking at control groups—parents who do *not* abuse their children— to see how many of *them* were abused. In other words, the researchers studied only those who were victimized by the cycle, not those who had broken free of it. When such studies finally were done, the results were quite different from what the child savers had theorized. After reviewing the literature, Cathy Spatz Widom, professor of criminal justice and psychology at Indiana University, found that fewer than 20 percent of abused children go on to abuse their own children. Widom concluded that "little convincing empirical evidence exists that the cycle of violence is a powerful phenomenon."[78]

The widespread acceptance of the cycle theory has had tragic consequences. As noted earlier, it has helped divert attention from the real, poverty-related causes of most abuse and neglect. But also, as is often the case with child saving, the worst harm has been done to those who really have been abused.

In one case, a mother's boyfriend was charged with abuse solely because he had been abused as a child.[79] An NCPCA publication warns parents to watch out for adults who were abused as children because they might be a danger.[80] Some abused children believe the theory themselves and resolve never to become parents.[81] Surely people who were abused as children have suffered enough. They do not need still another burden thrust upon them by their erstwhile "saviors."

One needs to take only the briefest look at any child-protective-services system in the country to see the one great, overwhelming flaw in the medical model as a plausible explanation for child maltreatment. If, in fact, child abuse is an illness, if it's a mental health problem, if it can strike anyone because of what's wrong inside them, then *what are all those poor people doing caught up in the child-protective system,* to the virtual exclusion of everyone else?

In the nineteenth century, the answer was easy: child abuse is a function of genetic inferiority and so is poverty, so naturally poor people are the target of child saving. But such theories are no longer acceptable. And since the obvious explanation, that child abuse is caused by or confused with poverty, is unacceptable to the child savers—they needed to come up with something else. And they did.

Like the tailors in the fable of the emperor's new clothes, the child savers simply invented a whole group of child abusers that only they are wise enough to see. With no supporting evidence they simply declared it a fact that middle-class and wealthy families abuse and neglect their children just as much as the poor do, but only the child savers have been able to see this. Hence was born what Leroy Pelton, former assistant to the director of the New Jersey Division of Youth and Family Services, calls "the myth of classlessness."[82]

Thus, Vincent Fontana writes, "Men and women in every walk of life, in every economic circumstance, of every degree of education, and of many different types of background, form the ranks of child abusers."[83] A pamphlet distributed by social services agencies in at least two states declares, "Child abuse can happen *anywhere:* In poor, middle-class, well-to-do homes. . ." (emphasis in original).[84] And the New York State affiliate of NCPCA declares, "Child maltreatment crosses all ethnic, social, and economic lines."[85]

This is another example of a statement by child savers that is not entirely false. If child abuse *never* crossed class lines, Lisa Steinberg would be alive today. But it is absurd to leap from this to the conclusion that there exists a gigantic group of invisible child abusers, equal in numbers to those found among the poor, especially when one considers the extent to which child saver definitions automatically define-in poor people.

Yet, in twenty-five years or more, the press has never asked for proof of the myth of classlessness; it simply has been accepted as fact.

It should not be necessary for those who disagree to have to prove a negative—that most of the "invisible" child abusers don't exist. Fortunately, however, there is a wealth of evidence that they don't.

The theory underlying the myth of classlessness is that the only reason we don't see the same amount of maltreatment among those who are not poor is that they have fewer chances to get caught. They are less likely to come in contact with the police or other public agencies employing mandated reporters, and they rely on private physicians who, it is said, are less likely to characterize an injury to a child as abuse.

Richard Gelles, for example, cites a study in which seventy-six pediatricians were given almost identical case records and asked if an injury was caused by abuse. The only difference in the records was that some described the child as black while others said the child was white. The result: The black child was 33 percent more likely to be reported as "abused."[86] But Gelles then leaps to a conclusion unsupported by the data: that the disparity proves that rich white people are getting away with child abuse. Given the history of bigotry that has infested child saving for more than a century, it is far more likely that poor black families who have done nothing wrong are being overreported.

Two case histories, both from Children's Hospital Medical Center in Boston, illustrate the point.

The first case involves Geraldine Churchwell, a black single parent who brought her asthmatic daughter to the Children's Hospital emergency room for treatment. The woman had an excellent record of caring for her daughter, as attested to by the allergist the child regularly saw. The hospital demanded that the mother institutionalize the child at a residential treatment center. Showing considerably more skill and initiative than many child-protective workers, Churchwell came up with an alternative: outpatient treatment at a clinic the mother was familiar with where her daughter could be treated by black therapists, an after-school program, and a homemaker. She also asked for help to find better housing. But in a lawsuit, Churchwell says the hospital turned down her plan and blackmailed her into accepting its own. If she did not institutionalize her child, a child-abuse report would be filed on her. As a result, Churchwell writes, her daughter wound up in an institution where the only blacks on the staff were "serving food and cleaning."[87]

What are the odds that Children's Hospital would have treated a middle-class white family the same way? The second case suggests the answer.

That case involves Perri Klass, M.D., an intern in the same hospital's pediatric cardiology unit. One night her husband called to say he would be rushing their son, then two and a half years old, to the emergency room —the same emergency room Geraldine Churchwell had used—because the boy had two cigarette burns below his eye. As Klass herself wrote, "a cigarette burn is about the most suspicious injury a child can have."

The father explained that the child was burned when he went running down the aisle of a restaurant and ran into a man who was waving a cigarette around. The parents received enough of a grilling about the incident for Klass to write about the experience in the *New York Times Magazine,* but that's all that happened. The child was not taken away. The family was not listed in a central registry. Child Protective Services wasn't even called.[88]

So, yes, there are artificial disparities in reporting rates. But they don't prove what the child savers say they prove.

More fundamentally, however, the gap in the rate of abuse and neglect between rich and poor is simply too great to be explained away as an artifice of the reporting system. And for this, the evidence is overwhelming:

—While the study cited by Gelles found a 33 percent disparity in reporting blacks versus whites, that disparity was far less than the huge preponderance of child-abuse cases among the poor. The National Incidence Study (NIS-2), referred to at the start of this chapter, found that abuse was up to 500 percent more prevalent among the poor and neglect was up to 1200 percent more common among the poor—clearly a much wider gap than can be accounted for by reporting differences alone.

—Furthermore, NIS-2 did not limit itself to cases reported to Child Protective Services in the sample jurisdictions studied. It also surveyed numerous other agencies in a cross-section of American communities. While some of these agencies probably have a predominantly poor clientele, most serve a cross-section of the population.

Professionals in these agencies could report cases to NIS-2 without identifying children or parents by name. Therefore, they did not need to worry that this would lead to intervention that would do more harm than good, or that they would be jeopardizing confidential relationships—two of the things that sometimes deter people from reporting their suspicions to CPS. In addition, "community professionals at [the non-CPS agencies] served as 'sentinels' by remaining on the lookout for child-maltreatment cases during the study data period."[89]

—The University of New Hampshire study also referred to at the start of this chapter used a cross-section of families, ensuring that rich and poor were represented in numbers proportionate to their representation in the population at large, and still found twice as much abuse in poor families.

—Although some kinds of abuse may be hidden, it is difficult to hide a dead child. Study after study of child deaths show far more deaths from abuse in poor households.[90]

—Studies in which all the subjects are equally open to public scrutiny (groups made up entirely of welfare recipients, for example) show that those who abuse tend to be the "poorest of the poor."[91]

—Similarly, when all children in a child-welfare system are looked at, "neglected" children are poor even more often than abused children. For example, a 1982 census of children in state care in Wisconsin found that 72 percent came from families with incomes under $10,000. For that group, "neglect" was the largest single reason for placement. But for the much smaller group from families earning $15,000 or more, none was placed in foster care because of "neglect."[92] If the child savers are right and all this invisible maltreatment is going on, why were Wisconsin authorities able to find at least a small number of middle-class abusers, but no middle-class neglecters at all?

Giovannoni and Becerra studied 949 families that had all come to the attention of child-protective authorities in four California counties:

> Certainly relative to the general population the entire parent group was skewed toward the lower end of the financial spectrum. However, [factors involving poverty] were two or three times more common among families in [neglect] categories than among those where this was not a part of the problem.[93]

But if classlessness is a myth, what accounts for the point made by Anne Cohn (and almost every other child saver) that the overwhelming majority of poor people don't mistreat their children?

First of all, when it comes to the child saver version of "neglect," Cohn may well be wrong. When neglect is defined the way the child savers define it, to include not having enough food for a child, or living in rundown housing, or not being able to pay the utility bill, or any one of a hundred similar things, by such definitions the majority of poor people probably are guilty of "neglect"—precisely because they are "guilty" of poverty. The difference between the poor parent who is reported, listed in a central registry, and has her children taken away for "neglect," and her impoverished neighbor may be nothing more than chance.

But that still leaves the question of parents who take out the intense frustration of poverty on their children. What about all the poor people who don't do that?

The first thing to note here is that the medical model falls victim to the same analysis. There are people with various forms of mental illness who don't abuse or neglect their children either.[94]

Moreover, if indeed child abuse is a mental illness, the child savers should be able to agree on what the illness is. But when Richard Gelles reviewed the literature, he found that "of nineteen traits [of a child abuser] listed by the authors, there was agreement by two or more authors on only four traits. Each remaining trait was mentioned by only a single author. Thus, there is little agreement as to the makeup of the psychopathology."[95]

But most important, this argument ignores the obvious. Some people are stronger than others, both physically and emotionally. Sometimes, physical strength is literally the issue, when it is a matter of keeping children safe in a poor neighborhood while holding down a job. Striking out at a child may be a function of sheer exhaustion. And even when the issue is mental strength, being less mentally strong is not the same thing as being mentally ill.

It is as if one were to take the entire staff of the National Committee for Prevention of Child Abuse and demand that they run a one-mile race while each holds a twenty-pound weight over his or her head. Some would finish the race, but some would collapse before the finish line. Would it be right to label those who did not finish such a race sick? Would they need years of "counseling"? Or would they simply need someone to come and lift the weight from their shoulders?

Perhaps the woman who leaves her small children alone to make a phone call would benefit from counseling. Maybe parent-education classes would help, too. But wouldn't it make more sense for someone to just come up with the money to get her a phone?

When they're really pressed on the issue, even the child savers admit that their position is untenable. The American Humane Association acknowledges that abusing families "tend to be involved in deprivation of necessities or neglect more frequently than any other kind of maltreatment, *which likely is related to their economic status*" (emphasis added).[96]

Sometimes, when child savers are caught with their facts down they simply deny saying what they said—or they maintain that the rest of us misunderstood them. Thus, Anne Cohn writes that when she and her colleagues said child abuse "crosses class lines," they never meant to imply that child abuse is equally prevalent in all classes.[97] But in reviewing the literature, Richard Gelles found that child savers repeatedly made just that claim. He writes: "Authors advancing the psychopathological model make a special effort to point out that social variables *do not* enter into the causal scheme of child abuse" (emphasis in original).[98]

Furthermore, if Cohn's position when pressed is that child abuse is not represented equally across class lines, it certainly isn't the message her group is conveying to the public.

In 1989, NCPCA gave its seal of approval to an episode of the television series "The Equalizer" in which a wealthy father brutally beat his young daughter for no greater reason than the sadistic joy he derived from it. The episode concludes with assurances that the girl, now safely rescued, will instantly be placed in a loving adoptive home. No sooner do the closing credits conclude than series-star Edward Woodward is back urging viewers to write to the National Committee for Prevention of Child Abuse for further information.

NCPCA's own material carries the same message. In one pamphlet Cohn herself outlines an eight-point "approach to preventing child abuse." Seven and a half of the points involve "educating" or "counseling" the parents.[99]

Cohn's group sends the same message to the children themselves. The group helped prepare a special *Spider-Man* comic book designed to teach children about emotional neglect. In one story, Susan's mother has no time for her. Is it because she's holding down two jobs to try to make ends meet? Is it because she was just cut off the welfare rolls due to a computer error and has to fight her way back? No way. The comic book implies that Susan's mother is one of those high-powered career women who doesn't know her place. She's seen at the dinner table looking through papers from her briefcase while poor Susan is trying to talk to her.

Eventually, we find out why Susan's mother has no time for her. She's been too busy "work[ing] with movie stars."[100] Aren't we all.

It was Norman Polansky and his colleagues who explained, perhaps unintentionally, why child savers cling so tenaciously to the "medical model." They write:

> Thus far, in discussing treatment, we have recognized public reluctance to intervene forcibly in families on two counts. One stems from respect for the Bill of Rights in our Constitution; the other from humane concern for the feelings of mothers, fathers, and children whom the intervention affects. Yet these values conflict with the desire to rescue the child.
>
> A way to resolve the conflict, of course, is to treat the state of functioning in the family as an aberration, a kind of sickness. *Ill people are not expected to be handled in the same way as everyone else* (emphasis added).[101]

*   *   *

There is one strand of modern child saving that, as far as I can tell, has no nineteenth-century counterpart.

Running through much of modern child saving, there is an undercurrent of hostility toward the very idea of families as a unit of societal organization. Among the saddest examples is a sort of unholy alliance between child savers and some feminists seen in some of the recent feminist scholarship on family violence.

Linda Gordon concludes her excellent historical study of child welfare with a surprisingly benevolent view of the child savers. In part this is because Gordon's study was not only about child maltreatment, but about violence against women as well. She writes:

> Women gained much from child protection agencies. Indeed, the inadequacy of means of caring for children outside their original families has meant that women may well have gained more, because children gained so little, from child protection work.[102]

Gordon says that the whole concept of "family autonomy" is a myth. She argues that family autonomy really means male-head-of-household autonomy and that family privacy means leaving men free to abuse women and children.[103]

Child saving agencies weren't so bad when there was a strong feminist movement—in the late 1800s and today, Gordon says. It was when feminism was in decline that child savers turned their attention from abuse committed by men to neglect defined as the responsibility of women. Thus, though Gordon offers no specific recommendations, her conclusion suggests a reluctance to curb coercive intervention into families that I find at odds with much of her own research. Gordon's analysis has several flaws:

—It is based on a research sample that is inherently skewed toward abusive families: case records from a child saving agency.

—In its description of family autonomy and family privacy it sets up a straw man, suggesting that those who believe in these concepts want to abolish, rather than merely limit, coercive intervention.

—It implies that because women sometimes asked for child saver help, this was the dominant reason for intervention. Her own research makes clear that often this was not the case, and there was a lot of intervention into families that were not abusive. Gordon emphasizes the cases where women sought out help. But nothing in modern calls to restrict coercive intervention and promote family preservation suggests that help should be denied when it is sought. It is forcing "help" on families—men, women, and children—when it does more harm than good that is of concern.

—It implies that now that there has been a resurgence of feminism, attention among child savers has switched back to cases of abuse. That is not so. Abuse cases are used now the way Gordon herself notes they were used a hundred years ago—to attract public support. The overwhelming majority of child saving still involves the cases where women are blamed, cases of neglect.

—And finally, there has been a crucial change since the period Gordon studied, which ended in 1960. Thanks in large measure to the efforts of feminists, women are not forced to stay in bad marriages to the extent that they used to be. For that reason and others, there are far fewer two-parent households among the poor. This means that when today's child savers barge into a family and destroy its autonomy and privacy, it is often a family headed by a woman that is destroyed.

If Gordon is suspicious of the family, Elizabeth Pleck is out to wage war on it. In *Domestic Tyranny: The Making of American Social Policy against Family Violence from Colonial Times to the Present,* she writes: "The single most consistent barrier to reform against domestic violence has been the Family Ideal."[104] As Pleck sees it, the ideal has three components: belief in domestic privacy, conjugal and parental rights, and the belief in family preservation—all of which add up to inevitable and automatic oppression of women.

"It follows, then, that the desire for personal autonomy, especially among women, would threaten family stability," Pleck writes. Among the concepts Pleck ridicules is the idea that ". . . the home is the only setting where intimacy can flourish, providing meaning, coherence, and stability in personal life." Since Pleck believes that "reform against family violence is an implicit critique of each element of the Family Ideal," she would just as soon abandon any efforts at family preservation altogether in favor of "a variety of programs that increase or strengthen the alternatives to maintaining the family."

The hostility to the family among some feminists is partly a backlash against some "friends" of the family that it could do without.

In the 1960s, during the height of the protests against the Vietnam War, the Far Right captured the flag and used it, sometimes literally, to hit over the head protestors who were engaging in an activity as American as apple pie—dissent. Rather than take back the flag, people on the Left reacted by burning it, becoming hostile to a symbol they should have embraced as their own.

In the 1980s, the Far Right did the same thing to the family. They used a concept they labeled "family values" to justify opposition to the Equal Rights Amendment, to abortion, and to day care, in short, to anything that promised the "personal autonomy" called for by feminists such as Pleck. And many feminists have reacted much as the anti-war protestors did. Rather than take back and redefine the concept of the family on their own terms, they have reacted with hostility and disdain to the whole idea.

But just as Richard Nixon's idea of America was not America, Phyllis Schlafly's idea of the family is not the family.

And it is a delusion for feminists to believe they will find any more sympathy from today's child savers than from those who, as Gordon has documented, sabotaged day care for poor women and insisted that a woman working out of the home was always a woman neglecting her children. Recall the questions on the first version of the Childhood Level of Living Scale, which gave a mother a brownie point if she "expresses feeling that her job is the housework" and took one away if she complained that her job was harder than her husband's. Recall the child saver comic book's portrayal of the neglectful career woman. "A very disturbing part [of the child-welfare system] is how victims of domestic violence are treated," says attorney Diane Redleaf. She cites a case in which "a woman was threatened with having her children removed because she hadn't prevented [her abusive husband] from breaking into her house."[105]

New York City Family Court Judge Leah Marks tells of a case she presided over in which a terrified mother went to a Child Protective Services office because her husband was beating her and sexually abusing the children. As soon as the woman left, the worker began an "investigation"—by calling the husband and telling him what his wife had said. The next day the woman called the caseworker and said it had all been a mistake, asking him to please drop the whole case. Two years later, the woman was hauled before the court. The charge: neglect. The reason: the woman had "allowed" her husband to sexually abuse the children.[106]

Jacquelynne Bowman, Managing Attorney for Family and Individual Rights at Greater Boston Legal Services, recalls a case in which "it was very clear that the mother did not harm the children; her boyfriend did. She got a restraining order against him. . . . Nobody was saying the mother was bad." But the child savers took her children away from her anyway. "She had had a very very close relationship [with the children]." . . . Bowman said, "She was saying, 'I never spent a day in my life away from those two kids.' "

At the time the woman was pregnant. Complications developed— Bowman believes because of the stress—and she had to be hospitalized for three months, making even visits with the other children impossible. After the birth, she remained in a severe depression. She gave away the baby. Now, Bowman says, "she's homeless and wandering the streets."

The woman's treatment at the hands of the child savers is "a very, very typical situation," Bowman says.[107]

There will always be cases in which it is necessary to separate children from their parents. But it is important to work to keep most families together because, like it or not, children need them.

"I have been both the child sent away from parents and the parent who was advised that I should give my child up for his own welfare," writes Maya Angelou.

> I survived the first condition by love and luck and resisted the second by the same interventions. . . . I was 22 years old and my son was six when a school psychologist informed me that my cabaret singing jobs were bad for my son. I was told he was hyperactive and would be better left with a foster family, for he needed security. I decided that wherever he was, I would be his security, and although we traveled from Hawaii to New York to Cairo to West Africa over the next ten years, we were together and neither of us was seriously the worse for our perambulations. We shared tears, frustrations, anger, love and laughter. . . .
>
> How much more strain is put upon the child who is uprooted and thrust among strangers with whom he has no mutual history? How is it

possible to convince a child of his own worth after removing him from a family which is said to be unworthy, but with whom he identifies?

When any child, vulnerable as the season's first snowflake, is handed into a strange atmosphere, even into a rare, sensitive and caring environment, the question which afflicts the newcomer is always, "If I wasn't good enough for my own family, which they say is no good, how can I be accepted here, before strangers?"[108]

Maybe the family isn't the *only* place "where intimacy can flourish, providing meaning, coherence, and stability in personal life." But it's still the best bet. For most of us it is still home—"the place where, when you have to go there, they have to take you in."

The biggest problem with trying to make a case against families comes when one tries to come up with good alternatives. Elizabeth Pleck, for example, can think of very few, and most prominent among them is "vastly expanding and improving foster care and adoption. . . ." But what is foster care except the substitution of one family for another—and quite likely the substitution of a male-headed family for a female-headed one at that.

One need not believe in "the Family Ideal" to believe in the need to replace child saving with family saving. One need only regard families the way Winston Churchill regarded democracy: Families are the worst form of societal organization—except for all the others.

4

The Numbers

Here are some statistics about child abuse you don't see very often:

—Between 95 and 99 out of every 100 women were *not* sexually abused by their fathers or stepfathers during their childhoods.[1]

—More than 99 out of 100 children are *not* beaten up by their parents every year.[2]

—More than 97 percent of all children are *not* abused or neglected in any way in the course of a year.[3]

These figures do not come from obscure sources. They are from the same studies that child savers themselves cite repeatedly. But they are from parts of those studies that child savers choose to ignore.

If there were a hotline to which abuse of statistics could be reported and a statistics-protective-services agency that could investigate such abuse, America's child savers would have their rights to their calculators permanently terminated.

The numbers bandied about most often are taken out of context, and numbers that call the approach of the child savers into question are ignored. Indeed, there is some evidence that the bias of child savers who edit the relevant scholarly journals is so strong that they unconsciously censor studies that do not support their preconceived notions.

Where then do the numbers we hear so often come from? They come from factoring in people like James Norman.

When Norman had his children taken away because he could not pay his utility bill, he became a statistic. In fact, he became a statistic as soon as someone phoned a child-protective "hotline" and alleged that Norman's children were maltreated.

From that moment on, James Norman became a "reported case." From then on, whenever news accounts say that there are two million "cases" of child abuse "reported" every year, they are talking about James Norman. They are also talking about Elene Humlen. The moment the school nurse called the Department of Children's Services to report her suspicions, the Humlen family became a "reported case" of child abuse. The parent who lost her child because the home was in poor condition and she couldn't afford a new pair of glasses is a "reported case." So is the parent who asked for a baby-sitter for her ten-year-old and had the child taken away instead. So is the woman who lost her child after she was kicked out of two apartments because of "no children" rules.

When people read news accounts about two million "reported cases," what image pops into their heads? Two million bruised and battered children? Two million potential Lisa Steinbergs? In fact, there are very, very few Lisa Steinbergs among those two million "reported cases." The majority of those two million are actually Chris Humlens—children who were not maltreated at all. And of the remainder, the majority are the children of people like James Norman, parents guilty of nothing more than poverty.

If such distinctions were drawn, the climate of public opinion that gives the child savers so much power would not exist. So when child savers talk numbers, they draw no distinctions. If people believe two million children are brutally beaten and tortured every year, it's easy to make everyone a suspect and allow for sweeping laws that set the stage for what happened to the Normans and the Humlens.

This does not mean that child abuse is a minor problem. The United States is a very big place. There are 64.3 million people in this country aged seventeen and under.[4] That is the number against which every other number must be measured. As a result, even a small percentage is still a big raw number. But a close look at child-maltreatment statistics suggests that the nature of the problem and the necessary solutions are very different than what the child savers would have us believe.

Before looking at specifics, it is important to define some terms and draw a crucial distinction.

A key theme of this book is that coercive intervention into the life of a family is harmful in and of itself. Therefore, any decision to intervene must weigh the harm of the intervention against the harm of the alleged maltreatment.

Once child abuse is alleged, a child-protective juggernaut rolls into action and enormous harm can result: Children can be traumatized by interrogations, strip-searches, and possibly needless removal from their homes. Given these potential consequences, child abuse as defined by law can't be allowed to become synonymous with anything that anyone might consider bad child rearing.

For example, I personally am opposed to corporal punishment (though I don't consider it child abuse)—at least I think I am. My daughter is only two-and-a-half years old as this is written and I have never really been put to the test. I am certain that I oppose any form of spanking other than an open hand on a clothed bottom. And I have no doubt, in terms of my personal values, that any spanking that leaves a bruise is abusive. So is any act of slapping or punching—even if it is done only once in the heat of anger. But for reasons I will explain in succeeding chapters, I also have no doubt that attempts to make this sort of personal standard the legal standard for child abuse—the standard that triggers coercive intervention—have done tremendous harm to thousands of children.

I mention this now because in this chapter I will use terms that offend my personal values and, I suspect, those of many readers. I will describe as "minor" or "less serious" conduct that violates those values. I use those terms only in the context of the higher standard that must be set for coercive intervention.

I offer a similar caveat concerning numbers of cases. Child abuse is *not* "almost as American as apple pie." But it is not rare either. The lowest numbers one can reasonably come up with still leave more than 1,100 children dead of abuse every year, 21,000 suffering major physical abuse, and more than 100,000 sexually abused.

The problem of child abuse is serious and real. It's the solutions that have been phony. The first step toward honest solutions is to try to get honest numbers.

*   *   *

The data that are used—and misused—most often come from two sources: the National Incidence Studies, which I referred to in the previous chapter, and an annual survey conducted by the American Humane Association (AHA).

The AHA tabulates cases of maltreatment reported to Child Protective Services agencies. Every year, the AHA gathers as much data as it can from as many states as are willing to give it. For the total number of reports, all fifty states, the District of Columbia, Guam, Puerto Rico, and the Virgin Islands are included. For other data, such as the type of maltreatment and the number of substantiated cases, the number of states from which data are available varies.

According to the most recent complete AHA report, 2,086,112 children were reported to be abused or neglected in 1986.[5] (In 1987, the number rose to 2,178,000, but the federal government stopped funding AHA's efforts to break down and analyze the data;[6] therefore, for the sake of comparability, except as otherwise noted, I will use the 1986 numbers.)

With that number comes the first major mistake commonly made by the media and often encouraged by the child savers.

A 1988 Associated Press story, apparently drawn from this data, began as follows: "From broken hearts to broken bones, more than two million children were abused and neglected across the United States last year."[7]

The reporter confused reports with cases—in other words, he mixed Christopher Humlen in with Lisa Steinberg.

A report is simply an allegation, something anyone can make by phoning a child-maltreatment hotline. The report can be made anonymously, and there need be no supporting evidence at all. After investigation, some effort is made to classify the report as true or false. Typically, states use terms like "substantiated" or "indicated" for true and "unsubstantiated" or "unfounded" for false. Once "indicated" the name of the accused is entered into a computerized central registry, sometimes for life.

It takes very little to indicate a case. It does not require a court hearing of any kind. A caseworker, usually acting entirely on his or her own, makes the decision. And nothing resembling proof is required. The worker need not be convinced beyond a reasonable doubt; there does not even have to be a "preponderance of the evidence"—the lowest standard of proof a court ever uses. Typically, the worker need only think she has "some credible evidence" that abuse or neglect occurred—or might occur sometime in the future, what AHA calls "at risk" cases.[8]

AHA combines this all into one table, so there is no way to tell how many indicated cases nationwide actually involved harm to the child. In New Jersey, however, where such a breakdown does exist, more than two-thirds of all *indicated* cases (67.7 percent) involved no actual injury to the child.[9] Douglas Besharov believes that at least half the indicated cases nationwide fall into the "at risk" category, including many that he describes as "junk neglect."[10]

When AHA published its 1982 data, this distinction was at least made clear in the headings accompanying the table showing the indicated and unfounded rates. By the time the 1984 data were published, the term "at risk" had been eliminated, and readers were left with no clue that this distinction exists.[11]

But despite the ease with which a case can be indicated and despite the low level of evidence required, according to the AHA data for 1986 only 40 to 42 percent of reports nationwide were indicated. The other 58 to 60 percent were unfounded.[12] (By 1987, according to AHA, only 37 to 40 percent of reports were indicated.)

For a while, the child savers simply ignored this number, and the media didn't raise the issue. But in recent years, the number of unfounded cases has begun to attract more attention, so the child savers have switched from ignoring it to trying to discredit it.

Thus, Anne Cohn writes that "*most* child abuse reports are 'unfounded' or 'unsubstantiated' because workers do not have enough evidence to present a case in court . . . or they do not have services to offer the family, or their caseload sizes are too high to take on another investigation" (emphasis in original).[13] Other commentators have cited the lack of training and experience of most child-protective workers and the practice in some states of listing a case as unfounded if the accused can't be located.

Cohn's assertion about "present[ing] a case in court" is a red herring, since the workers make the "indicated" determinations on their own. Her contention that "most" cases are labeled "unfounded" for that or similar reasons is a reflection not of the data but of the guilty-until-proven-innocent mentality of the child savers. Cohn's assertion about not indicating a case where no services are available may have some validity in that it can sometimes spare a worker some effort. But it is important to indicate a case if something really did happen in order to have a record if something happens again; so, it is unlikely that this problem is widespread.

Some of the other reasons for concluding nothing happened when it really did, commonly called "false negatives," have more validity. One cannot argue, as I do, that there is widespread incompetence in Child Protective Services without acknowledging that sometimes such incompetence will lead to failure to find real abuse. Similarly, CPS agencies are so flooded with reports that investigations are sometimes delayed past the time evidence could be found. So clearly, there are false negatives. But, as Aber and others have pointed out, for every false negative, there is at least one *false positive*—someone who is wrongly "indicated" as a child abuser—and probably a whole lot more.[14]

There are several reasons:

—The arguments about heavy caseloads and hasty investigations cut both ways. Just as these problems can lead to missing real abuse, they can lead to missing exculpatory evidence. A county Social Services Commissioner in New York notes that, contrary to the statewide trend, the proportion of indicated cases in his county is going up. But he says he doesn't know if that's because "people are having more problems, workers are better trained, or they're so overworked that they're indicating a case so they can move on to the next case."[15]

—In some cases, a parent is wrongly labeled an abuser on purpose, because it may be the only way to provide any services to a child in trouble. A study of reports to child-protective-services agencies concluded that "many of the reports made to CPS may reflect the fact that child-welfare services are accessible only through an imputation of abuse and neglect."[16]

For example, New York State law requires the provision of services to families in which a child is in imminent danger, and the state reimburses localities for 75 percent of the cost. Where such danger does not exist, localities can refuse services, and, when they do provide them, the state pays only half the cost. Because a finding of abuse or neglect is a major way to "prove" such risk, a New York City study concluded that "labeling of clients may be exaggerated, given the higher reimbursement rate for mandated cases."[17] Similarly, a study of the CPS system in Philadelphia concludes that "children [are] declared dependent just to secure needed services. . . ."[18]

"A protective case gets first dibs on services," says Jacquelynne Bowman of Greater Boston Legal Services. "A number of workers admitted they [indicated a case] to get services."

Geraldine Churchwell says that's what happened to her. Churchwell is the woman cited in the previous chapter who charged in a lawsuit that she was forced to institutionalize her child because Children's Hospital was threatening to report her to CPS if she didn't. After she gave in, the institution reported her to CPS anyway—in order to get services for her daughter.[19]

Massachusetts workers confirmed the practice. Some towns are rich in services for families and some are not, says Scott Scholefield, a CPS supervisor in Fitchburg. If a case comes in from one of the poorer towns, he says, "it's more likely to be screened in" in order to get services to the family.[20]

—As noted earlier, the AHA data for "indicated" cases include those where nothing has happened yet, but might in the future. Besharov estimates at least half the "indicated" cases fit this description.

—Among the most important reasons for false positives is what Besharov calls "defensive social work." Put yourself in a caseworker's shoes and imagine the following scenario:

A child has just been beaten to death by his father. Child Protective Services had previously investigated the family and found no problem. Because the child was white and the family was middle class, the press has taken an extraordinary interest. Editorials ask, "Who let Johnny die?" State legislators promise to "crack down on child abuse" and are preparing to call your boss on the carpet at a public hearing. The local district attorney has ambitions for higher office. He's talking about convening a grand jury and bringing criminal charges against the workers involved in the case.

The next time you go out to investigate a complaint, what are you going to do?

"The dynamic is simple enough," Besharov writes. "Negative media publicity—and a lawsuit—is always possible if the child [is left at home and] is subsequently killed or injured; but there will be no critical publicity if it turns out that intervention was unneeded—and how could people tell anyway?"[21]

"The easiest thing, the safest thing for me from a 'save-my-ass' point of view, is to get that kid out of that home," says Foster Cline, a child psychiatrist and director of Evergreen Consultants in Evergreen Colorado. "Because that's a lot less likely to be questioned than leaving a kid in the home, and then if abuse takes place, I'm dead in the water."[22]

"Public pressure says the primary way to protect children is to remove them from their homes," says Robert Schwartz, executive director of the Juvenile Law Center in Philadelphia. "No judge or worker is going to be blasted for placing a child in foster care. . . . The politics of the field preys on the workers."[23]

Besharov quotes a program director who was indicted for "allowing" a child to be killed: "Upon learning of the indictments, caseworkers and their supervisors became aware of their own vulnerability. As a result . . . for a while more children were removed from their homes. Supervisors told me that these removals seemed unnecessary but that caseworkers were afraid."[24] At another agency, Besharov writes, indictments caused "tremendous, agency-wide panic. As rumors about the case spread, morale plummeted and children were removed from their families at the slightest hint of danger."[25]

A recent United States Supreme Court decision (*DeShaney* v. *Winnebago County*) giving workers some immunity if their failure to remove a child leads to serious injury does not redress the imbalance. The case affects only federal lawsuits. States remain free to do what they want, the press remains free to pillory workers, and district attorneys remain free to bring criminal charges.

Such cases are extremely attractive for prosecutors and civil attorneys. Their client is a defenseless child and they will have strong public support. Conversely, as the Humlen case shows, workers are immune from liability if they wrongfully remove a child, and there is rarely any good press in going to bat for some inarticulate poor person who says she really didn't neglect her child and asks that the child not be taken away. As a practical matter the scales of justice are tilted strongly toward removing children unnecessarily.

Perhaps the most vivid example of defensive social work, and what it does to children, is the Washington State foster-care panic of 1987.

In September 1986, three-year-old Eli Creekmore of Everett, Washington, was kicked to death by his father. The child had been repeatedly removed from his home, only to be returned time after time. The case caused the same kind of sensation in Washington State that the Lisa Steinberg case caused all over the country. Extensive media coverage of the Creekmore case included an edition of ABC's "Nightline" and a nationally broadcast public-television documentary.

State legislators debated numerous proposals to improve the system. Those that involved actually improving services by spending more money were largely defeated. Those that made legislators look like they were "cracking down on child abuse" without actually spending a dime were passed. Thus, state law was amended to emphasize that the safety of a child was more important than preserving the family. The change was based on two popular misconceptions: that removal always equals safety and keeping the child in the home always equals danger, and that family preservation and child safety are inherently at odds with each other. Both these fallacies and the terrible consequences of the foster-care panic on Washington State's children will be dealt with in later chapters. For now, I will look only at the bottom line:

In July 1986, two months before Eli Creekmore died, there were 5,254 children in foster care in Washington State, a number which had been fairly steady for the previous several years. Three years later, the number soared to 6,384.[26] According to the Washington State Governor's Commission on Children, because of the Creekmore case, "Caseworkers have become more cautious and tentative in the exercise of their assigned responsibilities, especially the retention of children within the home. . . . Due to the perceived and/or actual civil and criminal liability . . . caseworkers may be recommending out-of-home placements in marginally substantiated cases."[27]

John Weeden, foster-care program manager for the state's Department of Social and Health Services, estimates that 50 to 75 percent of the foster-care increase is directly attributable to reaction to the Creekmore death.[28] Elizabeth Monroe, a Washington State Public Defender, recalled a conversation with a police detective investigating a spanking: "The detective says to me: 'I have to pursue this as far as I can, and I'm recommending the book be thrown at this client. She spanked her kids too hard, there were marks on [them]. And the reason I'm doing this is after Eli Creekmore, I just smell it when it's here. I know it, and I'm not going to be held liable if something happens.' "[29]

Of course some may feel defensive social work is good because at least it is keeping children safe. In Chapter 7, I will explain why it does nothing of the kind.

The mass of evidence suggests that the number of innocent families wrongly indicated at least equals the guilty families who are missed and probably far exceeds it.

In two states where parents are permitted to appeal a child-abuse finding, the results are startling.

In New York State, about 50 percent of indicated findings are over-turned on appeal, even though the hearing officer uses the same low standard of proof as the caseworker.[30] In Florida, during one six-month period, an astounding 92 percent of indicated determinations were overturned. When the administrator of Florida's central registry for child maltreatment was asked about this, he replied, "Everybody makes mistakes."[31] These numbers need to be examined with some caution. Only a very small number of people listed in central registries appeal (in New York, it's about 5 percent), and it seems reasonable to assume that the sample would be skewed toward those who have the best cases.

The same cannot be said, however, about what the National Incidence Studies found. One of the things these studies did was to second-guess child-protective workers.

In a letter to the editor of the *Wall Street Journal,* Deborah Daro of the National Committee for Prevention of Child Abuse wrote about part of what NIS-2 found: "Nine percent of the cases determined to be unfounded by Child Protective Service workers did indeed involve mis-treatment that had resulted in significant harm to the child."[32]

Daro is right, but she is telling less than half the story. NIS-2 also concluded that 61 percent of the cases indicated by CPS *did not qualify as maltreatment* under NIS-2 definitions. In other words, there were more than six times as many innocent families accused as there were guilty families missed.[33] The information about the cases wrongly indicated appears in the same document, on the same page, in the same table as the information about cases that were missed—yet somehow it never made it into Daro's letter to the editor.

Perhaps this is because child savers consider the NIS definition too strict. That complaint arose after the first National Incidence Study in 1980. As a result, the second study actually contains two definitions, including a broader one specially included to meet child saver objections. But even under this looser definition, there were still more than twice as many innocent families wrongly declared abusive as there were guilty families who were missed (27 percent vs. 12 percent). This didn't get into Daro's letter either.

Where does all this leave us? Roughly back where we started. At least 60 percent of child-abuse reports—and maybe as many as 80 percent, when the so-called "at risk" cases are included—are false. Not "unfounded," not "unsubstantiated"—just plain false. And that means there were at least 1,306,800 false child-abuse reports in 1987.

That proposition will be vigorously disputed by the child savers, of course. But surely even the most ardent child savers can't really believe that no family is ever wrongly labeled abusive. Why, then, does child saver writing completely ignore this possibility?

Child saver publications repeatedly warn readers not to believe data about unfounded reports, even going so far as to suggest, as Anne Cohn did, that in most unfounded cases, the accused really did it. Yet, to read the work of NCPCA, AHA, and like-minded groups, one would not even know that a CPS worker could mistakenly "indicate" a report. An NCPCA "fact sheet" called "What Do We Know About 'Unsubstantiated' Child Abuse Reports?"[34] lists eight possible reasons for missing real abuse. It does not even acknowledge that wrongly accused families exist. The AHA has played similar games with numbers.[35]

The next step in analyzing the AHA data is to examine what kind of maltreatment is included among the indicated cases. The single largest category, bigger than all the others combined, is not physical abuse of any kind or sexual abuse or emotional abuse. It's "deprivation of necessities" defined as "neglecting to provide the following when able to do so: nourishment, clothing, shelter, health care, education, supervision or causing failure to thrive."[36] Though this definition, like some state laws, contains the phrase "when able to do so," such provisions are routinely ignored when cases are indicated, as illustrated by the studies and cases in the previous chapter.

This is the category where all those neglect-confused-with-poverty cases are logged. It is the category AHA itself acknowledges "likely is related to . . . economic status."[37] When James Norman became a statistic, he was counted under "deprivation of necessities." In 1986, deprivation of necessities constituted 54.9 percent of all reports, indicated and unfounded.

Another 8.3 percent of reports concerned "emotional maltreatment" defined by AHA as parental (or other caretaker) behavior "which causes low self-esteem in the child, undue fear or anxiety, or other damage to the child's emotional well-being." Obviously, a definition this vague is susceptible to the same kind of misuse by child savers as is "deprivation of necessities." An AHA guide for caseworkers does not clarify the situation. According to the guide, emotionally maltreated children are "denied normal experiences that produce feelings of being loved, wanted, secure, and worthy." Characteristics of a separate but similar category, "demoralizing circumstances," include "immature parents," "failure to individualize children and their needs," and "values in home conflict with society."[38]

The problem is made more complex because the behavior a child displays that allegedly shows emotional neglect is the same behavior that an emotionally disturbed child will display through no fault of the parents.[39] This prompts child savers to try and make their judgments based on how the behavior of the parents stacks up against their personal prejudices.

When CPS workers were asked to list behaviors they considered to be emotional maltreatment of a child, they included singling out one child for more punishment and chores and fewer rewards; forcing the child to wear clothing "inappropriate" for his or her age or sex; not providing "security or stability" for the child; barring the child from extracurricular activities "without sufficient reason or alternatives"; and using "excessive" threats or psychological punishments.[40]

In other words, the judgment of a parent concerning who is best suited to do the chores, what clothes a child is to wear, what constitutes stability, when the child can stay after school, and how much "psychological punishment" is too much is to be supplanted by the judgment of a CPS worker who usually has no training in child development, little experience in child-protective work, and possibly no children.

Some of these grounds may well be reasons to offer help, but what could be more foolish than to allow a child to be thrust into foster care, about the most unstable existence around, because the parents are not providing enough "stability"?

Unfortunately, the same survey found that turning down child saver help also should be grounds for an emotional-neglect finding.

Finally, we come to the easier-to-define categories of physical and sexual abuse. Sexual maltreatment constituted 15.7 percent of all reports, and minor physical injury constituted 13.9 percent. "Minor physical injury" is defined as "twisting/shaking, minor cuts/bruises/welts or any combination thereof which do not constitute a substantial risk to the life and well-being of the child." In contrast, the kind of physical abuse people immediately think of as child abuse, defined by AHA as including brain damage, burns, broken bones, or "severe cuts/lacerations/bruises/welts," constituted only 2.6 percent of all reports.[41]

Boiling it all down, out of every one hundred reports alleging child abuse or neglect:
—at least fifty-eight are false;
—twenty-one are mostly poverty cases (deprivation of necessities);
—six are sexual abuse;
—four are minor physical abuse;
—four are unspecified physical abuse;
—three are emotional maltreatment;
—three are "other maltreatment";
—one is major physical abuse.

Out of the more than two million reports of maltreatment in 1986, according to AHA's data, there were 21,000 cases of major physical abuse and 132,000 cases of sexual abuse.[42] That translates into one out of every three thousand children suffering serious physical abuse and just over one in five hundred sexually abused. These totals are remarkably similar to those in the National Incidence Studies.

Earlier I explained how the National Incidence Studies were done, and I alluded to the fact that NIS-2 used two different definitions of maltreatment. Here's how that happened:

When the first National Incidence Study was done, the study counted only children "who experienced demonstrable harm as a result of maltreatment."[43]

But though it might seem logical that a study designed to determine the amount of child abuse would count only abused children, child savers demanded that the so-called "at risk" cases be counted as well. So the researchers conducting NIS-2 did it both ways. In fact, they made the new definition so broad that they automatically included any case in their sample that a CPS agency substantiated. Under the new definition, only cases from other sources would be second-guessed.

Here's what happened. NIS-2 found that under the old definitions there were 1,025,900 maltreated children in America in 1986. Under the new, broader, take-CPS's-word-for-it definition, the number rose to 1,584,700 children either maltreated or at risk.

Naturally, these were the numbers that grabbed the headlines.

But NIS-2 also divided the reports into "serious" maltreatment and "moderate" maltreatment.[44] The result: Of the more than one million cases counted, there were 1,100 fatalities, 157,100 cases of serious maltreatment, and 740,000 cases of moderate maltreatment under the original definitions.[45] Under the revised definitions, the number of serious cases barely rises at all—to 161,000. The increase comes almost entirely from the "moderate-maltreatment" category which rises to 952,000 and from adding the "at risk" cases.[46]

The bottom-line number, 161,100 cases of serious maltreatment in 1986, is remarkably close to the combined total for serious physical abuse and sexual abuse found by AHA, 153,000.

NIS-2 also tells us that we don't need a broad definition of child maltreatment to uncover the really serious cases for which coercive intervention is essential. When the NIS researchers broadened the definition, the number of serious cases discovered barely increased at all.

The other major sources of data about child abuse are studies that use survey research techniques to try to find out how many children in America suffer some form of child abuse either in a year or during their entire childhoods.

These studies have suffered from one or both of two major problems: extremely broad definitions of maltreatment and/or failure to distinguish between abuse by immediate family members vs. abuse by distant relatives or strangers. Some of the studies also suffer from methodological problems.

A bigger problem has been the misinterpretation or selective use of data from the studies by child savers and the press. Different studies have produced vastly different results, but only the studies that purport to reveal huge numbers of maltreated children get any publicity.

One of the first such studies was done by David Gil in 1967. Defining child abuse as "when an adult physically injures a child, not by accident but in anger or deliberately" with no definition of the word "injures," Gil asked a cross-section of Americans if they knew of families where abuse had occurred.[47] Extrapolating from the results, Gil concluded that between 2.53 and 4.07 million children might have been abused the previous year. But when another researcher, Richard Light, restudied the data using different underlying assumptions but retaining the same broad definition, he came up with a figure only about 10 percent as high as Gil's—between 200,000 and 500,000 cases.[48] Gil himself acknowledged his numbers were unreliable and probably too high, adding: "Physical abuse cannot be considered a major killer and maimer of children."[49]

Another University of New Hampshire study involved interviews with more than 6,000 parents concerning their child-rearing practices. Projecting their findings to current census data, the study found that slightly more than 348,000—six in a thousand—children are "beaten up" by a parent every year. (This term was not defined in their questionnaire, but the researchers assume that respondents took it to mean "something more than just a single blow.")[50] But that still means that 994 out of 1,000 American children do not get beaten up by their caretakers every year. The same study found that 98 out of 100 homes are free from all forms of what the authors call "abusive violence."[51]

Survey research has gotten the most attention in the area of sexual abuse. The statement "one out of three girls and one out of ten boys will be sexually abused" has been made so often, most people surely believe it. But these figures are from those among many different studies that came up with the highest totals. Many studies report much lower totals but get little attention and rarely are mentioned by child savers, and some of the studies that do produce high numbers use extremely broad definitions that lump together a single instance of witnessing a stranger exposing himself to repeated forcible rape by a parent.

Among the most publicized studies is one conducted by Diana Russell in which 930 women were asked during lengthy, in-person interviews if they had been sexually abused before the age of eighteen. It is from this study that the "one-out-of-three women" figure is derived, since it found that 38 percent of the women had experienced some form of sexual abuse during their entire childhoods (not in a single year).[52] Obviously, if these numbers are correct, sexual abuse is a problem of horrendous proportions.

But it is misleading to use this gross figure to argue for unlimited coercive intervention by child savers.

That's because the 38 percent figure includes far more than sexual abuse by parents or siblings. When only abuse by fathers and brothers is counted, the figure drops to 6.5 percent. When fathers (and stepfathers) alone are counted, it's 4.5 percent. (Mothers and sisters accounted for only .4 percent of sexual abuse of women.)

What this means is that, according to Russell's findings, at most from five to seven in one hundred women ever were sexually abused by someone who should be under the jurisdiction of Child Protective Services—a parent, stepparent, or, in some cases, a sibling.[53] That's still a figure that should provoke anger, concern, and action. But seven in a hundred is not the same as one in three.

Furthermore, more than one-third of the incest cases in Russell's study—36 percent—involved "forcible . . . [or] nonforcible sexual kissing, *intentional* sexual touching of buttocks, thigh, leg, or clothed breasts or genitals" (emphasis added), a definition that leaves room for possible misunderstanding. If these cases are not included, the total for which CPS intervention could reasonably be invoked drops to between three and five in a hundred.

And other studies have found lower numbers. A study by David Finkelhor, a researcher sympathetic to the child savers, found that only 1 percent of the women he surveyed were abused by their fathers. Although a much higher percentage—8 percent—reported some form of sexual experience with a brother, Finkelhor asked about all forms of sexual experience, everything from "playing doctor" to rape—not just abusive experiences. A second Finkelhor study found that 5 percent of the women surveyed reported being sexually abused by a relative.

A Texas study found that 5.4 percent of those surveyed, men and women, had been abused by an adult. A second Texas study reported that 4.3 percent of those surveyed, again, men and women, had had a sexual experience of any kind with a family member. And a South Carolina survey found only 1 percent of women surveyed reporting sexual abuse by any family member.[54]

Russell argues that any study with results different from hers is methodologically flawed. She cites one other study as coming up with numbers similar to her own. But Richard Gelles and Murray Straus, researchers sympathetic to the child savers, write, "There has yet to be a national survey that meets the normal standards of scientific evidence and can be used to determine a figure for frequency of sexual victimization of children."[55]

The problem with the survey research studies is less with the studies themselves than with what the child savers do with them. An NCPCA pamphlet reports only the gross totals of the two Finkelhor studies and breaks the Russell study down only by relatives and nonrelatives.[56] An NCPCA "fact sheet" says only that "studies of the general population of adults show that anywhere from 15 to 38 percent of females were sexually abused as children."[57] This kind of distortion is common even in what passes for "scholarship."

A case that deserves particular attention, since it has received a great deal of publicity, is a study of sexual-abuse allegations conducted by David P. H. Jones and J. Melbourne McGraw at the C. Henry Kempe National Center for the Prevention and Treatment of Child Abuse and Neglect at the University of Colorado School of Medicine.[58] The researchers looked at every case of sexual abuse reported to the Denver Department of Social Services in 1983, 576 cases in all. The department and the researchers agreed that 53 percent of the cases were indicated. Of the remainder, the researchers concluded that 23 percent were false and 24 percent lacked enough information to make a judgment. This was within one percentage point of the conclusions reached by the original caseworkers.

The 23 percent false figure is particularly significant because of where it came from. The Kempe Center is to scholars what the NCPCA is to the public, a center of child saver ideology. (It is named after the man credited with "rediscovering" child abuse and inventing the medical model to explain it.) The fact that even a study by researchers at the Kempe Center would find that almost one out of four sexual-abuse allegations could not even meet minimal standards for substantiation is highly significant. But this is not the way the researchers reported their findings.

The false reports fell into three categories: reports made in good faith that turned out to be wrong (17 percent), malicious reports made by parents (4 percent), and malicious reports made by children (2 percent).

Faced with such a high number of false reports, the researchers came up with the perfect child saver answer: They threw out their dictionaries and invented their own definition of the word "false."

Apparently following the lead of the Denver DSS, which came up with the categories, under the new, child saver definition, all the false reports that were not malicious were simply deemed not to be false. A new name was invented for them: "unsubstantiated suspicion." They also gave a new name to the malicious reports, calling them "fictitious."[59] The result: The child savers could now claim that out of all the child-abuse reports in Denver, only 6 percent were false!

At least people who read the entire study could figure out what was going on. But those who read only the one paragraph abstract at its beginning—which is what a reporter working on a tight deadline probably would do—wouldn't have a clue.

Indeed, the abstract further distorts the data by simply leaving out all the cases where there was "insufficient information." That skews the percentages, increasing the proportion of indicated cases from 53 percent to 70 percent. That was the only number for such cases given in the abstract. The only number given for false cases was 8 percent. The reader is left with the impression that 70 percent of all cases are true, and only 8 percent are false.

You can imagine what happened when the child savers got hold of this information. Under the heading "the 'problem' of false reports" (emphasis in original), an NCPCA pamphlet tells readers to, "note that this study, which is one of the few of false reporting, found that only 8 percent of reports were false."[60] It would have taken only eight more words, something like, "Another 17 percent were false, but not malicious," to at least put the study in context. But these words never appear.

And, of course, the Kempe Center study is not the only one to look at false reports of sexual abuse. (See Chapter 6.) But just as child savers only publicize studies concluding that real abuse is common, they publicize only studies concluding that false allegations are relatively rare.

The problem is compounded by what happens when scholars who do not share the child savers' biases try to get their work into print.

William Epstein, a social worker and consultant in social policy in Washington, D.C., wrote an article purporting to assess the effectiveness of a child saving intervention—removing the child from the home—in curing children's asthma attacks. But the study was a fake. The people Epstein really tested were the editors of "scholarly" journals concerned with social-work issues.

Epstein sent his "study" to 140 journals. Half got a version concluding that the child saving intervention succeeded, the other half got a version stating it failed. The result: 53 percent of the journals that got the version saying child saving worked accepted the article for publication. Only 14 percent of those that received the version saying child saving failed agreed to print the article. Epstein's conclusion: "Social work exists outside the critical tradition of objective science. The referees of these journals are not able to apply objectivity or the standards of science."

Epstein's study suggests there may be a lot of research proving the failure of child saving interventions gathering dust on office shelves. As another scholar put it: "If your findings are not in print, they don't exist."

Equally instructive was the reaction of social-work leaders to Epstein's results. They did not thank him and pledge to clean up their act. Instead, for the crime of successfully fooling journal editors, they charged Epstein with professional misconduct and hauled him before a closed hearing to decide whether to kick him out of the National Association of Social Workers.[61]

One other example of misuse of numbers deserves mention. Whenever the use of coercive intervention for something other than physical or sexual abuse is questioned, child savers reply that this other form of maltreatment—whatever it is—"is even worse than physical abuse." Neglect is said to be worse than physical abuse because children can and do die of it when, for example, it involves failure to provide medical care or food. Emotional maltreatment is said to be worse because a torrent of verbal abuse can leave scars that take much longer to heal than broken bones.

Once again, the child savers have said something that is not entirely wrong. When neglect can include anything from starving children to sending them to a fast food restaurant, obviously there will be cases where neglect is worse than abuse. It is not true, however, that not letting a child stay after school for football practice is worse than physical abuse. They have used the extreme cases to justify sweeping definitions that allow intervention into vast numbers of cases where no serious maltreatment exists. And, as the NIS results prove, the sweeping definitions are not needed to get at serious maltreatment.

At the outset, I noted that even the lowest estimates of the amount of child maltreatment in America show that the problem is serious and real. So why do the child savers seem so determined to exaggerate? I believe there are two reasons.

First, it is what politicians and the press demand. Most stories get into a newspaper or on the evening news in one of four ways: They involve an event that has taken place in the past twenty-four hours and is of significant interest or importance, they appeal to the personal whims of an editor, they come complete with great pictures, or they represent a trend.

Child abuse sometimes fits category one, as when a rich, white child is killed, and it sometimes fits category two. It rarely fits category three. To ensure sustained attention, child abuse has to be a category-four story.

To get on the serious news and feature pages, a trend must be widespread, and it must be getting worse. But that alone isn't enough anymore. There are lots of widespread growing problems in America. For people concerned with any particular problem to be heard above the din of other clamoring interest groups, their problem has to be bigger and/or growing faster than anybody else's.

Indeed, when sources won't provide an inflated numbers themselves, reporters sometimes try to goad them into it. The dialogue goes something like this:

Reporter: How many people are affected?
Expert: There is absolutely no way to know.
Reporter: Well can you give some idea?
Expert: It's impossible, there are just no reliable data.
Reporter: Well, how about a ballpark estimate?
Expert: I just wouldn't feel comfortable doing that.

Reporter: Well, does it only affect, say, one hundred people nationwide?

Expert: Oh, no, it's certainly more than that.

Reporter: Well does it affect ten million people?

Expert: Oh, no, not nearly that many.

The reporter keeps going in this vein, and pretty soon he or she has a number. Politicians are equally likely to play this game.

In October 1981, John Walsh, whose son Adam had been kidnapped and murdered a few months before, testified before a United States Senate committee. "We were told not to come here without some statistics,"[62] Walsh said at one point. So he gave them some.

Walsh declared that fifty thousand children are abducted by strangers and disappear every year. Nobody challenged the number at the time. Some of the senators started using it themselves, and soon the estimate took on a life of its own. The real number of stranger abductions each year is no more than two hundred to three hundred.[63]

Several years later, Walsh admitted that "I can't defend those figures,"[64] but by then the panic he had helped to start had swept the nation. Pictures of missing children were plastered on milk cartons and mail from your congressman; some children's earliest memories now include being taken down to the shopping mall to be fingerprinted; fast-buck artists cashed in with games and gimmicks; a lot of children became terrified of every adult they didn't know; and a lot of adults became afraid to smile at a child.

If nothing else in this chapter illustrates the need to beware of child saver numbers, the missing children panic certainly should.

There is a second reason for the exaggeration. The child savers have demanded and largely gotten incredibly drastic "solutions" to the problem of child maltreatment. They have virtually unrestrained access to any home in America without a warrant; they can list the accused in a central registry of alleged abusers, sometimes for life, on their own say-so; in many cases they have the right to take "temporary" custody of a child at will, with no hearing of any kind beforehand; they can deny the accused the right to face the accuser; and they can keep a child in custody indefinitely by meeting only the lowest standard of proof in American jurisprudence.

It takes more than ordinary numbers to stampede Americans into giving up so much of their liberty. It takes panic-inducing numbers. And that is what the exaggerated numbers put forward by the child savers are designed to do.

As Giovannoni and Becerra have written: "As in all politically sensitive matters, greater specificity and factual information are less likely to produce the desired emotional response."[65]

The chapters that follow look at the consequences of this panic.

5

Innocent Families

On a late-spring afternoon in 1986, Susan Gabriel got into her car and drove into the mountains near her home in Colorado Springs, Colorado. She parked the car next to a ravine and "found a nice, flat rock." Then she swallowed "a whole bunch" of tranquilizers and some codeine left over from recent oral surgery. She washed it down with some wine cooler and lay down on the rock to die.

Nineteen-eighty-six should have been a good year for Susan Gabriel. The year before she had met her husband Clark and married him after a three-month engagement. But only six weeks after they were married, in February 1986, Clark Gabriel was accused of sexually abusing Susan's nine-year-old daughter, Sara, from her first marriage.

Susan Gabriel survived her suicide attempt, and the whole family survived their ordeal at the hands of the child savers. Clark was acquitted of the abuse charges, and his name was expunged from the state's central registry. A new county social services director even named Clark to a review board to handle complaints against the agency. The Gabriels formed a chapter of Victims of Child Abuse Laws and try to help other families.

But vindication came at a high price. They lost custody of their daughter for three years, they spent thirty thousand dollars to defend themselves, and the stress caused Susan to have a miscarriage.[1]

The Gabriels were victims of a system in which workers, when they are trained at all, are trained to assume that all parents are guilty; they are conditioned to close their eyes, their ears, and their minds to anything that would indicate otherwise. They work in a system that gives them virtually unlimited power to intervene in the lives of families with virtually no accountability for the consequences. The power is given based on the false premise that only parents can hurt children, while child saver intervention is harmless.

Children have virtually no protection from their saviors. Based on nothing more than an anonymous telephone call, children can be brutally interrogated, strip-searched, and taken terrified and screaming from their homes at the sole discretion of an untrained "protective" worker.

To the child savers, that's the way it should be. Says Mary Goodhue, chairwoman of the Child Care Committee of the New York State Senate: "If [investigators] are wrong, well they shouldn't be. Too bad. Everybody makes mistakes."[2] Sara Gabriel was a victim of one of those "mistakes." And she is not alone. Glenn Joyner wrote of two other such cases in *Woman's Day*:

For Bob and Kathy Alexander, the nightmare began when their eleven-month-old daughter, Kristin, fell over a fat pencil on the kitchen floor. Because she continued to cry, Kathy rushed her daughter to her pediatrician, who diagnosed a barely perceptible spiral fracture of the lower leg. But the pediatrician did not have the facilities to put the leg in a cast, so the family went to a local emergency room.

Many doctors and CPS workers are told in their training that a spiral fracture automatically means abuse. Often it does. But it is simply not true that such fractures are never accidental.

The doctor at the emergency room refused to believe the Alexanders, and even though X-rays revealed no prior injuries, he called the parents liars, accused them of abuse, and called CPS. At midnight, CPS arrived and took immediate custody of Kristin. Her parents were allowed to ride with the crying, fearful child until they got to the foster-care facility. But when Kathy Alexander asked to nurse her terrified daughter to sleep, the child savers refused.

Kristin stayed at the foster home for four days. Her mother was not even allowed to bring breast milk to her, and the forced weaning made the little girl sick.

Eventually, two other doctors backed up the Alexanders' account, and the doctor who brought the original charges admitted the injury could have occurred the way the Alexanders said it did. All charges were dropped. But for several months afterward, Kristin suffered from temper tantrums and chronic diarrhea. And she rejected the mother whom, she thought, had rejected her.[3]

For Robin and Bob Johnson of Apple Valley, California, it began when Robin took her four-year-old daughter, Sandy, to her pediatrician because the child had a vaginal discharge. Solely because such discharges are "uncommon" in young children, the pediatrician reported the family to CPS.

Sandy, who had recently seen a videotape about child sexual abuse, denied that anything like that had happened to her. When she was interviewed by a CPS worker using "anatomically correct dolls," she denied it again. But the pediatrician called again and demanded action after a lab report identified the discharge as *Gardnerella vaginalis.*

Although this bacteria can be sexually transmitted, it can be transmitted other ways as well and it is quite common. One of the nation's leading experts said, "The presence of *Gardnerella* means absolutely nothing! Zero! And anyone who suggests that its presence is an indicator of sexual abuse has no idea what he's talking about."

What's more, a second laboratory said the first lab misidentified the bacteria—actually it was another common bacteria that is not sexually transmitted at all.

But none of this stopped the child savers.

On March 8, 1985, as Robin Johnson cowered in a corner with her daughter, two CPS workers and two sheriff's deputies converged on the Johnson home.

"Open up, Mrs. Johnson, we know you're in there," a deputy yelled. Robin finally let them in when they threatened to break down the door. "You can't take my baby," she screamed. "I won't let you." But they could and they did, pulling Sandy from her mother's arms and hauling the screaming four-year-old away.

Six months later, all charges were dismissed. But before that happened:

—Sandy's ten-year-old sister was interrogated three times at her school and left in tears each time. The first time she was asked, "Do your mom or dad ever lock you in closets? Do they beat you with whips or chains? Do they ever touch you in private places?" By the third interrogation, they were telling the ten-year-old they thought she had been molested, and she probably would be taken from her parents.

—Sandy herself was put through four more physical examinations in thirteen days and at least three psychological evaluations. At least seventeen different people asked her if she had been molested, and she always said no. Only one of the physicals allegedly found evidence of abuse, and that was based mostly on the erroneous lab report. The doctor who performed that exam is paid ten thousand dollars a month by CPS to do such exams and testify in court about them.

—The Johnsons lost their truck, their camper, and their home to pay attorney's fees. At a legislative hearing in 1986, Robin said, "Winning our case cost us everything except each other." But she spoke too soon. Robin Johnson is outgoing and a fighter by nature. Her husband is more reserved.

The strain of the incident destroyed the marriage. The child savers had created two more children of divorce.[4]

And there have been other such cases:

—In Orange Park, Florida, Mary Thomas was arrested on charges of aggravated child abuse and jailed for three days, because a doctor alleged she had waited too long to get treatment for a severe blister on the toe of an eighteen-month-old foster child in her care.

The doctor wrote a memo saying that the toe might have to be amputated. He wrote the memo three days after the toe had healed to the point that the child was released from the hospital—and he wrote it based solely on photographs and a telephone conversation with another doctor. He never examined the child himself.

All charges were dismissed and Thomas's name was expunged from the state's central registry.[5]

—In Baton Rouge, Louisiana, a child was forced into foster care for three days after her mother's car broke down, and she was two hours late picking her daughter up from school. Agency officials said they were "following normal procedures."[6]

—In Hennepin County, Minnesota, police removed two children from their parents before Child Protective Services had done any investigation at all. The removal was apparently based on an anonymous call followed by a secondhand account from police who had questioned the mother and neighbors. Those neighbors, according to court records, "later asserted that the questions asked and reports made by police were distorted and designed to corroborate [the] allegations."

The mother pleaded for an investigation by CPS. But no worker visited them until after the charges had already been dismissed by the courts. At that time, the worker concluded that the report was unfounded.[7]

Cathleen Dillon McHugh is the grown daughter of a New Jersey man falsely accused by the state's Division of Youth and Family Services (DYFS) of sexually abusing her adopted sister. In addition to raising his own children, the man had been a foster parent with an unblemished record. By the time all charges were dismissed, Dillon McHugh says, it was too late:

> Here was a man that DYFS destroyed. He's 65, retired, and never even had a traffic ticket. My older sister and I will never forget seeing him behind bars for no reason. My parents are heartbroken and my dad lives in fear that someone could falsely accuse him again.
>
> Their house was always alive with the sound of children. Always, you would visit and my dad would be reading a story or playing a game with one child and my mom would be feeding or dressing another one. Now their house echoes with silence for they are too afraid to take care of children.
>
> DYFS not only lost a great set of foster parents, which they have

a shortage of, but through their incompetence have torn a family apart. It is only our strong love that enabled us to survive this traumatic and unnecessary ordeal.[8]

Just as most cases labeled "child abuse" are not cases of brutal beatings, most of the more than one million false accusations made annually do not lead to the kind of harm suffered by the Gabriels, the Alexanders, or the Johnsons. But even when investigators do no more than question all parties involved and then close the case, they do cause harm.

Looking for Symptoms

The problem begins with the panic-inducing numbers cited earlier. They are used to urge all of us to report even the slightest suspicion of maltreatment to the child savers.

But how do we know? Serious physical abuse is easy enough to spot, but other forms of maltreatment are not. So the child savers have come up with lists of signs and symptoms that we all are supposed to watch for. Most of them revolve around a child's behavior. Such symptoms can be signs of child abuse or neglect—and they can be signs of dozens of other things.

For example, a brochure from a group called Childhelp USA says that signs of maltreatment include: "consistent lack of cleanliness or an intense obsession with cleanliness . . . behavior which indicates apathy or depression . . . behavior which is anti-social and hostile in nature . . . child . . . refuses to participate or dress appropriately for physical activities and/ or appears to spend extended periods of time in a fantasy world."[9]

In other words, report the parents of any child who is too tidy, too messy, too loud, too quiet, too imaginative, or too uninterested in sports.

An examination of six commonly available pamphlets turned up seventy-one different "behavioral symptoms" of sexual abuse alone, many of which turned up in just one of the pamphlets.[10] There is hardly a child in America who has not experienced at least one of the symptoms at one time or another. They include: clinging, anxious, irritable behavior; nightmares, bedwetting, fear of the dark, difficulty falling asleep, or new fears; increase or decrease in appetite; drawings by the child that are scary or use a lot of black and red; poor relationships with friends; difficulty in concentrating at school; low self-esteem; and emotional upset.

The pamphlets also included suggestions concerning when parents should be considered suspect. These included parents who: were abused as children (the cycle theory again); have difficulty relating to people their own age and are socially isolated; are overly protective or jealous of children; fail [to keep] appointments; overreact severely to any sex education their children might learn at school; [fathers who have lost a] wife by divorce, separation, or death; or are stepfathers (that alone is enough to make you suspect).

Some of the pamphlets include disclaimers warning that several symptoms should be present before suspicion is aroused and/or that the symptoms are reasons to ask questions, not to jump to conclusions. But others have no such disclaimers.

Sometimes the pamphlets say more about the groups who wrote them than about the problems they purport to address. Only one pamphlet, for example, mentions "lack of cooperation with agency" as a symptom of an abusive parent, and in this pamphlet it's mentioned twice. The pamphlet was written by the New York State Council of Family and Child Caring Agencies (COFCCA). (In a similar vein, a pamphlet that admonishes parents to, "Listen to the professionals you consult, value their advice and follow it rather than retreating into a defensive shell," comes from the National Association of Social Workers.)[11]

The COFCCA pamphlet also says any parent is suspect if he or she "believes in corporal punishment" or displays an "overinvolvement in religion." It also warns that an adolescent's development is "delayed" if he or she displays the following: "inability to fit in with peer group; overly self-conscious; confusion over identity, values and goals"[12]—in other words, if the adolescent is behaving like an adolescent.

"Intake workers are accepting reports from teachers and others that 'Mary is shy in class' or 'Mary is overfriendly,' " says Douglas Besharov. "[Behavioral indicators] alone . . . are an insufficient basis for a report. There are many other explanations for such behavior. It is essential that this point be made. Otherwise every shy or overfriendly child in the country will be reported."[13]

A social worker at a hospital that specializes in doing child sexual abuse evaluations reports, "We are getting more referrals involving children who have shown one or two indicators and whose parents have taken these as signs of obvious sexual abuse. Through our evaluations we are able to determine that these are isolated behaviors or are significant for other reasons. . . ."[14]

But children are not just being reported and evaluated. On the basis of such flimsy evidence, they also are being taken away from their parents. Peter Strubel, who used to train CPS workers in Colorado, says workers would look at symptoms that fit a so-called profile of an abuser, "and if you hit on maybe six of the ten items, you're a child abuser, no question."[15] Adds Robert Moro, the CPS supervisor in Massachusetts, "There is so much sex abuse paranoia within the Department of Social Services that if a child is exhibiting two or three behavioral indicators, throw in a couple of circumstantial evidence-type issues, add a dose of resentment and resistance [by the accused], and you've got grounds for placement."[16]

Calling the Hotline

Once someone has read the symptom lists, the next question is whether or not to phone in a report. All fifty states have toll-free numbers that can be called to report suspected child maltreatment. Some states operate a statewide central system; in others, reports are taken by local CPS agencies. Every state requires most professionals who come in contact with children, including doctors, teachers, day-care workers, and many others, to report their suspicions or face possible prosecution. In nineteen states, all citizens are required to report.

The laws generally require a report when the reporter has either "reasonable cause to believe" or just "reasonable cause to suspect" child maltreatment. But the drumbeat of the child savers urges reporters to cast an even wider net. A publication from the National Committee for Prevention of Child Abuse includes the following question and answer:

> [Question:] How sure must I be before I report?
> [Answer:] There is no rule. If there is serious doubt, resolve that doubt in favor of the child and report.[17]

Perri Klass, the pediatric resident in Boston, writes, "Some doctors, especially those without children of their own, are inclined to consider certain injuries, say a broken bone, as de-facto evidence of parental neglect."[18] Contrast this view with what Dr. Spock has to say on the subject. In the latest edition of *Baby and Child Care,* he writes: "If a child is so carefully watched that she *never* has an accident, she is being fussed over too much. Bones may be saved, but her character will be ruined" (emphasis in original).[19]

And if this isn't enough, every sensational case of a child-abuse death is followed by news accounts that, with 20/20 hindsight, insist that someone should have known what was going on. That makes mandated reporters in particular fearful of letting anything go by.

Professor Michael Wald of Stanford Law School, one of the nation's leading experts on child abuse law, told the California Legislature that his sister, a preschool teacher, and her colleagues fear prosecution if they don't report when a child is displaying "sexually inappropriate behavior," even though nobody really knows what that is in a preschool child.[20] A Michigan study found that mandated reporters are calling the hotline, "not because they have a reasonable cause to suspect child abuse/neglect, but to protect themselves from the potential of criminal or civil liability."[21]

But some child savers would like to instill even more fear: "Some of us have said, 'We're tired of all this nonsense. Let's just get a good case [of failure to report] and prosecute to show that this won't be tolerated,' " says Loretta Kowal, executive director of the Massachusetts Society for Prevention of Cruelty to Children.[22] (Although such prosecutions are rare, they do happen.)

Given the symptom lists that cover almost any child, the insistence by child savers that the slightest suspicion be reported, and the fear on the part of mandated reporters, it's hardly surprising that the system is inundated with false reports.

Once someone has decided to report, the call is taken by a worker at a child protective hotline. Every state does things a little differently, but in most states a process of classification is allowed, at least in theory. This means the hotline operator decides if the facts alleged would, if true, constitute maltreatment under state law.

Of course, state laws are so broad that almost anything could be included, and, like most CPS workers, the hotline operators usually have little training or experience. So, like so much else in the child protective system, what happens to a call to the hotline depends on who answers the phone.

In New York, calls are taken by a statewide hotline based in Albany and by countywide offices for the Rochester and Syracuse areas. The state legislature's Commission on Expenditure Review gave twenty-three hotline operators (twelve in Albany, three in Rochester, and eight in Syracuse) a series of hypothetical cases and asked if they would classify them as reports of maltreatment. The results: The Syracuse and Albany operators chose the same percentage of cases as reports—but they often chose different cases; the workers in Rochester were far more likely to classify cases as abuse than those in Syracuse and Albany; and even the Albany workers alone often disagreed with each other.

In one case, for example, all the Rochester workers said yes, this is a report of child abuse; seven of eight Syracuse workers said no, it's not; and the Albany operators split eight yes, four no.[23]

"It sounds like people have their own subjective, idiosyncratic criteria," said Charles Ewing, the Buffalo law professor and child psychologist. "That means whether there is an investigation depends on who takes the call. No system can function properly that way."[24]

New York is not alone. "I work out of a very affluent area," says Brett Cabral, a CPS supervisor in Massachusetts. "We screen in . . . things that Boston would be laughing at the person phoning in the report."[25]

But there is one common thread. Hotline workers are repeatedly told by their bosses to "err on the side of the child"—which means erring on the side of the system.

Cases that have been screened in and sent on to investigators include:

In New York: A woman's complaint that a child threw a basketball "intentionally with excessive force" at another child, apparently her son, hitting him in the stomach and leaving him bruised and in pain.[26] In New Hampshire: A CPS investigative worker ran out of time to check out serious cases while he looked into a case in which a twelve-year-old-boy had pulled down his six-year-old sister's pajama pants.[27] In Massachusetts: A man who had abused his wife and children reported his wife's new boyfriend on charges that the boyfriend was using drugs and allowing the children, age eight and ten, to walk one block through an open field to a swimming pool alone. Brett Cabral said his bosses forced him to investigate that case because "Those kids shouldn't be walking to the pool." It turns out, "The house is perfectly clean, the place is wonderful, the boyfriend seems pretty on target. We just intruded on these people's lives for no reason."

Other emergency services systems do not work this way. They recognize that the only way to ensure that help reaches those who really need it is to establish a screening mechanism and set priorities. (See Chapter 11.) The rationale for such overintervention is in part that, as the director of New York's hotline puts it, "It doesn't hurt to look."

But sometimes it hurts a lot.

The Investigation

Danny Meyer suffers from dyslexia, which impedes his writing, and aphasia, which impedes his speech. He was withdrawn and doing poorly in school. Then Danny Meyer discovered running. He ran first with local high-school students, then in the Boston and San Francisco marathons.

Running marked a turning point in Danny's life. "His confidence has increased unbelievably," says his father, Gary Meyer. "His speech has improved greatly, his reading ability has improved by leaps and bounds, and his personality has changed significantly. He's a completely different child." That account was confirmed by Danny's school principal and his doctor.

After moving from Los Angeles to Webster, New York, a suburb of Rochester, Danny Meyer decided he wanted to run across the entire North American continent. And he did it, between June and November 1983, when he was eleven years old.

With the approval of his family doctor, Danny started in Vancouver, British Columbia, and finished in New York City. Then-mayor Ed Koch greeted Danny at City Hall, Governor Cuomo sent him a letter of congratulations, and the New York State Assembly passed a resolution honoring him. But to the Monroe County Department of Social Services, Danny Meyer was just another "neglected" child. His school district had accused the Meyers of "educational neglect," because Danny had missed school to complete his run. The county Department of Social Services agreed, and the Meyer family is now listed in the state's Central Register of Child Abuse and Maltreatment.[28]

This was done in spite of the fact that Gary Meyer had driven more than a thousand miles, from Thunder Bay, Ontario, to Webster, to pick up school assignments for Danny when it was clear he was literally running late. And they did it despite the fact that even after Danny returned in early November, the district had not yet found a place to put him, because he was a special-education student. Danny Meyer had to wait another week to return to school, this time at the insistence of the same school district that had charged his parents with neglect.

"It's insane," said Kenneth Herrmann, a former county CPS director and professor of social work at the State University of New York at Brockport. "Given the child's situation, you would think the school district would be saying it's a wonderful thing. I can't understand the ineptitude of a county that would say there is educational neglect here."

In fact, there may be an explanation, at least for the school district's filing a complaint. The Meyers had been arguing with district officials, trying to get a better special-education plan for Danny. They believe the neglect complaint was the district's way of retaliating.

Because Danny returned to school after completing the run, CPS took no further action. But they had done enough. "[My wife] Jean has had a lot of trouble with her heart and this has caused a lot of stress," Gary said. "She's been to the doctor a number of times."

In December 1983, the Meyers were within days of finalizing the adoption of Korean triplet boys, when they told the caseworker for their adoption agency about their listing in the central registry. (She would have found out anyway, because adoption agencies always check central registries as part of their home studies.)

Said Jean Meyer, "When Gary told [the caseworker] she closed her notebook and couldn't get out of here fast enough." The adoption-agency caseworker said this was just coincidence. Another family, who better met the qualifications of the Korean agency with which her agency deals, happened to turn up at the last minute wanting to adopt triplet boys.

And what did all this do for Danny? "Danny came home from school in tears saying that the kids were teasing him because his parents are 'child abusers,' " Jean Meyer said.

Neither the school district nor the county Department of Social Services would comment on the Meyer case at the time. (Since then, the department has come under new management.) But one of the Rochester area's leading child savers was glad to comment.

"I wasn't upset when I heard that the department filed a report," said David Ambuske, director of the Children's Division of the Rochester Society for Prevention of Cruelty to Children. As far as Ambuske is concerned, the child savers can decide when and where Danny Meyer can run. "If he liked running, he could have run in the Rochester Marathon and let him carry a little sign," Ambuske said. Never mind the testimony of Danny's principal and his doctor about all the good the run did, Ambuske just knew there was something wrong. "I felt in my own gut feeling that this boy was being exploited," Ambuske said. "Many cases of neglect come down to a feeling. Call it a second sense or something." In fact, given the breadth of current laws, a "gut feeling" is all the child savers need to do to any family what they did to the Meyers.

There is no such thing as a "harmless" child-abuse investigation. Even when the case is ultimately ruled unfounded, it is only after a CPS worker has interrogated both the parents and the child, which, as Chris Humlen found out, can be terrifying in itself.

Even when no maltreatment is found after interrogating the family, the CPS worker is likely to go on to question relatives, baby-sitters, teachers, friends, neighbors, and anyone else they can think of who might have had contact with the child. They will probably have complete access to the child's school and medical records as well.

Kathy and Alan Heath, another Rochester-area couple, were put through that ringer three times.[29] Each time they were accused of abusing their seven-year-old son, Jeffrey (all names in this case have been changed at the family's request). Each time, the accuser demanded that her name be kept secret from the Heath family. Each time the case was ruled unfounded only to be followed by another report. The Heaths believe the false reports were part of a campaign of harassment by an "unstable" neighbor. Door-to-door salesmen turned up uninvited, a chimney sweep showed up (though the Heath house has no chimney), and they were thanked for a "pledge" to their local public television station that they had never made. All of this the Heaths said they could tolerate. It was only the false accusations of child abuse that caused real pain.

The first time the caseworker came, "She spent almost two hours in my house going over the same allegations over and over and over again," Kathy Heath said. "She went through everything from a strap to an iron, to everything that could cause bruises asking me if I did those things. [After she left] I sat on the floor and cried my eyes out. I couldn't believe that anybody could do that to me."

But it wasn't just Kathy Heath who was questioned. At age seven, Jeffrey Heath went through what his parents say was the same sort of interrogation. By the time they were reported for the third time, Alan Heath refused to allow his child to be put through it again. So the worker went to Jeffrey's school and had him pulled out of class and taken to the principal's office for questioning. "My son told me: 'She asked me if my mommy loved me, if your mother hit you, abused you.' " He returned to class terribly upset. "He kept coming up to [the teacher's] desk, wanting to talk to her." The teacher and the principal, who said he was present for the questioning, denied that the experience was traumatic for Jeffrey.

The worker also made the rounds, questioning friends, neighbors, even strangers who were potential witnesses. All were told that the Heaths were under investigation for child abuse. "Telling a person on the street that someone might be a child abuser and starting gossip of it is like telling somebody that you raped someone," Kathy Heath said. But when she asked the worker to please go back to the people she had spoken to to tell them that the family had been cleared, she was told: "That's not my job. All I have to do is what the rule book in front of me says I have to do."

The process was repeated three times, even though the department knew all the reports were coming from the same person, and even though they knew the accuser had at least once given a phony address and phone number.

The Heaths consulted an attorney, Larry Koss, but Koss found there was nothing he could do to help. "My clients' privacy, my clients' rights were being played with, and there was just no protection. It was like running into a giant marshmallow."

The Heaths wrote to state and county officials about their case. They got no response. As for what to do about their neighbor, the Heaths said the county child-protective agency could offer only one piece of advice: Sell your home and move out of the neighborhood.

While the Heaths were denied the right to confront their accuser, Mary Ellen Abrogast was denied the right even to know the accusation.

Abrogast, who lives in Massachusetts, adopted her grandchildren after her son was divorced. When the son remarried, he sued for custody. According to a lawsuit she filed, Abrogast was accused of emotional abuse because of the custody fight, but she was denied all access to her files to find out anything more about the accusation. The report was substantiated without the worker ever making a home visit or seeing the children. A second report was made and substantiated—again, with no visit to Abrogast's home.

Abrogast had a job working with the elderly at the time. Because of the substantiated reports, she was forced to take an indefinite leave of absence.[30]

Massachusetts Social Services Commissioner Marie Matava says in court papers that her agency did not release any information to Abrogast's employer, however the papers do not indicate if the employer was questioned during the investigation.[31] The department offered no further response to a request for information that would rebut the facts as stated by Abrogast.

What happened to the Meyers, the Heaths, and the Abrogasts are not extreme examples of the harm child savers can do. On the contrary, these are the run-of-the-mill cases. The Heaths, for example, got off about as easily as an accused family can.

The children in these families suffered no harm until the child savers intervened. As a result of that intervention, they suffered very real harm. They suffered harm because the privacy of the family was violated.

It has become fashionable in child saver circles to deride the very idea of family privacy. "We are constantly being told to keep our noses out of other parents' lives," says James Garbarino, one of the "experts" who equates corporal punishment with child abuse. "But being a parent is a social act, not a private act."[32]

"[Child rearing] is not a private matter between only the parent and child," says Elizabeth Robinson, a clinical psychologist in Washington State. "It is important to all of us how that child is raised. This is tomorrow. This is our future."[33]

What this rhetoric overlooks is the fundamental role that family privacy plays in protecting children. In a thousand ways, large and small, parents allow children to grow up to be healthy and secure by assuring them that the family can and will protect them from outside forces that might hurt them. Is there a parent alive, for example, who has never given a big hug to a small child frightened by a thunderstorm? But every year, camouflaged by the rhetoric of "protecting the future" and child rearing as a "social" act, child savers show more than a million children that they have no security. Thanks to the child savers, these children find out that when push comes to shove, their parents cannot protect them from a hurtful world.

Goldstein, Freud, and Solnit write that children "react even to temporary infringement of parental autonomy with anxiety, diminishing trust, loosening of emotional ties, or an increasing tendency to be out of control. The younger the child and the greater his own helplessness and dependence, the stronger is his need to experience his parents as his lawgivers—safe, reliable, all-powerful, and independent. . . . When family integrity is broken or weakened by state intrusion, [the child's] needs are thwarted and his belief that his parents are omniscient and all-powerful is shaken prematurely."[34]

It is striking how often parents who have never read experts like Goldstein, Freud, and Solnit say the same thing in their own words:

"I trusted my parents explicitly," says Kathy Heath. "I knew they loved me. They had control over things. When they took my son into the principal's office, I had no control over whether they could do that or not. Mother's a fixer in these kids' eyes. Mother couldn't fix it this time. Mother had no power." Another mother, whose children were taken for five weeks and then abused in foster care, said: "I used to tell the kids, you've got nothing to ever worry about, nobody can ever hurt you, don't worry about the bogeyman, you're safe here with Mom and Dad. You can't tell them that now."[35]

This does not mean that the right of family privacy can be absolute. But it does mean the criteria for infringing on that right must be something more than a child saver's "gut feeling." And it means that it *does* hurt to look.

Harassment

Cases like the Meyers' and the Heaths' also illustrate how easily the system can be used to harass innocent families. When the issue of harassment is raised, it is generally in the context of divorce and custody cases. But more than that is involved.

In the nineteenth century, people blackmailed their neighbors by saying: "Don't cross me or I'll report you to the Cruelty." In the 1980s, at the Florence Heights housing project in Northampton, Massachusetts, a tenant explained: "One thing people do here, if they don't like their neighbor, is to call the child protective."[36]

When more than one hundred CPS reports in the Rochester area accidentally became public, some were found to include comments by workers such as, "Unfounded. Former girlfriend of father probably made the report"; "Boyfriend reporting to get back at her, no basis for the complaint"; or "seems to be a neighborhood feud."[37]

"We can go in with the pretty clear understanding that it's an anonymous report with no clear basis of concern, but we have nothing to tell the parents, to say 'this is your recourse,' " says John Peers, a caseworker in the Rochester area.[38]

In Pennsylvania, out of eighteen reports made by landlords in 1988, none was indicated,[39] suggesting that the hotline may also be a tool in landlord-tenant disputes.

It is impossible to know how many false reports are malicious. For example, a report by the National Association of Public Child Welfare Administrators says on one page that false reports are "often" used to harass the innocent, but two pages later the same report says only "a small number" of false reports are malicious.[40] Even Besharov, who is strongly critical of the system, estimates that only 5 to 10 percent of all unfounded reports are made maliciously,[41] but that equals between 65,000 and 130,000 cases of harassment per year. And others believe the number is higher. A legislative committee in Missouri estimated that 15 percent of all calls in the Springfield area are harassment calls.[42] And John Peers estimates that one out of four anonymous reports he investigates turn out to be ill-motivated in some way. A study done by Michigan child-protective officials concluded, "Divorcing parents and their attorneys often attempt to use CPS motivated by their own custody objectives."[43]

All states allow people to make their reports anonymously. Callers don't even have to disclose their identity to the worker taking the call.

According to the American Humane Association, about 9.4 percent of all reports are made anonymously.[44] But it does not say what percentage of these prove to be valid. Data from states and cities that do provide such breakdowns and from one national study show that more than three out of four anonymous reports are false.[45] A study of reports involving only physical abuse in Baltimore found that only 15.5 percent were indicated.[46]

A study of every anonymous report, involving all kinds of maltreatment, received in the Bronx in 1978 and 1979—1,037 in all—found that only 12.4 percent were indicated, and none of these involved death or serious injury.[47] The authors write, "One case was indicated for 'diaper rash,' one case for welfare fraud, and two cases because the apartment was 'dirty.' " The authors conclude that anonymous reports should not be accepted, because they drain limited resources away from more urgent cases.

Strip-Searching

The harsh questioning and embarrassment families may face when victimized by a false report can be only the beginning. Child-protective workers have virtually unlimited power to enter homes, search them, and strip-search children, looking for evidence of abuse and neglect.

Technically, there are some situations in which parents may refuse entry into their home or refuse to allow a strip-search of their child. But there is no legal requirement that child-protective workers inform parents of these rights, making them largely worthless. Furthermore, the exercise of one's "right" of refusal can itself become grounds to suspect abuse and go ahead with the search anyway.

When a Washington State man insisted that deputy sheriffs produce a search warrant before they entered his home and checked his son's back for welts, the deputies forced their way in, handcuffed the father, and examined the son. No welts were found. The report was false. But when the man sued, a federal appeals court ruled that because the man would not allow the search, "the deputies could reasonably conclude that [he] was attempting to hide past abuse" and do the search anyway. In other words, the right exists as long as you don't exercise it.[48]

That is typical of the trend of court decisions. When it comes to allegations of child abuse, the courts have virtually repealed the Fourth Amendment, which prohibits "unreasonable searches and seizures" and requires that searches be done only after authorities have obtained a warrant based on "probable cause." Courts have carved out an exception for "exigent circumstances"—situations where authorities believe an emergency exists and there is no time to get a warrant from the court. Courts are divided over the amount of evidence authorities must have to justify their belief.[49] But the child savers argue that these limits don't apply to them. And so far, they've been winning.

The "H" family, a poor Chicago couple and their two children, six-year-old Lee and seven-year-old Marlena, had been engaged in a year-long argument with the children's school principal over whether the children could have lunch at home. According to court records, the principal allegedly "ridiculed" the parents, and when a doctor agreed they could feed their children at home, the principal reported the family to the Illinois Department of Children and Family Services, alleging that the children were abused and "malnourished."

On October 26, 1982, at about noon—two months after the complaint was filed—a child-protective worker appeared at the home of the "H" family. She demanded the right to search the house and implied that the children would be taken away if the parents did not comply. She began searching the kitchen to see how much food there was in the house. She found there was plenty. She then announced she would have to go to the school to question the children.

She met first with the principal, who told her the following: "Both parents usually are angry when they come to school. Something strange is going on with this family. Today, the children are the cleanest they have ever been since school has started. Other students indicated that Lee is tied up for punishment. They have never observed bruises on the children."

Apparently based on nothing more than this conversation, the worker demanded that the children be brought to her. According to a lawsuit brought by the family in federal court, the worker first tried to goad the children into saying their father was "mean" and that the children might be afraid of him because he is "big." "That's just because you don't know him," Marlena replied.

Then, according to the lawsuit, "The children . . . were stripped in a room in clear view of people who were working in the principal's office and in a room where others continually [went in and out]. Both the boy and the girl were forced to strip in the same room, despite the fact that the parents indicated that the little girl was shy." Then the children "were turned around like they were two pieces of meat" and repeatedly forced to open their legs and bend over as they were examined by the caseworker. After all this, no evidence of abuse or neglect was found and the case was ruled unfounded.

In an interview, the school principal said she didn't remember why she filed the report, but she denied any ill motivation. In its papers, the DCFS said the strip-searches took place in a closed room and that they were done with the parents' consent (even though the parents were never told they could refuse and were afraid they would lose their children if they protested).

At about the same time the "H" family, represented by Patrick Murphy, brought its suit, the Illinois chapter of the American Civil Liberties Union filed a class-action lawsuit in federal court alleging that warrantless searches of homes and strip-searching of children are "routine" practices in most child-abuse investigations. Neither Murphy nor the ACLU asked that all such searches be halted, only that the constitutional standard of "probable cause" be enforced. Murphy sought damages for the "H" family. The ACLU sought a preliminary injunction barring searches without probable cause until a full-scale trial could be held on its lawsuit. Prisoners and accused criminals already have such rights, the ACLU argued, surely children are entitled to the same protection.

DCFS has refused to comment on these cases because they still are in litigation. But in one of its briefs, the agency inadvertently let slip that strip-searching is not an exception used where there is strong evidence of abuse and other investigative techniques have failed. Strip-searching is standard operating procedure. The agency gave itself away when it said that any restriction on strip-searches "would immediately bring the child-abuse-hotline investigations to a halt." Obviously, if strip-searching is used only rarely, the whole hotline process need not come to a halt. Only if strip-searching were a part of almost every case could curbing the practice have such widespread effect.

In fact, a probable-cause standard would not require that any investigations be stopped. CPS workers would have to do a better job of gathering other evidence before forcing children to undergo the emotional trauma of a strip-search.

That trauma can be severe. Ner Littner, a prominent Chicago child psychiatrist who testified for the ACLU, said in an interview that even the best adjusted children suffer temporary "upset, sleep difficulties, nightmares, and difficulty eating" after such an experience. For what Littner terms the emotionally "vulnerable" child, the experience is like a nightmare come true and can significantly worsen and prolong whatever emotional disturbance the child already has. Sometimes, the damage is permanent.

And the problem is not confined to Illinois.

In Jersey City, New Jersey, Althea Clark (not her real name) and her two preschool-aged children suffered through five separate midnight raids by CPS workers and police.[50] Each time the children were awakened, taken from their beds, and stripped naked by Mrs. Clark at the CPS worker's insistence. Each time the worker stared at the children, looking them over from head to toe. Each time she found nothing, and each time the report was labeled "unfounded." Mrs. Clark believes the calls were made by a relative bearing a grudge.

In Iowa, the governor killed a proposal by the state's Department of Human Services to authorize workers to strip-search and photograph school-children without their parents' knowledge. It turned out workers had been doing it anyway, without authorization, but they wanted it made legal because of lawsuits by parents.[51]

A Massachusetts lawsuit includes a case where, "The report was anonymous and called in against a squeaky-clean family," according to the family's lawyer.

The case involved Marlene and Frank McKesson and their children, four-year-old Michelle and five-year-old Gerry. (All names have been changed to protect the privacy of the children, who are now ten and eleven.) The lawsuit alleges that:

> Although the investigator was able to observe that Michelle and Gerry showed no signs of abuse, she insisted on undressing both children. Michelle was frightened to the point of hysteria by the prospect of a stranger's undressing her. . . . [She] was frantically frightened during the entire procedure and for weeks afterward had fears and nightmares from the experience.
>
> When Marlene McKesson suggested calling the children's pediatrician instead [of strip-searching them] the investigator said she had already done so, without the McKessons' knowledge or consent, and had received excellent reports.

The child abuse report was, of course, unfounded. Part of the reason Michelle was so upset was because she had been taught never to take off her clothes in front of strangers.[52]

Leaders of the caseworkers' union in Massachusetts say they are now fighting against a State Department of Social Services proposal—developed in a panic after a highly publicized abuse death—to increase the use of strip-searches. "As an agency, Massachusetts spends a large amount of money on sex abuse training that says to children, Your body is your own, if you don't want anybody to touch you you don't have to let that person touch you," says Ed Malloy, a CPS supervisor in Weymouth. "[Now] the department . . . wants to have workers walk into the home and demand the parent show the child" with little or no evidence. "To have a social worker walk in and say to the parent in front of the child, you need to do this . . . and the parent jumps. That undermines the ability of the parent to protect that child."[53]

Obviously, if the real purpose of strip-searching was child protection, it would not be a routine practice. But that's not the real purpose. Strip-searching is not done to protect children. Strip-searching is done because it is more expedient for child savers.

In Massachusetts, more strip-searching was proposed to take the heat off the agency after a sensational death. In its Illinois lawsuit, the ACLU alleges that caseworkers are "rated on the speed with which they initiate and complete investigations." As everywhere else in the country, those workers have enormous caseloads. "Simple common sense leads to the conclusion that the workers in these circumstances will conduct searches as a matter of expedience, whether or not the searches relate in any way to the state's protective goals," the lawsuit states.

What is scariest about the child savers' enthusiasm for strip-searching, aside from their failure to notice that it can harm children, is the unchecked, untrammeled power to which they claim entitlement.

In briefs submitted for the Illinois cases, the DCFS claims it has the right to strip-search any child at any time based on any information in any report to the child-protective hotline, regardless of its substance or its source. (They do say parents should be offered the option of having their doctor perform the search, though there is no indication this offer was made to the "H" family.)

And what about the Fourth Amendment? Sorry, the Illinois child savers say, that applies only to accused criminals and prisoners. Innocent children aren't covered. The reason is the same one child savers used to justify the abuses of the juvenile court: We're only here to help you. Because the purpose of the search is allegedly to "help" the child, neither a child nor his or her parents has the same right to refuse it, absent probable cause, that an alleged murderer or rapist has.

The DCFS fallback position is that even if the Fourth Amendment does apply, warrants are not required under the "exigent circumstances" doctrine. In child abuse cases, DCFS argues, any report—no matter what is alleged and no matter how flimsy the evidence—is always such an immediate emergency that the circumstances are always exigent. Why then did the DCFS wait two months before investigating the "H" family?

In response to both the "H" family and the ACLU lawsuits, DCFS also argues that the parents "consented" to the strip-searches and the searches of their homes. Yet the DCFS also opposes requiring workers to tell parents that they may have some right to refuse. DCFS argues that requiring this would make it too hard for the worker to "build rapport" with the family. "Without harmonious communications," the DCFS brief says, "the investigation may well deteriorate into an adversarial process."

That child savers would make such arguments is depressing enough. What's really frightening is that courts are buying them.

It was in the context of the ACLU strip-search case that U.S. District Court Judge John A. Nordberg wrote, "this court finds that the life of even one child is too great a price to pay" to require more evidence before stripping children. By such logic all protections afforded criminal defendants should be eliminated. The right to counsel, the right to trial by jury, the right to a trial at all, the right to appeal, and a hundred other rights all create the danger that "even one child" might die. Indeed, there is no question that except under "exigent circumstances" a stranger accused of murdering a child could not be searched without a warrant.

Yet Nordberg ruled that although searches done for child abuse are "searches" within the meaning of the Fourth Amendment, the "exigent circumstances" argument always applies. He ruled that some vague guidelines established by DCFS are all that are needed to regulate such searches. Not only is a "probable-cause" standard unnecessary, the judge ruled there can hardly be any standard at all. "It is simply not possible to define a standard which must be met in every case . . ." Nordberg wrote. He also noted that the procedure proposed by the ACLU would "require more manpower and a larger budget. . . ."

In the "H" case, U.S. District Court Judge Nicholas J. Bua went further, accepting the notion that children have no Fourth Amendment defense at all against being strip-searched by child-protective workers. Bua dismissed the "H" family's complaint without even allowing a trial.

The cases were consolidated on appeal. The appellate court threw out the "H" case, ruling that the workers involved were immune from liability, and it upheld Nordberg's denial of a preliminary injunction to the ACLU. But the appellate court also ruled that strip-searches of allegedly abused children are Fourth Amendment searches, and it expressed some skepticism concerning the lower courts' reasoning in both cases. The ACLU case is back in the district court. But even if the appellate court were to uphold the ACLU someday, the state could appeal to the United States Supreme Court, which in recent years has been strongly inclined to give wide latitude to infringement by government on the rights of individuals.[54]

And some child savers have called for giving workers even more power. The late Nanette Dembitz, a former New York City Family Court Judge, called for allowing caseworkers to enter the home of any poor family (she specified recipients of Aid to Families with Dependent Children, or AFDC) at any time to check on their children even if no complaint at all had been received.[55] Until her recent death, Dembitz, like Vincent Fontana, was considered part of the mainstream of the child-protection movement and seemed to be on every New York City reporter's "A list" of people to quote on the topic.

*   *   *

Once the CPS workers get into a home, chances are that, if they have been trained at all, they have been trained not to investigate and find out if maltreatment occurred, but to assume that it did and then try to prove it.

David Chadwick, M.D., director of the Center for Child Protection in San Diego, California, told a state legislative committee that the job of his clinic was as follows: "We do evidentiary examinations *in order to prove abuse*" (emphasis added).[56]

A 1978 handbook says the job of CPS workers is to "aid the prosecution to establish a case against the perpetrator."[57]

A videotape used to train workers in California includes the following statement: "You *never* want to say that a kid is *not* a victim of sexual molest, because, in fact, eighteen months down the road that child may talk. And then if the defense attorney gets a hold of the case records . . . he says, 'You said a year ago that this wasn't happening.' You don't want that in the case record. You don't want it on the child's mind" (emphasis added).[58]

Similarly, Mary Case, the medical examiner in Missouri, said during a training lecture that "[If I cannot testify with medical certainty] that that is an inflicted injury . . . I am going to say I don't know. I am going to call it undetermined. Later on, new facts may be brought in, somebody may confess . . . but once you have called it an accident and somebody comes in and confesses, that would be embarrassing."[59]

"Indicated" or "Unfounded"

After interviewing and strip-searching the children if they feel it's warranted, it is up to workers with this sort of training to decide if the case should be "indicated" or not.

Indicating a report does not necessarily lead to the loss of one's children. It may not even lead to required "counseling" or other hoops to jump through in order to avoid losing the children. But it still can have serious consequences.

—The record often is permanent, and it makes it more likely that the children will be removed if there is a subsequent report.

—State laws vary, but day-care centers, and adoption agencies are usually required, at a minimum, to check central registries when screening potential employees or families. Although in some cases they may be allowed to hire or place a child with someone even if he or she is listed, realistically, who would do it? Furthermore, if the accused already works with children, chances are the employer will be questioned. If the report is later substantiated, chances are the employee will be fired.

—Although the records are theoretically confidential, the security of any confidential record depends on the integrity and the competence of those who maintain it. We journalists, for instance, make our living in part by getting people to furnish us with information they're not supposed to reveal. The more people with access to such information, the greater the chance of it leaking out. Philip Brockmyre, former coordinator of Child Protective Services for the Rochester, New York, area and a defender of the status quo, says there's "a powerfully long list of people that have access to [child abuse] information. So confidentiality is, in increments, becoming a myth."[60]

More people having access to confidential information also increases the chances of accidental disclosure. Brockmyre's comments came in response to the revelation that "confidential" records about more than a hundred cases of alleged child maltreatment were discovered in and around a dumpster in back of the county courthouse. The records had been forwarded from Brockmyre's department to the county District Attorney. When the D.A.'s office didn't need them anymore, nobody bothered to shred them before they were thrown out. Both indicated and unfounded cases were included.[61]

By design or by mistake, the word has a way of getting around. For instance, according to Marjorie Heins, an attorney with the Massachusetts Civil Liberties Union, child-care referral agencies have an informal policy called "red circling." When they find out a day-care center has been the subject of a child-abuse report, a red circle goes around the name and they refuse to refer parents there.

All of this means it is vital that the decision to indicate a case be made by a well-trained professional applying clear laws and regulations, with a fair chance for the accused to appeal. None of these safeguards exists consistently in Child Protective Services today and most hardly exist at all.

Since the laws themselves are so broad that, as one commentator noted, "every family in the country could be made out to be the proper subject of court jurisdiction,"[62] the workers are on their own. Just like the worker who took the call to the hotline in the first place, the investigators make their decisions based largely on their whims and prejudices—or as David

Ambuske might say, a "gut feeling."

People accused of child maltreatment are, as Giovannoni and Becerra put it, "at the mercy of their accusers' interpretation of these terms."[63] Adds Michael Wald: "Hundreds and thousands of social workers, police officers, probation officers, [are deciding] what is appropriate child rearing."[64] A study of case records in Philadelphia found that "each individual worker had adhered to his or her own, often inconsistent criteria for assessing family function and children at risk."[65]

This leads both to unfair labeling of the innocent and to missing cases of real maltreatment.

"They go by their feeling about the people," says Irwin Levin, an outspoken CPS supervisor in New York City, who exposed how widespread malfeasance in his agency contributed to the deaths of several children. "If they're satisfied that the parents seem okay, they stop doing a complete investigation and kids fall between the cracks."[66]

This all results in some absurd examples of substantiated cases.

In Florida, those cases included:

—Foster parents were labeled child abusers because they would not allow their foster children out of the house after 6 P.M. and would not let them watch television after 7:30 P.M.

—A teacher was labeled a child abuser because he disciplined a student by making him put his head down on the desk. When the child continued to lift his head, the teacher held it down for a short time with his hand.

—A mother was labeled a child abuser when, distressed by the constant thievery of her daughter, she took her to the store she had stolen from and introduced her as "my daughter the thief." Later, after the daughter stole five thousand dollars worth of her mother's jewelry, the mother sewed the pockets of her daughter's clothes shut and wouldn't let her carry a purse.[67]

One result of the lack of standards is that the determination of whether a family is maltreating their children may depend on where the family lives. In Massachusetts, says Robert Moro of the caseworkers' union, some areas are known for substantiating cases others won't. "Don't get investigated in Weymouth," Moro says. "They're famous for substantiating everything and naming everybody."

With no standards and no training, workers look for something obvious to get hold of. That may explain the near obsession child savers have with whether a house is messy.

Levin says too many of his workers "immediately associate" a dirty home with neglect or abuse. Conversely, the attorney for the mother of a little boy who died in foster care believes obvious signs of trouble in the home were missed because it was neat and clean. The foster parents were black, and the home was in a ghetto. The lawyer believes problems were missed because of a form of racism. "The thing you read over and over and over again in the reports on this house is how clean it was," said the attorney, James Trumm. "If this had been a foster home in Wellesley they wouldn't wax poetic about it's being clean—they'd expect it to be clean. They'd go beyond the facade." Instead, Trumm said, "These white cops and white social workers coming in were expecting to find a hellhole, and they were so surprised to find a place that was clean and neat" that they looked no further.[68]

Indeed, as the survey of Baltimore doctors and the case of Geraldine Churchwell also suggest, the racism that infused the child-protective system in the nineteenth century is still very much a factor in decision-making.

James Louis, a law guardian for children in New Jersey, recalls a case in which a Hispanic father began beating his children. The children were immediately removed from the home. The worker never noticed that the abuse only began after the father had suffered a head injury at work— the results of which could be treated with medication. Louis recalls: "When the worker was questioned about why she missed it to see if something could be done, she said, 'Those people shouldn't have their kids anyway because those people have too damn many kids.' "[69]

As for the right to appeal, as of 1985, CPS workers in only seventeen states were even required to tell the accused that the alleg·'on was indicated, and he or she was being listed in a central registry[70] ar.d only seven allowed the accused an administrative hearing to appeal.[71] Since 1985, Florida has added an appeal mechanism and New Hampshire was forced to do so by court order. Massachusetts added a procedure that draws a bizarre distinction: It allows the accused a hearing to claim they are not guilty of a given act of maltreatment, but refuses to allow anyone to challenge a determination that abuse occurred. Although the state Department of Social Services claims anything more would have a "chilling effect" on caseworkers,[72] the caseworkers' union joined civil liberties groups in fighting for a broader appeals process, according to union leaders. Says Robert Moro: "We're rushing to judgment here. We're asked to be Columbo in ten days [the time limit for substantiating a case]. We make mistakes. They deserve a second look."

Nor are you necessarily off the hook if the worker decides the case is "unfounded." Thirty-nine states or territories keep unfounded reports as well as substantiated reports—leaving them vulnerable to the same access, authorized and unauthorized.[73]

And the child savers want to erode protection for innocent families still further. The late Judge Dembitz chaired a committee that recommended changing New York State law so that only people who could *prove their innocence* by clear and convincing evidence would not be listed in the state's central registry. (The rest would be listed as either substantiated or incomplete.)[74]

Removing the Child

If workers decide to indicate a case, they must then make the most crucial decision of all, whether or not to remove the child from the home. Workers are no better prepared and have no better guidelines for this decision than for any of the others they are supposed to make.

Child savers argue that the courts serve as a line of defense against having children unjustly removed from their homes. Anne Cohn writes that "courtroom standards are quite demanding. . . ."[75] In fact, courtroom standards range from minimal to almost nonexistent.

But more important, child savers don't need a court to take children away from their parents. There are two methods by which child savers avoid even the most minimal scrutiny.

The first is to con parents into a "voluntary" placement. In some states, more than half the children in foster care were placed there by "voluntary" agreement—and as many as half of them never return home.[76]

Sometimes voluntary placement is the child welfare system's version of plea bargaining: Accept voluntary placement and we won't drag you into court and label you a neglectful parent. Or worse: Surrender one of your children voluntarily or we'll go to court to get all of them.[77] An American Bar Association report calls coerced "voluntary" placement, "a recurrent problem."[78]

Saddest of all are the cases where parents come forward on their own seeking help and are conned into giving up their children to foster care. The parents don't realize that once the immediate need is over they can't just get their children back by asking. The act of voluntary surrender has given the child savers the power to sit in judgment and determine if the parent is "worthy" of the child's return.

Several studies have found that up to half the children who stay in foster care for more than six months as a result of "voluntary" placement never go home.[79] Yet in many states, a child can stay in "voluntary" foster care for six months or longer before a court ever holds a hearing to see if the placement was truly voluntary or if continued foster care really is needed.[80]

Lawyers representing children in Washington, D.C., say that children placed voluntarily for what was supposed to be no more than ninety days wind up in foster care for years at a time without any court review at all.[81]

"Although it's called a voluntary placement agreement in no way is it a voluntary placement," says Jacquelynne Bowman of Greater Boston Legal Services. "They're told [the child will be kept longer] if we go through the court system, and here [with a voluntary placement] you have a right to terminate the agreement in three days." What the worker doesn't say, Bowman adds, is that the child savers can go to court and object to such termination, forcing the parents into a difficult fight to win their children back.[82]

Witnesses at legislative hearings in Massachusetts said, "Frequently they placed their children with [the Department of Social Services] through voluntary agreements and then felt that they had been deceived. . . . [T]hey were not allowed to visit with them, did not know where they had been placed, and their children were not returned to them within the time frame to which the parents had agreed."[83]

"I've seen it," says Robert Moro, the Massachusetts CPS supervisor, of the practices Bowman describes, practices Moro calls "a little sneaky. Any time an agency exists there are going to be abuses of power and we abuse it, too." Moro says the workers have "a Machiavellian justification: it's a dog-eat-dog world, we're trying to protect kids, this is the only way we could do it."

Leroy Pelton, formerly of the New Jersey Division of Youth and Family Services, cites cases including one in which a mother agreed to have three children removed because, the mother said, "If I didn't I'd be taken to court and lose all five children." In another case, a mother was told if she did not sign away her children they would be taken permanently by the court, "but if she did sign the children would be returned to her in a couple of months." More than eighteen months later, the children still were in foster care.[84]

In her years on the bench, New York City Family Court Judge Leah Marks has seen it happen time and again: "A person comes in with a reasonable problem and instead of trying to help that person with the problem [the caseworkers] will say, 'Why don't you place your kid, and then we can worry about the problem?'

"I've seen them place children because [the parents] didn't have housing at the moment, but then, when the parent comes back and says: 'Well, I have housing,' instead of just giving the child back, they say: 'We have to investigate your housing; we have to find out how good a parent you are.' The whole system is twisted so children are kept in who never should have been kept in."

Case in point: Charlene L. Charlene was a high-school dropout who wanted to return to school to learn a trade so she could get off welfare. She went to the New York City Department of Social Services seeking help with the care of her four children, two sets of twins aged three and four. Instead of offering day care or a homemaker, the worker suggested foster care. The worker promised that Charlene could visit her children whenever she wanted and bring them home when she was ready. "Everything she said sounded great," Charlene said. But her children were abused in foster care. And when Charlene asked for them back, the child savers said no. It was four years before they let Charlene have her children back. "I put them into care because I wanted better things for them," Charlene said. "But by my putting them in, they suffered an experience that no one would want to experience. I have to live with that."[85]

Judge Marks offers two examples from her own court:

In one case, two children were in the care of an aunt after their parents had died, though the aunt did not have formal, legal custody. The aunt had financial problems and sought help from the Department of Social Services. "They did not advise her to get welfare," Marks says, "they did not even advise her to apply to become the children's foster parent and receive payment for caring for the children. Instead, they had her sign a voluntary placement agreement." When the aunt tried to visit the children in foster care she was told she had no legal right to do so. She was kicked out of their lives. A year later, the DSS came to Judge Marks and asked that the children be legally freed for adoption. They told Judge Marks that there were "no interested relatives" seeking the children. By the time the aunt found out, it was too late. The children had been adopted.

In the second case, a mother had surrendered an infant and a toddler during an emergency. The mother spoke only Spanish. The city placed the children with parents who spoke only English. Four years later, the Department of Social Services came to Judge Marks and asked that she terminate the mother's parental rights. It seems the mother and children were not getting along—they weren't communicating well.

Judge Marks's advice to parents: "better to go find a friend who can take a child for a day or two, because once you sign those papers . . . you may never see your child again."[86]

If a parent resists "voluntary" placement there are, in theory, three methods for removing a child anyway. The first is to wait for a full-scale court hearing. The second, in cases where there is an imminent danger of serious harm to the child, is to rush to the courthouse or call a judge on the phone and get permission on the spot. The third method, where the circumstances are even more dire, is simply to take the child then and there. Out of fifty-five states and territories, twenty-nine allow a caseworker to remove a child from the home instantly, and law enforcement officers can do it in fifty-one jurisdictions.[87]

Of course, this power isn't supposed to be used unless the child faces a major risk of suffering serious harm even in the time it would take to call a judge and explain the situation. But, like all the other laws concerning child maltreatment, the protective-custody statutes are full of vague language. In some states, the same vague standards used to determine whether a child has been abused or neglected are enough to take a child into immediate custody. Other states use criteria like "danger from the child's surroundings" or "apparent danger of harm."[88]

And, at least in major cities, workers snatching children on their own—the method that's supposed to be the last resort—seems to be the method of choice.

"They use the emergency power routinely—and they shouldn't," says Florence Roberts, Family Law Director for Brooklyn Legal Services. When New York State studied a sample of such cases, auditors found that in 43 percent of them, the worker didn't even leave the required written notice to the parent explaining what they had done with the children and what little the parent could do about it.[89] In California, "It's extremely unusual to have a court order first," says Jane Henderson, who heads the staff of the California State Senate Select Committee on Children and Youth. "By and large they use their temporary custody power," adds Pamela Mohr of Public Counsel. Irwin Levin, the CPS supervisor, says many workers avoid seeking a court order before removing a child "because it's easier."[90]

And some New York City workers apparently don't even know they're supposed to go to a judge at all.

Former NCCAN director Douglas Besharov writes that in the mid-1970s, "The [New York City] agency's manual failed to instruct workers to determine whether there is time to obtain a court order before removing a child without parental consent, as required by state law. . . . Six years later, workers from the same agency were again being sued for illegal removal practices and, again, the agency's manuals still inaccurately described the statutorily required procedure."[91]

By 1989, city officials were bragging about a new "academy" that was supposed to vastly improve training. But, according to Lisa Clampitt, a former CPS worker who went through the academy, nobody ever taught her to try and get a court order before removing a child. "Basically, you removed the kids and gave the parents a form that said they should appear in court the next morning if they wanted to have their say," Clampitt says. "The child is removed before there is any legal action."[92] Where possible, workers are supposed to consult with a supervisor, Clampitt says, but "some of the supervisors are remove-happy."

Someone certainly was remove-happy in the case of a twenty-eight-year-old deaf woman living with her two children at a center for battered women in New York City.

Center officials felt the mother was having trouble taking care of the children. They called the city Department of Social Services expecting that they would provide help, such as a homemaker. But apparently no homemaker was available right away. So that very day, in another example of how child savers mistreat women as well as children, a caseworker scooped up the children and had them placed in foster care. No one even explained to the mother what was happening. "I never signed permission for them to be taken," the mother said in a court affidavit. "I believed they were being taken to school. When they did not return in the evening, I became upset and I have been very upset ever since."[93]

Even where a judge's order is required, as in Colorado, it is almost always a rubber-stamp procedure. "I don't ever remember the judge saying no," said Joe Pickard, a former CPS attorney. In his county, Pickard said, the lawyers always made the calls, but in other counties workers themselves got the same results: "The worker would call and say, 'Judge, I've got somebody here who's got bruises and the parents don't have an explanation' and the judge says, 'Take him. You're reliable. I know you.' "[94]

It is then up to the parents to go to court and fight to get their children back. In some states, they get this chance within twenty-four hours. In other states, it can be a four-day wait.[95] At least that's what the law says. In the case of the deaf woman cited above, somehow that never happened. It took a court order obtained by the ACLU Children's Rights Project to get the children back three weeks later.[96]

Even when the child savers obey the law and the hearing is held, the deck is stacked against the family. First of all, before the parents get to utter a word, the judge usually has received a written report from the people who took the child. In that report, they make their case and suggest what the judge should do about it. Once the hearing begins, CPS is usually represented by a lawyer employed by the county or the state who specializes in this sort of law. On the other side are one or two tired, scared parents, often poor and inarticulate. If they have a lawyer at all—and workers sometimes try to con them into not getting one—they probably just met him or her outside the courtroom.

"Primarily only the department [of social services] presents evidence," says Gary Seiser, a former juvenile court commissioner (the equivalent of a judge) in Riverside County California. "They're the only ones prepared."[97]

Lisa Clampitt says when she was a child-protective worker, she sometimes went up to the parents she was supposed to oppose and explained things to them they should have been told by their own lawyers.

The parents—and their children—are thrust into a process that is more like an assembly line than a justice system. Cases race by in four minutes or less. "There's not a lot of repeat argument," says Seiser. "You have to make it once and make it good." And the judges don't have what Seiser calls "the luxury" to "sit back calmly and reflect on the evidence. . . . You have to make a decision and move onto another case." The hearings are run "for the convenience of the system players . . . not for the parents or the child," says Pamela Mohr of Public Counsel. "I've been with a child and after the hearing the child will say, 'Was I ever mentioned? Did they talk about me?' "[98]

Given all that, it's not surprising that parents almost never get their children back after the initial hearing. Mohr says at least 90 percent of children taken by workers on their own authority are kept in care after the first hearing. It may be a long time before the next hearing. In California, says Mohr, it's supposed to happen in fifteen days. "In fact, two months is very good. Most of the time it will be a lot longer. We have a horrible continuance rate here. I've seen it take a year or two."

The bottom line: Child-protective workers effectively have the power to remove a child for weeks, sometimes months, solely on their own authority. Difficult as that is for parents, it's a lot harder on the children.

Children do not perceive time the way adults do. For a child, a separation from a parent feels much longer than it does to an adult. The younger the child, the longer the time seems. Goldstein, Freud, and Solnit write, "Emotionally and intellectually, an infant and toddler cannot stretch his waiting more than a few days, without feeling overwhelmed by the absence of parents. He cannot take care of himself physically, and his emotional and intellectual memory is not sufficiently matured to enable him to use thinking to hold onto the parent he has lost. . . . For most children under the age of five years, an absence of parents for more than two months is equally beyond comprehension."[99]

Yet two months is the minimum many children can expect before there is even a serious court hearing. And for someone like little Jennifer Humlen, trapped in MacLaren Hall before she was even a year and a half old, her eight-day stay was like an eternity.

And it all happens to children who suffered no harm at all until the child savers intervened. After doing a special study of the child-welfare system in Chicago, even the American Humane Association concluded that in fully half of all "emergency" removals, there had been no maltreatment.[100]

When a formal hearing is finally held, it is very different from a criminal trial. The burden of proof is neither "beyond a reasonable doubt" nor even the next highest standard, "clear and convincing." The child savers need present only "a preponderance of the evidence"—colloquially defined as 51 percent—to keep children away from their parents.

Nor is it clear what has to be proven. Because the laws are so vague, judges, like everybody else, are largely on their own. Lawrence Aber writes that the decision to remove a children from home and place them in foster care is "the most powerful, least restricted form of modern state intervention into the heart of family life." In one study, three veteran judges were asked to review actual case files and make "rulings." They agreed on what to do less than half the time. And even when they agreed, they cited very different reasons. Aber writes, "Each judge seemed to use his own unique value system."[101]

Like CPS workers, juvenile court judges don't always have the training and experience for the job. Although some judges seek election or appointment to the juvenile court because they have practiced juvenile law and it's what they are interested in, that is not always the case. In some jurisdictions, judges are rotated through a number of courts. In others the judges serve only part-time and are not even lawyers.[102] In other jurisdictions, the juvenile court is seen by judges as something they must endure pending promotion to someplace better.

"Judges see family court as kiddie court, not as important as the criminal and civil courts at City Hall," says William Norvell, who heads the Dependent Children Unit at the Public Defender's office in Philadelphia. "There's a constant shuffle of judges seeking transfer out. . . ."[103] Ira Schwartz, former administrator of the federal government's Office of Juvenile Justice and Delinquency Prevention, writes, "Many judges, particularly the most able and well-respected ones, view assignment to the juvenile court as 'punishment'—something to be avoided. As a result, too many judges who are elected or assigned to the juvenile court bench are either incompetent or ill suited for the job."[104]

Family court often becomes the place where new judges go to make their mistakes. For example, for nearly a decade federal law has required that child savers make "reasonable efforts" to keep families together before asking a court to place a child in foster care. But, according to a publication co-authored by the National Council of Juvenile and Family Court Judges, many such judges "remain unaware of their obligation to determine if reasonable efforts to preserve families have been made. Other judges routinely 'rubber stamp' assertions by social service agencies. . . ."[105]

When Susan and Clark Gabriel's daughter Sara was removed from her home in Colorado Springs, Colorado, it was supposedly an "emergency."[106]

On the morning of February 12, 1986, Susan Gabriel sent her younger daughter off to school as usual. But Sara, who had just turned nine, did not come home. Instead, she was taken into custody by the El Paso County, Colorado, Department of Social Services. Susan would not see her daughter for four days and would not have her back as part of the family for three years.

Susan had married Clark Gabriel just six weeks before. It was her second marriage, and her older daughter, then fifteen, was upset by it. Her older sister's problems were upsetting Sara, and her schoolwork was starting to suffer. Sara also said she was afraid of her teacher. Susan told Sara to talk to the teacher about that. That talk took place on February 12. In talking about her family, Sara mentioned that she did not like it when Clark Gabriel tickled her.

That was enough. Teachers are mandated reporters. They are trained to watch for changes in behavior and assume they are signs of abuse. They know that a stepfather is always suspect, because that's what child saver literature tells them. Obviously, this was a case of what Clark Gabriel now calls "felony tickling."

By the end of the day, Sara Gabriel was in custody, and her mother had been called down to the county Department of Social Services to talk to a caseworker.

Susan Gabriel recalls: "The caseworker said my daughter told them my husband had molested her. . . . She said he had tickled her. I said where? On the knee and the belly button . . . [the caseworker] said this is molesting. I hardly had time to recover when the next thing she said was: 'If you don't show complete support for your daughter, you might never get your daughter back again. You have to believe your daughter.' "

Susan Gabriel said the worker "strongly advised" that she divorce her husband. When Susan said she'd only been married six weeks, she says the worker replied, "Then it shouldn't be much of a problem."

Gabriel says the worker also advised her not to get an attorney "because it would make you look guilty."

One week later, Gabriel says, the worker called her in again and said: "It slipped my mind. Your husband really did touch your daughter between the legs." Difficult as that may be to believe, a police report written on March 24, when Clark Gabriel was arrested, lends credence to Susan Gabriel's account.

According to the report, on February 12 Sara Gabriel was interviewed by Officer Gurule of the Colorado Springs police and by Dick Brown and Barbara Midyett, civilians who work for the police department's Youth and Victim Services Division. During this interview, Sara Gabriel said nothing to indicate she had been touched in any but an innocent way by her father. She specifically denied being touched on her genitals or between her legs. The report specifies that "that was all of the information that was obtained by Officer Gurule at that time."

"At a later time," the police report says, Barbara Midyett contacted detective Mark Teasdale and told him something she apparently had not mentioned before. Midyett claimed that she had interviewed Sara Gabriel at school before Officer Gurule ever got there. In this earlier, previously undisclosed interview, Midyett alleges that Sara told her her father "had touched her in the vaginal area on the outside of her underpants." Midyett said Sara repeated this during another interview with Midyett at the offices of Youth and Victim Services.

The police report does not explain why Midyett apparently never mentioned the purported earlier interview to Officer Gurule. Midyett says she did mention it, but it is not reflected in the report because the report covered only the interview she and Gurule did together. Midyett acknowledges that she took no notes during either of the interviews she said she did alone.

Before Clark Gabriel's arrest, Susan Gabriel says she was repeatedly pressured to get him to plead guilty—without knowing to what. Six days after Sara was taken, the Gabriels still could not get a copy of anything stating what he was accused of doing. According to a "memo for [the] record" Clark Gabriel wrote immediately after talking to a caseworker, when he asked the worker for the written information, she laughed at him.

Through all this, Sara Gabriel was with strangers. "They didn't tell me where they were taking me, not 'till I was there," Sara said in an interview. "They said this is your home, at least for now."

Sara said whenever she would get upset about not being allowed to go home, the caseworker would say, don't blame us, it's your mother's fault for not divorcing your father: "[They'd say] your mom . . . should have kicked out your stepdad."

Eventually, Sara did change her story and said that one night, while she was in a sleeping bag on top of her bed, Clark Gabriel did try to touch her in the manner described in Midyett's report. She says she changed her story because repeated interrogations had scared her. "They'd ask a question but they wouldn't let me answer it. They said: 'You were tickled here, right?' I'd say no and they'd look at me like, 'Are you sure?' I was afraid, so I'd say yeah. I was afraid because I didn't know what they'd do to me. They were so powerful. They had a policeman with them."

After ten days in foster care, Sara Gabriel was placed with her natural father, Susan Gabriel's ex-husband. Eventually she would tell him and her therapists why she lied about being abused.

Sara Gabriel underwent two psychological evaluations before her stepfather's trial, both by therapists approved by Child Protective Services. The first evaluation "documented some significant psychological problems in Sara that might have caused her to produce a false allegation . . . [including] a great deal of sensitivity to interpreting affection in a sexual fashion, and difficulty processing feelings." The second report was inconclusive, stating that Sara "may be vulnerable to misperceiving events that happen in her environment" and has a tendency to "misperceive" the obvious. The report

also noted that Sara showed "clear signs of having been traumatized"—
but this was four months after she had been suddenly taken from her
family, placed in foster care, and repeatedly interrogated.

Susan Gabriel could not see her daughter until four days after she was
taken. At the first visit, Sara "sat on my lap and cried. She kept asking:
'Why can't I come home?' But I couldn't tell her because [the caseworker
said] if I talked about the case there would be no more visits at all."

Visits took place three times a month, always with a strict fifty-minute
time limit and always under guard by a caseworker. Sara would start out
"very stone faced, like she was trying to be very stoic." Then she would
break down and cry and cry again when her mother had to leave. After
Sara phoned her mother to say the charges were not true and she hadn't
been molested, CPS cut off all phone calls between them.

There were several hearings from March through June. "I was so upset,
I made a lousy witness," Susan said. "They'd keep saying, 'You have a
lot to lose because you still live with him.' They were constantly putting
me down because I supported him and wouldn't leave him."

The Gabriels fought with—and fired—their first lawyer. He had once
worked for the DSS, and the Gabriels say he kept trying to get them
to accept a plea bargain because the agency was so hard to fight. By June,
they started to fight with each other. That was when Susan Gabriel attempted
suicide.

She doesn't remember what happened after she took the pills, but
she thinks she must have vomited them up. She was hospitalized for three
days.

Then something extraordinary happened. The prosecution offered the
Gabriels an incredibly good plea bargain: deferred prosecution for three
years, and then, if there were no further problems, dismissal. Clark Gabriel
did something more extraordinary. He refused. He would settle for nothing
less than complete vindication. The judge found this so unusual that he
insisted that the Gabriels get a second opinion from J. Gregory Walta,
the judge's former law partner and a man with no prior connection to
the case. This is what Walta wrote:

> I have reviewed the Clark Gabriel file and cannot recommend to him that
> he accept the deferred prosecution offered in this case. I realize that a deferred
> prosecution is rarely offered and that in many ways, it is equivalent to
> a dismissal of the charges. Indeed, in most cases, I would strongly urge
> the defendant to accept such an offer.
>
> The problem with this case is that it is quite clear that Gabriel is simply
> not guilty of these charges:
>
> 1. The child initially did not make allegations of sexual abuse, even
> though directly questioned by a school teacher and later by police and

social service workers.

2. The allegation was made only after she was privately questioned by social service workers, a situation that I have seen before.

3. The child has since admitted she initially told the truth and was lying to social service workers when she alleged sexual abuse admitting this to her foster mother and on more than one occasion admitting it to her mother.

4. The response of Social Services has been, not to reassess the validity of the charges or their own interviewing techniques, but to limit the child's contact with her own mother.

5. The psychologist who has evaluated the child has voiced doubts about the truth of her allegations.

6. The psychologist who has evaluated the defendant indicates that he does not fit an abuser profile and the psychologist doubts the truth of the charges against him.

7. Social services has placed the child in "incest therapy," the tendency of which is to reinforce the allegations, not to question them.

This case fits a disturbing pattern in which child protection workers induce the child to make allegations not originally made, then resist the child's efforts to recant, and ignore reports by qualified experts questioning the truth of the child's allegations.

This case should not be kept alive by deferred prosecution or otherwise. If it is not dismissed I must reluctantly recommend that the defendant undergo the risks of trial.

If he prevails, I strongly recommend that he file suit against the Department of Social Services, the individual caseworkers involved, and, if case law permits, against the District Attorney's office and the prosecutors involved (emphasis added).

The case finally came to trial in November 1986. Susan Gabriel gives this account, all of it confirmed by one of the jurors, who spoke on condition of anonymity:

In addition to all the other evidence, the defense was able to show, through a reenactment and drawings of Sara's room, that it would not have been physically possible for events to have transpired the way the prosecution said they did.

After just five minutes of deliberations, eleven members of the jury were ready to acquit while the twelfth took a little longer because she wondered if perhaps there was some evidence the prosecution had not presented. Some of the jurors hugged the Gabriels and said they were sorry about what they had been put through. But it wasn't over.

Child Protective Services agencies are not bound by the rulings of criminal courts. They can bring their own neglect or abuse charges, which cannot lead to jailing the parent, but can lead to permanent loss of custody of the child. At these hearings, the prosecution must meet the much lower "preponderance of the evidence" standard.

That trial was scheduled for early 1987. By then, Susan Gabriel was pregnant. She says her new lawyer was warning that " 'There is no way the judge will let you have custody back if [your ex-husband] asks for it.' I had visions of them coming into the hospital room and taking away the new baby."

Then, two days before a pretrial hearing Susan Gabriel found out the child she was carrying had died. "I think it was the stress," Gabriel says. "I was so depressed I said I was willing to offer a deal" that allowed her ex-husband, Larry Dickinson, to retain custody of Sara in exchange for dismissal of the abuse charges against Clark. Eventually, however, the Gabriels were allowed liberal visitation and then one day, three years after the ordeal began, Susan Gabriel says she got a call from Dickinson. By then Sara was twelve-years-old, five foot eight, and starting to get into fights. "My ex called me and said, 'I can't handle Sara anymore. Take her back.' " Dickinson's version is different. He says he relinquished custody because Sara "was longing for [her mother's] attention and contact. . . . We all felt it was in her best interests to go back to her mom." The Gabriels also won a fight to have their names removed from the state's central registry, and, as noted at the beginning of this chapter, a new, reform-minded head of the county Department of Social Services has named Clark Gabriel to a citizen review board that will handle complaints against his agency.

For this, he was sneered at by colleagues at a conference he attended who asked when he decided to "get in bed with VOCAL."[107]

*   *   *

Even the worst child savers don't set out to hurt children on purpose. So why do they hurt so many children at all? Why would a child-protective worker strip-search children with no evidence that they had been harmed? Why would they spoil the greatest triumph of an eleven-year-old's life by labeling him neglected? Why would they not allow a mother to nurse her baby before she is taken away? I think there are several reasons:

—Typically, CPS workers have little training or experience. Like the public at large, they believe they are "erring on the side of the child." If they are wrong, they figure they can always give the child back. The notion that the intervention itself is harmful, especially if the child is placed in foster care, is an alien one.

—The law itself offers these untrained workers no guidance. They are free to exercise almost unlimited discretion.

—To the extent that they are trained at all, the message they get— overt or implied—is that most parents really don't know what they're doing. This message comes through, for example, when they are taught that all use of corporal punishment is wrong.

—They are taught, again overtly or by implication, that virtually all accusations are true, that "children never lie," and that they are supposed to be advocates for the child more than investigators. Accused parents, on the other hand, are either mentally ill or evil incarnate, so why listen to them? When the child savers took away Kathy Alexander's eleven-month-old daughter without even letting Alexander nurse her to sleep, they did not see a loving mother. They saw a vicious "child abuser" who they were convinced had fractured her little girl's leg. It was easy to deny her request without it ever occurring to them that they were hurting the child. After all, how could a child possibly get comfort from such a person?

—All public pressure is on the side of intervention and removing the child from the home.

—Almost the entire process is done in secret. The accused often does not know the accuser or even the accusation. The court hearings are held behind closed doors. Child saving agencies and their workers are largely immune from lawsuits, leaving the falsely accused with almost no legal recourse. In short, there is no accountability.

—People who go into child saving tend to be people who crave power over others. The child-protective system gives them power that is virtually absolute. And we all know what absolute power does.

The "corruption" of the child savers is not a selfish corruption—at least not in the traditional sense of the term. Opponents of the child savers sometimes make the mistake of alleging a conscious conspiracy of some sort, often for financial gain. If only that were true, dealing with the child savers would be a lot easier. One could at least appeal to their consciences. But child savers believe they *are* acting in accord with the dictates of conscience. Justice Louis D. Brandeis wrote:

> Experience should teach us to be most on our guard to protect liberty when the government's purposes are beneficent. Men born to freedom are naturally apt to repel invasion of their liberty by evil-minded rulers. The greatest dangers to liberty lurk in insidious encroachment by men of zeal, well-meaning, but without understanding.[108]

The absolute power of the child savers has bred self-righteousness and arrogance. It comes through in numerous ways. Some are subtle, like the California doctor who says his clinic does exams "to prove abuse," or when a caseworker says she likes to limit visits between parents and their children because it's like "dangling a carrot" before the parents to make them toe the line.[109]

The arrogance even comes through on the order form for publications from the National Committee for Prevention of Child Abuse. The form declares that if you accidentally pay more for your publications than you were supposed to, anything up to ten dollars "will be considered a donation to NCPCA" unless you specifically request otherwise when placing the order.[110] Who but child savers would make you specify that you are *not* donating to their cause?

Sometimes it's less subtle. There is a CPS investigator in Florida who is so quick to tear children from their families that he has been nicknamed "Cap'n Hook." It's considered a compliment.[111]

There are a lot of Cap'n Hooks out there. In 1988, the Association for Children of New Jersey conducted an intensive study of that state's child-protection system. It included reading samples of case records and talking to all of those involved, including the parents. The Association's Assistant Director, Cecelia Zalkind, told the New Jersey Legislature about what the parents told her group:

"A feeling of powerlessness and helplessness pervaded each of these stories. Many parents expressed the feeling that they had no one who could advocate for their interest and rights in a system that they found at best confusing and, more often, arrogant. Many were fearful of reprisals if they complained or even asked questions."[112]

Paulette Patterson knows the feeling of helplessness and powerlessness. Disabled and confined to a wheelchair, she had her three children taken from her when the family was evicted from their apartment. Patterson was told she could not see or talk to her children until she found adequate housing. When she asked her caseworker to help with her search, she was told that the agency "helps children, not parents."[113]

Another caseworker told researchers that parents whose children are in foster care are "creeps."[114]

Although he says his county has now changed, even a county CPS administrator admits, "We did an incredible amount of damage to these children." Dennis McFall, Program Manager for Children's Services in Shasta County, California, told a legislative committee, "There was an image of little old ladies in tennis shoes running around practicing wishful thinking [by removing children from their homes]. That image was essentially accurate."[115]

Not only are parents expected to cooperate with their saviors, they are practically expected to worship them. According to one social-work text:

> As the client tells of himself and his feelings, he gives over or deposits something of himself in the caseworker; as he feels at one with the caseworker's responses, he begins to take back into himself some of the caseworker's attitudes, qualities, and values. . . . Thus a client may be nourished and fortified by his feeling of union with his caseworker that not only

has augmented his sense of wholeness, but also may considerably alter his inner reactions and overt behavior.[116]

What such an approach suggests is what Eileen Anderson suggested in her essay on therapists and power discussed in Chapter 3: that a large part of child-protective work has as its unconscious goal not helping the child, but making the helpers feel good.

Certainly that helps explain one of the most pervasive and bizarre phenomena in child-protective work. Virtually every case history I have seen has one thing in common: At some point, a deal—a plea bargain—is offered: Just agree to our treatment plan, let us "counsel" you, attend some "therapy," take a few "parenting" classes; in short, let us run your life for a little while and make us feel good by "helping" you, and no matter what it is we're accusing you of, you can have your children back. Insist on your innocence, on the other hand, and we'll do everything we can to be sure you never get your children back.

This helps explain not only the harm done to innocent families, but also the seemingly inexplicable decisions that sometimes are made to return children to parents who really are abusive over and over again.

After three-year-old Eli Creekmore was kicked to death by his father—after repeated previous beatings and placements in foster care—a spokesman for the Washington State Office of Children and Family Services explained that the people who kept sending Eli back to his father, "were all pretty well convinced that he was truly repentant."[117]

Unfortunately, no one told Laura and Bill Dickerson the rules of the game when they arrived at Arapahoe County District Court in Littleton, Colorado, on October 18, 1985, to try and get their thirteen-year-old daughter, Dawn, back.[118]

She had been taken two days before directly from her school. It was another one of those so-called emergencies. Her parents were not even contacted about the alleged abuse until that evening, after Dawn was already in foster care. Eventually, the case was dismissed, the Dickersons' name was removed from the central registry, and they even won a $2,500 settlement and a very grudging letter of apology from the county. But at that first hearing everything was still new and bewildering.

According to a transcript of the hearing and a prehearing report submitted to the judge, caseworker Anne Parks offered a plea bargain: If the parents agreed to therapy, promised never to use corporal punishment, and stayed under indefinite child saver supervision, Dawn would be returned within a week—as soon as everyone had just one session of therapy.

Unfortunately for Laura Dickerson, she tried to respond to this with logic: "Your honor," Dickerson said, "if I may say, respectfully, if I am such a danger to my daughter, [that she had to be instantly removed] then you mean to tell me that an hour of therapy would alleviate all this danger?" Conversely, Dickerson asked, if it is safe enough for Dawn to return after just one therapy session, why couldn't she have her daughter back right now?

The caseworker's response implied that if Dickerson didn't stop asking logical questions, she might not get her daughter back for a very long time. "Your honor," the caseworker said, "I am going to be reluctant to leave these recommendations as is if the parents are not going to agree that this is going to be helpful and the way to resolve the situation. . . . If they're going to be resistive . . . we may need to look at other options. I'm real reluctant to have these entered as orders with the kind of resistance that the Dickersons are indicating at this point."

The case was postponed. It would be eighteen more days before Dawn was returned. In the meantime, Laura Dickerson said, Anne Parks told Dawn that her mother didn't want her back. And the county Department of Social Services tried to bill Laura Dickerson $177.61 for her daughter's foster care.

The Dickersons had so much trouble because Laura Dickerson had, in the words of VOCAL attorney Allen McMahon: "failed the attitude test."

Joe Pickard brought the Dickersons' civil suit. He says what happened to them "happens all the time, but usually outside the courtroom, not on the record. They didn't know [Laura Dickerson] had that kind of backbone."

*   *   *

After the trauma is over, after the children are safely back at home, after the legal bills have been paid, after the pieces of something resembling a normal life have been put back together, victims of false allegations often complain that they were "guilty until proven innocent." In fact, to the child savers, you can never be proven innocent.

After their ordeal had ended, the new Director of Social Services in El Paso County invited Clark and Susan Gabriel to talk to a group of child-protective workers and supervisors.

Susan Gabriel remembers what happened: "At one point I said, 'I will always be guilty in your eyes, because I did not respond the way I was supposed to. To you I'll always be a bad mother.' Of course I wanted them to tell me I was wrong about that.

"They just nodded their heads, yes."

6

Sexual Abuse

When it was discovered that the most popular teacher in affluent suburban Guilderland, New York, had sodomized at least one of his students,
the townspeople quickly rallied 'round. Unfortunately, a lot of them rallied 'round the abuser.

Just ten days before a huge retirement picnic planned in his honor,
Bruce Sleeper pled guilty to a charge that a former student of his at
Farnsworth Middle School had performed fellatio on him. The girl was
thirteen years old.

The county District Attorney says he accepted the plea to spare children from having to testify at a trial. He alleges that Sleeper had been
preying on his students for more than a decade. But listen to Guilderland
resident James Cleary: Before the plea bargain, Cleary said, "I think the
real question should be, Can this really happen to someone who is so
popular? I think the question should be: How true are these accusations?"
After the plea bargain, Cleary said: "Even though he pleaded guilty I still
can't believe it."

Cleary is an elementary school principal and a member of the Albany
County Legislature.[1]

There is nothing unusual about what happened in Guilderland. Not
only the community at large, but a child's own mother may refuse to believe her child was abused by the father or other relatives. Many victims
of child sexual abuse face the risk of being victimized a second time if
they come forward because the people they thought they could trust the
most might betray them.

"Sexual abuse changes your life in every conceivable way," one victim wrote. "Self-hate and feelings of inferiority become a part of you. There is no way to recover your lost childhood. You go through life feeling dirty and worthless, as if it was your fault."[2]

When the issue is child sexual abuse, everything is ratcheted up a notch. There is more denial that it is happening at all, more revulsion when it is finally faced, more insistence that it is happening everywhere, and more hype from media that can cloak prurient interest in a veneer of civic responsibility.

Faced with so much resistance from a public, and, at one time, from fellow professionals who believed children *always* lied about sexual abuse, is it any wonder that the people who work with abused children now insist that children *never* lie? But like so much else the child savers have done in the name of protecting children, their approach to sexual abuse has backfired.

After telling us that children never lie because they wouldn't know what to make up, the child savers taught children exactly what they would need to know. They told the public to view any change in a child's behavior as a possible sign of sexual abuse. And they taught their fellow "professionals" never to doubt anything that came out of this process.

This is particularly dangerous in sexual abuse cases. More than in any kind of abuse except emotional abuse, caseworkers, judges, and juries often must rely solely on what the child says—or is alleged to have said—and how the "professionals" evaluate it. And in the midst of the hysteria the child savers have spread about sexual abuse, state legislatures have been making it easier to obtain convictions on just such "evidence." The result has been large numbers of false allegations—almost never because small children deliberately lied, but because they misunderstood honest affection, were caught up in a bitter divorce or custody dispute, or were convinced they had been abused by the "experts" questioning them.

Self-proclaimed "experts" in child sexual abuse have seriously maintained that there is a national network of satanic-cult child abusers linked to day-care centers across the country, who abduct, molest, and kill children. This despite a lack of evidence so total that the FBI's expert on the subject says that if it were true it would be "the greatest crime conspiracy in the history of man."[3]

For six months, Tom Charlier and Shirley Downing, reporters for the *Commercial Appeal* in Memphis, Tennessee, studied thirty-six of the so-called "mass molestation" cases from around the country. In an extraordinary series of articles they found not an epidemic of ritual child abuse, but "a nationwide epidemic of hysteria." As the *Commercial Appeal's* managing editor put it in introducing the series: "We obviously suspect that most of the accused in most cases of ritual child sex abuse are innocent."[4]

Though many of the "mass molestation" cases involved allegations of abuse by people other than parents, the assumptions and the techniques used by child-protective workers and law enforcement agencies in investigating these cases are the same guiding principles used in all sexual-abuse investigations. The only difference is, because of their large scale, practices normally kept secret became part of the public record and the press brought it to public attention.

And it is not just innocent families who suffer. The very same techniques that allow the child savers to railroad the innocent can also, when they are exposed, allow the guilty to go free.

And there are effects on all of us. Parents become suspicious of teachers and teachers become suspicious of parents. Children are denied normal affection from day care and school teachers afraid that their actions will be misinterpreted. At the same time, they are taught lessons in sexual-abuse "prevention" programs that may leave them fearful. Such lessons may be the only sex education some of them ever get. What effect will all this have on the emotional makeup of these children when they grow up? Even researchers who support the child savers' approach admit they don't know.

*   *   *

"We know that children do not make up stories asserting that they have been sexually molested."—Kathleen Coulbourn Faller, co-director, University of Michigan Interdisciplinary project on Child Abuse and Neglect.[5]

"Children never fabricate the kinds of explicit sexual manipulations they divulge in complaints or interrogations."—Dr. Roland Summit, inventor of the "child sexual abuse accommodation syndrome."[6]

"Children do *not* invent stories about their own sexual abuse."—pamphlet distributed by Albany County (New York) Rape Crisis Center (emphasis in original).[7]

"Children don't lie."—Therapist testifying in the case of "John C," Superior Court, Marin County California.[8]

Such assertions are the foundation of much of what is said and done about child sexual abuse. One must always, it is said, "believe the children." If such assertions are correct, then some of the implications are startling, to say the least.

If children don't lie, then Bakersfield, California, is a hotbed of cannibalism.

If children don't lie, there is a secret underground amusement park near Fort Bragg, California. You get in from the ocean by submarine.

If children don't lie, then they are being flown from their day-care centers all over the country in planes to be molested, then returned in time to be picked up by their parents. Some of the molesters don't need a plane. They can fly through the air all by themselves.

If children don't lie, then a child in Missouri killed a justice of the Supreme Court.

If children don't lie, then then some children in El Paso, Texas, had their eyes removed—and then put back.

All of these statements have been made by children in connection with a sexual-abuse allegation.[9] Yet as with everything else the child savers say, when they say that children don't lie they are not entirely wrong. The chances that a pre-school-aged child would be inclined or even able to suddenly fabricate, out of whole cloth, a detailed account of having been raped or sodomized are extremely remote. Under such circumstances, it's true: children don't lie. Under such circumstances, it is reasonable to "believe the children."

But those are not the circumstances under which most sexual-abuse allegations arise. Very young children do not pick up the phone themselves, call the state hotline, and explain how and when they were abused. In one way or another, unless the child is an adolescent, and often even then, the story is filtered through one or more adults.

—Adults may have done a presentation about what constitutes abuse, after which a child may go up to an adult and say "that happened to me."

—An accusation may be brought to child-protective workers by an adult who claims he or she was told something by a child. The notorious McMartin Preschool case in Los Angeles started this way.

—An accusation may not surface at all until after a child has been asked leading questions or been bribed or bullied by questioners.

—An accusation may come from a parent in the midst of a bitter divorce. The accusation may be true or it may be malicious or it may be an honest mistake.

In assessing the veracity of any allegation of sexual abuse by a young child, the real question is not, Did the child lie? The question is, What did the adults around that child say and do?

The cornerstone of the belief that children don't lie is the assumption that young children don't know enough about sexual acts to make something up. Indeed, just knowing too much about sex is considered one of the behavioral indicators of sexual abuse. But how much knowledge is too much? Some parents try to duck their children's early questions about sex; others answer candidly. Some parents use euphemisms; some don't. Some parents are attentive to what their children watch on television; some are not. Some parents are lax about nudity in the house; some are not.

Nor do we know how much small children know or want to know. For example, a study by Alvin Rosenfeld, Director of Child Psychiatry at the Jewish Child Care Association in New York City, found that almost all children between ages two and four, boys and girls alike, had tried to touch their mothers' breasts and genitals. Sixty-eight percent of the boys and 57 percent of the girls had tried to touch their father's genitals. Rosenfeld says the findings indicate that children are more sexually curious than had previously been assumed. Yet this type of normal behavior has been "introduced in some child custody cases as supportive evidence of molestation. . . ."[10]

Furthermore, even if the lack-of-knowledge argument was valid a decade ago, the statement that children don't lie because they wouldn't know what to say is often followed immediately by the recommendation that all children repeatedly be taught the difference between "good touch" and "bad touch" starting in preschool. Such information would not allow a child to fabricate a graphic account of intercourse or oral sex unless told what to say by adults. But sexual abuse includes much more than that. In New Jersey in 1987, for example, 44.6 percent of all substantiated sexual abuse cases—by far the largest single category—involved "fondling."[11] Rosenfeld's experience shows that, to child savers, sexual abuse can include innocent touching. And according to the National Committee for Prevention of Child Abuse, children may be considered sexually abused if they can hear their parents making love in the next room.[12]

This still does not mean small children are running around fabricating stories. It does call into question some of the "behavioral indicators" that sometimes are used when a child hasn't said anything, and it does suggest that if other practices are present, such as coercion or leading questions, a child might be willing and able to "fill in the blanks."

The second reason child savers say children don't lie is that children have no reason to. When it's the word of the accused against the word of the child, writes Faller, "who has a vested interest in lying and who in telling the truth?" Faller argues that children bring only misery on themselves by bringing the charge, and so would have no reason to do it. But what about the adults around the children? If there's a parent seeking custody, or a district attorney with political ambitions, or simply a child saver who honestly believes she must rescue all children whenever anyone says those children have been molested, then Faller's question must be looked at in a different light.

And there are times when children may in fact be the ones with the vested interest in lying. Defense attorney Roy Howson cites a case in point. Six-year-old Sally was very close to her father when her parents separated. After the separation, Sally's home life became a lot less pleasant. Both parents, now living apart, became depressed and moody and had little time for her. Then Sally found out that after a friend, also a child of divorce, accused her father of sexual abuse, her mother started lavishing attention on her. Shortly thereafter, Sally made the identical allegation against her father. And immediately, she reaped the same reward. Rather than facing rejection and trauma at every turn, not only her mother, but the entire child-protective system, lavished praise and attention on Sally.[13]

The children-don't-lie argument is flawed on its face. But by the time it reaches the front-line child-protective worker it has been exaggerated beyond even the original intent of some of its proponents. It happens because of a phenomenon similar to the children's game of "telephone," in which a group of children line up and whisper a message from one to the next. By the time it's reached the end of the line the message bears little resemblance to the original.

In protective services it works like this. The few people who actually know a lot about sexual abuse of children—or say they do—give a lecture to top CPS officials from all over the country. During the lecture, they explain that a very young child exposed to no other influences will not spontaneously make up a story of having been abused. The top CPS officials take this back home and tell it to their top supervisors, who tell it to their lower-level supervisors, and so on. By the time it reaches the untrained, inexperienced CPS worker on the street, it becomes, no matter what the age or the circumstances, "children don't lie." Ever. Period. A teenager wants revenge against a teacher for a failing grade? It doesn't matter. Children don't lie. Believe the children. An adolescent is tired of strict discipline at home so she says she's abused there? It doesn't matter. Children don't lie. Believe the children.

For child savers, there is only one exception. When children say they have *not* been abused, then *don't* believe the children. As the prosecutor in a New Jersey "mass molestation" case explained, "To believe a child's *'no'* is simplistic" (emphasis in original).[14]

In a field that requires so many difficult complex decisions, "when someone hits upon a fad . . . [people] turn to it like a shipwreck survivor clinging to a life preserver," says Robert Schwartz of the Juvenile Law Center in Philadelphia.[15]

This helps explain the widespread acceptance and misapplication of something called "The Child Sexual Abuse Accommodation Syndrome." The syndrome was first postulated by psychiatrist Roland Summit in 1983 in the child savers' "scholarly" journal, *Child Abuse and Neglect: The International Journal.*[16] The article is considered required reading for child-protective workers.[17]

Summit states that abused children go through a five-stage process:

The first two stages are secrecy and helplessness. The child is terrified to disclose or resist the abuse because of the threats of the abuser. Then comes "entrapment and accommodation" as the child tries to live with his or her torment. If the child can be brought to tell, the disclosure will be "delayed" and "unconvincing" because of the child's fear. Once the disclosure is made, all the adults will unite in a conspiracy of anger and disbelief so painful that it inevitably prompts the fifth stage: a false recantation.

This is another one of those things child savers say that isn't always wrong. Common sense suggests that there are many cases that would logically proceed in the manner Summit describes. Many, but by no means all.

The accommodation syndrome makes sense when:

—The abuse is committed by a parent (almost always the father), another close relative, or someone else so well-regarded that the parents might absolutely refuse to believe it.

—The father has a close relationship with the mother, who won't believe the child.

—The disclosure was made spontaneously by the child, who could no longer tolerate the torment.

—It turns out that, in fact, all the adults to whom she turns turn against her.

But not all, probably not even most, cases fit this pattern. When parents are divorced, for example, the mother is likely to support the child against the father. In some cases the mother may have encouraged or fabricated the allegation in the first place as a weapon in a custody fight. Even if the parents do stick together, "professionals" are now far more likely to believe any allegation without question than to automatically turn a deaf ear. (Witness what happened when "Sally" made up her story.)

The syndrome does not apply to cases where the accused is not a parent. The syndrome does not apply when the allegation is made only because of relentless pressure by interrogators. And the syndrome does not take into account cases that develop from honest misunderstandings, which can happen when a child confuses "good touch" with "bad touch" after a sexual-abuse-prevention presentation.

Even some of Summit's fellow child savers don't buy his "syndrome." "It doesn't appear in even the majority of cases," says Lucy Berliner, director of research at the Sexual Assault Center at Harborview Medical Center in Seattle. "It's an exception."[18]

Summit's original article, though appearing in a "scholarly" journal, is anything but scholarly. It cites no empirical evidence whatsoever, only Summit's own impressions and those of some other clinicians. The lack of evidence is disguised by writing that eschews the objective language and facts of the scholar in favor of a hyperbolic diatribe that is especially startling in the pages of a journal that purports to be scientific.

"Children generally learn to cope silently with terrors in the night," Summit writes. "Bed covers take on magical powers against monsters, but they are no match for human intruders."

Summit writes that any disclosure by any child will be met by "an adult conspiracy of silence and disbelief." Of course a parent will never side with a child, Summit writes, since the whole institution of marriage is built on a rather shabby foundation: "Marriage," Summit writes, "demands considerable blind trust and denial for survival." Summit warns clinicians not to doubt a child just because the circumstances described seem impossible (such as abuse with multiple witnesses nearby): "The more illogical and incredible the initiation scene might seem to adults, the more likely it is that the child's plaintive description is valid."

Any verdict of innocent is a "continuing assault on the child." Three times Summit suggests that any hint of disbelief under any circumstances will jeopardize any child's "emotional survival." Even conveying doubt is risky: "Anyone working therapeutically with the child . . . may be tested and provoked to prove that trust is impossible. . . . It is all too easy for the would-be therapist to join the parents and all of adult society in rejecting such a child. . . ." Such nonbelievers often are holding themselves "aloof from the helplessness and pain of the child's dilemma. . . ." Indeed, Summit implies that anyone who doubts his theory shouldn't be allowed to evaluate children at all: "It is countertherapeutic and unjust to expose legitimate victims to evaluations or treatment by therapists who cannot suspect or 'believe in' the possibility of unilateral sexual victimization of children by apparently normal adults."

Repeatedly, Summit calls upon professionals to abandon their roles as objective evaluators and become "child advocates": "[Children] need an adult clinical advocate. . . . The specialist must help mobilize skeptical caretakers into a position of belief, acceptance, support, and protection of the child. The specialist must first be capable of assuming that same position."

Once having read an article like Summit's, or worse, hearing about it second-hand, how could the typical child-protective worker possibly be an investigator in any true sense of the word? The whole message of the article is that anyone who expresses the skepticism needed for an investigation of any abuse allegation under any circumstances is little better than a child molester himself. Those who express no doubt, on the other hand, are heroes standing up for defenseless children against the adult conspiracy. What a great boost for a young child saver's ego.

The result is that the charge of sexual abuse becomes impossible to defend against no matter who is making it and no matter what the circumstances.

Does the charge come from a divorced parent but the child denies it? Pay no attention. The syndrome says children always deny it but it's always true anyway. Does the child make the accusation but only after intense pressure? Well of course. The child won't "admit it" any other way. That's the nature of the syndrome. Does a child deny abuse, then "disclose" it under high-pressure interrogation and then deny it again? Pay no attention to those denials. Its just a false "recantation." The syndrome, you know.

For young children, whether or not they are telling the truth may depend more than anything else on how they are questioned. The so-called "mass molestation" cases reveal how children can be induced to accuse people of abuse. They also illustrate a series of problems that pervade the child savers' model for sexual-abuse investigations. This is what happened in some of those cases:

Bakersfield, California

In June 1984, a five-year-old girl told her mother that her father and another man had molested her.[19] A year later, the case had grown to include dozens of victims and allegations of cannibalism, murder, and satanic rituals. Twenty-one children were taken from their homes.

The California Attorney General's office issued a scathing report concerning the conduct of the investigation. The report puts much of the blame on one zealot caseworker who virtually took over the investigation from the county Sheriff's Department.

The report includes this dialogue between the worker and a suspect:

> Worker: . . . if [children] are mad at their dad that's when they may say physical abuse, but they're not going to say sexual. It just doesn't happen. So we do believe the children—okay, that you are involved.
> Suspect: So no matter what I say doesn't even matter then?
> Worker: Well, yeah of course it matters, but our stand is that we believe the children. At all cost, 'cause that's our job and that's what our belief is.

Many of the interviews were done by sheriff's deputies who had not received the specialized training required under state law. According to the report, the deputies "violated basic law enforcement standards and techniques for interviewing young victims. Deputies generally did not question the children's statements and they responded positively . . . only when the children revealed new allegations or said something to reinforce their previous allegations. They applied pressure on the children to name additional suspects and victims and questioned them with inappropriate suggestions that produced the answers they were looking for. . . . Deputies interviewed six of the children ten or more times each, with one child the subject of twenty-four interviews. . . ."

During the interviews, the deputies would tell the children what happened and get upset if the children didn't confirm it. One thirteen-year-old said later: "I told them nothing had happened, but they kept after me and after me and after me, over and over and over. So I finally said something had happened so they would stop bugging me about it."

According to the Attorney General's report, "Most of the arrests were based on the victim's statements alone. There is no documentation to show that any background investigation other than criminal checks was made."

The report also describes a "photo line-up" in which children were shown pictures of several people, one of whom was a suspect. In one case, the report states, the identification was "obtained under questionable circumstances. The victim initially could not identify the suspect from the line-up. The deputy left the room for a few minutes, leaving the social worker with the child, and was surprised to learn upon returning to the interview room that the child could now identify the suspect. The tape recording of the interview does not include the line-up portion of the interview."

Things finally wound down in Bakersfield when suddenly one of the children said the zealot social worker was herself part of the satanic cult that was molesting children. During the next six months two other children named the worker, as well as a Deputy District Attorney and a sheriff's deputy. Unlike virtually all the other accusations, these led to no arrests.

As for the allegations that started it all, the Attorney general's report found:

—No physical evidence was uncovered to indicate that babies had been killed.

—Several alleged homicide victims were found alive.

—There were no reports of any missing babies or young children in Kern County that corresponded with the victims named by the children.

—No bodies were found in various grave sites described by the children. . . .

—Deputies searched two lakes where alleged bodies were deposited but no remains were found.

—In fact, no evidence was found to prove the children's allegations, and evidence was developed that disproved the children's statements.

Twelve people were convicted in the Bakersfield cases, and all of those convictions are being appealed. But the district attorney refused even to prosecute another fifteen people, because the evidence developed by the Sheriffs and the child protective workers was so flimsy.

Jordan, Minnesota

The Jordan case began with James Rud, a garbage collector and convicted child molester.[20] In September 1983, the children of Rud's live-in girlfriend accused Rud of molesting them. Rud was arrested and charged.

But the Scott County District Attorney, Kathleen Morris, did not stop there. At her instigation police began questioning friends of the children who first made the charges, and friends of their friends. Initially, the children did not say much. Then Morris took over the questioning, and the accusations grew. Eventually, sixty children made accusations; twenty-six of them were removed from their homes and twenty-four adults were charged.

After being offered a plea bargain so generous the court ultimately refused to accept it, Rud implicated eighteen other alleged child abusers.

According to a state investigation, "Rud claimed to have obtained and reviewed copies of police reports regarding other defendants" before accusing them. "It is interesting to note that in Rud's 113-page statement, the only individuals identified by him were those whose names had been in the police reports, all but one of whom had already been charged with a crime."

Rud took two lie detector tests. One was inconclusive, and he flunked the other. When the first and only case came to trial, Rud was unable to point out in the courtroom one of the people he had accused in his statement. Finally, Rud recanted the statement, claiming he had made it to get a lighter sentence and to please Morris.

After she lost her first case, Morris dropped all the other sexual-abuse charges. She claimed that proceeding with them would jeopardize an even more important investigation: Some of the children had made bizarre allegations of ritual murder. None of the allegations checked out.

With the help of the FBI, the Minnesota Attorney General's office reviewed the handling of the Jordan cases. The report found that the Jordan case had been botched in much the same way as Kern County authorities had botched the Bakersfield case. The children were subjected to repeated interviews—sometimes up to thirty times. The Attorney General's report stated:

> According to experts, children may interpret repeated interviews as demands for more or different information than they have already given . . . [One child] had steadfastly denied any criminal sexual conduct on the part of his parents until he had been placed with new foster parents who questioned him extensively.
> . . . In many cases children were removed from their homes and isolated from all family contact for prolonged periods, even though the children denied having been sexually abused. In some instances, the children did not "admit" that their parents had abused them until several months

of such separation, marked by continuous questioning about abuse. In the most extreme cases, these children were also told that reunification with their families would be facilitated by "admissions" of sex abuse by their parents and other adults.

(Recall Kathleen Coulbourn Faller's question: Who has a vested interest in lying and who in telling the truth?)

"The Scott County cases raise the issue of how long and how often one can continue to question children about abuse before running the risk of a false accusation," the Attorney General's report said. The report found that the problem was compounded by the repeated failure of the people doing the interviews to write down what the children had said, making the claims of Morris and the police all the more suspect.

The report found that parents repeatedly were arrested and charged even when their own children strongly denied being abused. Often charges were leveled before anyone had been interviewed or any attempt had been made to find evidence.

As for the murder charges, one child eventually admitted that "the idea of the homicides came into his head when Scott County investigators questioned him about a black or mulatto boy who may have been cut or tortured. He said he got the idea of ritualistic torturing from a television program he had seen. He stated that he had lied about the murders because he wanted to please investigators."

Kathleen Morris was voted out of office and is appealing a "reprimand" by the State Board of Professional Responsibility. But first, she had more than her allotted fifteen minutes of fame. She was described as "gutsy and driven," a "pioneer in the cause of protecting children." She became a national celebrity and was considered an "expert" on interviewing children. She says if she had it to do over again, she wouldn't change anything but the outcome. "I don't apologize for what I did in the Scott County Cases. I don't regret any of my decisions."

Manhattan Beach

In the most notorious "mass molestation" case of all, the first charges were not even brought by a child.

In August 1983, Judy Johnson, a parent of a child at the McMartin Preschool, told local police that her son had been sexually abused by Raymond Buckey, a teacher at the school and grandson of its founder.[21] Johnson died in 1986. She had a history of mental illness. She made all sorts of bizarre charges, including an allegation that her son had been sodomized by an AWOL marine—who also sodomized the family dog.

The child himself said nothing directly to police. They arrested Buckey but released him for lack of evidence. Then they sent a letter to two hundred parents telling them Ray Buckey may have molested their children and describing in explicit detail what he might have done.

Of course the parents panicked and swamped the small Manhattan Beach Police Department with calls. The charges grew and grew. There were charges of animal sacrifice, exhumation and mutilation of bodies from cemeteries, trips to churches for satanic rituals and airplane flights. No evidence was found for any of it. Even after a $10,000 reward was posted for any pornographic pictures or videotapes of the McMartin children, none turned up. When children said there were secret tunnels under the preschool, police pulled up the floors and dug. They found nothing. The investigation spread to sixty-four other day-care centers; seven of them closed. All of them were in the same area as McMartin—the area to which parents sent their children after McMartin closed.

Seven employees of the school, including the owner, Peggy McMartin Buckey, were indicted in what authorities said was the largest child-sex ring in the country. They were charged with three hundred counts involving one hundred children.

They were immediately convicted in the press. On the April 20, 1984, edition of "ABC News Nightline," for example, substitute anchor Hodding Carter declared, "All of those accused have pleaded not guilty. But there is no question in the minds of investigators that children were abused over a period of many years. How could it have gone on undetected?" Reporter James Walker went on to declare that the McMartin story is about "how even the very young need to be listened to and believed." A *Los Angeles Times* story flatly declared that "they have told their secrets, the little ones and the adolescents, of rape and sodomy, and oral copulation and fondling, slaughtering of animals to scare them into silence and threats against them and their parents."

In a scathing, four-part critique of media coverage, including that of his own newspaper, *Times* media critic David Shaw wrote that the press "often abandoned . . . fairness and skepticism. . . . [T]he media frequently plunged into hysteria, sensationalism, and what one editor calls 'a lynch mob syndrome.' "

In January 1986, a newly elected Los Angeles County District Attorney dismissed all charges against five of the defendants, calling the evidence against them "incredibly weak." Three years later, a jury acquitted the remaining defendants on fifty-two counts and deadlocked over thirteen more. As this is written, the prosecution is retrying Raymond Buckey on twelve of those counts.

It was the longest criminal trial in American history, and the most expensive. So far it has cost more than $15 million. And so far, no one has been convicted of anything. Of the three assistant district attorneys originally assigned to the case, one quit the case when she began to have doubts about the defendants' guilt, and another, Glenn Stevens, was fired after declaring publicly that none of the defendants was guilty beyond a reasonable doubt and much of the case was "hogwash." He has sold his story to a film producer.

Once again, the way children were questioned was at the heart of the problem.

The children were sent to the Child Sexual Abuse Center at the Children's Institute International (CII) for what "Nightline" called "sophisticated play therapy" that would allow the children to "share their secrets."

The center's director, Kee MacFarlane, would dress up in a clown costume, sit on the floor with the children, talk to them through puppets, and make statements like "we can pretend." It all creates an image of "fantasyland," says Stevens. And the children quickly learn what is expected of them. Instead of open-ended questions, MacFarlane and other employees would ask if particular people did particular things. A simple nod yes then would be enough. "No" answers were rejected, with questions repeated over and over. "Yes" answers were rewarded with high praise and statements that "your parents will be so proud of you." The parents were indeed proud and would reward their children with presents or treats.

For children who are abused, being forced to relive the experience is traumatic. But for children who had not been abused, playing with puppets and a lady in a clown suit and getting rewarded for "right" answers is a game. The children would tell each other how the "game" worked, and they would know what was expected of them when they met with MacFarlane and the other workers at CII.

Particularly since the verdict in the case came down in early 1990, MacFarlane has tried to justify her techniques as necessary in order to provide a supportive environment to help children disclose alleged abuse, and to provide therapy for the children.

But when children did not give MacFarlane the answers she wanted, her approach was anything but therapeutic. Suddenly, the lady in the clown suit turned mean. This is how MacFarlane questioned an eight-year-old boy:

> MacFarlane: I thought that was a naked game.
> Child: Not exactly.
> MacFarlane: Did somebody take their clothes off?
> Child: When I was there no one was naked.
> MacFarlane: We want to make sure you're not scared to tell.

Child: I'm not scared.

MacFarlane: Some of the kids were told they might be killed. It was a trick. All right Mr. Alligator [the puppet the child is using], are you going to be stupid, or are you smart and can tell. Some think you're smart.

Child: I'll be smart.

MacFarlane: Mr. Monkey [a puppet the child had used earlier] is chicken. He can't remember the naked games, but you know the naked movie star game. Is your memory too bad?

Child: I haven't seen the naked movie star game.

MacFarlane: You must be dumb!

Child: I don't remember.

Jurors said it was this sort of questioning that made it impossible for them to convict anyone. Said one juror in frustration: "The children were never allowed to say in their own words what happened to them. To me that was crucial."

There have been other such cases around the country. In Oregon, a state hearing examiner found that when a child wanted to retract an allegation against a day-care-center operator, she was told by caseworkers that unless she stuck with her story they would take her away from her mother.[22]

In Sacramento, California, a six-year-old girl said that when she denied being molested by her uncle, a police detective "yelled at me and called me a liar. . . . She just wouldn't believe me, no matter what." The girl said she was offered ice cream if she would "tell the truth"—meaning accuse her uncle—but if she didn't, the detective said she would have to "do it the hard way" and have a medical examination. The detective denied all the girl's statements.[23]

In El Paso, a police detective displayed his gun and handcuffs while asking these questions of a child:

Detective: Who went to that party?

Child: I don't know, I don't know.

Detective: Oh, you do too know.

Child: I do not.

Detective: Yeah, you do.[24]

In another El Paso case, child-protective workers were called because a child was crying in class. When the child explained that she was upset because her mother had had the family dog put to sleep (because of illness, the mother said), the worker asked neighbors if the mother or any of her friends had been involved in ritualistic animal slaughter.[25]

In some cases, children don't need to say anything to be declared sexually abused. Conclusions are drawn based on how they play with "anatomically correct" dolls. "I call them anatomically incorrect," says Sherry Skidmore of the California State Psychological Association, because the genitals tend to be exaggerated.[26] That's bound to attract the attention of a curious child, say Skidmore and other experts. As one put it: "If you give a child two toy cars to play with, and he crashes one car into another, does this mean he's been in a car wreck?"[27]

The child savers insist that cajoling, bribing, and blackmailing small children while repeatedly telling them what happened to them and demanding confirmation—all that doesn't really matter. Says Kee MacFarlane: "I just don't believe that we have this incredible power to influence children . . . and that they will not only acquiesce to what we're saying but will go on to elaborate on it in great detail."[28]

But research indicates that that is exactly what does happen.

Skidmore cited this example, in which the child was under far less pressure than those questioned by the child savers. It concerned a description of a woman the child had seen who was *not* wearing a poncho or a cap:

> Q: Was the woman wearing a poncho and a cap?
> A: I think it was a cap.
> Q: What sort of cap was it? Was it like a beret or was it a peak cap or . . . ?
> A: No, it had sort of—it was flared with a little piece coming out. It was flared with a sort of button thing in the middle.
> Q: Was it a peak like that, that sort of thing?
> A: Y-yes.
> Q: That's the sort of cap I'm thinking your meaning, with a little peak out there.
> A: Yes, that's the top view, yes.
> Q: Smashing. What color?
> A: Oh, I think, uh, it was black or brown.
> Q: Think it was dark, shall we say?
> A: Yes, it was a dark color, I think. I didn't see her hair.[29]

Not only did the child "acquiesce" to what the interviewer was saying, to use MacFarlane's words, the child did indeed go on to elaborate on it in great detail.

Other child savers have argued that children are susceptible to suggestion—but no more so than adults. This is not reassuring.

According to Elizabeth Loftus, a professor of psychology at the University of Washington in Seattle specializing in the study of memory distortion, "scores of studies" have found that, when it was suggested by an interviewer, "people have recalled nonexistent broken glass and tape recorders, a clean-shaven man as having a mustache, straight hair as curly, and even something as large and conspicuous as a barn in a bucolic scene that contained no buildings at all."[30] As this is written, the government of China is setting out to convince one billion Chinese—including thousands of eyewitnesses—that the 1989 massacre of student protestors in Tienanmen Square never happened. Loftus believes they may well succeed. Compared to that, convincing an eight-year-old that he saw "naked games" should be literally child's play.

Of course not every sexual abuse case relies on behavioral symptoms, or even on a child's testimony, alone. Sometimes there is said to be visible medical evidence of abuse. But new research shows that much of what had previously been thought to be signs of abuse can also be found in children who have not been abused.

John McCann, a professor of pediatrics at the University of California, San Francisco, examined the vaginal and rectal areas of 250 children with no history of sexual abuse. He found wide variation among the genitalia of the girls studied, including features previously thought to be present only when children are abused. Until McCann's study, doctors had simply been diagnosing abuse based upon assumptions that sexual organs would show trauma and heal with scars in ways similar to other parts of the body.[31]

*　　*　　*

Each of the so-called "mass molestation" cases represents a triple tragedy. In Jordan, for example, there were all the children taken from their families and brutally interrogated. Second, there were the families destroyed. The only defendants to go to trial have divorced, others lost their jobs, and others have legal bills they'll probably never be able to pay. But there is a third tragedy as well. The Attorney General's report notes that "some children in Scott County were sexually abused"—not just by James Rud but by others who received immunity and were given therapy instead of jail. Because the investigation was so badly done, there is no way to know if any of the people whose cases were dismissed actually were guilty. If any are guilty, they owe their freedom to Kathleen Morris and the child saver mentality.

As the report notes, "The City of Jordan should also be listed among the victims of the so-called sex-ring cases. [We] simply do not believe that accusations of such widespread abuse were accurate. The citizens of Jordan, most importantly the children, both those who were abused and those who were not, have suffered as a result of these public accusations."

Just as in the Jordan case, what happened in the McMartin case is a tragedy on every level. Innocent families were disrupted and children who had not been harmed may have been convinced that they were. And we will never know for sure whether any of the defendants was guilty or not. As former prosecutor Glenn Stevens explained to the *Commercial Appeal*: "People ask me, 'Well, do you think anybody did any molesting?' My best answer is, 'I don't know.' . . . It may have happened, but if it exists, it is buried under the bungling of the initial investigation, the mishandling of the District Attorney's office and the way the children were . . . interviewed."

It was not only the poor interviewing techniques that ruined the chance to convict more of the guilty, if indeed they exist. In Jordan and in Bakersfield, the insistence that children don't lie not only prompted investigators to accuse the innocent, it also made them sloppy about trying to gather additional corroborating evidence that might have made it possible to get more convictions.

*   *   *

When confronted with all the holes in the "children don't lie" theory, the child savers react just as they do when confronted with the holes in the "child abuse crosses class lines theory"—they deny having said it.

Lucy Berliner has written, "Obviously, not everything children say about sexual abuse is true and professional writing has always acknowledged some proportion of untrue reports."[32]

"Of course some kids lie," Berliner said on another occasion, but "there is no shred of evidence that kids lie about sexual assault any more than adults do."[33]

Because sexual abuse so often leaves no physical evidence, child-protective workers and courts have become heavily reliant on the "expert" testimony of psychologists and psychiatrists. Such testimony also is crucial in other child-abuse proceedings, such as physical- and emotional-neglect cases. Such reliance gets judges and juries off the hook when the time comes to make some very tough decisions. If King Solomon were alive today, he probably would not have made his famous custody decision until he had ordered up psychiatric evaluations of everyone.

New Jersey law guardians Marguerite Rosenthal and James Louis write that "the more deference that is paid to the characterization presented by an 'expert,' the easier it can become to ignore evidence to the contrary."[34]

"Nobody likes to make the tough calls," Louis explained in an interview. "If some expert comes in and is forthright enough . . . legal principles developed through legislation and common law go by the board."

But the field of psychology simply isn't up to the job. Psychology is part science, but it also is part art, and even, arguably, part religion. There is no evidence that psychologists, psychiatrists, and social workers can reliably make the judgments required to determine whether children have been abused or neglected. There is considerable evidence that they can't. Bruce Ennis and Thomas Litwack reviewed scores of studies of the psychiatric decision-making process. Their conclusion: Judges and juries who rely on "expert" psychological testimony would do just as well if they tossed a coin.

Polygraphs are far more reliable than psychiatrists, the authors conclude, yet polygraphs are not reliable enough to be used in court.

Over and over again studies have found that when diagnosing identical patients in identical settings, no two psychiatrists would agree more than about half the time. Among the reasons:

—Training in psychiatry predisposes practitioners to find mental illness, and the biases of the school—or sect—in which one gets one's training virtually predetermines what "illness" one will find in a patient.

—Diagnosis often is influenced by the setting. If a patient is already in a hospital, he or she is more likely to be diagnosed as mentally ill.

—In studies where psychiatric residents were given different information about a patient's income, they were more likely to diagnose mental illness if they were told the patient was poor.

—Diagnoses were heavily influenced by the practitioners' own prejudices—and their own personality problems.

—Perhaps most important, a patient who criticizes the mental health profession (failing the "attitude test" again) is more likely to be diagnosed mentally ill than a patient who "flatters" it.

Ennis and Litwack conclude: "There is good reason to believe that psychiatric judgments are not particularly reliable or valid, and that psychiatric diagnoses and predictions convey more erroneous than accurate information." The authors blame not only psychiatry, but also legislatures and courts who have been "seeking easy answers where there are none."[35] A second survey of the literature, completed in 1988, reached the same conclusion. In a wire-service interview, the authors even repeated the coin-toss analogy.[36]

A *Georgetown Law Journal* examination of so-called expert testimony specifically in sexual abuse cases found that the experts are no more reliable than the broad, vague, symptom lists described in the previous chapter. One "expert" testified that the typical incest victim shows regressive behavior, acts like a younger child, and becomes withdrawn. Yet other experts say the typical victim acts like an older child and behaves aggressively. One "expert" testified that he believed a thirteen-year-old girl's allegation against her stepfather in part because a "sense of fairness, I think, made it unlikely that she would make up a story just to get back at somebody."

The problem is that, as with the symptom lists, behaviors said to "typify" abused children can also typify any number of other problems. The

Georgetown article concludes that, except under the most extreme circumstances, so-called expert testimony about "typical" signs of abuse or "typical" behavior of abused children is too unreliable and should not be admitted in court.[37]

At a minimum, the so-called "experts" ought to have some expertise. Yet Kee MacFarlane, for example, who says she "can't believe" children are overly influenced by leading questions, has only a masters degree in social work. She is not a psychologist or psychiatrist. Glenn Stevens, the former prosecutor, said that although MacFarlane never claimed such credentials, "she enjoyed having herself held out as a child therapist and an expert when in fact she doesn't have a license other than a driver's license."[38]

MacFarlane also acknowledged deliberately not reading articles by at least one prominent critic of her work "mainly out of self-protection." (Some experts frequently used by the defense haven't read their critics either).[39] Experts used in major cases in New Jersey and Chicago were later found to have exaggerated their credentials.[40]

A rare insight into what goes into an "expert" evaluation that a child was abused is provided by a deposition given in December 1987 by James Monteleone a professor of pediatrics and head of the Sexual Abuse Management Unit at Cardinal Glennon Children's Hospital in St. Louis. During the deposition, Monteleone acknowledged that:

—His program will never say that a child is *not* sexually abused. "You can never say they've not been sexually abused—never."

—There is no procedure manual for performing sexual-abuse examinations at his clinic.

—Training in sexual abuse for doctors at the clinic is optional. "And it's taught by word of mouth, like most medicine is."

—Medical histories of patients generally are not taken. There is not even a form parents can fill out to let the doctor know if symptoms sometimes associated with abuse might have predated the alleged abuse. "We don't check off forms. It's poor medicine."

In the deposition, Monteleone says he based a diagnosis of sexual abuse solely on "Strong behavioral indicators; night terrors, sleep disorders, fears of falling asleep, handling and touching." (Later he said there "might" have been other factors as well.) He acknowledged that many of the factors he listed are common among children whether they have been abused or not, and that he never checked to see if such symptoms predated the alleged abuse of the child he was examining.[41]

The defendant in the case discussed by Monteleone was acquitted.

Once you become famous as a child-abuse "expert," it seems nothing can change it. Nor, it seems, can even the most extreme views give pause to the reporters who quote the same "experts" over and over again.

In 1984, Kee MacFarlane told a Congressional Committee she believed there was a national conspiracy of child pornographers operating day-care centers as a cover. "I believe we are dealing with an organized operation of child predators designed to prevent detection," she said. "The preschool, in such a case, serves as a ruse for a larger, unthinkable network of crimes against children. . . . I don't know if what we're dealing with can be called organized crime, or if there is an entity that uses schools as procurement places. But I do know that hundreds of children are alleging that they were pornographically photographed during their entire time at preschools, that they were taken far away to do so, sometimes so far away that they were taken on planes."[42] The fact that in all these cases, not one pornographic picture had turned up apparently was irrelevant.

Roland Summit, inventor of the "accomodation syndrome," says he believes the satanic-cult theories.[43]

The National Committee for Prevention of Child Abuse effectively "convicted" all the McMartin defendants in a 1986 "fact sheet," and then went on to say that "one ongoing, federally-funded study is investigating over 30 cases of sexual abuse with multiple perpetrators and multiple victims in day care settings."[44]

NCPCA's New York affiliate distributed an interview with an "expert" who warned that "the more bizarre the story, the more reality there may be to it."[45] Often this type of belief is based on the idea that such stories, with so many wild allegations in common, couldn't possibly crop up all over the country unless they were true. In fact, that is exactly the reason they should be viewed with skepticism.

The tales told around the country are "urban legends." As Charlier and Downing explained in their series, the term is used

> . . . to describe fascinating and colorful tales that spread rapidly across the nation, usually with little change in detail, but which rarely can be traced to any actual event.
> Well-known examples include the person who inadvertently kills a pet while trying to dry it off in a microwave oven and the child who bites into a razor-blade-laden apple given to him on Halloween. Both tales, according to researchers, were launched without any known authenticity.

Although not cited by Charlier and Downing, another example is the rumor that surfaces repeatedly about the Procter and Gamble Co. being linked to devil worshipers because of the thirteen stars on the company logo. Since this tale has turned up all over the country in almost identical form, by child saver logic, it must be true.

Charlier and Downing report that the myths about a day-care conspiracy got several assists in spreading across the country. National news media gave enormous attention to the bizarre stories told by the children in the McMartin case, and investigators and parents in different cities began getting in touch with one another and holding conferences. As they returned to their hometowns, these people began asking children if particular things they had heard about had happened to them.

There are other reasons as well. The stories told by children have roots in everything from myths that date back to the early days of Christianity, when Romans accused Christians of mutilating babies, to stories told by the McMartin children about naked priests and nuns (which have roots in century-old anti-Catholic bigotry), to concerns children often have about urination and defecation when they've only been toilet trained for a relatively short time. Traditional American racial fears also have played a role in some of the stories.

Kenneth Lanning, the FBI's child abuse expert, tells about a policeman who had made a child-abuse-prevention presentation to some young children. He asked them what would happen if they got in a car with someone they didn't know. "What amazed him was the length and the detail and the depth of the stories these children told: He'd get in the car and [the stranger] would take you to some secret house and take you down in the basement and tie you down to the floor and rip your clothes off and rip your nose off and cut your ears off and chop your penis up," Lanning said. For all these reasons, plus the lack of physical evidence, Lanning is convinced that the conspiracy that MacFarlane and other child savers believe in so fervently just doesn't exist.[46]

None of this means that no child has ever been abused in day care. It does not even mean that no child has ever been abused by people mumbling incantations, wearing robes, and burning candles. The United States is a very big place and there are plenty of sick, evil people out there. The child savers might even have inadvertently given some of them ideas. What it does mean is that the reporters at the *Commercial Appeal* in Memphis are right: Most of those accused are innocent—and an enormous amount of time, money, and effort that could have gone into combatting real child abuse has been wasted.

But as Susan Gabriel found out, one can never prove innocence to the satisfaction of the child savers.

Lucy Berliner writes, "Even when a person is not convicted or where legal actions are dropped, it is not proof that there was no abuse or that the person is innocent." Berliner singled out Dr. Lawrence Spiegel, a New Jersey Clinical Psychologist who, after being cleared in both criminal and juvenile court, wrote a book about his experience. Berliner's statements appeared in a publication of the American Bar Association, of all places.[47]

And here is how NCPCA's Anne Cohn explained away what happened in Jordan, Minnesota. Her description, in its entirety:

> Investigatory problems coupled with other legal and logistical problems appeared to get in the way of a full hearing on the case. For example, one child on the witness stand under intense interrogation seemed to change or drop the allegations, and soon thereafter charges against all the parents were dropped.[48]

A former prosecutor in Maine writes, "I once had a caseworker boast . . . that she *knew* all abuse disclosures were true and it wouldn't matter what evidence there was to the contrary" (emphasis in original).[49]

Professionals who disagree with the child savers get blackballed.

A Nashville Tennessee psychiatrist who has done several court-ordered evaluations stopped getting referrals from the state's Department of Human Services after he disagreed with them on a case.[50] Experts in other cities report the same sort of thing happening to them. It is, of course, standard operating procedure for both prosecution and defense lawyers to call expert witnesses who can be relied on to bolster their cases. But that happens after the initial investigation. During the investigation, the purpose of consulting an expert is to benefit from his or her expertise, not to have one's prejudices reinforced.

Even scarier than what happens to consultants who disagree with the child savers is what can happen to investigators, or even friends and relatives of the accused, who dare to express doubt. In the Jordan case, a frightening pattern emerged. Each time someone was arrested, a few friends and relatives would come to his or her defense. Almost as soon as these friends and relatives went public, they also would be arrested. Then more people would come forward to defend the new accused—and they would be arrested.

In a case involving a Memphis day-care center, the same interviewing techniques used in McMartin and the other similar cases were used. A social worker and a police detective both began to believe the children were telling workers what the workers wanted to hear. Both began to have doubts regarding the truth of the allegations. Both then became suspects.[51]

Kenneth Lanning, the FBI expert, believes the reason some child savers refuse to listen to any other point of view is simple: They went into child saving because they were abused themselves. They go at their task with a "hidden agenda"—recruiting the children they question "to the brotherhood and sisterhood of the sexually abused."[52]

In the McMartin case, a girl who repeatedly insisted she had not been abused was told by two interviewers from Children's Institute International that they had been abused as children and that she would feel much better if she told someone about what had happened.[53]

When Kee MacFarlane herself was asked under oath if she had been a victim of child sexual abuse, she refused to answer. The judge who heard her refusal said she would consider it an acknowledgement that MacFarlane had, in fact, been sexually abused.[54]

If nothing else gives pause to people willing to embrace the ideology of the child savers, consider this: The professional disciplines that now tell us children never lie are the same ones that used to tell us children *always* lie.

In 1936, a special committee of the American Bar Association advised judges to always order psychiatric exams in sexual abuse cases, because it was so well known how prevalent lying was among purported victims. The report said: "The erotic imagination of an abnormal child of attractive appearance may send a man to the penitentiary for life. The warnings of the psychiatric profession, supported as they are by thousands of observed cases, should be heeded by our profession."[55]

In 1988, the ABA's National Legal Resource Center For Child Advocacy and Protection issued another report. The report again included recommendations for more admission of psychiatric evidence, as well as eliminating many "due process" protections for defendants. But this time, the recommendations were included in a volume that maintains children almost never lie.[56]

The ABA and the psychiatrists got it wrong in 1936, and they've got it wrong now. The whole question of "lying" is a red herring. When a child says he got his Christmas presents from Santa Claus, he isn't lying. But it doesn't mean we should believe in Santa Claus.

Even without the undue influence of the child savers, both children and adults can make honest mistakes. Even the Kempe Center study cited in Chapter 4 showed that such mistakes combined with deliberate false reports accounted for 23 percent of all reports. Here's an example of how that can happen. A child-protective agency received the following information from a caller to a CPS "hotline" concerning a young girl:

> The victim and the suspect have been seen holding hands and walking while the suspect had his arm around the victim. The source also stated suspect used to live with the victim's mother and the victim. He has moved out in the recent past but visits the home every day. The source also stated the victim goes away with the suspect for long periods of time. Source stated victim wears dresses, tights, and shoes. Source said it is rumored by children that the victim may be sleeping with suspect. No other information is available. . . .

That was enough to prompt both Child Protective Services and the police to investigate. Here's what they found out:

—A doctor found no evidence of sexual abuse.

—The man is a friend of the family.

—According to both mother and child, when he sleeps over, he sleeps on the couch.

And why was the little girl so nicely dressed when the man took her out? Because he was taking her to church.[57]

The problem may be compounded by the well-intentioned efforts of child savers to prevent abuse through school-based education programs designed to help even the youngest children distinguish between "good touch" and "bad touch." There are more than two hundred such programs available, but they were rushed onto the market. No one knew whether they worked. No one knew what side effects they could produce. Ten years after most of the programs began, there still is little evaluation, and much of what does exist is self-evaluation by the creators of the programs.

Even proponents of these "prevention" programs concede there is little evidence that they prevent anything. But they do get some children who have been abused to come forward and report it. Bruce Sleeper, the teacher in Guilderland, New York, was caught after some of his students saw a sex-abuse prevention program.[58]

But some of the prevention programs also show signs of doing what most child saver activities do—backfiring. They are producing both true reports and false reports, particularly among younger children. Sometimes the errors are relatively harmless. A first-grade girl, who had been told she had the right to say "no" if an adult tried to make her do something that made her feel uncomfortable, told her parents she had the right to say no to anything they wanted her to do—including cleaning up her room.[59] Other misunderstandings can be more serious. At about the time of Sleeper's arrest, authorities just across the Hudson River, in the city of Rensselaer, were concluding that children who claimed they had been abused by a substitute teacher had confused normal affection with "bad" touching.[60]

Sherryll Kerns Kraizer, who designed a prevention program that tries to avoid some of the potential pitfalls, tells of a kindergarten child who had been taught at school about his "private zones." "That night, when his father swatted him on the bottom on his way up to bed [the child] turned to him and said, 'Daddy, I'm sorry, but my teacher said that's my private zone and you can't touch me there.' "[61] It's a funny story. But had the child told his teacher instead of his father it could have been tragic. Teachers are mandated to report alleged abuse.

An eleven-year-old in El Paso was concerned about her father's alcoholism. She didn't want him home on the weekends, when he would typically get drunk, so she made up a story that he had sexually abused her in order to get him jailed. She said she got the idea from a "good touch bad touch" presentation at her school.[62]

Jill Duerr-Berrick, of the Family Welfare Research Group at the University of California at Berkeley, directed a study of the impact seven prevention programs had on preschoolers. The study concluded that the programs were virtually worthless for that age group and should be scrapped. Duerr-Berrick said the study found no benefit from the programs and some harmful side effects. Before the programs were taught, all of the preschoolers reacted positively to descriptions of normal parent-child behavior such as tickling, bathing, and being tucked in at night. After the programs, between 10 and 20 percent showed signs of regarding the same activities negatively.[63]

Some prevention programs involve all forms of child abuse, not just sexual, and in at least one case the National Committee for Prevention of Child Abuse has gone on record as preferring confusion to anything that would interfere with child saver ideology. The group opposes any effort to distinguish between physical abuse and corporal punishment. According to NCPCA, anything that sounds like it condones corporal punishment "doesn't belong in a child abuse prevention presentation."[64] Recently NCPCA has gone further. In another *Spider-Man* comic, the group urges children to report their parents to another adult whenever they are hit in any way, even if they are spanked. If the first adult doesn't intervene, they are told to keep reporting the parents to another and another.[65]

Further confusion—and fear—results when prevention programs shy away from explicit descriptions of what it is they are supposed to prevent. Many such programs refer to "bad touching" as touching areas that a bathing suit covers. In addition to being potentially confusing, this sends the message that, as one author writes, "You can talk to me about sexual abuse, it's not your fault, there's nothing wrong with you. But your body is so bad that I can't even say what is underneath your swimming suit."[66]

Given the traditional American skittishness about sex education in the schools, warnings about not being touched may be the only sex education some children get. Even David Finkelhor, a leading sex-abuse researcher from the child saver camp and a strong proponent of school-based "prevention" programs, has wondered what will happen to these children as they grow older and have to deal with their own sexuality. He writes, "How many of the children exposed to these programs get the idea that sexual touching is always or almost always bad or dangerous, or exploitative?"[67]

Sherryll Kerns Kraizer writes that "there is a growing possibility that [these programs] may not be in the best interests of children, that children may be more fearful, mistrustful, and insecure after these prevention programs are presented than before. There is a possibility that we are, in the name of prevention, taking away our children's right to feel safe and grow up viewing the world as a fundamentally nurturing place where people sometimes get hurt."[68]

I do not believe prevention programs should be abolished, but they should not start until elementary school—and a major national effort needs to be made to evaluate them objectively and find those that do the most good with the fewest side effects.

Even as our children are learning all about "bad touches," they are getting fewer "good touches."

The panic created by the child savers has led some people who care for children to withdraw some of the normal affection they used to show them. All over the country, teachers talk about how they tell children to "give yourself a pat on the back," instead of giving the child a hug. In Waukeegan, Illinois, after a teacher was charged with sexual abuse and two parents brought lawsuits, the school superintendent wrote a letter to all teachers advising them not to touch their students. The Chicago Teachers' Union issued a set of "self-defense" guidelines for its teachers. Number one was, "Use discretion when touching children for purposes of praise, reward, or comfort." Teachers also were advised to hold all conferences with students in public areas with an adult witness, and never to transport students in their cars. At day-care centers, directors "are starting to shy away from people who do a lot of touching," says one center director in Chicago. "We're losing out on people who have that natural warmth. Kids need to be touched, but we're cutting down on it out of our fear and trepidation."[69]

"It's had a tremendous chilling effect," says Louise Stoney, policy and program director of the New York State Child Care Co-ordinating Council. "There's a very big fallout and a big concern among staff in centers who are nervous about even taking children to the bathroom."[70] The scare also is driving away the relatively few men who might be willing to work in day-care centers, and, Stoney says, some centers hesitate to hire men at all. That reinforces the stereotype that child care is "women's work."

Even some fathers have become more hesitant to show normal affection, especially divorced fathers taking their children on visits. "It terrifies some fathers, especially weekend fathers," says Diane Schetky, a psychiatrist who has written extensively on sexual abuse. "They're afraid to have their child sit in their laps."[71]

During the early 1980s, at the height of the "missing children" scare, while children absorbed these messages, some also were being taken down to the shopping mall to be fingerprinted and ate their breakfast cereal with a picture of a missing child staring back at them from a milk carton.

What is this all going to add up to as these children grow older? Possibly the worst consequence of all—making children *more* vulnerable to sexual abuse instead of less.

James Garbarino, another researcher very much in the child saver camp, nevertheless warns that "the more you define making physical contact with kids as being extraordinary or something that makes one suspicious, the more you leave the field open to people who want to touch kids for the wrong reasons."[72]

One other consequence of the child saver's efforts should be noted. They gave insurance companies an excuse to jack up premiums for day-care centers, making day care that much harder to get, especially for poor people—which means more latchkey children and more allegations of "lack of supervision."

*   *   *

Much of the publicity about false allegations of sexual abuse surrounds divorce and custody cases. Attorney Thomas Albro describes such allegations as "the nuclear weapon[s] of marital custody battles." Diane Schetky says "the way to get courts to notice is to yell sexual abuse. And it works. Courts cut off visitation rights."[73]

No one knows how often these cases actually arise. An American Bar Association survey, based on a survey of courts, concluded that the problem was "small" but "growing."[74] (And the survey was part of a document that included only articles favorable to the child saving point of view.)

But a great deal can happen before a case ever reaches court. Attorney Steven Merrill of Fairfax County, Virginia, says he has seen "plenty of cases in which just the threat [to allege sexual abuse] has been used to gain leverage in custody."[75]

"Parents have discovered that they can assist their chances of obtaining custody of their children if they lodge a complaint of child abuse against the spouse," says Loren Suter, deputy director of the California Department of Social Services Division of Adult and Family Services. "The counties . . . are having to spend much more of their time in those kinds of issues."[76]

Even at Cardinal Glennon Children's Hospital in St. Louis, where abuse allegations clearly are not greeted with skepticism, there is now concern about time wasted on false reports arising from custody cases. Writing to a legislative committee, Wayne Munkel, a "medical social consultant" for the hospital, estimated that 10 to 15 percent of all the evaluations done there were brought on by such disputes. "It is clear that parents and lawyers have determined that the only way to deny permanent visiting privileges of another spouse is to allege child abuse or sexual abuse. . . . Those who are expressing their hostility and anger towards their ex-spouses have now found a way to do just that. . . . Many times I feel lawyers . . . are fishing for evidence to use in the divorce case." Munkel said the staff's "greatest fear" was that a real case of abuse would be missed because so much time was spent on false reports.[77]

Of course, just because an allegation is brought during a custody dispute doesn't mean it's false. Different studies have put the percentage of false reports in such situations at 20 percent, 36 percent, 55 percent, and 77 percent.[78] The key variable may well be the bias of the researchers going in—which is one more reason to avoid reliance on "expert" psychiatric testimony in court.

Like everything else the child savers have done, the hysteria they have created over sexual abuse has had its worst effects on children who really are abused.

Botched investigations in cases like McMartin and Jordan, Minnesota may have let the guilty go free. When hoaxes are exposed, they cast suspicion on all children who say they have been abused and make it easier for the public to retreat back to denial of a very real problem.

Recently there have been charges that the problem of false allegations in custody cases is beginning to produce a backlash. Instead of automatically believing the charge, some judges are said to be automatically disbelieving. If so, the blame rests squarely with the child savers who started the hysteria. They have managed to find one more way to destroy children in order to save them.

As the report of the Minnesota Attorney General on the Jordan case concludes: "The best way to protect children is to conduct investigations in a responsible manner."[79]

7

Foster Care I

When one observes, first hand, the physical violence, criminality, dilapidation and miserable poverty with which many potentially neglectful urban families are bombarded all the time, the notion that a well-meaning young caseworker might add a significant threat is ludicrous.

—Norman Polansky, et al.,
Damaged Parents, p. 14

Christmas Eve 1985: The ground floor of the home of Ralph and Naomi Peterson was filled with Christmas cheer. Friends and relatives were there for some traditional holiday merrymaking.

While the adults partied downstairs, they couldn't hear the terrified sobs of Angela Bennett, the foster child they were supposed to be taking care of.

Three boys, two of them sons of the Petersons' friends, the third, another foster child—were taking turns raping Angela. She was nine years old.[1]

A "well-meaning young caseworker" had Angela taken away from parents whom a therapist would later describe as "excellent." The worker stood up for Angela's "children's rights." She made a "child-focused" decision and got a court to "err on the side of the child" by placing Angela in foster care with the Petersons.

Angela didn't tell her foster parents about the rape on Christmas Eve or about the six other times the Petersons' other foster child, Gerald, had raped her. Gerald threatened to beat her up if she told. The Petersons had done nothing before when Angela told them how Gerald had beaten her and pushed her down the stairs. And when Angela's parents, upset by the bruises they saw, told the caseworker she wouldn't listen. So Angela said nothing.

The rapes were not discovered until nearly two years later during a medical examination. By then, Angela had been home, then placed again, first in a foster home, then in a psychiatric hospital.

But discovery of what Angela had been through did not lead to her getting help. It only led to more trauma at the hands of her protectors.

The child savers were unwilling to accept the idea that Angela had been raped while under their "protection." Angela's mother tape-recorded a telephone call from her daughter in which Angela described being pressured to say she had been abused by her father and brother. "They were taking away my toys and stuff," Angela said. "They keep on pressuring me and they say that you sexually abused me." Angela said the hospital staff told her her parents didn't really want her back. And they told her she'd never return home unless she accused her father and brother.

When Angela refused, the child savers changed their tack. They began telling Angela over and over again that she was responsible for her own rape. In another tape-recorded telephone conversation, Angela told her mother how Louise, her caseworker, "said I had been raped because I wanted it to happen. . . . Louise said I was seductive and inappropriate. . . . [She said I was walking] in a sexual way. In a provocative way. I thought I was just walking the right way."

After two weeks of pressure, including the loss of privileges in the hospital's behavior-modification program, Angela gave in to Louise's demands to write a letter to her parents: "Dear parents," the letter said, "I didn't really get raped and it was half of my fault and I'm sorry for lying."

Then, accompanied by Louise, Angela was allowed to visit her parents and repeat her story. Afterwards, Angela said, the caseworker was jubilant. "She had a smile ear to ear. . . . She went up to my room and said, 'Whenever your mom says you were raped, correct her because you weren't really raped.' " Later Angela called her parents from the hospital and explained why she had written the letter. She never wanted to be raped. "I hated it," she said. "[I felt] dirty."

Angela wrote a short essay about foster care for a school assignment. She wrote: "The foster home is very scarey [sic] and it is dirty trash and a sewer. . . . It is a very dark and lonely place to stay."

*   *   *

Joanne Huot knew something was wrong.[2]

She didn't buy the explanation for the huge bruise she found along the spine of her two-year-old son, Joseph, when she visited him in a Philadelphia foster home on Thanksgiving Day 1987. She didn't believe the child "fell."

She didn't believe it three weeks later when Joseph was hospitalized with a "seizure."

She pleaded with the child savers to let her have her son back, but no one would listen. After all, this was a "neglectful" parent, an "unfit" mother talking.

In October 1987, Joseph had been taken from his parents because they had been fighting. No one ever accused either parent of maltreating Joseph.

No one offered the Huots help with their marital problems. Instead, they defended Joey's "children's rights." They made a "child-focused" decision. They "erred on the side of the child" and placed him in foster care.

On January 26, 1988, Joseph Huot was rushed to Philadelphia's Nazareth Hospital in a coma. There were bruises on his back and massive swelling of his brain. At 2:00 P.M. the next day, Joseph Huot died.

Two months later the foster parents, Walter "Sonny" Hairston and his wife Maryanne were arrested and charged with Joseph's death. It was only after the child died that the agency responsible for his care learned that it had "erred on the side of the child" by placing him with a man who, six years before, had spent five years in jail for rape, aggravated assault, and burglary.

"I trusted you!" Joey's grandmother shouted at the Hairstons when the jury's verdict—guilty of involuntary manslaughter—was announced. "Joey's lying in his grave," she said later. "I don't have a grandson, Susie doesn't have a brother, my daughter doesn't have a son."

*   *   *

Sara Eyerman was born three months premature. She weighed only two pounds. She survived and became a happy, playful infant. But she hadn't made up all the ground she had lost at birth. She was smaller than the other kids, and she was fragile.

When Sara was eighteen months old, a call from a worried neighbor brought in Child Protective Services. They were suspicious of Sara's small size, and they didn't like it when Sara's mother phoned the family doctor on one occasion instead of taking her in to his office the way the caseworker told her to. (The doctor had no problem with this.)

So a well-meaning young social worker took Sara away and placed her in a "specialized" foster home where supposedly she would get extra care to see if she would develop better.

About six weeks later, Sara began running a high fever. But instead of acting immediately, the child savers set up a doctor's appointment for two days later. On the way to the doctor's office, Sara stopped breathing. A nurse from the "specialized" foster home rushed her to a hospital, and ran inside yelling "pulmonary arrest!" But it was two late. At the age of twenty months, Sara Eyerman was dead. The cause of death was viral pneumonia.

"She should have been in the hospital two days earlier when she had a 104.8 temperature," says Sara's mother, Angie. "When she was home, she went to the emergency room if her temperature got over 101. I didn't care if they laughed at me when I got there or not. One time I took her when she was cutting a tooth. . . .

"I kept her alive for a year and seven months. They had her for six weeks and three days and she died."[3]

*   *   *

"Children don't go to heaven when they are removed from their parents," says J. Lawrence Aber, of Columbia University. "They go to the foster-care system."[4]

You would hardly know there was a difference between heaven and foster care by reading the newspapers or watching television news.

News accounts that chronicle the horrible abuse of a child often begin like this one: "In her previous life, the little girl suffered abuse so horrendous that it was the stuff of tabloid headlines for days. But in Nanna's loving arms, the past seems so far away."[5] (Nanna is, of course, the foster parent.) To the extent that foster care is portrayed at all, it is portrayed as the happy ending.

A lot of people who work in the system, and the foster children themselves, know better. They know that for thousands of abused and neglected children—and many who were wrongly believed to be abused or neglected—foster care is not the happy ending, it is the tragic beginning. It is not where the nightmare ends. It is where it starts.

To understand why the child savers do so much harm, foster care must be brought front and center.

Foster-care systems are so badly run that nobody even knows exactly how many children are trapped in them or how much they cost. All we know is that taxpayers spend billions of dollars to destroy the lives of hundreds of thousands of children. Foster care does not work in practice, and cannot work even in theory.

—Even under the best of circumstances, removing children from their families and tossing them from stranger to stranger is inherently harmful.

—Circumstances are rarely the best. Many children spend their days jammed into overcrowded, violence-plagued offices, and their nights being dragged through city streets in search of a bed for a few hours of sleep.

—Any notion that foster care is a temporary safe-haven until a child can be returned home or adopted is a myth. The most recent national data are from 1985, when the system worked much better than it does today. Even then, 39 percent of foster children spent two years or more in care—easily enough time to destroy family ties.[6]

—Foster care is not a haven. Often it is not even safe. Most people assume that removing children from their parents means removing them from danger and placing them in safety. Often, it is the other way around.

Foster care can never be "good" for a child. There are times, however, when it can be *less bad* than any other alternative. There are children who really need foster care. But it is unlikely that more than one-quarter to one-half of the children now in foster care really need to be there.

Foster care "scars those it ensnares . . . fragments families and sabotages their eventual reconstruction," writes Ruth Hubbell in her study, *Foster Care and Families.*[7] Says Susan Carter, Executive Director of the National Association of Foster Care Reviewers, "The foster care system is morally and politically bankrupt."[8] Even a report written by staff at the San Francisco Department of Social Services asks: "Is the injustice we pull children from worse than the injustice we place them in?"[9]

Richard Krugman, M.D., Director of the Kempe Center in Denver, is fond of defending the child saving status quo by telling people that "no child ever died of a social work evaluation." He's said it to *U.S. News and World Report,* and he's said it to the *Washington Post.*[10] I assume, however, that he has never said it to Angie Eyerman. Although the death certificate for her daughter Sara says "viral pneumonia," the real cause of death was a social-work evaluation. Joey Huot also died of a social-work evaluation. And so have many others.

Those who see making it easy to put a child into foster care as "erring on the side of the child," those who say they are defending "children's rights," those who want to make coercive intervention easy because they say they are "child focused," must be held to account for the consequences of laws that make foster-care placement so easy—consequences like the rape of Angela Bennett and the deaths of Sara Eyerman and Joseph Huot.

—They must be held to account for the case of Henry Gallop and Aaron Johnson of Boston.

After social-work evaluations, the mothers of the two children, who are not related to each other, were conned into voluntarily placing the children in foster care. The child savers allowed an agency whose license had lapsed to place the children in a home which had been a source of repeated problems for several years—but which was spotlessly clean. According to a report by a committee of the Massachusetts Legislature, "Both mothers said they thought they would have continuous communication [with the state's Department of Social Services], the foster parents and with their children during the placement period. Each mother thought they would be allowed to visit with their children." In fact, "The parents stated that they had not seen their children at any time during the placement period, did not know where the children had been placed, [and] did not have any contact with DSS or the foster parents. . . ."

As a result, they were never told, for example, that over a five-month period, Henry Gallop had been hospitalized fifteen times "for problems that included seizures, pneumonia, difficulties with breathing, ear infections, cuts, vomiting, and burns that were said to be caused by radiator steam."

Henry was the first to die. Even then, a DSS supervisor decided not to tell Aaron's mother about Henry's death because she would be "needlessly worried." Three months later, Aaron was also dead. An inquest determined the children had been poisoned but could not determine if it had been done deliberately. An emotionally disturbed adoptive daughter of the foster parents was charged with killing Gallop after a friend of the girl told the *Boston Globe* that the girl said she had killed him.[11]

—They must be held to account for the case of Gladys Campbell, age two, of Philadelphia. After a social-work evaluation, someone "erred on the side of the child" and placed Gladys in a foster home sixty miles away in New Jersey.

When police were called to the foster home, they found a hole in the wall in Gladys's room. The hole was so deep that they could see the lathing behind it, and they observed that some of the slats were broken. The damage to the wall was caused by the force with which Gladys Campbell's foster mother threw her against it, crushing her skull.

During her months in foster care, relatives tried repeatedly to find out where Gladys was so they could visit, but the child savers refused to tell them. Gladys's grandmother finally found out when a worker called her to tell her Gladys was being rushed to a hospital. "He said, 'She has a fractured skull,'" the grandmother recalled. "And that's when I screamed. . . ." Gladys died the next day. The foster mother pled guilty to aggravated manslaughter.

"I blame myself for letting them take the child. We were too trusting," the grandmother said. "It haunts me today knowing [that if she hadn't been placed in foster care] she would have lived."[12]

—They must be held to account for the case of Eugene D. of Louisville, Kentucky. After a social-work evaluation, someone "erred on the side of the child" and had Eugene removed from his mother when he was nine months old.

At the time, Eugene weighed seventeen pounds. Eight years later, he still weighed seventeen pounds. During his entire time in foster care, his weight never topped nineteen pounds. His bones were sticking out and skin was flaking off.

Eugene, who suffers from cerebral palsy, and two other disabled children were placed with a fifty-five-year-old woman who had no training in caring for special-needs children and depended on foster-care payments for her livelihood.

Child-protective workers had received at least nine warnings about Eugene from doctors, nurses, and school personnel. They were told about how Eugene repeatedly missed doctor's appointments, they were told about the time he came to school with roaches in his clothes, they were told about the broken leg he sustained at age two that went untreated for ten days—and that doctors believed was not caused by accident. Yet he was not removed from his foster home. In fact, Kentucky's child savers were planning to make his placement in the foster home permanent.

Eugene's mother finally was able to get him back, and she now is suing state child-welfare officials. In response to her suit, the state's child savers maintain that Eugene received "loving, competent care."[13]

—They must be held to account for the case of four-month-old Corey Greer of Treasure Island, Florida.

After a social-work evaluation, somebody "erred on the side of the child" and placed Corey in a foster home that would later be described by police as "filthy and overcrowded." The home was licensed for four children. By the time Corey Greer died in his crib of dehydration, twelve were living there. The foster mother was convicted of manslaughter and third-degree murder.

Corey Greer might have survived the overcrowding, if only he had been white.

According to a witness at the foster mother's trial, the foster mother told her that touching black children "just gives me the willies." According to the witness, the foster mother referred to Corey Greer as "a big black blob."[14]

—They must be held to account for the case of Juan and Julie D. of New York City, twins who were born with AIDS.

The twins' grandmother was caring for them when they were diagnosed. She wanted to keep on caring for them, but the problems became overwhelming, she couldn't handle it all alone, and the city would offer no help even though she was entitled to such help under New York State law. Instead, after a social-work evaluation, someone decided to "err on the side of the child" and place the children in foster care. No foster home could be found, so the D children were placed in an institution for disturbed teenagers.

Though they were only eighteen-months-old, Juan and Julie had no cribs, only beds to sleep on, and they ate on the floor. They were also abused.

When Julie's grandmother found her with a face full of black and blue marks, they were moved to another home. At that home, Juan wound up badly bruised, and Julie had what appeared to be cigarette burns on her body.[15] The foster parents neglected Juan's medical needs, leaving him in severe pain and possibly hastening his death in 1985. Julie died two years later.

While the grandmother cared for Juan and Julie, she got $300 a month in welfare payments. The foster parents who abused them got $1,500 per month.[16]

In some of these cases, the children really did need to be placed in foster care. Even the lawyer for Henry Gallop's mother says she was not able to take care of Henry at the time he was placed.[17] But nothing any of these parents may have done to their children—and most had done nothing to them at all—compares with what the child savers did to them when they "erred on the side of the child."

That's because the children were placed in a system so overloaded with children who don't need to be there that there is no room to give children who really have been abused the care that they needed. It is another example of the iron law of child saving: Those who need help the most suffer the most.

Most foster parents do not murder the children in their care. Most are dedicated and caring individuals who open their homes and their hearts to troubled children whom others turn their backs on. And just as it is unfair to draw conclusions about natural parents based on horror stories, so, too, is it unfair to draw such conclusions about foster care.

But that's about as far as the analogy goes. That's because there is evidence that abuse in foster homes, while not the norm, has become sufficiently widespread to be of serious concern. And because though a good family—be it biological parents or adoptive parents—is vital for a child, foster care by its very nature is harmful, no matter how good the foster family is.

The cases described above are not typical of foster care. But this case, summarized from a longer account in *Foster Care and Families*, is:

Mrs. Carey was severely injured in an automobile accident. With no close friends or relatives to help her, she agreed to a child saver's suggestion that she "voluntarily" place her three children in foster care.

The children were separated not only from their mother, but from each other. Two were in separate foster homes, the third in an institution. The oldest child, a fourteen-year-old boy, ran away from his first foster home and back to his mother's trailer. He was taken to a second foster home.

All the children were placed so far from Mrs. Carey that she could see them only once a month when the agency had time to arrange visits. She was not allowed to arrange any on her own. She was not trusted with the foster homes' addresses. All mail had to be funneled through the agency.

The social worker handling the case considered natural parents "creeps for having put their children in foster homes." She added: "I have to get over that."

Two years later, Mrs. Carey was fully recovered from her accident. But the child savers wouldn't let her have back the children she had voluntarily placed. "They tell her she must first find better employment and better housing. Maybe then she will have her own children back in her own house—she does not know."[18]

"I consider every child who is removed from his natural parent to be emotionally disturbed just because of that separation, not counting the series of crises that may have led to the necessity of it," says Jeanne Collins, supervisor of the Substitute Care Unit of the Outagamie County [Wisconsin] Department of Social Services.[19]

"How would you feel if I came in and said: 'I'm from a certain agency and we're pulling your wife out?' " asks child psychiatrist Foster Cline. "Sometimes we pull things on kids we wouldn't pull on adults."

Every parent who has ever left an infant with a baby-sitter, even for an hour or two, knows that the child sometimes becomes terribly frightened. He has no way of knowing that the people who are leaving him, his only source of comfort and nurture, will soon come back. But what happens when they *don't* come back? When an infant is moved, Cline says, it can "decay the very foundation of personality. . . . At that time a child is learning how to love and learning basic trust. If he's moved in the first eighteen months, the research says he will face severe emotional trauma as far as forming loving bonds later."[20]

Similarly, when child psychiatrist James Robertson studied very young children separated from their mothers, he found that:

> In this initial phase, which may last from a few hours to several days, the young child has a strong conscious need of his mother and the expectation, based on previous experience that she will respond to his cries.
>
> He is grief-stricken to have lost her, is confused and frightened by unfamiliar surroundings and seeks to recapture her by the full exercise of his limited resources.
>
> He has no understanding of his situation and is distraught with fright and urgent desire to find his mother. He will often cry loudly, shake the crib, throw himself about, and look eagerly toward any sight or sound that might prove to be his mother. . . .

> In the second stage, despair gradually succeeds protest. This is char-
> acterized by a continuous conscious need of his mother coupled with an
> increasing hopelessness . . . He is withdrawn and apathetic, makes no
> demands on the environment and is in a state of deep mourning for his
> mother—grief of the greatest intensity.
>
> This is the quiet stage which is sometimes erroneously presumed to
> mean that distress has lessened, that he is "settling in." . . .
>
> In [the denial] phase, which gradually succeeds despair, he shows more
> interest in his surroundings, and this may be welcomed as a sign that he
> is becoming "happy." It is, however, a danger signal. Because the child cannot
> tolerate the intensity of distress, he begins to make the best of his situation
> by repressing his feelings for his mother, who has failed to meet his needs,
> particularly his need for her as a person to love and be loved by. . . .
>
> Finally, if his stay is lengthy . . . he will in time seem not only not
> to need his mother, but not to need any mothering at all. . . .[21]

When children are a little older, they face an added burden. They are not old enough to understand what's going on, but they are old enough to assume that what is happening must be their fault—that somehow they did something so terrible it caused the breakup of their family.[22]

The child savers do nothing to ease the trauma of removal. "The way they take children is appalling," says Diane Redleaf of the Legal Assistance Foundation of Chicago. "The way to minimize the trauma would be to prepare the child, let them see where they are going . . . try to explain what was going on in a way that made sense to the child. They don't do any of that."[23]

And sometimes they do a lot worse. Albert was ten when he talked about the way he was taken from his mother four years before:

After child-protective workers questioned him and his mother, "They came back. With cops. Then they barged in the door and grabbed my mom and threw her against the wall and put the handcuffs on her." Albert remembers swearing at one of the police officers because they wouldn't let him kiss his mother goodbye.[24]

Often the first foster home is not the last. The trauma is compounded by multiple placement. Nationwide, in 1985, more than 26 percent of all foster children were placed in three homes or more.[25] Although it's the most recent data available, this figure comes from a time when conditions in foster care were far better than they are today. More recent state data paint an even grimmer picture. In Maryland, for example, in the year ended September 30, 1988, 57 percent of the children in care had been in three or more placements, and 35 percent had been in four or more.[26]

Goldstein, Freud, and Solnit write, "Where children are forced to wander from one environment to another . . . resentment toward the adults who have disappointed them in the past makes them adopt the attitude of not caring for anybody. . . . Multiple placement . . . puts many children beyond the reach of educational influence and becomes the direct cause of behavior that the schools experience as disrupting and the courts label as dissocial, delinquent, or even criminal."[27]

"Three agency replacements and you have an agency-made sociopath," says Charles Gershensohn, Senior Evaluation Analyst at the Center for the Study of Social Policy in Washington. "This child will never trust an adult again."[28]

Children need a "consistent nurturing figure," says Pat Glass, a Seattle therapist who specializes in counseling foster and adopted children. "Everything the child is learning about how the world works is reflected through the eyes of that figure. That's where we get our conscience. That's where we get our view of ourselves. And later, when we see children in the system and say, 'This kid has no self-esteem, he hates himself' . . . we're looking back at a child who got the message that they weren't valued."[29]

Kenneth Herrmann, professor of Social Work at the State University of New York at Brockport and a former county Child Protective Services director, recalls a former foster child who told him: " 'I felt like a bag that kept being left on different people's doorsteps. . . . I wrote a poem about being a box that kept getting mailed to the wrong address.' "[30]

Patrick Murphy, former head of the Juvenile Office of the Legal Aid Society of Chicago, says multiple placement turns children into "emotional pulp. I can't tell you the hundreds of children who turn into male and female prostitutes at fifteen and sixteen, not just because it's a way to make a buck, but because they feel it's all they're good for—not because of what happened to them in the home, but because of what happened to them in the system."[31]

Or as a former foster child put it: "I felt I was in a zoo and I was being transferred to another cage."[32]

Yet, incredibly, sometimes child savers move a child in retaliation against foster parents who speak up too strongly on behalf of the children in their care when the interests of the children conflict with the interests of the agency.[33]

Foster care doesn't only harm children taken from "good" families. On the contrary, in some cases the disruption of foster care can be even more harmful to a child who really was abused in his or her own home. As the authors of a report on foster-care institutions in New York City put it: "The attachment of the child to the parent is not something that the parent earns, but rather something that the child needs."[34]

That doesn't mean that no child should ever be removed from his or her home or that every child who has been removed should be returned. It means that when the children really have been abused, they have an even greater need for a placement that is stable and secure. And they can't get that from a foster-care system overloaded with children who don't need to be there.

Children who have no real home often wind up no better off as adults. In the Minneapolis area, between 14 and 26 percent of homeless adults are former foster children.[35] Between 25 and 50 percent of the young men in New York City's shelters for the homeless are former foster children.[36]

It isn't just the experts who issue warnings about foster care. There are plenty of present and former foster children who keep trying to tell us themselves.

Except for the fact that she doesn't smile very often, except for an expression that seems to say, "keep your distance," Anne Williamson is very pretty. She's blonde and blue eyed—the sort who people would have been lining up to adopt as a baby. The scars are on the inside.

When I first interviewed her in 1976, she was a twenty-one-year-old student at the State University of New York at Albany. She had come to Albany to be near the state legislature, so she could lobby to change the foster-care system. That's why she told her story willingly, despite how hard it must have been.

She chain-smoked throughout a two-hour interview. She always maintained her composure and never raised her voice. Her anger was expressed in words that suggested ice more than fire. The ability to keep in control is very important to Anne Williamson. She says it's what allowed her to survive foster care. By the time she was nine years old, Anne Williamson had lived in nine different foster homes:

> You're left hanging. And you wonder: Is my mother going to come and get me? Am I going to be [left] here? What's going to happen to me? Who am I? Who's kid am I? Is this my mother? Is that my mother? They're not my parents. But she's not either because she never comes.
>
> When you spend your life going from place to place and knowing you're not going to be in any place for very long, you learn not to reach out, not to care, not to feel. I knew that if I reached out to my foster parents or to the other kids or to schoolteachers or to friends in school, very shortly I would have to leave and never see them again—never even get a chance to say goodbye. . . . If you don't get involved you can't get hurt. And that was my revenge on the world.
>
> I still don't want other people to see what I'm feeling if I'm upset. I don't cry very often, but when I do I will not do it in front of other people. I am still very insecure in my friendships. I am never quite able to accept that this or that person likes me for what I am. Because I'm too scared. Maybe it's going to go wrong [like] the things that happened before.
>
> My bitterness is not that I went through what I did . . . my bitterness

is that I don't think it should have had to happen. There was no reason why my family's life should have been destroyed. I can look at a caseworker, and the one thing I want to say to them is: you personally are responsible for the destruction of many lives. . . . It happens to be traumatic to be taken from your home and be put somewhere else, and it's even more traumatic when you compound it with doing it millions of times.

Two things helped Anne make it through the system: A tenth set of foster parents who finally gave her a permanent home and that ability to keep her rage bottled up inside her. Her five brothers had neither. "They didn't stop. They kept going with the multiple placement." By now, Anne says, "between them, they've been in every prison in New York State.

"Short of a miracle, they'll all remain dope addicts, or nonproductive people. I shouldn't even use the term people. They're not people. . . . They've had every emotion ripped out of them so they're not people as far as I can see."

Anne said she wanted to go on to law school and become "a child-advocate lawyer" like Marcia Lowry who then, as now, headed the Children's Rights Project at the American Civil Liberties Union, "and work with kids in the family court who are getting a bad deal." And, in spite of everything, she "still had hope" for her youngest brother, who was seventeen.

I got back in touch with Anne Williamson about three years later. Things had changed. With one semester to go, she had run out of money for college and had to drop out. She was trying to start a small business with a friend. She said it had been important to her to talk about foster care when she did, but she didn't want to talk about it anymore (which is why, though I have used her real name in the past, I have not done so here). And her youngest brother was back in jail, charged with rape.

Says Anne Williamson: "The people that I've seen, the kids that have emerged, [from foster care] are . . . dead. Their hearts are functioning. The ol' heart's pumping the blood around. But they're basically dead inside. It's been killed. Either they had to kill it to survive physically, or somebody else killed it in them. Whatever it is that makes people human."

Others tell similar stories.

Boyd A. was in five different foster homes over five years between the ages of seven and twelve. He had been placed "voluntarily" by his mother when she was hospitalized after being beaten by Boyd's father. But when she was well, the child savers wouldn't give Boyd, his two brothers, or his sister back because they weren't satisfied with the housing his mother was able to find. At one point, they actually returned the children to their abusive father because he had an apartment and their mother didn't.

It took a lawsuit brought by the ACLU's Marcia Lowry to reunite

Boyd and his mother. At the age of twelve, Boyd told a congressional committee about his experiences at the hands of the child savers:

> They took almost five years away from my life. That's almost one-half of my whole life that I spent just waiting to come back to my real family.
>
> It was terrible to be put in lots of different homes with lots of strangers, knowing they wouldn't let me be with my mother. I wanted to be with my mother and my brothers and sister.
>
> I had a lot of social workers. I had so many I can't remember them all. They all said they wanted to help me, but I think that was a lie. They never paid attention to me, or what I wanted or needed.
>
> One time I ran away from a foster home and back to my mom, but the social workers wouldn't let me stay. That made me feel very bad. The only help I wanted from the social workers was to go back to my mom, but they didn't help us with that.
>
> I was in so many foster homes I can't remember them all. I do remember one home they put me in because the foster parents only spoke Spanish. I don't speak Spanish.
>
> I am supposed to be in seventh grade, but I am in fifth. Every year that I was in school, I would change to another school. . . . [Other kids] would tease me about being a foster kid. They say, "Ha, ha, I have a mother." I used to feel like if they got a mother, then they're all more special than me.
>
> The worst fear was never seeing my mother again. The foster care people are trying to tell my mother that she's not—that she's not good enough right now? She's good enough for me anytime.
>
> I have nightmares. I had a nightmare that a cop came and took me back to foster care and I never got to see her again.
>
> It's hard for me to tell you how bad foster care is. My mother used to come visit me a lot when I was in care, and when she left, it felt like the whc.. world was leaving me.[37]

"If you want to see a waste of human resources, you just look at this family," Lowry told the committee. "These are bright children who could really be very productive citizens in this country and we have spent a lot of money to do everything we can to keep them from growing up healthy and productive."[38]

Them and many, many others.

David Wagner. Age eighteen. Six placements in ten years: "They say I'm emotionally disturbed and I guess, based on how I feel, that's true. If you had grown up in the foster care system like I have, you'd be disturbed too."

Maria. Age sixteen. Multiple placements over four years: "They told me, 'leave your home, live in the system, you'll have better opportunities.' I haven't had any of that. I expected a home. One steady home. Someplace at least that I could call home. I didn't care so much if the parents didn't accept me as their child, but at least there'd be someone to care for us."

Linda P. Age twenty. Six placements in two years: "When you are a kid and you go through something like that, you don't know what's happening, but you have feelings. And the feeling you have is no one wants you."

Jamal. Age sixteen. Number of placements unknown: "I'm a sixteen-year-old kid. Who's going to adopt me? So I've turned hard. I'm a rock now. I'm not letting them get to me. You can call that disturbed if you want, but that's the way it is."

Joseph. Age eighteen. Fifty placements between ages nine and seventeen. Multiple suicide attempts. Became a prostitute: "No one listened. They don't care. As long as you're out of their hair and they don't have to write any more paperwork on you they're satisfied. I had no love, no caring, no anything. When people paid me to be with them I thought that was the affection I needed."

Kathy. Age eighteen. Grew up in foster care: "When you're in foster care, you can't find no love."[39]

And things are getting worse. Now, not only must children try to cope with multiple placements, they must endure having no home at all, or one so crowded and dangerous that conditions are unbearable.

After several years of steady decline during the first half of the 1980s, the number of children in foster care at any one time suddenly soared upward again, overwhelming the system. Now children are routinely crowded into foster homes beyond their licensed capacity.

The crowding that contributed to the death of Corey Greer is not unusual, as children are squeezed in wherever a bed can be found. In Florida, according to a 1989 report by the state's Auditor General, 10 percent of all foster homes were overcrowded. Not surprisingly, the report found that "placements made under these conditions are generally unsuccessful. . . ."[40] At least a quarter of the foster homes maintained by the District of Columbia are overcrowded.[41] In Boston, a foster parent says she has had six infants placed with her at one time, some of them in poor health. Another says the Department of Social Services routinely lies about the severity of the children's problems. "DSS will tell you anything to get you to take the kids," she says.[42]

And many children can't get into a foster home at all.

Hundreds of New York City children spend their days jammed into overcrowded rooms in city offices—there is simply no place else to put them. At night, workers frantically attempt to find a place for the children to stay. They move from home to home or from institution to institution night after night, often carrying their belongings in plastic garbage bags.

"Those who are forced to endure the night-to-night program often spend their mornings at one foster care agency, their days at one of the field offices, and their evenings at a different foster care facility or at [a central office]," wrote U.S. District Court Judge Mary Johnson Lowe, upholding a lawsuit against the system. "If an overnight assignment is identified by a caseworker after their arrival at [the central office] the child would then be 'transported' to yet another facility. The children in the night-to-night program do not have something as basic as a place to hang their clothes or put a toothbrush."[43]

Children are shuttled all over the city, sometimes traveling for an hour and a half at a time from placement to placement. When they get there, they sometimes are turned away at the door.

In one two-month period, one thousand children were placed at least five separate times. In many cases, they endured nine placements. At least one child was placed sixty-five times. Judge Lowe cited some examples:

> From May 7 to July 9, 1986, Richard S. was sent on overnights 15 times. From May 7 until June 30, Johnny H. was assigned 25 times. From May 13 to June 23, Sharmaka B. received 20 overnights, from May 15 to July 10, Kasonga K. was assigned 16 times. Faith C. was sent on overnights 17 times between May 27 and July 8. Carmen G. experienced 14 overnights between May 7 and July 3. Charles D. was on overnights 11 times between May 7 and May 29. Between May 14 and July 7, John A. was assigned 17 times. Adriane G. was assigned to overnights 11 times from May 16 through July 7. Nigel R. was sent on overnights 12 times between May 27 and June 16. Between May 29 and June 30, Louis D. experienced 18 overnights. The list goes on.[44]

Even a child-protective worker who had removed three small children from a "crack den" only to see them split up and sent on overnights for three weeks said: "The middle child—he was eight years old—started talking about suicide. I felt I was doing more damage than the environment they were in."[45]

The offices where these children are confined generally have one room for infants and toddlers, another for teenagers. Judge Lowe's decision and a subsequent report by the investigator she appointed, Ronald Garnett, paint a picture of children who are growing up malnourished in every sense—physically, mentally, and emotionally.

The rooms called "nurseries" are not worthy of the name. Often they are overcrowded with so little for the children to do that the staff makes them take long naps to fill the time. Sometimes, the nurseries are filled not with toys but with office furniture. At one office, "Children up to twelve years old were kept in a single room with two cribs, two desks, and a chair. . . . When it was overcrowded in the nursery, caseworkers kept children in playpens." At another nursery two children shared a crib.

There is no running water in the nurseries. Children are bathed in water from buckets brought from elsewhere in the buildings, or they are taken to the public rest rooms and bathed in the sinks. The food doesn't have enough meat for growing toddlers. Some of the nurseries have roaches.

At one office, the teenagers were initially held in the basement. "The basement has a concrete floor, no windows, and a fan without any other system of ventilation. . . . The temperature reached ninety-two degrees in the office above them." At another office, forty-seven teenagers were placed in a 22-by-17-foot room. In many cases the rooms had no air conditioning, even on days when the temperature was in the nineties. "However, uniformly, offices of administrators were air conditioned, comfortable, and spacious." Another adolescent room was furnished with three chairs and a small table. Nothing else.

In one office,

> Staff conceded they had no special training or facilities to provide services to a blind child regularly present as an overnighter. On the day of my visit, the child was lying alone in a cubicle, outside the teen room, which staff called "isolation." His belongings were strewn under a chair in a corner.
>
> Often there is little for the children to do except fight. No site has been unscathed by the acts of violence and vandalism which have occurred at all the teen room sites.

At some facilities, the violence is "pervasive." Garnett had to break up one fight himself.

Garnett concluded that there is "a bureaucratic barrier" between the people who set up the system and "the real world of the teen and nursery rooms. [Staff] expressed frustration at how the 'bosses downtown' could allow young children to be warehoused in the field offices and under the conditions observed. One caseworker asked . . . 'If a child is taken from a home, no matter how poor or unsuitable it is, is being brought here any better?' "

The city is "effectively transforming a portion of [its] foster children into homeless children," Judge Lowe ruled. "The overnight system's inherent instability as well as its inevitable lack of any coordinated supervision of basic needs or support has resulted in physical, emotional, and psychological harm to the children exposed to it." The judge agreed with a child-protective worker who testified that any parent who treated his or her children the way the city was treating the children in its care would be promptly charged with neglect and hauled before a court to have the children taken away.[46]

Yet despite the court ruling, by mid-1989, conditions had worsened.

Some children never got a bed for the night at all. They slept on desks at a city office.[47] In 1990, overnighters still were "a substantial problem" according to one of the lawyers who sued over the issue.[48]

Overnighters do not exist only in New York City. In Florida, according to the auditor general's report, "Some children are kept in emergency shelter facilities, hospitals, and other temporary settings until a foster home can be found."[49] Children have had to spend nights sleeping on office floors in Orlando, Daytona Beach, and Miami, where the evidence was videotaped by a television crew. When a supervisor tried to deny it, the reporter bluntly told her viewers, "She is lying."[50]

"We have kids stacked up like cordwood in Broward County," says Midge Sinclair, who chairs a group that investigates complaints against the agency that runs the state's foster-care system.[51]

"Want to learn about child abuse?" says Miami Juvenile Court Judge William Gladstone. "Find out what the State of Florida does with its kids in shelter care."[52]

In Baltimore, according to the Maryland Foster Care Review Board, "children are placed in whichever home has an empty bed, even if it is just for a night or a weekend. Sometimes the child has to be re-placed in another home and another. This constant short-term placement and re-placement is destroying children."[53]

"I spend so much time simply trying to get a child placed somewhere, anywhere," says Diane Weinroth, an attorney in Washington, D.C. "They will be sitting in the child-protective-services office and there won't be a placement for them."[54] If there is still no placement by nightfall, they sleep on the office floor.[55]

In San Francisco, 20 percent of the children housed in the city's "emergency" shelter were there for seventy-six days or more. "That's incredible," said Karen Tefelski, a volunteer with the California Children's Lobby. "The child is there, sometimes in a dormitory-type setting, no services, nobody familiar, maybe getting put in a van and getting dropped off to school one day; getting picked up, hoping that it might go to a foster home the next day or maybe back to its family. . . . That a child has to wait for seventy-six tomorrows is absolutely appalling."[56]

In Philadelphia, the city's child-protective agency can't even keep enough disposable diapers on hand for the babies that spend hours at a time at city offices. As in New York, older children wander the halls dragging their belongings around in trash bags. Said one supervisor: "I've seen more of those trash bags than I care to remember." Sometimes, a child will spend the night on a cot, right outside the office where the "hotline" calls are taken.[57]

Massachusetts workers say they have "overnighters" as well.[58] In Chicago, children sleep in an office appropriately located on Dickens Street,[59] and it was a six-year-old from Louisiana who asked of the foster parent who would care for him for just one night: "Is it all right if I call you Mommy tonight?"[60]

In Los Angeles, of course, children are confined at MacLaren Hall. And in other communities, children are mixed in with accused delinquents in juvenile detention centers. Sometimes, children allegedly abused or neglected actually are kept in jail until someplace else can be found.[61] In Fort Lauderdale, a thirteen-year-old boy sexually assaulted a four-year-old boy while both were being held in the county Juvenile Detention Center. The four-year-old was there because his mother was hospitalized and couldn't care for him. The thirteen-year-old was there because he had been sexually abused and there was no place else to put him.[62]

And finally, when all else fails, child savers put children in cages.[63]

Clifford Masse, a nine-year-old autistic child, was one of them. New York's child-protective agency, the Child Welfare Administration (CWA),[64] took charge of Clifford when his mother became overwhelmed by the demands of caring for him. They shut him away on a hospital ward in Brooklyn. The hospital did not have the staff to give Clifford the attention he needed. So they locked him up for hours at a time in a crib with a hard plastic cover. When he became strong enough to break through the cover, they shot him up with sedatives. "We have videotapes of him coming to school like a zombie," a social worker at Clifford's school said. Clifford's mother visited him daily, watching over him for long periods of time. Finally, she sought help from the President of the New York City Council whose staff ultimately got Clifford placed in a special school in Delaware.

Clifford was one of more than a hundred mentally disabled foster children shut away in New York City hospitals. Another was a six-year-old boy who lived in an almost empty room on a locked psychiatric ward. His caseworker ignored six requests to appear in family court and explain why nothing was being done. She finally showed up when threatened with arrest. It turned out she was almost completely unfamiliar with the case— and the little she thought she knew she had gotten wrong.

Warehousing a foster child in a city hospital costs between $12,000 and $27,000 a month. Had even the lower amount been given to Clifford's mother, it would have been enough to have two home health aides take care of Clifford twenty-four hours a day seven days a week at $8.00 an hour each. But when foster children are kept in hospitals, federal, state, and other city funds pay for it. It doesn't cost the Child Welfare Administration a dime.

Disabled children are not the only ones for whom a hospital substitutes for a home. In big cities all over the country, including Philadelphia, Los Angeles, San Francisco, Chicago, Washington, D.C., Miami, and New York, a new term has been added to the child-welfare lexicon: *boarder babies*. These are infants who must stay in the hospital because the child savers claim they can't be sent home with their mothers, and no place else can be found for them. Like Clifford Masse, some have lived in cages, their only nurturing coming from busy nurses working in shifts. Some learned to walk while tethered to their cribs.

As noted earlier, a study by the office of former New York City Comptroller Harrison J. Goldin found that the single biggest reason such children couldn't go home was because the parents didn't have adequate housing—in fourteen of the ninety-seven cases studied it was the only reason.

The study tracked the ninety-seven boarder babies through the first three years of their lives—the time when they most need the security of a permanent home. Nineteen were moved two or more times after leaving the hospital, and another sixteen were likely to experience that many moves. Three children were abused or neglected by their foster parents. Two of them were twin girls. According to the report, "In three-and-a-half years they have seen four homes, had two extended hospital stays, and been neglected or abused by two or three caretakers. Their chances for ever learning to trust, to love, perhaps even to care about another human being are virtually nil. And they still don't have a home."

In another case, a child with severe neurological problems had to wait ten weeks in the hospital before the Child Welfare Administration would authorize surgery. Then he waited another eight weeks because, although his foster mother was willing to take him back, the private agency handling the case "wanted to institutionalize him for fear of adverse publicity if he died." The child wound up in an institution where his doctor predicted he would "vegetate." In a second report, the comptroller's office found that the foster mother regularly visited the child in the institution and might be willing to take him home if she could get sufficient help. But CWA "remains unaware of her interest and has offered no assistance."

After the comptroller's first report was made public, the CWA responded the way bureaucracies always respond to such documents. They said the report was out of date and they had since made great improvements. But when the comptroller's investigators went back a year later to check, they found plenty of falsified records to make the system look better, but no real improvement.[65]

Of course, the child savers have a solution for all this. Since working with families is anathema to them, they've come up with an answer that's simple, obvious, and wrong. In the words of a retired Philadelphia judge: "bring back the orphanage."[66]

Apparently these people have been watching too many Father Flanagan movies. They have somehow reached the conclusion that the same federal, state, and local governments that gave us the nation's prison system, that gave us the juvenile justice system, and have dotted the landscape with hideous warehouses for the mentally ill and the mentally retarded, miraculously will come up with loving, humane institutions for foster children, many of whom are black and almost all of whom are poor.

Actually, we don't have to guess what a modern child saver orphanage would be like. The orphanage *is* back. And it's not Boys Town.

In Los Angeles, New York City, and elsewhere, bringing back the orphanage was the child savers "solution" to the boarder-baby problem. Infants and toddlers spend months in "congregate care facilities" where the work is done by staff working in shifts, and the workers sometimes don't even know the children's names.

Before New York City's seventeen shelters were closed under intense pressure from the state in late 1989, they housed an average of 135 children daily. The median age of the children was between twelve and fifteen months. One of the "homes" was a storefront.

An early *New York Times* account of a city facility described it this way:

> The children sleep in cribs lined up side by side in the back two bedrooms. They eat meals off styrofoam plates and wear throwaway bibs while shift workers tend to them as best they can, sometimes lining up highchairs and feeding two or three children at a time.
>
> At an age when most children fear strangers, these children cling to virtually anyone who comes near. An adult who sits in a chair is likely to be surrounded in a matter of seconds with toddlers begging to be cuddled.
>
> "Sometimes," said Elaine Peterson, who has worked in the house since it opened in August of 1987, "when there's time, I get on the floor with all of them. They just want to hold onto you. Even if all they get is a foot, they're happy."[67]

When the city comptroller's investigators visited the shelters, "The visitors were greeted by children who ran up to them and climbed on them, begging for attention. (One child, after sitting on a staff member's lap for ten minutes called her 'mommy;' when the staff person got up to leave, the child broke out in tears.)"[68] Upon further investigation, it turned out that these accounts were optimistic.

A group called the Public Interest Health Consortium for New York City obtained four hundred pages of reports on the baby warehouses done by the city's own health inspectors. This information was supplemented by interviews with shelter staff, parents, and foster parents. Among their findings:

—Health and sanitation practices were so poor that there were repeated outbreaks of infectious diarrhea. One such outbreak killed a one-year-old boy and a four-month-old girl. It was caused by "unsanitary diapering practices." The report concluded that there may have been more deaths, but record-keeping was too shoddy to be sure.

Inspectors found that "all but five of the shelters have had consistent problems with roaches, flies, mice, or rats. Food practices are often unsafe." The head of a City Health Department inspection team wrote: "We *know* how to prevent many of the medical problems they are encountering. We have implored CWA both verbally and in writing to make renovations to alleviate these inadequacies. We predicted that such an outbreak would occur . . . and CWA should expect such outbreaks to continue to occur if they ignore our recommendations and requests" (emphasis in original).

Another child died of meningitis, caused by an infection that can be prevented by routine immunization. As of February 1988, only 22 percent of children in the shelters were adequately immunized. A year later, the number *fell* to 9 percent.

Disease isn't the only hazard. Fire safety citations against just one shelter over a two-year period included: "Electrical wires and connections exposed to children; some staff not aware of emergency procedures; no usable phone; only one staff person present to supervise and evaluate children; smoke detector needs new battery; matches accessible to children; staff smoking against regulations." Other problems at the shelters included: "unshielded wall outlets, broken cribs, playpens, and high chairs; play areas with broken glass; toxic chemicals leaking from containers within easy reach of toddlers."

Emotional support for the children was virtually nonexistent. The shelters were staffed largely by untrained workers with no more than a high-school education. They worked in eight-hour shifts, so no child ever had a single caretaker to love him or her. The turmoil for the children was worsened by enormous staff turnover. Children at one shelter were cared for by twenty different workers in eleven days. Comments in inspection reports included: "Children should be held . . . when drinking from bottles; little communication between attendant and infants. Children walking around were spoken to only if they were doing something potentially wrong; outdoor area for play . . . is strewn with broken glass, garbage, and rocks, etc." The toys at the shelters often were dirty or broken, and the books were inaccessible to the children.

According to people in the system who spoke to the report's authors, the city found a way to make things even worse. Under pressure from the state to limit stays in the shelters to twenty-one days per child, the city started shuffling children from shelter to shelter in order to give the false impression that the deadline was being met.[69]

How does all this affect a child? A man who miraculously survived an institutional upbringing wrote this:

Now, I watch little kids, how they run to mommy's arms and fall asleep on daddy's shoulder. . . . I had no mommy and daddy like that. Just one set of stiff, white-uniformed different-feeling arms after another. I know many of those people cared, even loved. But there were too many of them, too many changing faces and voices and arms, and not one face, not one voice, not one enfolding embrace was mine. All mine.

I was just a toddling baby when the tenderness inside me began to die. I have no early dreams of laughter and warmth. I only remember feeling alone. Alone and afraid.[70]

Although the New York shelters closed in late 1989, chances are they'll be back. At various times, the city also claimed to have gotten its overnighter and boarder-baby problems under control, only to see them return. Typically, the city puts some effort wherever press and public attention are directed at the moment. The problem seems to subside, but actually it's just been moved somewhere else. In Los Angeles, as this is written, three baby shelters remain open with children warehoused at a cost of at least $2,300 a month for every child.[71] And again, the problem is not limited to big cities. There are three baby shelters in Rhode Island, according to Oryann Lima, a supervisor for the state's Department for Children and Their Families, though Lima hastens to add that "two out of the three are warm and nurturing."[72]

And the baby shelters are not the only new orphanages. Many of the "group homes" around the nation, originally designed for teenagers, now house younger and younger children. Some of these homes are excellent. Others are not.

A group home for retarded foster children in Brooklyn was furnished only with beds and torn chairs. Boys and girls aged seven to nineteen were mixed together in the home with little supervision. Sometimes as few as three staff were available for twenty-two children, including several that needed constant attention. For several months, the children were given only sponge baths because the bathtubs and showers were broken. The children had nothing to do but watch television. The city says the state should house these children in state institutions. The state says it doesn't have room. Considering that the city is doing "somebody else's work," said a CWA spokesman, "I think we are doing a remarkable job."[73]

*   *   *

The foster-care system operates under the peculiar premise that children are best helped by tearing apart their families, placing them with strangers, and then, supposedly, working to reunite them with their natural parents. In other words, we will push Humpty Dumpty off the wall and then try to put him back together. It should come as no surprise that there are rarely enough "horses and men" to do the job.

Once in care, both the children and their parents are largely abandoned.

Workers are overwhelmed by huge numbers of children who don't need to be in care but wind up there—and on their caseloads. More workers can't be added because resources are drained away investigating enormous numbers of false reports. That means the parents are left on their own at a time when they are least able to cope. The problems of poverty that often cause foster-care placement are also exacerbated by it. "If a child is moved, the parents are required to prove they are improving the physical conditions that led to the child being removed," says Lawrence Aber. "But it takes money to do that."[74]

But when a poor child is placed out of the home, the parents' welfare grant often is cut. That increases the likelihood that the parents will lose their apartment. And that means that even when the child is ready to return, the parents may not have an apartment that the authorities deem "suitable." The parents "also have to prove they are emotionally invested in the child," Aber says. "[That means] visiting, buying presents on the child's birthday, traveling—but that all takes money." Meanwhile, as noted earlier, the child savers are paying foster parents more to take care of a stranger's children than welfare recipients get to help them care for their own.

Even when workers have the time to try to reunite families, often they lack the inclination. "There is often an unconscious push by workers and foster parents to blame the parents," says child psychiatrist Foster Cline. The child himself is likely to blame the parents for the separation and get increasingly angry at them as the stay in care drags on. That is worsened "when the adults keep saying: 'it's lucky we got you away from those folks.' Then the kid says the same . . . and the system is saying that's all right."[75]

Caseworkers and foster parents tend to come from similar, middle-class backgrounds. They tend to identify more with each other than with the impoverished parent from whom a child has been taken. The middle-class foster family "becomes the standard against which the natural family is judged," writes Ruth Hubbell. "Though the original problem may be solved the worker begins to compare the foster and biological families and finds the biological family inferior" so new conditions are piled on one after the other before the parents can get their children back.[76]

"Once the child gets signed into care, all these workers evaluate the family and the child," and they find all sorts of new "problems," says Marlene Halpern of Community Action for Legal Services. Put any family under a microscope and that will happen, Halpern says, but only families with children in placement are subjected to such scrutiny.[77] In theory, parents are supposed to be involved in drawing up case plans designed to lead to reunification of the family. Halpern says 80 percent of the time, the parents are left out. The workers make little effort to visit the natural parents and almost none to help them with their problems—offering only the ever-popular "counseling."

"All their instincts are against [reunification]" says Diane Redleaf. "It's part of the bias against natural parents that exists throughout child welfare."[78] Halpern agrees. "[The workers] don't like the clients they have to work with, they like the foster parents better." As a result, even when the official goal is still reunification, sometimes only a few months after placement, "the unspoken goal becomes adoption." Halpern says she often finds comments like this one in case records only a short time after placement: "Though I explained to Mrs. so-and-so that the placement is temporary, she said she would be interested in adoption. She would make a fine adoptive parent." Asks Halpern: "What the hell is she discussing those issues for?"

In other cases, workers make no plans at all. The "goal" for a majority of New York City children ages twelve to twenty-one is never to even try and find them a family. Instead, the goal is "discharge to independent living."[79] As one study notes, that is often a code phrase for "giving them a [subway] token and the address of the nearest homeless shelter."[80]

"A youngster that I represented was about to be kicked out of foster care at nineteen or twenty, a graduate of high school [who] wanted to go to college, but there was no help for him from the social services system," says Washington, D.C., attorney Diane Weinroth. "His social worker told the judge that her discharge plan for him was to tell him how to get on general public assistance and Medicaid."[81]

The parent fighting for return of his or her child may encounter hostility not only from the caseworker, but from the foster parents as well. Some foster parents understand that when reunification is possible, their job is to support that effort and help bring the family back together. Others don't. In her study, Ruth Hubbell found that foster parents who wanted to be helpful often were shut out by the agency. "I don't know what would have to be done for him to return home," one foster parent said. "There's no plan that I know that we're working toward."

Others didn't want to help. "I would hate to see him go home," said one foster parent. "I don't think he would reach his full potential in life. He wasn't well supervised." Several foster parents expressed hostility to the natural parents. "I don't have much faith in their mother, they need a good adoptive home," said one. "The saddest thing in foster care is that they want to go home, but they would miss the regular routine of a good home," said another. One foster mother actually told her foster child "that his mother didn't care for him and would never change her life for him."

One foster mother censored her foster child's letters. "She writes, but her letters are full of lies," the foster mother said. "I read the letters if they are taped closed. Once I told her to rewrite it because it was full of lies. The caseworker reads the letters also, and gives them to the parents. But he explains the lies to them."[82]

The hostility of the entire foster-care system to parents is most apparent in agency policies toward visiting. Studies have repeatedly shown that the single most important variable in determining whether a child will return home or be trapped forever in what has been called the "no attachment zone" of foster care is whether the child is visited often by his or her parents. Frequent visits are also vital for reducing the trauma experienced by a child who is suddenly pulled away from everything comforting and familiar.

In a study he conducted, Stanford University law professor Michael Wald found that as the time in foster care dragged on, visiting declined. This was "very painful to the children. . . . Even when parents had not contacted the child for months or years, the child never gave up hope. As one seven-year-old boy who had not heard from his mother in two years said, 'Every time the phone rings, I hope that it's her.' "[83]

Visitation is so important that an American Bar Association report recommends that when a child is taken into custody without a hearing, using the "emergency" powers of the state, visits usually should take place *every day* until a trial is held.[84]

Yet the child savers make visiting as difficult as possible. Many states require agencies to arrange visits only once a month and then don't even follow through on that.

Such practices have probably destroyed the Saunders family in Illinois. After twenty-one-month-old Adam Saunders was taken into protective custody in 1983, his mother Deborah agreed to "voluntary" placement "because she was having difficulty caring for Adam as a single parent and wanted time to improve her circumstances," according to a class-action lawsuit in which she is a plaintiff. Only after the placement did Deborah find out that she would be allowed to see Adam only once a month for one hour. Once, even that was denied. Telephone calls she made to her caseworker pleading for more visits went unanswered. On Easter Sunday, 1984, Saunders went to Adam's foster home to bring him a chocolate Easter bunny. She was turned away at the door. Easter Sunday was not one of the scheduled visiting days.

Officially, the plan for Adam was that he would be returned to his mother. But after growing up without her for so long, Adam's mother is a stranger to him now. He doesn't even understand who she is anymore.[85]

Such cases are not unusual. Often children are placed so far from their homes that frequent visits are impossible. A New Jersey study found that 60 percent of foster children were separated from their siblings as well as their parents, and 30 percent were placed out of their home counties. Partly as a result, foster children were visited, on average, only five times per year. Typically, the first visit did not take place until they had been in care sixty days.[86]

New York City maintains six hundred foster homes in Suffolk County, thirty-five miles or more from Manhattan.[87] The poor families from which children usually are taken often don't have cars, and public transportation is inadequate and expensive. In Florida, children often are placed out of their home counties. In San Francisco, children regularly are placed fifty miles away from their homes. In Philadelphia, it's often 120 miles.[88]

Often such distant placements are a consequence of a foster-care system overcrowded with children who don't really need to be there. But California probation officer Dennis Lepak believes children are sometimes placed far from home on purpose, because "children placed far from home are easier to manage. When friends, family, and familiar surroundings are removed, the job of controlling the child becomes much easier."[89]

When visits are allowed, they often are permitted only at a dreary Social Services office, only under the watchful eye of the caseworker, only for one hour at a time and only during office hours—making it extremely difficult for poor working parents. This is partly a function of the enormous caseloads workers must carry. They have little time to shuttle parents and children back and forth, so it's easier to make everyone come to them. Marlene Halpern says it's also because the workers "don't want to go to the ghettoes" where the parents live.

Under the circumstances, when a visit finally takes place, it's hardly surprising that it will be strained. But, Halpern says, the child saver monitoring the visit will use the impossible conditions she helped set up against the parent. "She'll take out her notebook and write something like 'mother didn't relate well to the child.' " What do you expect, asks Halpern, "when you have a three-year-old who's been with a foster parent for a year and the natural mother is being watched by everyone?"

"We hate visits, we really do," acknowledges Robert Moro, the Child Protective Services supervisor in Massachusetts. "We can't get past the fact that it's a taxicab arrangement that has nothing to do with social work. It's an incredibly time-consuming process." Moro acknowledged that "sometimes the social worker will try to delay and discourage more frequent visits than might be clinically appropriate because they're trying to play Solomon with their time."

Child savers often talk—sometimes, it seems, almost gleefully—about how upset some children get after a visit. They use this to justify cutting off such visits. Although there are cases where this upset really is a result of being forced into contact with an abusive parent, most of the time it is nothing of the kind. Often it is the *separation* from the parent that causes the upset. A child placed in foster care goes through a grieving process similar to the stages of grieving when a loved one dies—denial, anger, bargaining, depression, and acceptance. If a child has a visit "during the denial or the anger stage," says Susan Carter of the National Association of Foster Care Reviewers, "the kid is angry, doesn't understand why it's happening, of course he's going to be upset if he sees [a parent] for two hours and then has to leave. That shows he's attached [to the parent]." As child psychiatrist Foster Cline noted, the child may also be blaming the parent for the separation, and the child savers may be encouraging such sentiments.

But perhaps the worst thing child savers do to children concerning visits is to hold the children hostage until parents change their behavior in ways of which the child savers approve.

In Erie County, Pennsylvania, for example, visits usually don't start until at least a month after placement, and then they take place under strict supervision at the child saver's office. When the parents start jumping through the hoops the child savers have set up, they may be rewarded with more frequent or less closely supervised visits. Says Becky Malinowski, a casework information specialist for Erie county, "If you make progress we can move the visits home, or change from supervised to unsupervised."[90]

Malinowski and others say visits at the foster home are also avoided— indeed the location of the foster home often is kept secret—because of hostility between the two sets of parents. Hostility which, they say, is of course all the natural parents' fault. Parents often "have negative attitudes toward foster parents because the foster parents are doing a better job raising their kids," Malinowski explains.

"I think that's horrendous, absolutely horrendous," says Michael Wald. First of all, Wald notes, such a policy is punishing the child for the alleged sins of the parents. In addition, "The notion these people have about handing out rewards shows something about their attitude toward parents as well— that they don't see that there is attachment, that there is an implication for the nature of the relationship just by visiting."[91]

"What it shows is an attitude that is not, We are going to work with you, but rather, We'll tell you what to do and you do it," says Susan Carter, who adds, "The way to getting cooperation is to give it."

"If the goal is reunification and the best way to reunify is meaningful visitation, you don't use your best tool as a lever [to force parents into] counseling," says Marlene Halpern. Indeed, Halpern says, there may be good reasons for parents not to "cooperate." A parent may feel uncomfortable getting counseling "from the same agency that's holding their child from them," Halpern says. Furthermore, Halpern says, if the parents get counseling through the child saving agency, anything they say may eventually be used against them in court. "I wouldn't trust them for two minutes," she says.

But, child-protective workers see nothing wrong with using visits as leverage. It isn't really punishing the child, explains Oryann Lima, a casework supervisor in Rhode Island, because "We can't give the child false hope he will go home if the parent isn't doing anything else [besides visiting]."[92]

In other cases, visits are used to "dangle a carrot" in front of the *child.* Says Dennis Lepak: "Most programs consider home visits to be a privilege, and visits are used as rewards for good behavior rather than as reunification tools."[93]

Faced with so much state-sanctioned maltreatment, the only recourse for foster children has been the courts. The only meaningful accomplishment of a 1980 federal law designed to reform foster care, says Marcia Robinson Lowry, Director of the ACLU's Children's Rights Project, has been that it has increased the grounds to bring class-action lawsuits in an attempt to force foster-care systems to change. A congressional report lists forty-six lawsuits pending or settled against child-welfare systems in nineteen states.[94]

Foster-care systems, or parts of those systems, are operating under court orders or settlements in New York City,[95] Kansas City, Baltimore, New Mexico, Georgia, and Massachusetts.[96]

"I have been a judge for twenty years," U.S. District Judge Joseph Howard wrote in deciding the Baltimore case. "During that time much human tragedy has passed before me; however none has so deeply touched me as the plight of these children."[97]

"Children have suffered unspeakable injuries to body and spirit," U.S. District Court Judge Robert Keeton wrote in the Massachusetts case. Listening to some of those horrors brought Judge Keeton to tears while presiding over it.[98]

Suits are pending in Louisiana, Kentucky, and Washington, D.C. There are at least three class-action lawsuits in progress in New York City alone. In Illinois, there are at least eight. Illinois's Department of Children and Family Services is presently being sued—or has already been held in contempt of court for:

—Failure to provide Spanish-speaking workers to families that speak only Spanish.

—Failure to provide services to teenage mothers in foster care.

—Routine strip-searching in cases of alleged abuse.

—Failure to provide preventive services to keep children out of foster care.

—Failure to assign a caseworker until thirty days or more after a child is placed.

—Failure to provide adequate visitation.

—Abysmal conditions in emergency shelters for foster children.

—Abysmal conditions in foster care after children are placed.

The suit over conditions in foster care, brought by the Illinois chapter of the American Civil Liberties Union, includes the following cases:

—A seventeen-year-old boy who had been in ten different placements over four years, including several placements in shelters. He faked a suicide attempt to get out of one placement. Although he is an honor student, he couldn't graduate from high school with his class because multiple placements had so disrupted his education.

—A fifteen-year-old boy with five placements in six months.

—A thirteen-year-old boy in foster care "as long as he can remember." The child was warehoused at an overcrowded, understaffed, violence-plagued mental health facility "which controls his behavior by administering strong doses of psychotropic medication."

—A seventeen-year-old girl with seven placements in a year. Twice she was kept in a locked ward in a mental institution long after mental health officials said she could be discharged, because there was no place else to put her. She was ignored for so long by her caseworker that she slit her wrists to get the worker's attention.

—Brothers aged three and six who were in eight placements in a year. In one foster home they were not adequately fed or clothed, in another they were hit by the foster mother, and in a third the six-year-old was sexually abused. The fourth placement was a good one, one where the foster parent demanded that the child get therapy for the sexual abuse he had suffered. For that, the worker labeled the foster parent a troublemaker and threatened to remove the children.[99]

"This case was brought," the Illinois Civil Liberties Union says in one of its briefs, "because plaintiffs want the defendant to stop mistreating them."[100]

More revealing than the charges brought in this lawsuit is the response from the Illinois child savers. They argue that after removing children from homes where the parents allegedly subjected them to physical or emotional maltreatment, the Illinois Department of Children and Family Services has *no legal responsibility whatsoever* for their emotional well-being and no responsibility for their physical well-being unless they are in a state institution, as opposed to a private institution or a foster home.[101] Indeed, at one point in their brief, the DCFS argues that the status of a foster child is analogous to that of a prisoner.[102] (Actually, DCFS is suggesting that foster children have fewer rights than prisoners, since, elsewhere in their brief, they acknowledge that prisoners have some right to physical safety.)[103] As the Illinois Civil Liberties Union states in its response, "It is effectively

[DCFS Director Gordon] Johnson's contention that he . . . is entitled to establish and maintain a child welfare system that routinely abuses the children who are entrusted to it."

The Illinois DCFS did not think up this defense on its own. Faced with so many lawsuits, they hired Skadden, Arps, Slate, Meagher & Flom, what Benjamin Wolf, the ACLU's lawyer, calls "the most expensive law firm in the city"—the one that charges "New York billing rates"—to defend them in four of the lawsuits. DCFS, which repeatedly pleads poverty when asked to help children, has paid more than one million dollars to Skadden, Arps, etc., to avoid providing those services.[104] Diane Redleaf, who has brought several suits against the DCFS, estimates that what the state pays the law firm for two hours of work would have paid James Norman's rent for a month.[105]

William Curtis, the DCFS chief counsel who worried that people like James Norman might become too dependent on the state, said his agency is depending on outside counsel because both his office and the state attorney general's office were too "overworked" to handle such complex litigation. Curtis said the fees are "very reasonable" given the amount of work involved, and he blamed the high cost on the Civil Liberties Union and like-minded groups for filing all those lawsuits.

Curtis said he was very pleased with the work the law firm was doing. "We got a lawfirm that specializes in corporate takeovers," Curtis said. "They really come on strong. They hit you with everything they've got. They use a team approach and they inundate." They also "make sure that we don't make an admission in one case that's going to hurt us in another or something like that."[106]

Judges have repeatedly, though not always, refused to buy the child savers' excuses. But, says Marcia Lowry, winning or settling the case is the easy part. Month after month, year after year, the child savers have to be dragged back into court and forced to obey the law.

Sometimes they respond, literally and figuratively, with contempt.

In the Baltimore case, Judge Howard blasted attorneys for the state for:

—Willfully violating a court order to provide information to the plaintiffs.

—Engaging in a "degree of evasiveness that is simply deplorable" in response to written questions from the plaintiffs.

—Initially claiming that the state did not compile figures on abuse in foster homes, then mysteriously finding this data several months later. The judge called the explanations for this discrepancy "disingenuous" and "of questionable veracity."

Judge Howard concluded that these and other abuses "are a virtual admission that they cannot rebut" the allegations of widespread abuse in

Baltimore foster homes.

The Baltimore case has now been settled, and one of the lawyers who brought the suit says that, though compliance has been slow, attorneys for the state are at least behaving themselves.[107]

Or consider what happened in the lawsuit over visitation in Illinois discussed earlier:

—On June 5, 1986, the DCFS signed a consent decree agreeing to, among other things, weekly visits—then promptly ignored their legally binding promise.

—On March 16, 1987, the plaintiffs sought to hold DCFS in contempt. DCFS did not even reply to the motion and repeatedly thwarted plaintiffs' efforts to obtain information.

—More than a year later, and after being forced to pay some of the plaintiffs attorneys' fees, DCFS admitted it had failed to live up to the consent decree and said negotiations had resumed.

—But, in February 1989, DCFS broke off negotiations and said, in effect: If you don't like it, sue us again.

In holding DCFS in contempt, U.S. District Judge Paul Plunkett declared that the child savers, "continually strung plaintiffs along, apparently hoping to be the victor in a war of attrition. . . . The court can only conclude that Defendant entered into the decree in order to simply get Plaintiffs off its back, yet never seriously intended to live up to it. We do not take kindly to what we perceive to be three years of bad faith conduct, conduct which was in blatant contravention of a court order."[108]

As this is written, DCFS is appealing the contempt judgment. Says Diane Redleaf: The Illinois Department of Children and Family Services is "a lawless agency."

*   *   *

The terrible things that foster care does to children are no secret. Yet no matter how much research is done, no matter how much is written about "boarder babies" and "nomad children," and no matter how many children come forward to tell what foster care did to them, child savers keep right on removing children from their own homes in cases where it's obviously going to do more harm than good. Why?

The answer, I think, is that child savers live in a foster-care fantasyland. They see in front of them children living in poverty, perhaps with a struggling single parent, and they fantasize that they can take the children away and place them in a nice middle-class suburban home with two cars, two dogs, and two parents.

The attitude among many workers is: "If you remove a child too soon, so what," says Jacquelynne Bowman of Greater Boston Legal Services. Bowman says one worker's reaction to the sudden removal of a child to foster care was, "Oh, well, she'll get used to it."[109]

"Workers . . . have images of cases and what they're going to do with them—and the resources that are out there don't particularly affect what the workers do," says Michael Wald. They don't "think through" whether there is an alternative to foster care or whether they have anything better to offer than the home from which they are taking the children.[110] Judges are no different. "In hearings on foster care placements," Ruth Hubbell writes, "judges balance evidence of the alleged shortcomings of a biological family against the assumed conditions in an optimal foster home. This is often a comparison between reality and fiction. . . ."[111]

One of the finest examples of self-delusion is Bourne and Newberger's argument, cited in Chapter 3, that it is all right to remove children solely because of poor housing conditions, since, of course, it is only "a stopgap measure until the inadequacy of the community's provision of shelter is remedied."

Even if the child savers could find a middle-class home for every poor child, they would do it at the expense of what they can't see and can't seem to understand—the love and trust that children like Boyd, for example, have for their parents. So they "fabricate success," as Malcolm Bush puts it, by denying, even to themselves, the trauma of foster care. Thus, a worker writes this about a child who has been moved from home to home:

"Initially, Betty didn't make a good adjustment in this placement. She was lonely for Mrs. Bond. Mrs. Taylor, the worker, has been working with Betty to resolve her anxiety about first leaving her natural placement and then the Williams."

But, Bush writes, "Betty's condition is unresolvable in the sense that the moves she has made cannot be reversed or expunged from her history, and they may not even be explicable in terms she would understand or accept. The language of [the caseworker's] record suggests, however, that she can achieve peaceful understanding of her loss."[112]

All of the trauma of foster care is, of course, compounded if the foster parents themselves abuse the child. At the beginning of this chapter, I cited several cases of such abuse and said that they are atypical. But how atypical they are is another question.

The foster-care system has its share of both "fools and heroes" according to Paul DiLorenzo, who heads the Support Center for Child Advocates in Philadelphia.

One of the heroes is the foster parent who cared for a sickly premature infant who needed six types of medication and three machines to keep him alive. For fifteen months, the foster parent, a registered nurse, cared for the child night and day, never sleeping for more than four hours at a time. The foster parent pleaded with Philadelphia's child savers for a machine she knew of that would both improve the child's care and signal when there was a problem, thus allowing the foster mother a normal night's sleep. The agency refused. Instead they suggested tying a bell to the infant's toe so that the foster mother would hear if the child went into convulsions.[113]

Perhaps because there are many such heroes among foster parents, and because it would complicate a story which would otherwise have clear villains (the natural parents) as well, I think the press has been reluctant to try and find out how many foster parents are a lot less than heroic. And certainly it is not something the child savers want to know. So very little is known about the extent of abuse in foster care.

On the one hand, foster parents are even more vulnerable to false allegations of abuse or neglect than the rest of us. They are not allowed to use any corporal punishment on foster children. And foster children are more likely than others to know how to manipulate the system and phone in false reports on their own. "My wife and I have been the subject of [maltreatment] allegations five times in the last ten years," says Arnold Herman, director of Foster Friends, Inc., a New Jersey foster parents organization. "The only reason that we are still foster parents . . . is that our love for the children in our home is just slightly greater than our hatred for the . . . investigation system."

Herman said new foster parents are told during training to expect to be investigated on a maltreatment charge at some point during their service.[114]

Nevertheless, the evidence that is available suggests that signs of abuse in foster care are much more than an artifact of the reporting and investigation process. It is a serious and growing problem that should weigh heavily in decisions concerning whether to remove a child from his or her own home.

"My experience over the last couple of years is that we have as much or more abuse in foster homes as we have in reabuse after returning children [to their natural parents]," says Gary Seiser, the former Juvenile Court Commissioner in California. Seiser says "a significant percentage" of foster homes, though not a majority, "are really very marginal, and local departments would not choose to use them if they were able to find better homes."[115]

In joint testimony, the National Center for Youth Law and the Youth Law Center told a Congressional hearing, "Our offices have become painfully aware of many situations where children's health and lives are in greater jeopardy in foster homes than they were while they were living with their families."[116]

"The rate of abuse in foster care is going up, and it's going up alarmingly," says Elsa Tenbroeck, administrator of children's services in San Mateo

County, California.[117]

"I think it's a lot more rampant than is known," says Pamela Mohr of Public Counsel. "I say that because of my own experience. . . . I've seen a lot more cases than I would expect to."[118]

"Foster care is like Russian roulette," says Lisa Clampitt, the former CPS worker in New York City. "The [foster] home could be 100 percent worse than where they are." When Clampitt complained about this to her supervisor, she says she was told, "You can't question your foster-care system."[119]

There are some indications of the rate of abuse in foster care that go beyond anecdotal evidence.

In preparation for one of its lawsuits against Illinois child savers, the Illinois chapter of the American Civil Liberties Union obtained that state's data on abuse in foster care through the state's freedom of information act. They found that, by the state's own estimate, the rate of abuse in foster care is double that of the general population. "Those statistics enormously underestimate the problem," says Benjamin Wolf, the attorney bringing the suit. In particular, Wolf says, the sort of abuse suffered by Angela Bennett—sexual abuse of foster children by other foster children—is grossly underreported. "Because of the chronic shortage of placements, all kinds of kids are mixed up together," Wolf says. "A sixteen-year-old may act out what was done to him on a five- or a six-year-old in the same placement. I would bet my life that goes on a lot and it's never reported to anybody."[120]

A 1981 study of foster children in Kansas City, Missouri, found that 57 percent of the sample children were placed in foster-care settings that left them "at the very least at a high risk of abuse or neglect."[121] That study proved sadly prescient. A follow-up report issued in October, 1987, found that 25 percent of the children in the newer sample actually had been victims of "abuse or inappropriate punishment."[122]

In Louisiana, another study found that 21 percent of the abuse or neglect cases examined involved abuse or neglect in foster homes[123]

One of the most comprehensive studies of foster-care abuse occurred in connection with the Baltimore lawsuit. In that case, Trudy Festinger, Chairwoman of the Department of Research at the New York University School of Social Work, led a team of reviewers who read the case records of 149 Baltimore foster children. Based on the Baltimore City Department of Social Services's own case records, Festinger's team found that forty-two of the children—28 percent—had been abused in foster care. In other words, the average child has better than a one-in-four chance of being abused each time he or she is placed—and 35 percent of Maryland foster children are placed at least four times.

Cases found by the Maryland casereaders included:

—A foster parent who stole her foster children's savings, left them unsupervised, and repeatedly hit a foster child on the head.

—A foster parent who repeatedly hit a child with her fists, and left a child who could not control his bladder in his urine-stained clothes, even sending him to school that way. Less than a year later, a second child with the same problem was placed in the same home.

—A home in which "street-smart teenagers" were placed with foster parents aged sixty-seven and seventy-four. While the parents were asleep, one of the teenagers sexually abused younger children.

—A home in which the foster mother fondled the foster children and the foster father had oral and anal sex with them. At least one child remained in the home for four months after abuse of other children was discovered.

—A foster parent who denied food to a pregnant foster child. The case record was so inadequate that the acting director of the Baltimore City Department of Social Services did not know if the home still was in use or not.

—A home in which the foster father severely beat a nine-year-old foster child with a belt and an extension cord. The child was not removed until two months after the abuse was discovered. After this child and others were removed, it also was discovered that the children were forced to wear clothing that was "dirty, old . . . [and] . . . unfit for wearing." They also were denied adequate food.[124]

That abuse in foster care is probably a lot more frequent than abuse in the general population shouldn't come as a surprise. Many of the reasons are not the fault of foster parents.

—Foster children usually come into a home with special problems, either because of maltreatment in their own homes or at the hands of the child savers or both. Feeling that they have been betrayed by so many other adults, they often will "test" their foster parents by provoking them.

—Child savers pressure foster parents to take more children than they can handle and often more than their licenses allow. Sometimes they don't tell parents about the children's problems. Or they place children with parents who obviously can't handle them and can't control what they might do to each other—like the Baltimore teens placed with elderly foster parents. All of this makes abuse of some type almost inevitable.

"We set up foster parents," says Robert Moro. "We shoehorn more people than should be in the home, we badger them, we play on their social consciences to take in more than they can handle . . . and as soon as a problem comes up we file [a maltreatment report] on them to cover the agency's butt. . . . I wouldn't want to be a foster parent in Massachusetts nowadays."[125]

The child savers make things worse by driving the best foster parents out of the system. The best parents are the ones who fight for their foster children, often become attached to them, and dip into their own pockets to help support them because the monthly payments are too low. But though the practice was supposed to have been abolished years ago, child savers still move children out of a home because they have become "too attached" to foster parents—when stable, secure attachment is just what the child needs.

And child savers often treat foster parents the way they treat natural parents—like dirt. They are put through the same bureaucratic wringer, and when they fight for their foster children's rights, like the Illinois parent mentioned earlier, they are often threatened with removal of those children. The difference is that foster parents don't have to put up with it. They can quit.

For bad foster parents, none of this is a problem. Foster-care payments are too low to care for a child well, but one can treat a child shabbily and still make a profit. If you don't care about kids you won't fight for them, and you are certainly not going to become attached to them. The system is tailor-made to attract the wrong people.

"The majority of the people who get licenses to be foster parents normally are doing it for economical reasons," says Gary Seiser. "Many of those people need the money."[126] Because of the low pay, says the National Center on Youth Law, "few competent individuals are interested in applying."[127] Shirley Wilson, a social worker at Hahnemann University Hospital in Philadelphia, says that today it is actually easier to place a sick infant than a healthy one because if the child is sick, the foster parents get more money.[128]

Perhaps what is really surprising is that the problem of abuse in foster homes isn't worse than it is and that so many good foster parents give so much of themselves in the face of so many obstacles. Even the most pessimistic data still show that the majority of foster parents don't mistreat the children in their care. If we were absolutely certain that the only children removed from their parents were those who really had been badly maltreated and could not be protected at home, then the risk still would be worth it. But we know that is not how the system works.

The main reason relatively little is known about the extent of abuse in foster care is that the child savers don't want to know about it.

"We were really appalled to discover that not all allegations of abuse in out-of-home placements are investigated, and in some instances there is almost a presumption not to believe the child," says Cecelia Zalkind of the Association for Children of New Jersey.[129] Pamela Mohr says there's "a tremendous burnout rate" among foster parents, and with so many children coming into care, "there are not enough foster homes to begin with [so] people don't want to believe it and don't want to close down the foster home."

"There are not that many [good foster homes] left," agreed James Louis, the New Jersey law guardian. "When you've got a live one, you want to keep them happy."[130]

Does this contradict the assertion that foster parents are especially vulnerable to false allegations? Not necessarily. Just as when dealing with natural parents, there is more than enough ineptitude in the system to allow for errors in both directions. The tendency may be to ignore complaints from natural parents or their lawyers and pursue, sometimes excessively, those that come in through the normal "hotline" process.

In New York City, the Department of Investigation, the agency charged with monitoring other agencies, studied abuse in foster care and concluded that it is "a growing and serious problem." Investigators found major problems with both the private agencies responsible for children's care and the Child Welfare Administration, which is supposed to investig te allegations of maltreatment in foster care. The department's 1982 report found:

—Agencies waited an average of seven days before reporting deaths to the CWA and nine days for other incidents. The delays often made adequate investigations impossible.

—If an agency claimed an injury or death was due to illness or accident, the CWA simply took the agency's word for it.

—Thirteen percent of the foster parents named in abuse allegations had arrest records, and 5 percent had convictions. Among child-care workers at group homes, again 13 percent had arrest records, and 7 percent had convictions. One worker had eleven arrests and six convictions.

—Agencies often failed to properly implement—and sometimes simply ignored—CWA recommendations to discipline employees and decertify foster homes.

The CWA "does not obtain medical reports for most cases, and . . . when it does obtain them, it has no staff capable of assessing the information," the report concluded. "Additionally, child protective investigators' attitudes regarding the nature of cases impede their effective detection of abuse. . . . Investigators . . . explain away cases all too readily as accidents/illnesses/incidents. . . ."[131]

A Florida child tried to get someone to pay attention to the abuse she was suffering in foster care by slashing her wrists. "I thought that if they saw me like that they maybe would pay more attention to me and the other kids." But they didn't. "You're just a paper to them, just a folder full of papers."[132]

A discussion of abuse in foster care cannot be confined to family foster homes. Although that is usually where abused and neglected children go first, as they get older, or if there is no place else to put them, or if the frustration of multiple placement leads to what child savers call "acting out behavior," or if the child savers are just tired of a particular child, a group home or a large institution is often the next stop. Though such institutions generally are for children labeled "delinquent" or perhaps "mentally ill," often this distinction exists only on paper.

When the child who was once a cute toddler or adorable eight-year-old becomes a rebellious adolescent, child savers can no longer derive the psychological satisfaction from "treating" him that they used to. So often, they wash their hands of him.

That's when they become the responsibility of probation officers like Dennis Lepak. "Children are railroaded into the criminal justice placement system on menial and trumped up charges." Lepak says. "Pushing aside a mother to get out a blocked door becomes an assault, coming in a window in a child's own bedroom becomes breaking and entering, and a ride in the family car is charged as auto theft."[133]

"They'll bait the kids," agrees Pamela Mohr. "They'll make sure he gets taunted by other kids and they won't do anything to interfere. . . . They'll keep baiting the child until he lashes out and they can ship the kid out . . . for the probation department to deal with."

Then they can wind up in a juvenile detention center or an emergency shelter while they wait for a placement—mixed in with juveniles who committed the most serious crimes. "The soft kids are put in with the real hard kids," says Lepak, "and the kind of sexual assault that happens in adult prisons goes on in juvenile hall."[134]

"We most recently had a staff member stabbed and two others severely assaulted," a clinical director at the emergency shelter in San Francisco reported. "We had a pimp who was using our girls in foster care to prostitute and returning them at night so he didn't have to feed and house them. More profit for the pimp."[135]

Or they can wind up in a place like the Western New York Children's Psychiatric Center near Buffalo.

A state investigation disclosed an inmate's "sex club" involving children aged five to twelve. It included an initiation rite involving children engaging in oral and anal sex with each other. The investigation found that senior officials at the center knew what was going on but in many cases did nothing to stop it. Officials did act in the four cases of sexual abuse of inmates by staff at the center.[136] Another New York study found that reports alleging child maltreatment occurred nearly three times more often in state facilities for the mentally ill than among the general population.[137]

Or they can wind up in a place like the Hegeman Diagnostic Center in Brooklyn. Hegeman and other such facilities are meant for short-term placement while children are evaluated. But after the evaluation there is often no place to go. So, places like Hegeman get backed up and overcrowded.

"It's really the equivalent of boarder babies for adolescents," says Karen Freedman of the advocacy group, Lawyers for Children. "We believe that assaults, sexual and otherwise, occur daily at the centers." For example, a twelve-year-old girl brought to Hegeman after being raped in a foster home was sexually abused by other girls at the center. Another girl, also twelve years old, "had her life threatened and every stitch of her clothing stolen at Hegeman," Freedman said. She says a worker at Hegeman told the girl's aunt, "I'm sorry, I cannot guarantee your child's safety."[138]

Or they can wind up in a place like the Montrose Juvenile Facility in Reisterstown, Maryland.[139] Patricia Hanges, a retired Baltimore police officer, was a church volunteer at Montrose, which housed children as young as nine. She described what she saw to a congressional committee: "Whether intentional or not, everything was done to break the spirit of the children," she said. They were subjected to constant verbal abuse and sometimes physical and sexual abuse as well; they could not phone home and all mail was censored; they were told when to stand up, when to sit down, and when they could go to the bathroom; they could not speak during meals; they were "cared for" by staff who needed only a high-school degree or equivalent to be hired; they lived in overcrowded, unsafe dormitories. A child with a dislocated shoulder waited three days before he was sent to a hospital for surgery—and then, only after his mother complained.

"The state of Maryland was treating our children in this manner . . . under the guise that we were protecting them," Hanges said. "Well, if that is protection, buddy, I hope they never protect me like that."

Hanges emphasized that "The children at Montrose [were] not hard core delinquents." They were children like James Guttridge, age twelve.

Guttridge's mother, Judy, first sought help for James when he was a small boy who had been diagnosed as hyperactive. But she said the state's Juvenile Services Agency told her they could give no help unless James got in trouble.[140] By the time he was eleven, James had started to get into trouble but just petty stuff, like trespassing. His mother insisted on a court hearing, thinking then James would finally get some help. That's when he was sent to Montrose:

> When he got there, I called the social workers and asked them if he was going to be evaluated. They told me yes. I said: I would like to have a report. [They said,] "Well, you are not getting any." . . . They told me he was no longer my son, he belonged to the State of Maryland and I . . . had nothing to do with what went on in his life anymore.
>
> I still called, and I still got upset. My husband said don't call there no more.
>
> Every Sunday I went [to visit. The bus trip from Baltimore took two-and-a-half hours.] By the time you get there it's a quarter to two and you

have to leave by 3:15.

> One Sunday we went there and he told me that a man there had made him [and four other boys] take all his clothes off . . . and all the other little boys in the cottage went around and got to touch them. . . . Two months later, I went and my son had bruises all over his back. . . . He told me the staff had picked up a chair and hit him with it.
>
> While I was there, the staff would holler, you could hear the confusion in back while you were visiting. It was dirty. It stunk. . . . They marched them back and forth like little prisoners.
>
> My son asked me one time, what would you do if I showed up at the house? I was stupid enough to tell him I would take him back [to Montrose] because I was going to do what the law wanted me to do, which was dumb.

One day in June, James Guttridge was punished by being placed in solitary confinement in "the pink room," a place that, Hanges said, "smelled of urine and feces so bad I had to hold my breath when I went into it in the summer months."

At midnight that night, Judy Guttridge got a phone call:

> My son had tried to commit suicide; [they said] he was fine, he was in the hospital. But when we got there he was not okay. He was unconscious. We were there all night and all day. He died that afternoon. . . .
>
> I wonder how tall my son would have been? How big? What would he have done? I just have all these feelings and they never are going to go away.

"Mrs. Guttridge wanted her son," said Patricia Hanges. "She visited him every week. Constantly called. Tried to help by bringing things to children who received no visitors. This mother wanted help from the system. James could have been served in his community with back-up services for his family rather than institutionalization."

Instead, taxpayers spent more than $3,300 a month so he could live—and die—at Montrose.

The death of James Guttridge did not stop Montrose officials from using the pink room. Hanges found out about it when another child started to cry and said, "Ms. Pat, don't take me back. They put me in the pink room and I see that little boy's ghost."

They also put Troy Chapman, age thirteen, in the pink room. Says Hanges: "He said, if you put me in that cell, I will hang myself." They put him in the cell anyway, and he carried out his threat.

Still another child, this one eleven years old, had tried to choke himself after being placed in another isolation room. He too had told the staff person who put him there that he would kill himself. The staff person replied: "Go ahead. That's one less little boy I'll have to worry about."

In the time since Guttridge and Hanges testified, Maryland officials ignored the cries of those who want to "bring back the orphanage" and closed Montrose down. But scores of Montroses still blight the national landscape.

"In the state mental hospital in South Carolina, children who attempted to commit suicide were stripped to their underwear, bound by their ankles and wrists to the corners of their beds, and injected with psychotropic drugs," says Mark Soler, director of the Youth Law Center in San Francisco. "In the Phoenix Indian High School in Arizona, Indian children found intoxicated on school grounds were handcuffed to the fence surrounding the institution and left there overnight. In a private treatment and special education facility in Utah, children were locked in closets for punishment, grabbed by the hair and thrown against walls, and given lie detector tests as part of their 'therapy.' "[141]

That there would be widespread abuse in such places should not surprise anyone. The workers directly responsible for the children at many group homes and institutions have only a high-school education.[142] Often, they are thrown into a home or onto a ward with little or no experience. At group homes in Washington, D.C., according to attorney Diane Weinroth, "They have got some very strange people working in these facilities. I don't know where they come from. But I will tell you this, there are no standards for hiring. I have never, ever, been afraid of one of my clients, but I have been afraid to go into some of these facilities at night and deal with the night staff alone."[143]

In a 1989 report, New York City's Council of Family and Child Caring Agencies decided it was worth admitting how lousy many of their member-agency workers are in an attempt to convince state and city officials to give them more money. The council's report states:

"A director of a residential treatment facility estimates that at his agency an average of two child care workers each month is fired due to poor performance. [The director states:] 'Many of these workers we could have predicted would not have worked out, but in most cases we're desperate to hire quickly to replace workers so that we can maintain proper staff-child ratios.' "

But look what happens when child savers are placed in the position of the accused rather than the accuser. In the same report, COFCCA agencies make a plea for far greater understanding and sympathy for workers who abuse children than they have ever shown to parents: "Under these conditions, there are more situations which create the opportunity for inappropriate intervention due to circumstances rather than intentional abuse or neglect."

The report goes on to bemoan how tough it is on a worker to be accused: "The result, however, is the same in that a worker, once reported, goes through a process of investigation which could be lengthy, threatening one's job security and personal integrity."[144] Similarly, when a New York State study charged that COFCCA agencies failed to report 84 percent of the maltreatment taking place in their foster homes and institutions, COFCCA complained that the study defined abuse too broadly and included "alleged" as well as confirmed cases.[145]

Judy Guttridge probably wishes someone had shown as much solicitude for her son. She recalled the last time she held him: "That night, he no longer belonged to Montrose or to the state, he belonged to me again, because he was dying. . . ."

8

Foster Care II

No one knows exactly how many children "belong" to the state on any given day. Nor do we know how much money is spent driving them to suicide or otherwise "caring" for them.

What we do know is that the number of children trapped in foster care is increasing, that at least half those children probably don't need to be there, and that the excuses the child savers have given for the increase won't wash. Foster care is not increasing because there is more real maltreatment of children, and, by and large, it is not increasing because of the current trendy explanation for every problem: drug abuse. Foster care is increasing because it is the way child savers like to deal with children—and because foster care is where the money is.

In 1989, the federal government spent more than eight times as much money on foster care as it did on programs to keep children out of foster care.

Foster-care systems, like all child-welfare functions, are run either directly by state agencies or by city or county governments, and the federal government hasn't bothered to keep an accurate count of how many children are in them. The best guess is that America's foster-care population peaked in the late 1970s, with perhaps half a million children in care at any given time. New state and federal laws, as well as public attention to the plight of foster children, led to a decline in the foster-care population during the early 1980s. But in recent years, the population has soared again.

At one point, the foster-care population may have been cut almost in half, to 267,000 in 1982. By 1985, it still may have been only 276,000, a difference that could have been due to nothing more than statistical error. Such error abounds. These numbers are based on a voluntary reporting system. Some states don't report at all, and the 267,000 and 276,000 figures are projections based on those that do.

The states that do report have considerable latitude in defining foster care. For example, when Oregon officials became embarrassed about having the highest placement rate in the nation, due largely to children placed in care and returned home within a week, they simply defined these children out and only reported children who were in care for more than a week. Kentucky only reports children in care more than thirty days.

The 276,000 figure is a "snapshot," that is, it gives the number of children in care on the last day of 1985. But a child who entered care on January 1, 1985, and left care anytime before December 31 would be missed by this count. When these children are added in, the total number in care rose to 452,000,[1] and that's when things were getting better. Now, it seems, they're getting worse.

A survey conducted by the American Enterprise Institute and the American Public Welfare Association found that, as of September, 1989, the foster-care population was back up to 360,000, with almost all of the increase taking place since 1987. More than half the increase occurred in just two states, New York and California. Today, one out of every three foster children lives in one of these two states. In New York State, at the end of 1989, the total number of children in foster care was about 52,000—slightly above where it was at its height during the late 1970s. (The 1989 figure includes 10,000 children placed with relatives.)[2]

We also don't know how much it all costs—the hotlines, the investigations, the foster care, and what little is provided in the way of services. My own guess, projecting from federal expenditures, is that foster care alone costs at least $5 billion per year, and, based on New York and California data, the entire system costs—very roughly—at least $7.2 billion per year.[3]

Whatever the exact numbers may be, this much is certain: Thousands of lives and billions of dollars are thrown away on foster care every year.

In theory, foster care is supposed to be the last resort for dealing with a troubled family. First, "reasonable efforts" are supposed to be made to keep the family together by providing "preventive services." A court is supposed to certify that such efforts have been made before a child is placed. Without such certification, the federal government isn't supposed to help pay for that child's foster care.[4] But for a hundred years, foster care, either in homes or institutions, has been the first resort. The promise of preventive services has been a cruel joke.

A study of 119 cases in four states found that courts made no "reasonable efforts" determination in 44 percent of the cases.[5] Since all a judge has to do is check a box on a form to claim that such efforts have been made, this figure undoubtedly underestimates the extent of the problem. In some cases, according to congressional testimony, judges have lied in order to keep the federal money coming.[6]

In California, according to a legislative committee, "Most counties . . . [have to] resort to removing children from the home and placing them in foster/residential care because sufficient funding is not available to provide alternative services to the child's family." In California, says probation officer Dennis Lepak, the chances of parents getting preventive services are "zero"—unless they can pay for the help out of their own pockets.[7] In New York City, parents are put on waiting lists for months at a time, "and in the meantime, we will have to remove your child promptly," says Suella Gallop, a CPS supervisor and spokeswoman for the caseworkers' union.[8] While she was attending the city's much vaunted "training academy" for child-protective workers, Lisa Clampitt says, "I asked every day: Can we get a list of resources [we can offer families]? They said you'll learn it eventually." Six months later, when Clampitt quit in disgust, she still hadn't been given the information.[9]

"There are frequent occasions when families have to be separated unnecessarily because services to maintain the family intact are unavailable," says Ken Doe, a CPS supervisor in Massachusetts. "We often get referrals from schools saying children are neglected because they're alone or have inappropriate caretakers after school," Doe says, but CPS has almost no money to pay for after-school day care and can reimburse baby-sitters only fifty-five cents an hour.[10] Similarly, recall the study of "lack of supervision" cases in New York City cited in Chapter 3. It found that in 52 percent of the cases studied, what was needed was the obvious: day care or baby-sitting. Yet the most commonly offered "service" was foster care, followed closely by those old child saver standbys "counseling" and "parent education."[11]

For a great many families labeled "neglectful," "preventive services" don't have to be very elaborate. "The services that are needed are not incredibly overwhelming," says Florence Roberts of Brooklyn Legal Services. "You may have a mother whose welfare case was closed. Now she has no food or money and the electricity was turned off. Somebody has to get the lights on and the case reopened. . . . Instead, it's so much easier to just go ahead and yank the kids."[12]

That's done even though preventive services are cheaper than foster care. Several experts have pointed out over the years that the single most effective "preventive service" is Aid to Families with Dependent Children. Yet states routinely pay more to foster parents to take care of other people's children than they will pay parents on welfare to help take care of their own.

In California, for example, welfare benefits are relatively high; a family of three gets $694 per month ($231 per person). But place those children in foster care and the foster parent will get a monthly minimum of $329 for each child. And, unlike welfare payments, the foster-care payment rises with the child's age. If a child is at least twelve, for example, the monthly payment is $423. And if the child is a little hard to handle, the foster parent gets an extra $175 per month. If the child is placed in a modern-day orphanage, the cost is much higher. Group-home rates in California typically run between $1,500 to $3,000 per month.[13] And, as noted in the previous chapter, a facility like Montrose costs $3,300 per month.

Where "preventive services" are offered at all, they are geared to the needs of child savers, not children. In the vast majority of cases, the only service offered is "counseling."[14] At best, counseling means that poor parents who need day care or better housing to keep their families together instead have to find extra money for a baby-sitter and bus or subway fare so they can go to a therapist's office and make the therapist feel useful by discussing their "deep seated" problems. At worst, "counseling" is a euphemism for offering nothing at all.

Counseling by competent therapists has helped millions of people overcome all sorts of problems. There are undoubtedly many cases where mental health problems do lead to abuse or neglect, and in such cases counseling is essential. And even when the problem is poverty, counseling can supplement more important services and help a family to cope. "Parent education" that is not patronizing and truly helps parents help themselves can also be a real benefit. But it is absurd to make these "soft" services the only attempt, or even the primary attempt, to preserve troubled families. The notion that nearly all families labeled neglectful need a lifetime of deep, intensive therapy is a myth that keeps a lot of child savers employed but does nothing for children.

A review of data the state of Louisiana was required to collect to comply with federal law gives some idea of just how far the reality of "preventive services" is from the theory. Among the findings:

—Two-thirds of the children were placed in foster care with no attempt to provide preventive services beforehand.

—Once in care, one-quarter of the children who were supposed to be returned home had needs identified for which no services were provided.

—Half the children in institutions did not need to be there, according to the state's own criteria.

—In more than half the cases, caseworkers did not visit children in care as often as required by law.

—One-quarter of the cases did not have the court reviews required by law; in New Orleans, this figure was over 50 percent.

—Where court reviews did take place, court orders for services were ignored in one-quarter of the cases.[15]

Susan Carter of the National Association of Foster Care Reviewers says there are three key problems in foster care: Either there is no plan for what to do with a child once the child is in care, there is a plan but there are no services, or the child never should have gone into foster care in the first place. Says Carter, "One of those three things happens in just about every case."[16]

All this leads, of course, to one fundamental question. Of the hundreds of thousands of children in foster care, how many could have stayed at home had services been available? Obviously, it is a question that is impossible to answer definitively. Any estimate of "what might have been" is inherently subjective. And the answer will vary in different parts of the country, since placement rates vary widely. The best that can be done is to canvass the educated guesses of the people who work in or study the system day in and day out and get their uncoerced ballpark estimates.

"Ninety percent of the cases . . . could be handled in the home with good quality workers doing good work," says Peter Strubel, who trained CPS workers in Colorado until he quit, fed up with the "indiscriminate" use of foster care.[17] At the other end of the scale, even Irwin Levin, the CPS supervisor in New York who generally favors sweeping laws and coercive intervention, says 25 percent of the children in foster care could be home if services were available. Nationwide, that would mean that, at any given moment, at least 90,000 children in foster care don't need to be there. And Levin's estimate is probably far too low. Lisa Clampitt, the former CPS worker in Manhattan, believes up to half the children placed in foster care are removed unnecessarily. Douglas Besharov believes "a majority" could be safely left at home if services were provided.[18]

In Los Angeles, lawyers at Public Counsel reviewed every abuse and neglect petition filed in that county during one week in 1987. They concluded that 30 percent were so groundless they never should have been filed at all. The director of Public Counsel's Children's Rights Project, Pamela Mohr, estimates that another 20 percent could be safely left home if their parents received welfare payments as high as what California foster parents get. And another 10 percent could be home with additional services, for a total of 60 percent.

The estimate from Diane Redleaf of the Legal Assistance Foundation of Chicago: 25 to 50 percent; from Charles Gershensohn of the Center for the Study of Social Policy: 70 percent; from Ben Wolf of the Illinois Civil Liberties Union: 55 to 90 percent, an estimate he says is based on comments made to him off-the-record by people in the system itself. Dennis Lepak, the California probation officer, estimates that even among children referred to the criminal-justice system half could be home if services were available.

One of those in the best position to offer an estimate is Peter Forsythe, Director of the Program for Children at the Edna McConnell Clark Foundation. Few good things happen in child welfare, but when they do, the Clark Foundation has usually put up the money for them. The Program for Children specializes in funding and evaluating programs designed to keep families together and avoid foster care. Forsythe is in a unique position to see what is being done and what can be done all over the country. He estimates that family-preservation programs could keep 50 to 70 percent of the children now in foster care safely at home.[19]

Of course the child savers don't see it this way. Whenever the foster-care population surges upward—as it is now—they have an excuse for it. It's always something beyond their control, and it's always the fault either of the parents, the children, or both. The latest trendy answer is drugs.

When the panic over child abuse met the panic over drug abuse, it was a marriage made in child saver heaven.

As this is written, we are in the midst of a media feeding frenzy over drugs. Americans can't pick up a newspaper or magazine or turn on their television sets without hearing about a nation "at war" with drug abuse. Stories carry headlines like: "Children Go Hungry as Food Stamps Feed Drug Habits, Vice."[20] If the public is under the impression that every foster child was born a crack baby, and every parent who loses a child to foster care is an addict, it's understandable. As long as the public is bombarded with such messages, who's going to argue with child savers who throw up their hands and say, "Of course we hate to see all these children coming into foster care, but what can we do? It's those drugs, you know."

This is another one of those cases where the child savers are not entirely wrong. Of course drug abuse is responsible for part of the increase in foster care. Cocaine and its cheap derivative, crack, are undeniable menaces. But their role also needs to be put into perspective. Statistics about drug abuse suffer from the same hype and distortion as statistics about child abuse.

It has repeatedly been asserted in news accounts that there are 375,000 newborns affected by parental drug abuse every year.[21] Since the number generally appears in stories about "crack babies," the public is left with the impression that, every year, 375,000 babies are born addicted to crack. But this number is a projection from a small survey of mostly big-city hospitals, which see a higher-than-average number of drug-abusing parents. More important, the survey asked only for the number of children born to mothers who had used any drug of any kind—including marijuana— to any extent during their pregnancy. It did not ask if the babies were born addicted or with any other ill-effects, and it was not limited to crack. Thus, in coming up with the statement that 375,000 newborns are "affected," crack babies are lumped in with perfectly normal children of mothers who may have occasionally smoked marijuana.

Douglas Besharov, the former director of the National Center on Child Abuse and Neglect, estimates that out of nearly four million babies born every year, the real number of crack babies is 30,000 to 50,000.[22] This figure is alarming enough, certainly, but it is only 10 to 14 percent of the total commonly used in news accounts. Even if one believes, as Besharov does, that parents who are full-blown crack addicts are largely hopeless and their parental rights should almost always be terminated, the number of such cases is not nearly enough to justify child saver claims that there is nothing they can do about all the children in foster care.

No place has been hit harder by the drug problem than New York City. In 1985, about 1,200 babies were born to drug-using mothers (again, that figure includes all illegal drugs, not just cocaine). By 1989, the number had soared to 4,800. But during that same period, the number of children in foster care more than doubled, from fewer than 17,000 to an estimated 38,000. Obviously, they can't all be crack babies.[23]

Of course, drug abuse can lead to foster care in other ways as well. But here, too, data indicate that the problem is serious and growing, but it is also exaggerated by the child savers. In 1989, the city expected to receive 10,271 allegations of child maltreatment involving drug abuse. On the one hand, this is almost four times as many such reports as in 1986. On the other hand, it still represents fewer than one-sixth of all child maltreatment reports in the city.[24]

A look at the city's foster-care population over the last fifteen years also puts the drug issue in perspective. The city's foster-care population reached a peak in 1975, with nearly 30,000 children in care.[25] The city's child savers insisted that there was nothing they could do. Of course, no child was placed in foster care unless it was absolutely necessary, they said. By 1981, the foster-care population was down to about 25,000.[26] This time, the child savers were absolutely sure it couldn't go any lower. Monsignor Robert Arpie, Child Care Director of Catholic Charities of the Archdiocese of New York declared that "only the most troubled youngsters are coming into care."[27] Yet by 1984, the foster-care population had fallen below 17,000.[28] Now, the foster-care population has soared again. But it was not until 1988 that it passed the 30,000 mark achieved back in 1975. And the current figures include placements with relatives, an option not available in the 1970s. If the reason the number is so high now is drugs, what was the cause in 1975, when no one had even heard of crack?

David Tobis, an expert on New York City's foster-care system at Welfare Research Inc., argues that the increase in the total number of children in the city system at any one time doesn't result from large numbers of new children coming into care. It results from so few children leaving care. In the wake of the drug scare, the pressure has been taken off child saving agencies, so they can keep children in care longer. They can also return children home without providing adequate after-care services, leading to an increase in the number of children who come back into care.[29] National data also show an increase in repeat placements.[30] The longer stays and the higher recidivism rate increase the number of children in care at any one time and overcrowd the system.

Other data also cast doubt on the drug-abuse hypothesis. The federal government's 1985 national survey found that in New York twenty-six out of every 10,000 children came into foster care at some point during that year, just one more than the national average. California was a little above average at thirty-two, but still far below states that had much less of a drug problem. The highest placement rate in the nation, at eighty-five— more than three times the national average—was Washington State, surely not the drug capital of America.[31] (Oregon would have been even higher had it not massaged its numbers as described earlier.)

Other disparities are even more striking. The placement rate in Minnesota, forty-four per 10,000, was nearly double that of neighboring Wisconsin at twenty-four per 10,000. Vermont, also at forty-four, was almost double Maine at twenty-six. South Dakota sent seventy-one children out of every 10,000 into foster care in 1985, Utah sent only fifteen. The lowest rate was in Texas with only six children placed for every 10,000. The rate of placement in Washington State was fourteen times higher than the rate of placement in Texas.

Of course, few people had even heard of crack in 1985. But people had heard of drugs. Yet the numbers for states with major drug problems often were lower than states that did not have such severe problems.

Even now, the rate of placement for children in the states hit hardest by crack, New York and California, is lower than the rate for Washington State back in 1985. (And the placement rate in Washington State is higher now because of the foster-care panic discussed in Chapter 4.)

Some of this can be accounted for by shoddy record-keeping and the games states play when they report their numbers to the federal government. But the disparities are too frequent and too glaring to be attributed to that alone.

Charles Gershensohn used to head the Evaluation Branch of the federal government's Administration for Children, Youth, and Families, the agency that compiled this data. Gershensohn says the disparities among states proves that the use of foster care has very little to do with drug abuse or anything else that is objectively wrong with a family. "The determining factors of children going into placement and leaving placement have more to do with the sociology of the community than factors of the child and the family," Gershensohn says.[32]

Data that will be discussed later in this chapter concerning how placement rates have varied over time during the twentieth century also show no relationship between placement rates and family problems.

What all this suggests is what numerous experts have observed by watching their foster-care systems firsthand: By and large, child maltreatment cases related to drug abuse are not replacing less serious cases that don't belong in the system, they are coming in on top of those cases.[33] Even Paul Jensen, a deputy commissioner of New York's Child Welfare Administration, has contradicted his bosses and acknowledged that "the systemic problems were there prior to crack and they will continue whether we are able to address the crack problem or not."[34]

Rather than being the primary cause of increased foster care, the very real problem of drug abuse has become a smoke screen child savers have used to take the pressure off them to keep families together—something they never really wanted to do and only did when that intense public and legal pressure was on. In fact, hysteria over drug abuse has allowed the child savers to expand their domain into families where they would otherwise have no excuse for butting in.

When people hear statistics about drug abuse, mothers, and babies, chances are the images that come to mind do not involve women like Theresa. Theresa lives in Nassau County on New York's Long Island. She was thrilled to learn she was pregnant in October 1987. She immediately called South Nassau Communities Hospital for a prenatal-care appointment. Although they couldn't see her until December 10, she took precautions on her own, even quitting her job as a bartender to avoid all the secondhand smoke. According to her doctor, Theresa kept all her prenatal-care appointments conscientiously and wouldn't even take an aspirin without checking with him first.

Indeed, Theresa made only two mistakes. Mistake number one: At her first prenatal-care appointment, she admitted she had smoked marijuana before she knew she was pregnant. She raised the issue herself because she was fearful for her unborn child. But, because of her admission, hospital policy required that the baby be tested at birth to see whether there were any drugs in his system. Had Theresa lied to her doctor, or merely kept silent, she would have had no problem.

Theresa made her second mistake just hours before the baby's birth. The pain of labor was excruciating, but the hospital said she wasn't ready to be admitted. She was getting "nervous and tense" because "it was my first baby. I really didn't know what it was all about." Theresa says a friend who is a registered nurse told her it wouldn't hurt the baby if she smoked a marijuana cigarette to relax. Unaware of either the upcoming drug test or its consequences, she did so.

The hospital social worker reported the test result to Child Protective Services. She said she did so only because state law forced her to. She did not think a referral was appropriate, and she did not believe the baby was at risk with his mother. But, because this baby was born in Nassau County, that didn't matter. In the wake of the national drug-abuse hysteria, the county adopted a policy that applies to any child whose system shows any sign of any illegal drug: automatic confiscation of the baby at birth— or at least before mother and child leave the hospital. The child may or may not be returned after a subsequent investigation.

The policy draws no distinction between a baby born addicted to crack and Theresa's child, who was born perfectly normal. Nassau's policy is: Take the baby first, ask questions later.

Theresa sued, and while an appeal was pending, the county gave her her child back.

The attorney from the Nassau County Attorney's office who defended the policy, Patricia Carroll, said her bosses would not let her release any court documents it filed rebutting the facts as described by Theresa and her lawyers, even with names deleted. Although there is no rule or law prohibiting such release and though the case was slated for argument before an appellate court that routinely publishes its rulings, the County Attorney's office claimed it would somehow violate "confidentiality." Child savers do this routinely when their behavior is questioned. Carroll recommended that I get the county's court papers from Theresa's attorney. Those papers largely confirm Theresa's account of what happened.[35]

Carroll said she successfully got the appellate court to dismiss the case as moot after the child was returned. She acknowledged she did that, in part, because "it was not one of our stronger cases."

In general, the county argues that any mother who has used drugs of any kind in any way during pregnancy has exercised judgment so poor that the newborn is automatically in sufficient danger to justify immediate removal. Then what about the "judgment" of mothers who are addicted to nicotine and ignore the explicit statement on cigarette packages that says: "Warning: Smoking by pregnant women may result in fetal injury, premature birth, and low birth weight"? Will we confiscate the child of every mother who smokes? What about the mother who drinks? No, not just alcoholics. Research indicates that only one drink a day during the early months of pregnancy may harm the unborn child.[36] Or the mother hooked on caffeine? Will we take away the babies of every mother who drinks too much coffee? And why stop with the unborn child? If it's poor judgment to smoke one marijuana cigarette, what about the judgment of tobacco-smoking parents who expose their children to eighteen years or more of secondhand smoke in the home?

In Theresa's case, the hospital was so appalled by the county's action that it kept the baby past the normal discharge date in the hope a court would intervene. But the court upheld the decision.

In one sense, Theresa was lucky. Her baby was temporarily placed with Theresa's mother, not with strangers. But during the crucial first days of her son's life, when parent and child have the best chance to form the emotional bonds that should last a lifetime, this mother was forced into a traumatic, frightening custody fight.

Infants recognize their mothers voices and take comfort from them virtually from birth. How do you explain to these infants why their mothers are not around for them? How do you explain that this is called "erring on the side of the child"?

Researchers have begun to view these first days and even hours as vitally important. It is part of the reason why hospitals now encourage mothers to keep their newborns with them and one of many reasons why breast-feeding now is encouraged. (Because her child was taken away and she didn't know when he would be returned, Theresa could not breast-feed him.)

Ray Helfer, the child saver who coined the word "parentectomy," has written, "When this sensitive period goes well the relationship between new parents and their newly born infant has the potential of progressing far beyond . . . expectations. . . . [W]hen this interaction goes poorly, a vicious cycle can develop when the infant and the new parent(s) do not engage, resulting in a degree of discontent and frustration which can lead to a breakdown in the interactions between [parent and newborn]."[37] Other researchers go further. Marshall Klaus and John Kennell write that "because the human infant is wholly dependent upon his mother or caretaker for all his physical and emotional needs, the strength of these attachment ties may well determine whether he will survive and develop optimally." Kennell and Klaus further believe that early separation of a newborn from his or her mother "may be a significant factor" in child abuse.[38]

None of this means that any newborn separated from his mother for any reason is doomed. If that were true there could be no such thing as a successful adoption, for example. It just means that social services commissioners should not go around deriding the very concept of bonding, as Nassau County's did in a letter to a newspaper.[39] And it means that Nassau County's child-confiscation policy is one more example of child savers jeopardizing the children they mean to help. It jeopardizes not only the children taken from their parents, but also many others by contributing to overcrowding in the county's foster-care system.

Nassau County's foster children stay in care longer and are bounced from home to home more often than the state average. In fact, children stay in care longer in Nassau County than they do in neighboring New York City. Caseloads are soaring while services lag behind. In 1988, Nassau County spent only $630,000 on preventive services. Upstate Monroe County, with only half of Nassau's population, spent $7 million. Crowding in the foster-care system is so severe that Nassau County has its own boarder babies.[40]

Nassau County is not the only place where fear of drugs has become an excuse for more child saving. A policy similar to Nassau County's is now state law in Florida. The law is the main reason one Miami hospital has twenty to thirty boarder babies in care every day.[41]

In Massachusetts, the usual search for cheap ways to placate the public after the highly publicized death of a child has led to new rules requiring a child-protective investigation of any report of any form of suspected drug or alcohol abuse, domestic violence, or criminal activity.[42] Yet, even as these guidelines were taking effect, millions of dollars were being cut from the budget for services for poor families.[43]

As Robert Moro, the caseworkers' union leader has pointed out, this means CPS must investigate whenever "a neighbor smells marijuana, overhears an argument, or reads about a recent arrest in the local newspaper." Moro notes that, had these guidelines been in effect when their children were younger, a CPS worker would have been dispatched to the home of Governor Michael Dukakis because of his wife's alcoholism and her twenty-six-year addiction to diet pills.[44] Were she a Massachusetts resident, a caseworker would also have had to check out the first honorary chairwoman of the National Committee for Prevention of Child Abuse—Betty Ford.

If drug abuse doesn't account for most of the recent rise in the use of foster care, what does? Two things. First, as we have seen, it's what child savers want to do. Second, because it is what child savers want to do, it is where the money is and always has been. This is illustrated by the history of foster care in the twentieth century.

A high point in foster-care placement in this country was reached in 1933, when fifty-nine out of every 10,000 children nationwide were in foster care. But, beginning in 1935, the placement rate suddenly dropped sharply, even though the nation was in the midst of the great depression. The reason is simple enough. Nineteen thirty-five was the year that Aid to Families with Dependent Children (AFDC) became law. Beginning that year, help to families in their own homes was partially reimbursed by the federal government, while foster care was still paid for by states, local governments, and private charities.

By 1960, the placement rate was down to thirty-eight per 10,000 children.

Yet by 1977 it had soared to seventy-five per 10,000. This happened during a period that was largely prosperous. Why? Because in 1962 Congress created a program under which AFDC payments followed the child into foster care. What's more, these funds were, and are, unlimited. The federal government still pays from 50 to 78 percent of the cost of foster care for poor children.

In 1980, Congress passed the Adoption Assistance and Child Welfare Act. The law said that federal reimbursement for foster care would be contingent on states first making "reasonable efforts" to keep children out of care. It also included a series of provisions designed to cap foster-care payments after increasing federal aid for preventive services. I believe this is the major reason for the drop in foster care during the early 1980s.

But, the year after this law was passed, Ronald Reagan became president. After failing to get the law repealed outright, the Reagan administration virtually abandoned enforcement efforts and never allowed preventive services funding to rise enough to trigger the cap on dollars for foster care. Funding for preventive services remained meager, while for foster care it remained an open spigot. In 1989, it is estimated that the federal government spent, at most, $124 million on preventive services. It spent more than $1 billion on foster care.[45]

Because of the Reagan-administration sabotage, the federal law has barely been worth the paper it's printed on. By the mid-1980s, the child savers noticed this. They knew the pressure was off. And once again foster-care rates are rising.[46]

Where counties are in charge of foster care, the same sort of incentives are often replicated in their relationship with the state. The results are seen in California, where the state tried to pass legislation controlling foster care but failed to change the financial incentives. The law failed, largely, I believe because California continues to reimburse counties between 95 and 97.5 cents for every foster-care dollar. For the people making the decisions, foster care is virtually free. For preventive services, counties get back 75 cents if the program is financed by the State Department of Social Services—but only until they hit a dollar ceiling. As with federal dollars, California dollars for preventive services are capped, but California foster-care dollars are limitless.[47]

According to Dennis Lepak, other agencies, like probation departments, that want to use preventive services get back zero.[48] Says Lepak: "Many probation wards who could stay in homes and receive services with their families are removed to make them eligible for state foster-care funds and the services those funds can make available. . . ."[49] [There is] a bottomless pit of placement money available for the asking. . . . All the incentives push the worker to remove the child . . . reasons are rationalized and families are broken."[50]

When the financial incentive is combined with what child savers are inclined to do anyway—take people's children away—the combination is unstoppable.

No change in law or in anything else is as vitally important to protecting children from foster care as is changing the financial incentives built into the system.

And this change can't be limited to the public sector.

In 1979, New York State changed its reimbursement system for local governments administering child-welfare services. The state made provision of preventive services as attractive as foster care. This helped to some extent. As noted earlier, the use of foster care in New York State dropped substantially. As bad as things are now in the state, they would be far worse had this change not been made. But several factors limited the effectiveness of this change.

—Prevention was only made equally attractive financially. Overcoming the ingrained habits of generations of child saving requires that prevention be much more attractive.

—As noted earlier, decisions on how to spend preventive-services dollars were made by the child savers themselves. The result was a lot of money wasted on "counseling."

—The services were not carefully targeted to children at imminent risk of foster-care placement. Families in need were helped, but not necessarily the families who needed help the most.

—Most important, the change in the law changed only the financial incentives for government. They did not touch the incentives for the scores of private child saving agencies that have a stranglehold on the child-welfare system in New York City—and that are part of the child-welfare systems in Chicago, Philadelphia, and other cities. Though they are run by private organizations, these agencies owe their existence almost entirely to public dollars from contracts with local governments.

In New York City, for example, child saving agencies are paid on a per diem basis. They get a fixed daily amount for each child. If the agency goes through the difficult process of returning a child home and succeeds, the reimbursement stops. If the agency goes through the equally difficult process of terminating parental rights and placing a child in an adoptive home, it gets a one-time flat fee. The easiest course of action—warehousing children in foster care—is also the most remunerative. The money keeps rolling in day after day after day.

Of course, the agencies get apoplectic when this is pointed out. All the agencies insist they never even notice the financial incentives when deciding what to do with the children in their care—all of them, that is, except one, which confessed in 1974.

A report by the Edwin Gould Foundation for Children stated, "The main reason for the lack of increased adoptions is that the reimbursement rate is still not high enough. . . . This fee level motivates many agencies to retain children in foster care, rather than place them in adoptive homes. . . . *[Agencies] may be forced to compromise the child's interests if the financial viability of the agency itself is threatened*" (emphasis added). The report goes on to state that agencies must keep their beds constantly filled to capacity with foster children in order to cover their overhead.[51]

"The per diem rate is an incentive to keep kids in care," says David Tobis, who tried to change the system when he was on the staff of former City Council President Carol Bellamy. "They keep kids in care to cover their expenses."[52]

Peter Forsythe, the director of the Clark Foundation's Program for Children, also cites financial incentives as a reason for overuse of foster care.[53] And Irwin Levin, the maverick CPS supervisor, put it this way: "The social work community lives off child abuse."[54]

But the best evidence of the influence of financing on keeping children trapped in foster care came from a man who was trying to deny this influence.

In 1976, the late Joseph Gavrin, then Executive Director of New York's Council of Family and Child Caring Agencies, drew this analogy: "It's also true of hospitals that they only get paid when the patient is in the bed, but that doesn't mean that hospitals don't try to get the patient out just as quickly as they can. And the same thing is true of the foster care agencies."[55] But in the intervening years, study after study has shown that, in fact, the amount of time patients spend in the hospital is dependent on whether hospitals are paid for every day they keep the patient. In fact, the evidence was so overwhelming that, in the years since Gavrin drew his analogy, the federal government stopped using a per diem system for reimbursing hospitals under Medicare. Presumably, Gavrin's analogy cuts both ways.

*   *   *

The private child saving system is also a cauldron of racial and religious bigotry, just as it was in the nineteenth century.

In New York City, that bigotry is another tragic legacy of Charles Loring Brace. In the nineteenth century, Catholics and Jews had to form their own agencies in order to protect Catholic and Jewish children from being stolen and shipped out to Protestant homes in the south and midwest by Brace's Children's Aid Society. Eventually, the Catholic and Jewish agencies grew to dominate the city's child-welfare system.

In the decades following World War II, the agencies got almost all of their money from the city, but they insisted on giving first preference to "their own." At the same time, the population in need of help was changing, with the greatest need among black Protestant children. Only after the wealthier Jewish and Catholic agencies had taken care of "their own" would they let any of these children in. Most black Protestant children wound up in the child-care equivalent of the back of the bus: overcrowded facilities run by inferior agencies that lacked the resources of the dominant groups.

The lengths to which agencies would go to restrict help to only "their own kind" was astounding. An administrator at the New York Foundling Hospital (the agency Vincent Fontana works for) testified that at least until the 1960s, when agency staff were unsure of a baby's race, they would take the baby to an anthropologist at the Museum of Natural History for a determination.[56] That practice may not have been stopped until the 1970s, when the anthropologist died.[57]

Agencies were also anxious to know exactly how dark a black newborn would be. It was believed that at birth the true skin color of black babies was most apparent in the genital area. So until sometime in the 1960s, workers went around taking the diapers off black babies to check out the color of their genitals.[58]

One would have thought discrimination would have abated as the number of white children in the system declined. No such luck. Agencies still fight for the remaining white children, and when they run out of whites they prefer light-skinned blacks. A court-ordered study of case records and interviews with workers found that the case records agencies read before deciding to take a child are filled with references to the children's complexions. "[The private agencies] always ask about skin shade," said one worker. "They will refuse children if they think the kid is too dark." "Agencies have vacancies, but not for dark black children," said another worker. "They also ask what kind of hair does this kid have? Is it kinky, is it straight, is it coarse?"[59]

The director of the ACLU's Children's Rights Project, Marcia Robinson Lowry, filed a lawsuit challenging this discrimination in 1973. The suit was finally settled in 1988, but, as of January 1990, Lowry said, the city and the agencies were not complying with the settlement. John Cardinal O'Connor said defending the right to discriminate had cost the Catholic agencies "a fortune"[60]—money that, presumably, could have been spent to help children.

Malcolm Bush found the same reluctance to take black children in Chicago. His data show that blacks are grossly underrepresented in private agency facilities. He quotes a former agency director who says Catholic Charities of Chicago blocked the creation of a public child-welfare agency in Illinois until the child-welfare problem became "too big and too black," and they wanted more of the black children taken off their hands. If this discrimination resulted in leaving the black children home, it might have done some good. But the black children simply got inferior foster care— or in some cases, jail.[61]

What it boils down to is this: Private child saving agencies have been among the last bastions of racism in the twentieth century. Their philosophy has been: We will take care of our own kind and for all we care other children can rot. Any agency that purports to be helping children but does not view all children as "their own kind" lacks the fundamental human decency to be involved with children.

There is another kind of discrimination practiced by child saving agencies. It is a practice commonly known as "creaming" (as in skimming the cream), in which the private agencies take the children who actually need help the least and discriminate against children they consider "difficult."

This has been a major contributor to the "overnighter" problem. Those hours spent each night trying to find a place for these children are often spent on the phone with private agencies who won't take them because they are considered too "difficult." New York City officials have practically begged the private agencies to send representatives to the makeshift shelters to look the children over so they'll see that the children really aren't so bad.[62]

Workers trying to place children have found that agencies sometimes keep vacancies secret, revealing them only to placement workers who can be trusted to send only children those agencies like. Conversely, agencies will reject children just because they were referred by a worker who has sent them "difficult" children in the past.[63]

Lowry says the two forms of discrimination are interrelated. Sometimes agencies use racial or religious grounds as an excuse to avoid taking difficult children, other times they say a child is too difficult to avoid a child of the "wrong" ethnic background.

Again, the problem is not unique to New York. A Philadelphia study found, "Some social workers and supervisors believe that many [private agencies], responding to a 'provider market,' accept only clients who are less difficult to serve."[64] A Florida study noted, "Many group and residential facilities are private organizations that have the ability to reject children proposed for placement, requiring caseworkers to 'shop around' for a facility willing to serve the children."[65] And in California, says Dennis Lepak, group homes engage in a different kind of creaming: Many won't take a child unless the county agrees to keep him or her in the group home for at least a year,[66] a demand that obviously flies in the face of efforts to reunite families as soon as possible.

In Chicago, a survey of five private agencies, conducted by one of those agencies, found that, on average, the agencies turned down more than half the children state workers asked them to take.[67] A Chicago worker trying to place children complained, "I only have teenagers and black babies and . . . they will take only young kids and white kids."[68]

A study Malcolm Bush conducted of case records in Chicago found that one child was rejected by four different agencies for the following reasons: Agency 1: "He is a behavior problem." Agency 2: "He is not retarded enough. He is too old." Agency 3: "He is too dangerous." Agency 4: "He is too young." Reasons given in other cases included: "He is not the best kind of child for our institution," or "she looks less appropriate than other candidates." The most common all-purpose excuse, Bush writes, is "structure." The agency simply says the child needs "more structure" or "less structure" and it is off the hook.[69]

Joseph Gavrin's counterpart in Chicago, Bob Ralls, Executive Director of the Child Care Association of Illinois, told Bush, "The private agencies are voluntary and they stand for a certain ideology. Some of them are sectarian and some of them have other ideologies, and as such they have a right to pick and choose."[70] Ralls did not mention that the "private" agencies run their foster-care programs with public dollars.

The notion that private agencies would behave so cruelly is hard for most people to accept. People understand why a corporation would pollute the environment in order to increase its profits, but child-care agencies are almost always nonprofit. Why would they mimic the most irresponsible corporate behavior? The question reflects a misunderstanding of the nature of nonprofit organizations in general and child saving organizations in particular.

Part of the reason it seems hard to believe that nonprofit agencies put their financial interests first is that the idea is often presented in terms of a conscious conspiracy. That's not how it happens. As any nonprofit organization matures, it is easy for it to lose sight of its original goal. Keeping the organization going, which once was a means to an end, becomes an end in itself.

I spent many years in the nonprofit sector of journalism—public television. Public television stations were often founded by people dedicated to bringing the public an alternative to what commercial stations had to offer. Yet increasingly such stations shy away from controversial programming, bump unpopular programs out of prime time, and run reruns of old commercial television series to build ratings. During a "pledge drive," one station I know of actually went on the air and told little children that if they didn't go get mommy and daddy and bring them to the TV to listen to their pleas for more money, the station might take away Sesame Street!

Slowly and subtly, this station had forgotten its original mission. Self-preservation had become an end in itself—and the end justified the means.

The child saving agency that acknowledges even to itself that it is placing its own interest first and the children second is extremely rare. Instead they construct elaborate rationalizations. We're not creaming, they say, we're *specializing*. And by using the medical model described in Chapter 3, they convince themselves that they are performing a useful service by "treating" these "sick" children. Bush found that child savers' case records are written "to deny the failure of interventions, to justify the refusal to serve 'bad clients,' and to justify the decision to extend hegemony over 'good' clients." This is accomplished in part, Bush writes, by:

> translating the language of ordinary men into a quasi-professional language which establishes the profession's hegemony over the client. [For example:]
> "This is a rather immature, impulse-ridden boy who does, however, respond to predictable external controls. The inability to control rather primitive aggressive impulses unless he were exposed to an understanding but firm and neutral environment does indicate the need for placement in a boarding school with reality-oriented rewards for acceptable functioning and immediate delivery of negative reinforcement for unacceptable aspects of his behavior."
> In short, the boy behaves badly, needs to be praised when he does well and punished when he misbehaves. The common language description of the problem, however, could put the solution in the hands of nonprofessionals. . . . The translation . . . steers the boy to the specialized services of the . . . agency.

In another case, an agency described a child who was doing extremely well without their "help" as actually being "sneaky and manipulative and in working with him one needs to look beyond the face value of his actions."[71]

For the child savers there is an additional reason to prefer "good" clients. As earlier chapters have shown, they have an enormous need for power over others. Bush sums it up this way:

> The reluctance of some private agencies to take difficult children does raise a crucial question about the definition of "private." When it allows an agency to accept public money while shunning responsibility for those who most need help, privateness is reduced to the protection of a comfortable existence. At the extreme, it becomes an exercise in self-gratification. The client exists to make the helper feel good; clients who cannot perform that role are rejected. At this point privateness loses all trace of civic responsibility and wears its most offensive face—the protection of privilege, or the privilege of enjoying the role of helper, while ignoring those who need the most help.[72]

If that seems too harsh, recall the words of the report from the private agency in New York City: "[Agencies] may be forced to compromise the child's interests if the financial viability of the agency itself is threatened."

Not all private agencies are inherently bad. The Homebuilders program, which I will describe in Chapter 10, was originally developed by a private, sectarian agency in Washington State from which it has since been "spun off." Private agencies can be an important source of innovation. They should be an adjunct to a strong public child-welfare system. But they must never be allowed to control it.

Even as agencies reject children who are "too difficult," child savers insist that they can't be expected to do any better because all the children they care for have become incredibly difficult to handle. (If blaming the parents doesn't work, blame the child.) Thus, they will say things like, "In general the children's problems are more difficult because increasingly they reflect the parent's inability or refusal to act for other than economic reasons . . . an increasing number are coming with scars in the form of serious behavior and emotional problems resulting from broken homes and parental irresponsibility."[73]

Once again, this is not entirely false. Obviously, as the problems faced by children increase, more of them will have more difficulty coping. But insisting that the children are tougher is also both a useful all-purpose excuse and a way to enhance the child savers' own prestige. It should be taken with a grain of salt—especially when one considers that the statement quoted above was made in 1949.

*   *   *

The foster-care tragedy is still another example of child savers trying to do good and having it backfire horribly. And once again, it is the children who really have been maltreated who are hurt the most.

Seriously maltreated children are those most in need of therapy and other forms of help. Yet that help is delayed or denied as resources are diverted to investigation of false reports and to unnecessary placement. Such children are also likely to be least desirable to agencies that "skim the cream" and turn away the rest, making them the most likely to wind up as overnighters.

Where children really have been seriously maltreated and where their parents are unable or unwilling to change, parental rights should be permanently terminated and the children should be placed in permanent adoptive homes. But the child savers have wound up making that more difficult as well.

Child savers often complain about the reluctance of judges to terminate parental rights. Often this reluctance is engendered by the judges' understanding of foster care. If judges could have confidence that children came into foster care only after intensive preventive services had been tried and failed; if they could have confidence that serious efforts had been made to reunify the family after placement, then they could feel comfortable about severing the legal relationship between parent and child forever. But judges know that's not true. They know children are thrown into foster care for little reason or no reason at all. And they know that both the children and their parents are largely abandoned after placement. And that's why many of them are so reluctant to terminate parental rights.

"There is definitely a connection between whether enough is done on the front end and whether you can terminate parental rights," says Susan Carter of the National Association of Foster Care Reviewers. "If the judge knows that everything has been done properly [to try to preserve the family] but it failed, he will feel better that at least he is making the right choice."[74]

Even when the judges are willing, the child savers often aren't ready. Because resources have been diverted to handle false reports and unnecessary placement, less time and fewer staff are available for adoptions. The results have included long delays in termination proceedings in Washington State and Philadelphia and dramatic drops in adoptive placements in New York City and Los Angeles. More than half the boarder babies studied by the New York City comptroller's office in 1989 were still in foster-care limbo, neither returned home nor adopted, four years after their birth.[75] Even when they were abandoned at birth, the study found that often, no effort had been made to terminate parental rights. In Philadelphia, "There is so much emergency work, these adoptions just don't get done," according to one of the lawyers who is supposed to do them.[76]

Often, the flooding of the system is a direct result of the defensive social work discussed earlier. "There's a public relations reason why agencies like this remove lots of children who don't have to be removed," says Benjamin Wolf. As so many others have pointed out, Wolf says they are terrified of the public reaction if they leave one child in his or her home and something goes wrong. But they know that thousands can suffer in foster care and no one will notice.

That is what happened in Washington State after Eli Creekmore died at the hands of his father and the system panicked, leading to a sudden, massive increase in foster-care placements. Suddenly, the foster-care system in little Washington State, which doesn't have a city with more than 470,000 people in it, began to bear a scary resemblance to New York City:

—A state report found that 30 percent of the petitions filed in the Seattle area seeking foster-care placement were for children who didn't need to be in foster care.[77]

—Children are routinely spending their days in offices while caseworkers search desperately for someplace to put them. "I can remember waiting to find a home with a baby in my arms, doing phone work, hoping the baby wasn't going to cry," said one caseworker.

—Children are being separated from siblings and moved far from their parents. Foster children from Everett, Eli Creekmore's hometown, are now placed at the far end of the next county, at least forty miles away.

—Children are becoming nomads. A teenager who was released from a juvenile detention center into foster care "seemed to be really trying [to turn his life around]," according to his caseworker. "But by the time we moved him for the fourth time in ten days, he'd lost it. He stopped trying to cooperate." He wound up back in the detention center. Another worker moved a well-behaved ten-year-old three times in a week because three children with serious problems had no place else to go. "That's a form of child abuse," said the worker. "Child abuse by the system."

—Caseloads have become unmanageable. A rule requiring monthly visits between caseworkers and children in care is routinely ignored. "It's an excellent idea and we should do it, but nobody does," said one worker. "We don't even give it lip service."

"I have a sixteen-year-old who came onto my caseload four months ago, and I have never seen the child," said another worker. "The brush fire isn't quite high enough. . . . I just hope it doesn't blow up."

—Children are put in inappropriate settings. One worker placed a boy she believed was dangerous with a family who had a younger child. "I felt really nervous about it and I told the parents," she said, "but that was the only placement that was available."

—Children who should be adopted wait a year for lawyers to get a termination petition together because they are too busy handling all the new children coming into foster care.[78]

We know what will happen to many of these children. Some will grow up to join the ranks of America's homeless. Some will become "emotional pulp." Some will fill our jails. But they will suffer in obscurity. No one will mourn for them like an entire state mourned for Eli Creekmore and an entire nation mourned for Lisa Steinberg. No one will be held accountable for their fate. No one will change any laws because of what will happen to them. No one will demand that we "err on the side of the child" by keeping more children *out* of foster care.

"If a parent abuses their child, if they neglect their child, if they abandon their child, they can be hauled into a court of law and penalized," says Anne Williamson, the former foster child. "As far as I'm concerned, the agencies should be in the same position. . . . As far as I can see, they violate the child abuse laws more than anyone else.

"To have a caseworker [hardly ever] see you . . . that's neglect. . . . If they just let me hang in foster care because for whatever reason they don't want to be bothered to find me a real home that I can call my own, that nobody can take me out of, that's abuse.

"But what can you do to them? Why shouldn't I have the right to make them account for what they do?"

9

System Failure

Even if innocent families never were harmed by the child-protective system, even if no child was ever wrongfully placed in foster care, and even if everyone agreed that the surrender of our civil liberties is worth the price, our present laws for protecting children still would suffer from one fundamental flaw: They don't work.

The child savers see the current laws as a trade-off. Says Jean Schafer, who ran the Child Protective Services system in Ohio: "I'd rather see a family disrupted than a bunch of dead children."[1] The child savers have managed to give us both.

The litany of failure is well known. Newspapers are filled with the stories of children who were known to Child Protective Services but died anyway. Either the child-protective system never knew how serious the problem was, or the child was returned to abusive parents and subsequently killed. Nationwide, 35 to 55 percent of all child-abuse deaths involve children previously known to Child Protective Services.[2] Such cases are the principal rationale for the child savers' constant pleas for more: Make even more people report, investigate even more innocent families, put more children into foster care more easily.

And every time there is a highly publicized death that's exactly what we do. Yet the deaths keep coming. It's time we learned that these cases don't mean we need to do more if it's going to be more of the same. In that sense, they mean we need to do less.

Some deaths can't be prevented, just as some crimes are impossible for authorities to prevent, and it's time the child savers admitted as much.

There will always be cases where there are no warning signs, or where those signs are apparent only with hindsight. But where a death or reinjury could have been prevented, certain factors are almost always present:

—The worker or workers handling the case had little education in child-protective work before they were hired, little or no training afterward, and little experience on the job.

—The workers were grossly overworked so they lacked the time for a thorough investigation. Or return of a child was predicated on providing certain services that the workers never had time to provide. Or they never even had time to monitor the family.

—A child saving bureaucracy grew so huge that communication broke down and no one knew who was doing what in the case.

Often, these factors are overlooked in the drive to find a scapegoat.

A lengthy news service report on factors contributing to a sensational child-abuse death in Florida did not mention until the next to last paragraph that one of the workers involved was carrying a caseload of forty-seven—nearly three times the number the Child Welfare League of America recommends. That information was considered so unimportant that editors receiving the story on their newswires were advised that it would be an excellent section to omit from their newspapers if they were short on space.[3] In a Mount Vernon, New York, case a child was returned to his mother with the stipulation that she be monitored with home visits twice a month. After the child died, it was disclosed that only one visit had taken place in six months.[4]

Almost all of the factors contributing to undiscovered abuse or to reabuse are a direct result of the system the child savers created. They have overwhelmed workers with false reports and trivial cases and flooded the foster-care system with children who don't need to be there.

Between 1981 and 1986, reports alleging abuse or neglect increased by 156 percent nationwide. State funds to deal with the problem increased by 2 percent.[5]

When child-protective workers have so many people tugging at their sleeves and yelling in their ears, how can the cry of one child in real need be heard over the din? Douglas Besharov, the former NCCAN director, writes:

> The system is so overburdened with cases of insubstantial or unproven risk to children that it does not respond forcefully to situations where children are in real danger. . . . We continue to squander scarce child protective resources on investigations of the ever-increasing number of unfounded reports. . . .
> Decision making also suffers. . . . After dealing with so many cases

of no real danger to children, caseworkers are desensitized to the obvious warning signals of immediate and serious danger.[6]

The criticism is not coming only from outsiders. In Massachusetts, Ed Malloy, a child-protective supervisor warns that the state's plans for even more intervention based on even less evidence "could significantly increase the risk to children in families where there is clear evidence of abuse and neglect by reducing resources and by reducing the time available to social workers to visit and help these families."[7]

*   *   *

For a child whose family is under investigation, for a child who has been abused, for a child in foster care, no one is more important than the caseworker. The child's future, sometimes his or her very life is at the worker's mercy. In a system that is effectively lawless, the caseworker is the law. The caseworker decides which child is mature enough to stay home alone after school and which child is not. The caseworker decides if the child care is "proper," if the home is "fit," and if the child's "well-being" is in jeopardy. Says Anne Williamson, the former foster child: "The caseworker is God."[8]

Yet caseworkers usually have none of the education, training, or support they need to do their jobs.

"The police department, the fire department, the ambulance service, all are emergency services, just like [Child Protective Services]," says Irwin Levin, the CPS supervisor in Brooklyn. But police officers and firefighters don't start on the job until they have gone through a rigorous training course—and received passing grades. They have to report in writing on everything they do, and their work is reviewed by trained supervisors. Says Levin: "None of that exists in Child Protective Services."[9]

The first thing to understand about child-protective workers is that, when you're lucky, you *don't* get what you pay for. CPS workers are expected to make life-and-death decisions as crucial as those of a surgeon, yet, in 1987, the estimated median salary for a child-protective worker was $20,952 per year. Ten states paid starting salaries of $15,000 or less. In comparison, the average salary for public relations people at state agencies was just under $27,000.[10]

In private agencies the pay can be worse. Nationwide, the median salary of social workers with master's degrees at private agencies is lower than the median for mail carriers and car salesmen. In New York City, the median pay for private-agency child-care workers is lower than the *entry level* salary for secretaries and toll collectors working for the state.[11]

For that kind of money, there's only so much you can demand in the way of education from the people you hire. Although people doing child-protective work are often referred to as "social workers," most states do not require their workers to have any social-work education before they are hired. Of forty-eight states responding to a 1985 nationwide survey by Kenneth Herrmann, Professor of Social Work at the State University of New York at Brockport in 1985, only four states required entry-level child-protective workers to have master's degrees in social work, and only twelve required even a bachelor's degree in social work. A bachelor's degree in anything was sufficient in twenty-two states. Three states required an associate's degree in anything, and the rest required a high-school education or had no educational requirement at all. A second survey, which obtained responses from twenty-six states and the City of New York, produced similar findings.[12]

In some cases, states that don't require a lot of education require that the people they hire have some sort of related experience—but usually not much. Herrmann's survey found only ten states that require more than two years of experience for any position. Two-thirds of the states require one year or less.[13] And experience is sometimes defined broadly. Lisa Clampitt got her job making life-and-death CPS decisions in New York City with a bachelor's degree in dramatic literature and eighteen months' experience as an editor for "Children's Express," a news service that uses children as reporters.[14]

At least five states require no educational background and no experience.[15]

And the trend has been in the wrong direction. According to Charles Gershensohn of the Center for the Study of Social Policy, in 1958 almost half of all child-welfare workers had master's degrees. Now it's down to 9 percent. CPS workers are "paid 'good neighbors' taking on family situations that most psychiatrists and psychologists would not tackle," Gershensohn says. "It's like asking a barber to do brain surgery."[16]

There is little on-the-job training to compensate for the lack of education and experience. When child-protective workers learn at all, they learn from their mistakes.

In Maryland, new caseworkers may be on the job for six months before they get any training.[17] In Michigan, only fifteen days of classroom instruction is offered—and none of it is mandatory.[18] A Philadelphia study found that "new workers may be assigned cases from the very beginning of their employment. Thus, a worker is frequently expected to conduct investigations and provide or arrange for services to families before receiving the training necessary to properly provide the services. . . . Supervisors bear the burden of training new social workers while juggling unassigned cases. Their options are to assign cases to workers too soon or risk catastrophes because some cases are not monitored."[19]

In California, "many county personnel currently performing child protective work have absolutely no professional training," according to Kim Thomas, legislative policy analyst for the California chapter of the National Association of Social Workers.[20]

A 1981 study of caseworkers in Wisconsin found that 23 percent of them had received no training in the state's Child Abuse and Neglect Act, 32 percent had no training in conducting investigations, and 39 percent learned no counseling techniques. Most of those who did get training got it only after they were already working with troubled families.[21]

New York City officials responded to repeated criticism of untrained workers by setting up a so-called "Child Protective Services Academy," where new employees get twenty days of training before going out on cases.

Lisa Clampitt went through the academy. "They started by saying: We're going to teach to the lowest common denominator so the stupidest people will understand. Any hopeful people would be bored and asleep." Clampitt says there was one message the academy taught over and over: "They would literally say it all through training: You have to cover your ass. Everyone's going to try and dump work on you and get you in trouble."

This lesson is reinforced on the job, according to a detailed study of Child Protective Services in New York City. Administrators interviewed for the study said, "CPS workers are governed by two principals: 1. Protect oneself in case of a fatality review and 2. Get rid of a case as soon as possible," preferably before thirty days, at which point the paperwork increases exponentially. Rather than cooperate with people responsible for providing services, protective workers are encouraged to rush each case off their desks and onto someone else's so, "If a child dies at least the record will show that they tried to hook the client up with services."[22]

There is one other noteworthy aspect of the so-called "academy." No one actually has to get a passing grade in anything in order to keep their jobs. Irwin Levin says there is no more accountability once employees are on the job. "No one ever gets a negative evaluation," Levin says.

Apparently, the New York City academy is not unusual. Says Larry Brown, Executive Director of the American Humane Association, "Training units often are the burial grounds for dying social workers."[23]

By the time her "training" was over, says Lisa Clampitt, "I felt incredibly unprepared for the job." Or as Brett Cabral, a longtime CPS worker in Massachusetts, put it: "When I started . . . I didn't know shit."[24]

"Child Protective Services . . . may do more harm than good unless adequate training qualifications are established," says Leila Whiting, a senior staff associate for the National Association of Social Workers. "We will say that we will offer help and support, but in reality we will give them an overworked, underpaid, untrained but well-meaning person who will not really know what to do."[25]

"We're sometimes offering the public a sham," says Kenneth Herrmann. "We offer them some program descriptions that look exceptional, but they're staffed with people that basically just don't know what the hell they're doing."[26]

But simply adding "more training" won't be enough, since it begs the key question of whether the *trainers* know what *they're* doing. It is not very reassuring to know, for example, that the State of California is paying to have hundreds of professionals trained in "child sexual abuse prevention" at Kee MacFarlane's Children's Institute International—the place that botched the interviews in the McMartin case.[27]

Or consider what passed for training at a workshop in Missouri.

On March 18, 1987, Mary Case, M.D., Medical Examiner for St. Charles County, Missouri, conducted a training session for child-protective workers. Case's comments included the following:

—"The state of the home is very important." A dirty home often reflects the parents "general attitudes towards life" and could well mean the parents are drug abusers.

—"Boyfriends are always suspicious characters, by the way, when they are baby-sitting."

—"Spiral fractures do not accidentally happen."

—"Three marks on that child's face, the probability that that child has been abused is almost 100 percent without knowing anything more. Just seeing three bruises on the face of a child."

—"I can accept one bruise on a child at a time. Any more than that I am going to want to see that child next week and see if this is some kind of repetitious pattern."

—"If you see a five-month-old kid with a bruise on it, somebody did that." (Contrast these views with those of Dr. Spock noted in Chapter 3.)

As noted earlier, Case also told the people she was training that she would never say a case isn't abuse, the only answers she gives in court are "yes" or "undetermined."

During the presentation, Case tended to flit from topic to topic, sometimes changing course in mid-sentence. Advice professionals should give parents to avoid causing accidental injury—such as not feeding small children certain foods or not bouncing a baby too hard on a parent's knee while "playing horsey"—was mixed in with practices Case clearly felt were abusive with no way for her audience to tell which was which. Case made a point of noting her strong opposition to all corporal punishment. And all of this was accompanied by gruesome slides of children who had been hideously abused.[28] It's hard to imagine anyone walking out of their training session with Case without thinking that almost everything is abuse, and almost every parent is guilty of it.

It's no wonder the people running worthwhile family-preservation programs like Homebuilders in Washington State say they have to "untrain" many of the workers who go to work for them.[29]

Child-protective workers aren't likely to stick around long enough to learn from experience. It takes at least five years on the job to learn to make the judgments required of a child-protective worker, says Peter Strubel, who used to teach them. But very few CPS workers stick around for five years.

On average, caseworkers in Washington State quit after only eighteen months.[30] In New York City, on average, 52 percent of the workers providing "preventive services," 48 percent of the foster-care workers, and 58 percent of child-care workers in foster-care institutions quit every year. Among child-protective workers the turnover rate averages 60 percent a year, though there is some indication that this is improving—it may now be down to "only" 40 percent.[31] In 1985, 61 percent of the CPS workers in Miami quit. In Fort Lauderdale, it was 78 percent.[32] Said a foster-care worker in Baltimore: "I'm leaving because I'm neglecting my own children and I owe them something too."[33]

Child-protective workers are not just inexperienced in child-protective work. Sometimes, they are also inexperienced in life.

A CPS worker is in a high-stress, low-paying job, has minimal qualifications, and is at the bottom of the career ladder. People attracted to such jobs tend to be just out of college, in their early twenties. This suggests that many CPS workers, at least when they start out, are not married and have no children of their own.

What little training they have gotten has taught them that any parent is a potential abuser, that most parents don't really know what they're doing, and that all parents are suspect. They will have no personal experiences against which to measure such dogma if they lack the counterweight of personally experiencing the difficulties—and the joys—of parenthood.

They learn that corporal punishment is always wrong, but have they ever had to discipline an errant child themselves? They learn all about what might make a parent hate a child, but they may have never experienced the love that most parents feel for their children. They may never have shared, as only a parent can, a child's pride in mastering a new task, a child's joy of discovery, or a child's fear when he or she thinks mommy and daddy are going away.

Perhaps it makes no difference. The only study I know of—and it dates back more than a decade—which tried to measure whether being a parent affected workers decisions did not find a correlation.[34] On the other hand, a study of state legislators found that their votes on issues involving family policy were strongly influenced by their stage in what the researchers called the "family life-cycle."[35] And recall the experience of the doctor in Boston who found that her childless colleagues considered any injury to a child at least an act of neglect, while her colleagues with children were more forgiving.

At a minimum, the topic deserves more research. So do two related questions: Are children who were maltreated themselves disproportionately represented among child-protective workers? If so, does the fact that their entire personal experience makes families inherently suspect have any bearing on their decisions, as the FBI's expert in child sexual abuse has suggested?

*   *   *

What kind of people would take a job as a child-protective worker, a job that comes with so much responsibility and so much heartbreak and so little reward? Probably two kinds of people: The very dedicated and caring and the very lazy and stupid. CPS agencies are filled with both.

Every child-protective agency has workers who stick it out despite of all the problems; people who work long hours and who bring wisdom, concern, and caring to each moment; people who put their careers on the line fighting the system, and sometimes put their lives on the line fighting child abusers.

"I've been threatened, bitten, spit at, and chased with a fire extinguisher," says a Florida worker. "My car was shot at twice."[36] A Wisconsin worker took the cases with which he was dealing too much to heart. He killed himself.[37]

Then there is the case of Irwin Levin, the CPS supervisor in Brooklyn. He exposed massive negligence and incompetence in the child-protective system in New York City that contributed to the deaths of at least eight children.

After nearly two years of pleading with his bosses to listen and to act, Levin finally went public. Only then did the city's Child Welfare Administration (CWA) investigate. But they didn't investigate Levin's charges— they investigated Levin. He was demoted two pay levels, costing him $2,000 a year in salary, fined a month's pay, and suspended without pay for four months. When these actions provoked public outrage, the CWA finally asked for a probe by the inspector general of its parent agency, the Human Resources Administration. That report found that all of Levin's charges were true. This led to revocation of the fine and the suspension, but Levin remains demoted. And CWA denied the findings of its own inspector general—suggesting that he had been "misled" by Levin. CWA threw in some character assassination along the way, suggesting that Levin had "emotional difficulties."[38] In a sense they were right: Irwin Levin gets emotional when his agency's neglect and incompetence allows children to die.

Levin has continued his public crusade for reform, even taking out an advertisement in the *New York Times* at his own expense. He believes his agency bungles half the cases it handles. "The situation at CWA is like a terrible, insidious disease you can't get rid of," Levin says. "Either you can leave, throw up, do yourself in, or do the system in."

What happened to Levin happens elsewhere as well. Speaking with her face and voice disguised, a Florida worker told WPLG-TV in Miami, "I am terrified of the administration. They have told me that if I didn't be quiet I would lose my job." Another anonymous worker said the Florida system is "run on fear and intimidation." In response, the head of Florida's Department of Health and Rehabilitative Services, Gregory Coler, said: "I don't believe that there has been any inappropriate intimidation."[39] He did not explain what sort of intimidation is appropriate.

On the other hand, every child-protective agency has people like the ones Lisa Clampitt worked with. "The people they would hire were the most incompetent people I was ever surrounded by," Clampitt says. "There were people deciding families' lives who didn't know how to use carbon paper. They'd spend half an hour debating: Does the shiny side go up or down?"

Clampitt recalled a colleague who could have placed a boarder baby in a foster home if someone could get the foster parents a crib. Clampitt said the worker was prepared to let the baby wait in the hospital a week rather than exert a little extra effort to find the crib. Clampitt came up with the crib in two hours.

Experiences like that led Clampitt to conclude that a lot of her colleagues were working in Child Protective Services because "$22,000 a year is a lot more than these incompetent people can get anywhere else."

Clampitt's perception of some of her colleagues is remarkably similar to Irwin Levin's. He has repeatedly urged the courts not to rubber-stamp the recommendations of his own workers. Why? Because "most often incompetent, unskilled, and poorly supervised staff are preparing ill-conceived recommendations based on prejudice and/or inadequate investigative efforts."[40] In one case involving a custody dispute, Levin says, "A staff person had a ten-minute interview with each parent, got no records at all," and then made his recommendation. In another case, CPS workers had overwhelming evidence that a mother presented a grave danger to her newborn infant. "But my staff never prepared a court case, no papers are there. . . . We've got to give the kid back to the mother because the staff screwed it all up."

Sometimes, the incompetence goes all the way to the top. When former head of Philadelphia's Department of Human Services Irene Pernsley was asked if she had "any familiarity" with the qualifications required to be a worker or administrator in her agency, she replied: "No, I don't." Asked if she knew what the duties of agency social workers are, she answered, "I have no familiarity with that."[41]

And sometimes, the actions of child-protective workers cross the line from the merely incompetent to the illegal. Among the abuses Peter Strubel says he observed firsthand:

—Workers who would throw a child into foster care if an accusation came in at 4:30 P.M. on a Friday so they could go home for the weekend. They would investigate to determine whether the child belonged in foster care on the following Monday.

—Workers who would make parents sign blank release forms.

—Workers who would falsify court reports, writing the report first in order to meet a deadline, presenting it to the court, and then going to see the child later.

Each of these practices was cited by at least one other person interviewed for this book from their firsthand experience.

Irwin Levin says there's no need to worry about the workers in his agency falsifying records. Says Levin: "Our workers were so incompetent, they didn't know what to lie about." But in some cases they did know. A New York City Comptroller's report found that in more than one out of five cases studied, workers falsified records "by altering dates and back-dating forms" in order to appear to be in compliance with deadlines that actually had been missed, sometimes by years.[42]

"Monthly visitation statistics . . . which our department relies on are inaccurate and inflated," says a Los Angeles caseworker. "Workers are forced to lie to find the happy medium between mandated activities and the avoidance of administrative pressures."[43]

Robert Schwartz, Executive Director of the Juvenile Law Center in Philadelphia, estimates that one-third of child-protective workers "are terrific and rowing upriver doing a real good job"; another third "*were* terrific" but have been beaten down by the system; and the last third never should have become CPS workers at all.[44]

Whether the caseworker is any good or not, he or she becomes the scapegoat for system failure. Says Robert Moro: "The public yells at the commissioner, who yells at the area directors, who yell at the managers, who yell at the social workers, who go home and kick the dog."[45]

The wide variation in the quality of CPS workers helps explain how the same system can intervene too much in some cases and too little in others. Thus, there are cases like one Levin cites in which a mother with cancer needed help around the house to keep her family together. She was assigned a homemaker, but almost lost that homemaker—and her children—when a caseworker failed to do the required paperwork.[46] Or the case of James Norman in which his family was destroyed in part because the worker couldn't do the simple arithmetic on a risk-assessment form. Or a case in Florida in which a parent was charged with abuse because a worker mistook a birthmark for a bruise.[47]

On the other hand, there's the case of Lillie Mae Ferebee, recounted by the *Philadelphia Inquirer*. Philadelphia's child savers bounced her from foster home to foster home for ten years, beginning when Lillie was four. Then they sent her back to her father. Lillie said that's where she wanted to go. But no one told Lillie that the reason she had been separated from her father was that he had been serving ten years in prison for raping a twelve-year-old girl.

The rape was so violent that police found blood and excrement on the bed, and the girl required surgery to repair her torn vagina. Court records described Lillie's father as a schizophrenic. His nickname was "Eerie." At his sentencing, he went berserk and struggled with twenty court officers, sending the judge fleeing from the courtroom. So it should have come as no surprise that within weeks of her return Lillie was beaten and, she says, raped by her father. He was acquitted of the rape charge. Lillie was removed from her father's custody after the beating. A year later, she was placed in foster care with a convicted murderer.[48]

The worker who returned Lillie to her father had no training in foster-care cases. Lillie's case was her first. In a court deposition, she explained her decision: "Well, to be perfectly honest," the worker said, "he said he wasn't guilty."[49]

If the lack of education, training, and experience aren't enough to guarantee system failure, one more factor is sure to do it: enormous caseloads. The Child Welfare League of America recommends that child-protective workers handle no more than seventeen cases at a time. Just try and find a child-protective agency that adheres to that standard.

A Washington State report, commissioned in response to the death of Eli Creekmore, found that the state's Department of Social and Health Services is a case study in how not to run a government agency. Leadership of the agency was described as, "non-accessible, distant, punitive and negative, arbitrary, and inconsistent. . . . In many ways the agency resembles a losing team whose players turn on each other and whose coach regards the players with resentment." CPS workers must cope with "substandard work conditions [and] high caseloads which far exceed any national standard."[50]

A member of the committee that wrote the report, Katharine Briar, subsequently was named to head the DSHS Division of Children, Youth, and Family Services. Two years later, I asked the executive director of the Washington Federation of State Employees if Briar and been able to change any of the conditions she had identified in the report. He replied: "No."[51]

A study of Philadelphia's child-protective system included these findings:

—State regulations call for maximum caseloads of thirty. Even that limit, far too high to begin with, was exceeded by 40 percent of the Philadelphia workers. One worker had a caseload of 104.

—It takes from three to eight weeks just to get something typed. If both a supervisor and an administrator swear that the requested typing is "urgent," it can be done in three to five days.

—Up to four workers share a single telephone. Workers pile case records on the floor because file cabinets and bookshelves are unavailable. Often, they have to bring in their own pens and paper.

—Unqualified staff are kept on past their probationary period. Once that happens, it's almost impossible to fire them.

—"The basic knowledge and skills necessary for functioning at a reasonable level of professional competence do not seem to be developed in many workers. . . . Workers did not feel competent that they fully understand how to detect whether sexual abuse [or physical abuse] has occurred. Some reported that they did not know how to interview a child who is the subject of a sexual abuse report. . . . Some workers said they did not fully understand what evidence is necessary to remove a child from his home."[52]

In Washington, D.C., in late 1989, half the caseworker positions were vacant and the remaining workers were handling an average of sixty-one cases each. One worker had 117 cases. Another had paperwork for seventy cases stuffed in a drawer—none had been investigated. In August 1989, there was a backlog of 185 uninvestigated cases involving 771 children. With caseloads that high, one worker said he handled the cases "by ignoring most of them." Other workers let visiting clients answer the phone for them. Said one worker: "I don't go to work, I go to war. If we help a child, it's by accident." In one case, foster parents kept getting checks for a foster child in their care but, for nearly a year, no caseworker ever visited. When the foster mother called to find out what was going on, she was told the city had no record of the child. He had been placed and, literally, forgotten.[53]

In Florida, some workers keep their files in their cars because they have no desks. The Department of Health and Rehabilitation Services admits to worker caseloads of forty to sixty, while other sources put the number for some workers at four hundred. In 1987, WPLG-TV found a backlog of hundreds of uninvestigated cases. Said one worker: "It's harder to fight the system than to do the work."[54] And even Gregory Coler, the agency director who abhors "inappropriate" intimidation, calls his agency, "a Mack truck with a shiny paint job and a Volkswagen engine."[55]

In Los Angeles, caseloads range from fifty to a hundred or more. According to a caseworkers' union leader, home visits "have been reduced to a physical sighting of the child or a parent and noting it on a form. All expectation of casework has been lost. Our management has lost sight of the fact that we are paid to do something a little bit beyond opening and closing cases and moving papers in and out of the system every month."[56]

In New York City, child-welfare officials came up with a novel "solution" to the caseload problem. In late 1988, then-mayor Ed Koch and his subordinates bragged that caseloads at the Child Welfare Administration had been slashed to 18.9, down from 35.5 the previous year. But Koch was playing a shell game. His numbers applied to the "protective/diagnostic" units, which get most of the press attention because they do the initial investigations. The "reduction" was accomplished by suddenly transferring huge numbers of cases from protective/diagnostic workers to "family service" workers, who are responsible for monitoring children whose families are being supervised. They already had heavy caseloads of their own. Those caseloads soared to anywhere from thirty-three to seventy cases per worker. Hundreds of families were ignored for months. "Cases were literally sitting in boxes, untouched," according to the president of the caseworkers' union. As City Council President Andrew Stein put it: The city "has been giving us a Potemkin Village statistic while children were dying."[57]

Several New York City workers described their experiences to *Village Voice* columnist Nat Hentoff:[58]

> I sometimes work until two or three in the morning, having started at 8:30 the previous morning. I've worked until 6:30 in the morning and been in court that day at nine. And during that time, I've been assigned new cases. . . .
> Case records? Case records? You somehow never seem to get them. Why? Because they're piled up in boxes. Nobody knows where anything is. So without the case record, you start from scratch. . . . You can't even learn what the allegations were and there's no way of finding out. . . .
> I run around trying to find a Xerox machine that works. I run around trying to find paper. They don't have supplies. . . . Half the new caseworkers bring in their own phones.

Said Irwin Levin: "We'll have dead kids on our hands for years."[59]

The chaos that has engulfed the New York City system is comprehensively described in a 214-page report by a group called the Neighborhood Family Services Coalition. It is remarkable both for its thoroughness and its insight. Two examples tell the story. I have altered the narratives slightly to eliminate a welter of confusing acronyms:

> A private agency accepted a referral from a child protective worker and assigned a social worker to the case immediately. The two workers met jointly with the client, Ms. Green, at which time she stated that she had struck her four-year-old son the previous day.
>
> The protective worker did not believe a report of suspected abuse was warranted because no bruises were evident, no previous reports existed, and the boy said his mother had not hurt him. The agency worker, nonetheless, believed the agency was mandated to file a report in such instances and asked the protective worker to do so.
>
> The protective worker assumed the agency was picking up the case and would begin work with Ms. Green immediately. The agency worker believed Ms. Green might be an abusive parent and decided to delay contact until protective services completed a full investigation.
>
> No report was filed, no investigation was performed, and no services were delivered to this family.

In the second case, a mother who was glad to cooperate with protective services—indeed she wanted their help—finally gave up after weeks of fighting the child-welfare bureaucracy:

> Ms. Richards, twenty-three, was reported to Child Protective Services for suspected neglect of her seven- and eight-year-old boys. The school initiated the report with allegations that the youngsters were frequently absent from school and extremely unkempt in their appearance.
>
> During the investigation, it was discovered that Ms. Richards had been a heroin addict for several years, but for the past two years she had been a regular participant in a methadone maintenance program. She said she began to feel overwhelmed by her responsibilities after her mother died six months ago and expressed a desire for counseling and help in learning to manage her household.
>
> The child protective worker informed Ms. Richards that she would be referred to a private agency for services. The protective worker telephoned the agency and requested counseling, parenting skills and possibly home-maker services for Ms. Richards.
>
> He was asked where Ms. Richards lived and whether or not she had a substance abuse problem. The protective worker said Ms. Richards lived within the agency's service area and that she was no longer a drug addict. The agency accepted the referral and Ms. Richards was instructed to go there the following afternoon.
>
> Ms. Richards had to cancel her appointment because one of her sons was ill. She rescheduled an appointment for the following week.
>
> When Ms. Richards appeared for her first appointment, an intake worker completed a psycho-social history. Ms. Richards offered the information about her methadone maintenance program. She was then informed that the agency could not work with clients who were in drug programs.

Ms. Richards was told to return to her protective worker to make an alternative service plan. When she did this, several weeks later, she was told her worker was no longer on the case and that her case had been transferred to another unit of the Child Welfare Administration for monitoring.

Several months later, the original protective worker, while speaking with the private agency about another case, inquired about Ms. Richards' progress. The agency had no record of Ms. Richards.[60]

Lisa Clampitt recalls what should have been a high point in her brief career as a child-protective worker. She spent a day with a Manhattan family in which the father would get drunk and abuse the children at night. "It was really a bad scene," Clampitt said. "The father was yelling at me. It was a creepy situation. I could have gone in and removed the children immediately. But I put in an entire day talking to the whole family." By the time she was through, Clampitt said, the father agreed to move out to his mother's house in Brooklyn, and the whole family had agreed to counseling.

"When I got back to the office I was really excited," Clampitt says. But her boss wasn't. "He yelled at me. He came down on me real hard." Why? Because it was "irresponsible" of her to spend a whole day on just one case.

Enormous caseloads also turn workers against the families they are supposed to help—if they are not against them to start with. "When you have a caseload of forty, you begin to believe that nothing works—because in your experience nothing did work," says Charlotte Booth of Homebuilders. "You begin to feel very negatively: These people can't change, I might as well take the kids now. Your frustration shows, and you start becoming a little more punitive, and the clients become punitive back."[61]

The lack of education, the lack of training, the overwhelming caseloads—none of this is taken into account in the legislation that gives almost unlimited discretion to child-protective agencies.

Goldstein, Freud, and Solnit write that current laws are based on "the fantasy . . . that only the most competent, most skilled and most sensitive lawyers, judges, doctors, social workers, foster parents, family helpers, and other personnel will implement the grounds for intrusion under the laws of child placement." Precisely because this is only a fantasy, "It is important to place a heavy burden of proof upon those who are empowered to intrude."[62] The current system is "built on a whole set of premises that just aren't there," says Michael Wald. "[It] assumes competence when there is a lot of incompetence. It assumes trained people when there are untrained people. It assumes adequate resources when there are inadequate resources."[63]

The typical American child-protective agency operates like a modern-day version of the Keystone Cops—only they fire real bullets.

The child savers' solution to all this is simple. Just give more money and more power to the people who have made such a mess of things already. There are two problems with this approach. First, it isn't going to happen. Indeed it can't happen.

"There will never be enough money for all the investigators that are needed if the reporting process is not reformed," says Douglas Besharov. If there was ever any doubt about this, the voters of Washington State settled it in November 1989. These were the people who were supposedly shocked by the death of Eli Creekmore. It turns out that they were shocked enough to broaden laws and flood the foster-care system, but not shocked enough to pay for it.

Just three years after Creekmore's death, a "children's initiative" was placed on the ballot. It would have forced the state legislature to appropriate $360 million a year for two years in additional funds for all kinds of services to help children, not just Child Protective Services. If the legislature could find no other way to pay for it, it would be funded by an increase in the state's sales tax of just under one cent.

The voters of Washington State had a chance to choose between paying an extra penny on the dollar when they made a purchase or letting more children die. They voted to let more children die. The children's initiative was defeated by a margin of two to one.

But even if the money were available, simply using it to fuel the present child saving steamroller would do no good. In New York City, for example, no one even keeps track of all the different programs funded under the label of "preventive services"; there is no serious attempt to evaluate them and no effort to direct dollars toward programs that have proved effective. "More money, more staff, higher staff qualifications, improved staff training all are undoubtedly necessary," says the Neighborhood Family Services Coalition report. "But these alone will not ensure the provision of needed services to all families at risk. To accomplish this, there must be a reconceptualization and restructuring of the city's network of services for families and children."[64]

"The question for Congress, I think, is . . . are you going to try and attach some strings to this huge amount of federal money that you are giving to the states to damage kids," says Marcia Lowry. "There is a shortage of resources . . . but I am telling you that if you put twice as much money into this system tomorrow, you would have twice as many screwed up kids."[65]

Public-policy debates are often framed in terms of spending more vs. spending smarter. In child welfare, we must do both. More money is essential. But it must be linked to a dramatic reduction in the scope of coercive intervention and the power of the child savers. The only way to get to the children who really need help, the only way to ensure that there will be fewer Eli Creekmores and Lisa Steinbergs, is to curb the horrendous excesses of the current child-protective system and strip it down to what it was meant to be in the first place: an emergency response system akin to the police, the fire department, or the emergency medical service.

The present deluge of false reports and unnecessary placements is directly responsible for the failure to meet the needs of children in real danger.

A California study stated flatly that "the increased number of reports that need to be investigated, combined with a shortage of needed services and a lack of interagency cooperation . . . have reduced the level of services provided to abused and neglected children."[66] In New York City, no more than 56 percent of the cases that investigators label "indicated" get any services at all.[67] Another New York study, this one with a statewide focus, concluded that the number of children needing services and getting them dropped from 75 percent in 1983 to 52 percent in 1985. That study, by the State Communities Aid Association, also found, "The CPS intake system does not distinguish between serious child abuse and other less urgent child welfare problems. . . . The child protective system focuses on intake and investigation of reports at the expense of services."[68]

What this means to individual children can be seen when, for example, a caseworker comes to court and asks that a child be kept in care for six more months solely because she hasn't had time to read the file.[69]

Or it can be seen in the caseload of Dan Wayment, a caseworker in New Hampshire. Cases he was assigned one day included a teenager who allegedly was being molested during weekend visits with her father and a case involving alleged sexual abuse of a first-grader by her twelve-year-old brother. Unfortunately, Wayment went to the case involving siblings first. It turned out to be the one described in an earlier chapter in which the sole act of "sexual abuse" was one instance in which the boy had pulled down his sister's pajama bottoms. Later that day Wayment was delayed in court. The next day was even busier. He wound up unable to get to the teenager before her next visit with her allegedly abusive father.[70]

Or it can be seen among the cases carried by one Boston CPS worker profiled by the *Boston Globe*. The cases included:

—A mother with children in foster care solely for lack of housing.

—A case involving a child "born with a rare, undiagnosed condition that required specialized medical care, tube feedings, and fifty diaper changes a day. . . . Under pressure to release the child for financial reasons, the hospital blamed the mother as an incompetent caretaker." The worker was forced to spend weeks finding specialized foster care for the child—and getting it approved "because you're asking for bigger bucks."

—A mother who had been accused of no maltreatment at all. She just wanted help getting herself and her five-year-old son out of the housing project where the mother had been raped and beaten and the boy had witnessed a murder.[71]

All of these families needed help. But none should have had to bear the stigma of a child-abuse investigation, and the worker should not have had her time diverted from cases of real abuse.

Even among CPS officials themselves, there is growing sentiment to curb the scope of coercive intervention.

From Michigan: Child Protective Services has been "inundate[d] with almost unlimited demands. The high rate of unsubstantiated complaints indicates a waste of manpower. Inappropriate complaints result in investigations which intrude on thousands of Michigan families. . . . [This] has its cost both in terms of family trauma and its impact on finite staff resources.

"A realistic understanding must occur about the limited capacity of CPS staff to identify, predict, and be responsible for the behavior of potentially abusive and neglectful parents and to protect all children from this behavior. . . . Otherwise, CPS will continue to face a growing avalanche of demands until program and staff are immobilized."[72]

Following the recommendations of a task force made up of Child Protective Services workers and officials, Michigan has contracted with the National Council on Crime and Delinquency to develop a set of risk-assessment guidelines to allow calls to be screened so workers don't have to go out on every case.[73]

From Washington State: "Child Protective Services staff are faced with violating policy by declining to investigate clearly low risk complaints or spending time and energy [on them] at the expense of having adequate time [for] more serious situations."[74]

From North Carolina: "Current legal definitions of neglect are so broad that protective services intervene in some situations where there is no substantial risk of harm to children. . . . This is reflected in the low substantiation rate and takes an inordinate amount of staff time for investigating situations where protective services are not needed or services to solve a problem are not available."[75]

In California, the deputy director of the state Department of Social Services, Loren Suter, told a legislative committee: "We believe that it's gotten to the point where workers cannot deal effectively with the needs of the children who are actually abused and neglected because we're spending a disproportionate share of our resources and staff time on unfounded or unsubstantiated reports. . . . The high washout rate suggests, at least to us, that the definitions of abuse and neglect may be too broad."[76]

A representative of the County Welfare Directors' Association agreed:

"At one time, the child welfare system's efforts to protect children from abuse and harm were hampered by a societal reluctance to report child abuse," said Lee Kemper. "Now the child welfare system's efforts to protect children are hampered by the voluminous amount of reporting that is occurring."[77]

And Kay Hill, a self-proclaimed "bleeding heart social worker," said that the inability to screen calls means that "frequently our staff wastes time on cases that that should not ever be seen by us. . . ."[78]

In 1989, the California Legislature responded. It narrowed the grounds for taking a case of alleged "neglect" to court or for taking custody of a child in so-called "emergencies" (though not for initiating some sort of investigation) and gave workers the discretion not to investigate every call in person.[79]

Even the American Humane Association's Larry Brown has warned, "If we don't tighten intake criteria for CPS, it will be swamped by all types of child welfare cases because we're the only available resource."[80]

The child savers' objections to narrowing intake criteria are twofold. First, they argue, any limits on what is investigated will lead to cases of serious maltreatment going undiscovered. In fact, more cases go undiscovered now, a point I will address in Chapter 11. The second concern is that restricting CPS to more serious cases will leave children with no recourse when the situation is not serious, but help may be needed to prevent problems from worsening (the continuum theory). This is nonsense.

Clearly families like those helped by the Boston CPS worker should not simply be left to their own devices. But those who want to undo the damage done by the child savers want only to limit *coercive* intervention. None of their proposals would restrict access to help for a family that wants help. On the contrary. One of the few ways to free up the money for programs that will provide real help to troubled families is by shrinking the child-protective empire.

One reason child savers oppose such an approach is that it undercuts their power. Ever since the days of mothers' pensions, child savers have opposed any "preventive service" that did not give them control over the lives of recipients. A related reason is that a lot of child savers don't know how to offer constructive help. Child savers have become too dependent on coercion; they don't know how to show poor people respect and deal with them as equals.

Voluntary services must be geared to what the recipients really need, not what child savers are most comfortable providing—in other words, more day care, homemakers, and emergency cash for utility bills and security deposits, and less "counseling" at a child saver's office. The services must be readily available in the recipient's community in a form that's attractive, not threatening. They can't force people to battle bureaucracy to try and get help, as happened to Ms. Richards.

Extensive outreach efforts are also necessary. Sitting in an office waiting for the families to come in won't be enough. As author Lizbeth Schorr has pointed out: "Families with few supports but great needs are often inept at using available supports, formal or informal. They often need help in using help."[81]

The next two chapters offer some ideas for how to make the child-protective system work and how to give poor families "help in using help."

10

Family Preservation

Child savers will tell you that there is a terrible tension between child protection and family preservation. They will talk about an "inherent conflict," about how they are on a "collision course." It's not so.

For the overwhelming majority of American children, including most of those alleged to be maltreated, there is no child protection without family preservation. Their best hope lies with their own families.

"The state can be a custodian, but not a parent," writes Malcolm Bush. "Children are sustained by the 'illogical' affection of their parents—affection and regard that outsiders would not give to children, particularly when they misbehave or if, by various criteria, they are unattractive. The state can never provide that affection and many surrogate parents cannot maintain it in the face of deviant behavior."[1]

Recall what Dennis Lepak discovered: "*No one* will value and protect another's child as they will their own." If we are serious about erring on the side of the child, we must begin by erring on the side of the family.

Child savers have been paying lip service to such ideas for most of this century. There were calls for what is now known as "family preservation" as far back as the first White House Conference on Dependent Children in 1909.[2] But the practice is far different. The orientation of practitioners, the financial incentives, and the law all encourage taking children away from their parents.

In tens of thousands of cases, family preservation does not require efforts that are elaborate, lengthy, or expensive. Placement rates and child-protective caseloads could be cut significantly by the simplest of means:

money for a telephone, a security deposit, a utility bill, emergency food aid or a baby-sitter; a good day care or after-school program. But, as Florence Roberts says, right now "it's so much easier to just go ahead and yank the kids."

Other cases are more complicated. They may require an array of different services, all of which must be made easily accessible to the parent in need.

For example, it is known that children born prematurely or with low birth weight are more likely to be maltreated, perhaps because they can be more difficult to care for. Therefore, one of the best preventive services around is the federal government's supplemental feeding program for Women, Infants, and Children (WIC). The program combines extra food aid and better prenatal care, and it has had dramatic success both in ensuring the birth of healthier children and in saving money that otherwise would have gone to expensive neonatal intensive care. But WIC is not available to everyone who qualifies. When the money runs out, eligible women are placed on waiting lists. Any politician who says he or she wants to "crack down on child abuse" but does not work to expand WIC to everyone who is eligible is either badly uninformed or lying.

After birth, programs that send visiting nurses to poor families have also had remarkable success, partly because the nurses do more than just provide "parent education." They also do things like make sure the new parent is signed up for food stamps and other "hard" services. Even the programs child savers like so much, parent education and counseling, have a role to play, provided they are designed to support new parents, not patronize them.

Fundamentally, the programs that are needed to reduce child abuse are the programs that are needed to ameliorate the worst effects of poverty. It would take another book to list them all, describe which ones work, and explain why they have not been put into widespread practice. Fortunately, this book already has been written, and I refer readers to Lisbeth Schorr's outstanding work, *Within Our Reach: Breaking the Cycle of Disadvantage*,[3] for a thorough discussion of these issues and a telling refutation of the notion that "nothing works."

As important as the specific services, is the way in which they are delivered. Schorr lists the key attributes of programs that work:

—They offer a broad spectrum of services, with an emphasis on "hard" services and meeting needs identified by the clients themselves.

—They cross traditional bureaucratic boundaries and they provide a coherent, easy-to-use package of services. As Schorr writes: "No one ever says, 'This may be what you need, but helping you get it is not part of my job or outside our jurisdiction.' "[4] Or, as Malcolm Bush has suggested, "multiproblem families" need multi-solution agencies.[5]

To help meet these needs, some states have begun to experiment with neighborhood service centers. These centers provide "one-stop shopping" for families needing help, rather than forcing them to fight myriad bureaucracies. Parents can go to one place, often within walking distance, to put their children in day care or an after-school program, see a doctor, get job training, attend a parent support group, get individual counseling, apply for food stamps and welfare, receive emergency financial assistance, and so on.

But what about those cases where a child really has been maltreated by the parents? Can such families be preserved? *Should* such families be preserved?

Often they should. Even child savers concede that most maltreating parents don't want to harm their children. Very few abuse them for the sadistic joy of it, and a great many children remain attached even to abusive parents. And there is no joyous foster-care fantasyland out there awaiting these children. As Michael Wald points out, for some children, staying with their families "is as important for them as an emotional, psychological issue" as it is for the parents. If no effort is made to keep the family together, "we are depriving some of the children, maybe a majority of the children, of a possibility to be in the home where, if the parents behavior can be changed, they will be best off in the long run."[6]

When the parents want to change, and when the children want to stay, there is compelling evidence that families can be preserved and the children can be kept safe. Much of that evidence comes from a pioneering program in Washington State.

From its start in 1974, through the end of 1989, the Washington State Homebuilders program worked with 4,856 families in which children were in imminent danger of being placed in foster care. Their record of success at keeping these children out of foster care is astonishing, at least until you take a close look at how Homebuilders works. Homebuilders applies common sense to child welfare—which, come to think of it, is pretty astonishing in itself.

The success has been made possible by what has been called "the SWAT team approach." Homebuilders spends only four to six weeks with each family. But what the program lacks in time, it makes up for in intensity.

Homebuilders workers have only two cases at a time. That means they can spend fifteen hours a week with a family, according to the program's assistant director, Charlotte Booth. Over a month, she says, "that equals a year's worth of conventional psychotherapy."[7]

The program has other unusual features:

—Intervention takes place at a crisis point for the family, when other efforts have been tried and failed and foster-care placement is imminent. Rather than this being too late, as child savers often suggest, Homebuilders has found that this is the best time to intervene. "Families are seen at a time when motivation to change and potential for growth may be at their peaks," Homebuilders officials write. "They are considerably more willing to experiment with new ideas and new behaviors than they are when their pain seems more bearable."[8]

—Intervention is immediate. A worker responds within twenty-four hours of referral. The workers are on call twenty-four hours a day.

—The workers stay on call throughout their work with the family. The family is given their worker's home telephone number.

—The worker goes to the family, instead of the other way around. It's easier to apply practical skills if they're taught to a parent in the home instead of in an agency office. In addition, Booth says, it's a question of "who has to be nervous."

—Workers are trained in several approaches to family therapy. That way, they don't become hostile to the families with whom they work because of their own initial failures. They don't start viewing poor families with contempt. "A client who is labeled manipulative by other programs is just one who simply isn't buying the therapist's approach," says Booth. "If we hit a barrier to one approach, we can try another. That way, we don't find ourselves not liking our clients."

But perhaps the most important ingredient in Homebuilders's success is the refusal to confine itself to throwing social work at problems. Homebuilders provides the traditional "soft" services, but workers also help families find day care and job training, teach practical skills, like how to use a bank account and help with financial problems. And it's all done by the same worker. Confronted by a family with a dirty home, the homebuilder will not lecture the parents or spend weeks trying to determine the deep psychological trauma the dirty home is "obviously" just a symptom of. The homebuilder will roll up his or her sleeves and help with the cleaning.

This approach has several benefits. First, and most obvious, as in the less serious poverty-related cases, the lack of certain hard services may be contributing directly to the maltreatment, as when lack of supervision is caused by lack of day care.

But there are many other benefits to providing hard services:

—It makes life for the family less overwhelming. As one evaluation of Homebuilders puts it: "In families drained emotionally and physically by economic and social crises, family members may be less able to engage in problem solving interventions than when they are relatively free of basic health and safety concerns."[9] In other words, first free the parent from the worry that her children don't have enough to eat, then worry about the psychological stuff.

—The hard services provided are the ones the parents identify as needing most. By helping to deal with these problems, instead of dismissing them as unimportant compared to the "real" problem, the homebuilder gives the client something a poor person almost never gets—respect.

At the same time, the homebuilder gains the parent's respect. "Most client families have already been through many therapists," writes Homebuilders director Jill Kinney. "They often believe the therapists cannot or will not really help. When a therapist provides a concrete service, the client is often surprised and grateful to see that the therapist actually can help. The client is often more willing to begin sharing information or to accept the workers' suggestions once the therapist has demonstrated that they do more than 'talk therapy.' "

At the same time, Kinney writes, the therapist learns a lot about the client while they work on "hard" services together, and the therapist can take advantage of "teachable moments" while providing concrete help. Kinney writes, "Clients often are the most willing to share information when they are involved in doing concrete tasks with their therapist such as washing dishes or traveling somewhere."[10] The hard services make it possible for the soft services to work. A homebuilder may teach a client how to handle the welfare bureaucracy or get better health care or special education for his or her child. The homebuilder provides the all-important "help in using help."

And how well does it work?

Although Homebuilders is run by a private agency, it is not allowed to engage in "creaming." The program takes only children who are right on the verge of foster-care placement and must take any child referred unless the program is full.

Since 1982, 88 percent of the families served by Homebuilders were still together a year after the intervention. The program has done two studies comparing the people they serve to control groups they had to turn away because the program was full. In one study only 24 percent of the children in the control group were kept out of foster care. In the other, none of the children avoided placement.[11]

Some have argued that while Homebuilders might be fine in Washington State, it can't work in a big-city ghetto, where the problems of poverty are even worse. In 1987, Homebuilders began proving these critics wrong. They set up a program in the South Bronx. After one year, 74 percent of the families they worked with still were together—not as good a record as Washington State, but still impressive.[12]

Homebuilders is also cost effective. In 1986, the program was paid $2,600 per case. (In 1989 it was $2,700.) Had the children been placed—and it's clear that most would have been—placement for a year in a family foster home would have cost $7,186, and a group home would have cost

$22,373 in 1986. Homebuilders has also kept children out of institutions which cost even more.[13]

Even the low caseloads of Homebuilders workers aren't as expensive as they seem. Though they carry only two cases at a time, the intervention typically lasts for only four weeks. Over the course of a year, a homebuilder typically carries at least twenty cases.

The following is one homebuilder's account of a single case. The case was referred to Homebuilders due to the concerns of a nurse, fearful about the family's daughter, who was about to be released from the hospital after being born prematurely.

> The nurse was also concerned about the family situation because their three-year-old boy had recently been diagnosed as hyperactive with some brain damage. Child Protective Services and the nurse were suspicious about the boy's three concussions over the past year. . . . The nurse wondered if the three year old and the baby shouldn't be placed in foster care. . . .
>
> [When I arrived at the home] the first thing I noticed was the smell of gas leaking from the furnace. The mother said she thought she had smelled gas, [but she had no phone and she] hadn't felt up to walking to a public phone to call for help. Her pediatrician had ordered her to get a telephone installed due to the uncertain condition of the baby, yet since her husband was out of work, they couldn't pay the installation fee. I suggested that the woman dress herself and her children warmly, open the window a little and turn down the furnace. While she did that, I went to a telephone and called the landlord to send out a repairman.
>
> When I returned, the woman talked about her situation. She said she had been very depressed since the baby's birth, and had often felt the child did not belong to her. She was also extremely upset about her son's "wild" behavior. She wondered if, like an uncle in prison, he didn't have a "bad seed" in him. She had been thinking that she would rather kill him now than see him grow up to be a murderer like his uncle.
>
> She was very thin, pale, and weak. She had a chronic cold. She had lost her front teeth due to poor health. Now 22, she had had . . . four miscarriages in five years of marriage. She said she was very lonely. Her husband was usually away from the house from mid-morning to late at night unsuccessfully trying to sell insurance. He had not sold a policy in five months.
>
> The woman told me that every counselor she had ever seen told her that her husband was "rotten" and she should leave him. But she said she loved him and he didn't beat her. . . .
>
> The woman had expressed fears about sitting alone at night with no curtains [in the windows] for privacy. She told me that one recent night a strange man had been peering in her window. She had been raped once before and was very scared it might happen again.
>
> The next day, we approached a local charitable organization and got the $25 needed to have a telephone installed. We also got two old bedsheets that could be nailed up as curtains.

On my next visit to the family, we focused a lot on the three-year-old son. The woman said she did not love him, and described a variety of what she labeled self-destructive and wild behaviors that he engaged in.

She reported incidents such as him throwing himself backwards off the furniture, touching the hot stove and laughing, turning on the kitchen burners, banging his head against the wall until unconscious, biting, scratching, and hitting other people. Although he was three, he still was not talking at all.

She was concerned that CPS would think she was abusing him because he hurt himself so much and because they locked him in his room at night. They did this because he only slept two or three hours at a stretch. When awake, he would go into the kitchen at night and eat until he vomited. She said she thought she should put him in an institution because she couldn't handle him. He would not kiss or show any affection to people. . . .

The parents had already voluntarily placed the boy once for 72 hours because the mother felt she "couldn't cope" with him. She was also afraid she might harm him because he made her so angry sometimes.

Before leaving, we made a list of what the mother could do if she felt her son's behavior was so bad that she would want to place him again. I let her know I thought it was a good idea to put him in his room sometimes, and explained the concept of time out.

The list also included calling me (their phone was to be installed the next day). We then made an appointment to take the son to Mary Bridge Children's Hospital Learning Center to see about enrolling him in a special school program. Finally, we talked about the mother getting some free time for herself. I volunteered to baby-sit for several hours later that week.

During the baby-sitting, I was alone with the children for five hours. I was able to observe a lot about the little boy. I observed him engage in some of the behaviors the mother had reported. However, by the end of the day, I determined he would respond to positive reinforcement and time out. I taught him to play a kissing game.

Information gathered that day was invaluable. It was proof for both me and the mother that the little boy could change, and he did care about people. The mother cried the first time she and her son played the kissing game.

During the second week of intervention, the mother began to talk more about her discontent in the marriage. She said that she knew her husband wasn't really working all the times he was gone. She expressed resentment over the fact that he dressed nicely while she had only one outfit, that he was free to play all day and night while she sat in their apartment, that he would not let her get a driver's license but also would not drive her places.

Feeling that she had reached a teachable moment, I began to talk about territoriality and assertiveness training. I also called the mother's [welfare] caseworker and got authorization to get her front teeth replaced.

The father began to be curious about what was happening, and decided to stay home to meet me one day. While his wife was at the dentist, he and I spent several hours talking. He shared his own frustrations with having to be on welfare. I told him how I wanted him to be part of the counseling process and he agreed to attend the next session. . . .

During the last weeks of intervention, we focused primarily on some behavioral child management skills. The son had begun attending the Mary Bridge school program and the mother rode the bus with him every day. I was pleased to see this, as it gave the mother a chance to watch the teachers and to make friends with the staff there. She began to report having some positive feelings about her son, and no longer felt she should send him away. She also began to feel much better about herself. She had temporary caps on her teeth and began to smile more. She was also beginning to gain a little weight.

As the end of the intervention approached, I explored with the mother ways she could continue counseling. She decided that she wanted to go back to a counselor at the mental health center. She had seen the counselor a couple of times right after the baby was born last summer and thought she could trust her. She made an appointment.

During the last week, I helped the family move to a better apartment in a neighborhood where they felt safer. It wasn't until after the move that the family found out the Mary Bridge bus would no longer be able to transport the boy to school. The mother became very upset but quickly [calmed down and began to solve the problem]. She talked with the counselors at Mary Bridge and followed their suggestion to see if the boy could be transferred to the Child Study and Treatment Center's day care program. He was put on the waiting list.

A follow-up call from this family several months later revealed that although there had been many upsetting events that had happened after I left, they were still together as a family.

The woman had been seeing her counselor and had continued to work on being more assertive. She and her husband were also going for marital counseling. The father had quit insurance and was in a job training program. The son was attending the new school, and the mother was participating in a parent education program required by the school.

They reported that the son was starting to talk and did not seem as "wild." The infant daughter was doing well.

Homebuilders has handled cases a lot more difficult than this one. But this case illustrates some important points about why Homebuilders succeeds where child savers fail.

First, consider the mother's condition when the homebuilder arrived at the door. What could be more indicative of a so-called "apathy-futility syndrome" than a woman too tired to get help when she smelled gas in her house? But instead of labeling, patronizing, sneering at, and writing off this woman, the homebuilder offered some concrete help and that led to immediate progress.

Second, the homebuilder started with the problems that the mother said bothered her. She did not belittle those problems or dismiss them as mere symptoms of something else.

Third, the homebuilder was on the scene long enough to see that the mother was telling the truth about the cause of her son's injuries. No regular CPS worker could have investigated long enough to find that out.

And finally, by the time the intervention was over, the mother was acting on her own initiative to get assistance with her problems. She had gotten the "help to use help" that she needed.

"I wish all caseworkers were like her," said a parent in one of the families helped by Homebuilders in the South Bronx. "I felt like somebody was caring. It is good when you can talk to a person and they can understand you."

Said another parent, "They did not put me on hold."[14]

Cheryl Powell's family, and Powell herself, also found a lifeline in Homebuilders. Herself a foster child bounced from home to home, Powell had been raped twice by age fourteen. She ran away from a foster home and lived on the streets. To get food, she would watch customers at pizza parlors and grab their uneaten pie crusts after they left. By age twenty-six, Powell was an exhausted single mother with three small children. Homebuilders intervened when she tried to kill herself by drinking a bottle of Pine Sol.

By the end of the Homebuilders intervention, she was in a job training program, she had learned how to care for the children and be more assertive in her relationship with her boyfriend, and she had discovered that it was a previously undiagnosed internal illness that had been leaving her so tired. "I know without these people I would either not be here or I would not have my family," Powell said. "Before, I thought I was ugly. Now, I like myself. . . ."[15]

Other programs across the country have modeled themselves on the Homebuilders approach. Partly as a result of the Baltimore lawsuit discussed in Chapter 7, such a program was set up in that city. A parent in the Baltimore program said, "When they came into my life, I was scared because I thought they was going to take my kids from me, but it don't work like that. They come to keep the family together. I think that everybody like me needs somebody like them. . . . They don't look down their noses at you because you don't have."[16]

One question arises immediately in the mind of anyone who is introduced to programs like Homebuilders for the first time. Given the difficulty of the cases they deal with, how can it possibly be safe for the child to remain in the home?

This is actually a two-part question. First, is it safe to leave the children at home during the intervention itself? Here, the answer is unequivocally yes. In fifteen years of work in Washington State and three years in the South Bronx, no child has ever been seriously harmed during the course of a Homebuilders intervention. Even the program administrators don't think that record will last forever, but I doubt that there is a foster-care program anywhere in America that can match this level of safety.

This success is not as surprising as it may sound. Unlike conventional caseworkers, Homebuilders spend a long time with their client families, long enough to spot what is causing crises to occur and teach parents how to defuse them. In addition, the homebuilders themselves are on call twenty-four hours a day—a ready resource for a parent who feels he or she is beginning to lose control. And if there is a crisis, "usually, the therapist can stay as long as necessary," says Charlotte Booth, "Four, eight, twelve hours."[17]

And finally, unlike the typical CPS worker who is untrained and sent out to fend for herself, almost all Homebuilders have master's degrees in social work, and they get lots of "back-up" from supervisors and administrators. For almost any family, a Homebuilders-type program is the safest of all available options during the intervention itself.

The second question is tougher: What happens after the intervention ends? Do the children remain safe?

Advocates of family preservation point to the large number of children still at home a year later as evidence of the safety of family-preservation programs. When the homebuilder leaves, the family is not abandoned. They remain under the supervision of Child Protective Services, which remains free to remove the child if problems recur. There are some obvious problems with this measure. The previous chapter illustrated some of the ways in which supervision can break down and renewed abuse can go undetected. Furthermore, everyone knows horror stories about cases in which CPS did nothing even after repeated warnings that a child was being abused. Common sense suggests that among the 88 percent of Homebuilders families that stayed together for at least a year, there are some where the children were in fact reabused and should have been removed.

So if the question is: Is family preservation perfectly safe? The answer is no. But the question should be: Is it safer than the alternative?

In 11 percent of the cases Homebuilders handled, foster care eventually was used anyway. That suggests that most cases are monitored and action is taken when it is needed. Charlotte Booth believes CPS generally keeps closer track of cases after they've been through Homebuilders if only because, should abuse recur, the Homebuilders intervention proves that "reasonable efforts" were made and therefore termination of parental rights is easier.

Furthermore, Homebuilders has now been around for sixteen years despite hostility from the child saving establishment. If large numbers of children who had gone through the program were turning up battered and bruised, you can be sure that establishment would have blown the whistle on it to the press and the public. (Indeed, they already try to blame family preservation for their own failures whenever they can get away with it.)

In addition, studies have begun to measure the results of family preservation by looking at more than just whether foster care was avoided. A two-year study of eleven family-preservation programs found that when children were not placed, there was a good reason for it. Most families showed dramatic improvements in their behavior by a whole series of measures.[18]

"A great deal of abuse and neglect that causes removal are situational crises," says Peter Forsythe of the Edna McConnell Clark Foundation. "They don't want to hurt kids. It happens because people haven't been taught to recognize their rising anger and express it normally, or they're overwhelmed. . . . They can't make their life work, but they want to make it work right. The notion that they're all nasty and should be strung up is an ignorant statement."

Furthermore, everything we know about foster care—the inherent emotional trauma, the shuffling from home to home, and the emerging documentation of abuse in foster homes—suggests that, if the children in Homebuilders and similar programs had been placed, more of them would have been hurt more often. "Kids go into foster care and come back abused," says Forsythe. "Nobody has a vaccination solution."[19]

And finally, we need to remember that the children we are talking about are only a small percentage of those labeled abused or neglected. Most were not maltreated at all—except by poverty.

The reaction of mainstream child savers to programs like Homebuilders is fascinating: silence in public, hostility behind closed doors.

Anne Cohn of the National Committee for Prevention of Child Abuse managed to write a 58-page pamphlet with 296 footnotes called *An Approach to Preventing Child Abuse*—and not mention Homebuilders once, even though the program had already been in operation for nine years when the pamphlet was written.[20] This is not altogether surprising considering that another NCPCA pamphlet, cited in Chapter 3, goes out of its way to deride the usefulness of "hard" services.[21]

Privately, child saver resistance to family preservation can be fierce. When Salvador Minuchin, probably the nation's foremost expert on therapy with families, wrote to three hundred New York City agencies offering to train their staffs at no charge, he did not receive a single reply. He did a little better writing to foster-care agencies: Four out of thirty accepted his offer. He began working with them in 1987 with funding from the Clark Foundation.[22]

In another example of agencies putting their own financial interests ahead of children, Charlotte Booth says agencies that specialize in residential "treatment" threatened to quit the Child Welfare League of America (CWLA), if that group endorsed a proposal to allow federal foster-care funds to be used for family-preservation programs. And, Booth says, CWLA caved in.[23]

And family preservation efforts sometimes are undercut in other ways as well. About one-third of Homebuilders families continue with some other service after the Homebuilders intervention ends. But sometimes, Charlotte Booth says, that actually does more harm than good. "The way we try to empower clients is not what [the system] wants in a client," Booth says. "I remember one particular client. She had been walked on and beaten down . . . and we worked very hard to get her to be more assertive. After our intervention ended, she went to a mental health center and said: 'I want to learn this, and this and this.' I got a call from the mental health center saying they didn't want to work with her because she was to‹ pushy."

The fact that they have not publicly criticized specific successful programs does not mean that the child savers have been silent on the matter of family preservation in general. On the contrary, family preservation has come under loud, sustained, and often successful attack.

Whenever a child dies after warning signs have been ignored or after he or she has been returned to an abusive home, the child savers come out of the woodwork, wagging their fingers and saying, "We told you so." Whenever a child dies the way Lisa Steinberg or Eli Creekmore did, the child savers say, "Don't blame us, that awful law forced us to do it." By "that law" they mean the federal Adoption Assistance and Child Welfare Act or similar state statutes.

There are two variations on this theme. In one, blaming the law is followed by the insistence that family preservation endangers children so the law should be changed. Thus, in another of her letters to the *New York Times,* the late Judge Nanette Dembitz declares that "a conflict in values" between child protection and family preservation "has been a basic cause in many cases of [children's] subjection to danger and damage."[24]

"Would you rather have them split up families where they could be helped and kept together," a doctor declares in a television documentary, "Or would you rather have some children that are seriously injured or die?"[25]

The second variation is even worse. It's the "with friends like these family preservation doesn't need enemies" problem. People who are running dreadful child-protective systems where overworked personnel make horrible decisions with tragic results misuse the principles of family preservation to cover their asses. It's not that we wanted to return the child, the bureaucrats say, the law forced us to do it.

But both the child savers and the bureaucrats know full well that there is nothing in any law that requires any child to be returned to an abusive family. The federal law says only that "reasonable efforts" should be made to keep a family together—reasonable efforts, not ridiculous efforts.

The National Council of Juvenile Court Judges, the Child Welfare League of America, the Youth Law Center, and the National Center for Youth Law have together written a comprehensive guide to the federal law for professionals in all parts of the child-welfare system.

The guidebook explains, "The law was intended to ensure 1. that no child be placed in foster care *who can be protected in his or her own home* and 2. that when removal is necessary, reunification be attempted before any other permanent arrangement is sought *unless it is not possible to reunify the family while protecting the child's safety*" (emphasis added).[26]

"The law is neutral," says Robert Schwartz of the Juvenile Law Center in Philadelphia. "It's used as an excuse, but it doesn't force anything. If a worker has any evidence a child is at risk the law responds to that . . . by removing them rather than the opposite. It's a convenient scapegoat."

Blaming the law is "a total misconception," says Susan Carter of the National Association of Foster Care Reviewers. "The reality is there is much more [trouble] going on in foster care that the public doesn't see. They don't see the damage that is done to some children in foster care, even in the best foster care, not even considering those who are abused [in foster care]."

"People are looking for scapegoats for their bad decisions when they blame the law," says Peter Forsythe. "The law, the regulations, nothing says return children to dangerous situations. That's pure baloney and hype and scapegoating and bad reporting. . . . I have yet to see a case where there was a death after a child was returned [when there was a careful assessment beforehand and adequate services provided afterwards]."[27]

Look into the circumstances surrounding sensational cases and one finds not a failed law, but a stumbling, bumbling child saving bureaucracy. Again, the reasons include failure to investigate, failure to deliver services, failure to supervise—all failures traceable directly to the overwhelming of the child protective system by false reports and overuse of foster care. Behind almost every avoidable child death is either a good child-protective worker who was too overworked to see what was going on, or a bad child-protective worker who never bothered to look. Lillie Mae Ferebee was not returned to her convicted rapist father because some law required it. Lillie Mae Ferebee was returned because her caseworker was an idiot.

"Family preservation can be a catch phrase that can be misconstrued," says Schwartz. "[A worker thinks] they said, 'Leave the kid at home, that's what they've been telling me' as opposed to, 'The mandate is to protect the child in the home whenever possible.' Even that mild nuance gets lost."

Furthermore, family preservation is a vital tool for protecting those children who *can't* stay in their own homes, again because scarce foster-care beds have to be saved for the children who need them most.

But even more important, family preservation means more than just keeping a child in his own family. Family preservation also means finding a permanent substitute family as soon as possible when a child can't be safely left at home. And the techniques of family preservation actually are the best and safest way to do that.

Here's why: Under the present system, both children who really need to be removed from their parents and children who don't are removed capriciously and thrown into foster care. No serious effort is made to reunify the family or even keep parents and children in touch with each other. Years go by, the children drift from placement to placement, and their chances of ever being returned home or adopted diminish. All this leads to the reluctance of judges to terminate parental rights discussed in Chapter 8. Contrast this to a system built around the principles of family preservation. Under such a system, families would have access to a wide array of support services, either on a voluntary basis or as a result of a substantiated allegation of maltreatment. If these services were not sufficient after three or four months, a program like Homebuilders might be tried for up to two more months. If that didn't work either, the children would be placed in foster care, but intensive work with the family would continue for another six months. If at this point the family could not be safely reunited—or if reunification is tried and the child is abused again—the family would get no more chances. Child-welfare officials would have easily met the reasonable efforts requirement and could petition for termination of parental rights.

Only one year would have passed, so the child would be less likely to have experienced multiple placement. The child is probably no less "adoptable" than before child-welfare intervention began. And the judge could act with the assurance that every effort had been made to keep the family together before he or she was asked to terminate parental rights.

Maryland's Foster Care Review Board, which monitors the status of children in care, has recommended that the state's entire foster-care system, as now administered, be scrapped and replaced with something very similar to what I've just described.[28]

As head of the ACLU's Children's Rights Project, Marcia Lowry has brought lawsuits seeking both better services to keep children in their own homes and quicker termination of parental rights. She sees these goals as complimentary, not as on a "collision course." Under the present system, Lowry says:

> Nobody is putting in the resources to do the kind of intensive work that is necessary. Then, because the family has not been given a fair shot, time passes and the courts are reluctant to terminate parental rights because

judges feel it is . . . unfair. . . .

Give the parent a fair shot—but a fair shot. Not, "Ma'am, go home and work on your self image." Real effort should be made to give services so the family can get back together, and if it does not work we have to be prepared to say, after a reasonable period of time, "Sorry, this kid has got to have a chance of his or her own."[29]

Such a system would not require enormous amounts of new money—though that certainly would help. It would require an enormous reallocation of existing resources from investigating false reports and needless foster-care placement to the provision of intensive family preservation services. As that suggests, family preservation must replace foster care as the core around which the child-welfare system functions. It cannot remain an underfunded add-on, made up mostly of pilot projects. If the car's a lemon, you can't fix it by adding a nice hood ornament. Because Homebuilders is such an add-on, handling only a limited number of cases per year, for example, Washington State still has one of the highest placement rates in the nation.

The case of Eli Creekmore, the three-year-old Washington State boy kicked to death by his father, is a case study in how child savers and bureaucrats use a tragedy to advance their own agendas. The Creekmore family had been through Homebuilders, and that made it easy to make family preservation the scapegoat for his death.

First came the attacks on the idea of family preservation:

A doctor who treated Creekmore declares during a television documentary: "They are supposed to protect children from injury and harm and neglect, and on the other hand, they're supposed to mobilize the resources of society to keep troubled families together, and I'm sure in almost every case they see, those two jobs they have are on a collision course."

On the same program, a psychologist says, "Some families are not worth preserving."[30]

Then came the bureaucrats ducking for cover:

The Secretary of Social and Health Services in Washington State explained to a legislative committee, "When I met with the staffs involved in [the Creekmore case] they continually pointed to what they regarded as a conflict in legislation." He went on to cite cases where legislators had complained about his department's intrusion on innocent families, as though this somehow excused its inaction in the Creekmore case.

And at the very end of the program, even as any viewer with a heart would be wiping tears from his eyes after hearing Eli's story, we are presented with a deputy attorney general who says: "I'm also hoping that people in—out of their justified concern in protecting children—that they don't go too far on changing or amending our law. I think our law is generally pretty good."[31]

But what actually happened in the Creekmore case?

Creekmore first came to the attention of Child Protective Services when his grandmother reported that he had been severely beaten. He was returned to his parents, and Homebuilders was brought in for four weeks. No one contends that Eli was hurt during the time Homebuilders was involved with the case. Indeed, those were probably the safest four weeks of his short, tragic life.

At the conclusion of every intervention, Homebuilders sends a letter to CPS describing the status of the family. In this case, Homebuilders warned CPS to be extra careful in monitoring the Creekmore family and to remove Eli from the home immediately if there was any further maltreatment.[32] Yet, within a month of Homebuilders' departure, Eli was being abused again. The owners of a home where he went for day care repeatedly called CPS. Relatives took photos documenting his injuries, yet CPS did nothing. Finally, Eli was placed in foster care once more, only to be returned home still another time.

The producer of the documentary about the Creekmore case took at face value the state's insistence that this was somehow a result of laws encouraging family preservation. At one point, the narrator of the program states, "The reports from Eli's grandmother and day care teacher had been minimized or ignored, at least in part because CPS was legally obligated to give the Creekmores every opportunity to resolve their problems before permanently removing Eli from their custody."[33] This is simply not true. The state is not obligated to offer "every opportunity," only to make "reasonable efforts." And that requirement had been fulfilled by the Homebuilders intervention. As soon as Eli was abused again—or even at serious risk of such abuse—CPS could have and should have placed him in foster care and gone to court seeking termination of parental rights. That this wasn't done is a function of overwork and/or incompetence at CPS, not anything in any law, nor any "conflict of values." But the coverage of the Creekmore case is typical.

"The media have the power to raise public consciousness or to reinforce old prejudices and fears," notes a report from the Clark Foundation. "When media simplify and sensationalize child abuse scandals, they help viewers and readers jump to the conclusion that children should be more readily removed from home. . . ."[34]

Lawrence Aber raised the same concern in writing about a Massachusetts case that was similar to the Creekmore case. "Had the editors anticipated that their call for prompt, effective action on child abuse reports would lead to premature, arbitrary separation of children from their families without consideration of alternatives, perhaps their news stories would have been worded differently. The media must learn to discipline itself to investigate not just the facts behind a tragedy, but the likely consequence of the inevitable recommendations that follow such a tragedy."[35]

The problem is compounded by the skill with which the child savers have hogged the media spotlight.

Most of us reporters are not experts in the subjects we write about. We're usually working under tight deadlines and we need to find quotable "experts" in a hurry. So we look at the last story written about the subject and call the people who were mentioned in that story. *Newsweek* media critic Jonathan Alter calls it "rounding up the usual suspects." In this field, the usual suspects tend to come from the child saving camp. Almost every story in New York, for example, quotes people like Anne Cohn, Vincent Fontana, and, until her recent death, Nanette Dembitz. The people who disagree can match them book for book, degree for degree, and credential for credential. But, except for Douglas Besharov, they either don't have much media savvy, don't like to deal with the press at all, or don't get into print or on the air because their views seem at odds with conventional wisdom. If every phone call a reporter has ever made to a Cohn, Fontana, or Dembitz, had been placed instead to, say, Malcolm Bush, Charlotte Booth, or Albert Solnit instead, America's understanding of child abuse might be completely different than it is today.

Also, Aber made a tactical error by beginning a sentence with the words, "The media must learn to discipline itself. . . ." That kind of talk always sends editors running for their First Amendment bunkers, from which they fire salvos of outrage at the interloper.

If the press doesn't understand the connection between what we have tried to do about child abuse and what happens to children in foster care, it's not surprising that the public doesn't either.

In addition to attacks from child savers, family-preservation efforts, like Homebuilders, have also come under a sort of friendly fire from people like Michael Wald.

Wald was among the first to link the harm of foster care to the excesses of child saving. His excellent model law restricting coercive intervention is discussed at length in the next chapter. But Wald is concerned that programs like Homebuilders are aiming too low. He writes: "If a child can be left at home without being seriously abused or neglected, the intervention is deemed successful. . . . We also seem to be preventing serious reabuse. But if we use such measures as academic, social, and emotional development, the case for family preservation becomes much less compelling."[36]

"Mike is confusing the role of family-preservation services [with] the possible role of a much broader array of services," replies Peter Forsythe.

Forsythe argues that family preservation can't take on all the functions that the rest of the child-welfare system has abandoned in favor of child saving.

Forsythe and others argue that family preservation is like an emergency room. It stops the crisis. Then other services must be made readily available to accomplish the changes that Wald wants to see. And programs like Homebuilders do teach families how to obtain whatever such help is out there. Jane Knitzer, who co-authored two evaluations of the South Bronx Homebuilders program, says: "Family preservation services are a very effective way of engaging families turned off by previous efforts. Then you have to work harder with other social service agencies so the philosophy is consistent. . . ."[37]

But Wald complains that the policies supported by Forsythe and others "haven't led anybody toward that [continuum of voluntary services]. All they've done is let the system look to what it can do minimally instead of what it can do maximally."

I think Wald is misplacing the blame. If the system has been doing only the minimum, it is not the fault of a small group of family-preservation advocates and their relatively small programs. It's the fault of a child-protective empire that has not been made to change. And there is a fundamental danger to "aiming higher" when the intervention into a family is coercive. Once you say you will use coercive intervention to do anything more than ensure a child's safety—if you try to use it to improve a child's academic performance, for example—you open the door to a massive reallocation of the nation's children from the poor to the rich. As Forsythe notes, if you took all poor children away from their parents and placed them with families who could afford to send them to elite private schools, you certainly could improve their academic performance.

Indeed, Wald said in an interview that his criticism of family preservation was not meant to suggest that he wanted to broaden the grounds for coercive intervention. Subjective evaluations of emotional well-being and criteria like academic achievement still should not be considered when deciding whether to force a child out of a family. That should only happen when the child is in serious danger of serious maltreatment. Wald says he only is suggesting that once the decision is made to intervene, help should be available beyond restoring minimal functioning to a family.

*   *   *

There are some cases that don't fit the family-preservation model. Though such cases get attention far out of proportion to their actual numbers, there are times when there should be no second chances. Period.

Exactly where one draws that line is not as clear-cut as it might seem initially. Often it is argued that one should simply apply the same standard as is applied to violence between strangers. If you slap a stranger, for example, it's a crime, so slapping your own child should be treated the same way.

There are some problems with this approach. First, though technically slapping a stranger is a crime, one is not likely to be punished severely for it, especially if it's a first offense. Second, even maltreated children sometimes want to go back to their abusive parents—indeed they sometimes insist upon it.

"I've had kids that were taken away from home say . . . I wish I'd never said anything because I'd be at home," says Dawn English, a foster parent in Washington State.[38]

Sandi Baker, Executive Director of the Sacramento Child Abuse Treatment Program, says she used to believe that "what should happen is that those rotten no-good parents . . . should just be expunged from [the children's] lives . . . me on my white horse, I would protect all these kids from those evil, horrible parents. So you'd put them in foster homes . . . and they'd run right back to the parent you'd rescued them from. So it finally dawned on me. Well, if they keep running back, maybe we ought to work with the family."[39]

This approach does not preclude punishing the abuser. A child can be returned after the parent has done some jail time and while that parent is still in a work-release program or serving some form of community service sentence.

There are times, however, when the child's safety dictates no second chances, even if the child wants to return and the parents claim they will change. I would draw this line at cases such as those where a child has been raped or sodomized or severely beaten by a parent, and, in the case of the beating, it was not a one-time aberration by a parent suddenly unable to control his or her temper. That is, there is clear and convincing evidence that the incident is a "first" only in that it is the first time the abuser got caught. In these situations, the child should be placed in foster care, parental rights should be terminated, and the offender prosecuted criminally.

And even if the beating did happen "only" once, or if there is a pattern of repeated abuse that is not as severe as I have described, but still serious; if the child does not want to go home, he or she should have an absolute right to stay away.

This is not the same thing as allowing any children who leave home because they think they're being made to do too many chores or too much homework to stay away. Nor does it mean that children should simply be taken at their word if they make up a story about abuse for which there is no evidence. Nor is it the same as taking all children at their word when there is evidence that the words have been put in their mouths by a vindictive spouse or by the child savers themselves.

And of course, even in less serious cases, if intensive efforts at family preservation are tried and fail, there should be no third chances.

There also need be no second chances where the parent "throws away" a child by kicking him or her out of the house, and someone else stands ready to adopt the child. Where adoption is unlikely, attempts at reconciliation are likely to be a better option than anything the foster-care system has to offer.

Similarly, in cases of abandoned infants, an intensive effort should be made for thirty days to find a parent or relative and find out the reason for that abandonment. If it turns out the child was abandoned because the parent is homeless, for example, they should be reunited and helped to find a home. On the other hand, if the parent isn't interested in the child and refuses to take him or her back, that should be the end of it. Parental rights should be terminated and the child put up for adoption.

And finally, there is the question of what to do about parents who are serious drug abusers. Earlier, I described the use of hysteria over drug abuse as an excuse for more child saving. But what about the parent who really is hooked on cocaine or heroin, who abused those drugs during pregnancy and gave birth to an addicted child?

The natural reaction is: Why bother? How could anyone who would do that to a child before birth possibly be a good parent afterward? What's more, the child is likely to be especially difficult to raise. There is evidence that the effects of drug abuse suffered in the womb will last a lifetime.

The answer is that one doesn't try to preserve such families for the sake of the parents. You do it for the sake of the child. If the parent doesn't raise this child, who will? A hospital? A "congregate care facility?" A succession of temporary foster parents? There are not a lot of people out there lining up to give permanent adoptive homes to premature, cocaine-addicted babies— especially if they're nonwhite as well. As columnist Ellen Goodman has written: "There simply is no way to save the babies if you throw away the mothers."[40]

In Los Angeles, a Perinatal Substance Abuse Council has set up programs to work with drug-abusing mothers and their children together.

They found that a large number of mothers want desperately to change. "I can't impress on you enough how much motivation a new mother can bring to turning her life around," the council's chairwoman, Kathleen West, told the annual meeting of the National Association of Foster Care Reviewers in 1989. "In many of the families, the mothers were not non-compliant. We were setting them up to fail." Women who were functionally illiterate, for example, were being told to go find a drug-treatment program and set up their own appointments. Once again, there was the need for help in using help.

The other key finding, not surprisingly, was that the same grinding poverty that is at the root of most child abuse, is at the root of a lot of drug abuse as well. Here again, West said, hard services made a big difference.

West's group didn't do all this for the parents. Los Angeles already had tried doing it the other way—automatically separating addicted children from their mothers. Says West: "The legacy is six-year-olds in group homes all over Southern California" and baby warehouses in Los Angeles like the ones in New York City.

West's group decided that working with families, even families with a drug-abuse problem, was a better alternative. Similarly, Marlene Halpern argues that it's a lot better to get a mother into treatment and let a newborn stay with "a mother who is clean now and has a home to take that child to and can bond with that child, rather than have the child moved from night to night. That's more disastrous for children."[41]

In most places, however, the addicted mother who wants to change is still set up to fail.

"When somebody says: 'O.K., don't take my child, I'll go into a treatment program, I'll do whatever you say'—that person needs to have treatment delivered that day," says Dennis Lepak. Instead, they wind up "on a five to six month waiting list."[42] A nationwide survey of eighteen big-city hospitals found that two-thirds of them had no place to which they could refer pregnant women for drug treatment. In all of New York City, as of 1989, there was only one residential drug-treatment program serving young mothers and their children. There are thirty beds for such women in all of Boston. Two-thirds of all drug-treatment programs in New York City refuse to treat poor pregnant women at all, and 87 percent have no services for poor crack addicts.[43]

Melinda Bird of the Western Center on Law and Poverty cites the case of a married, pregnant heroin addict living on welfare in a city with no drug-treatment program. At her own expense, the woman drove two-hours a day to a treatment program in the nearest large city, until she ran out of money to pay for gas. She missed enough sessions to be kicked out of the program. She went back on heroin and gave birth to a baby, who, though not addicted, had heroin in its system. The child was immediately removed from the mother and placed in foster care.

"After they took the baby away, she and her husband split up," says Bird. "She dropped into the street culture. She lost all reason to pull herself together."

Much like priorities in child abuse itself, priorities in drug treatment need to be reversed. Pregnant women and parents of young children need to be allowed to go to the head of the line for the limited number of places in current treatment programs, and such programs need to be expanded.

Where the parent of an addicted newborn refuses readily available treatment, or where he or she fails the program, that parent should be a prime candidate for having parental rights terminated.

Paradoxically, the people standing in the way of a system that would crack down on the brutal abuser and the addict who refuses to change are not the people who advocate family preservation. Once again, it's the child savers. Again, they don't do it on purpose. But they have so swamped the system that there is no time to find even the relatively low number of children who would be affected by such a crackdown, no time to pursue termination of parental rights when they are found, and no room for them in overcrowded foster-care systems.

In addition, a system that can impose severe sanctions as quickly as I believe it should will never take hold—indeed *should* never take hold—until judges and juries can be assured that child-welfare officials know what really happened in any given case, have had time to assess the situation, and, where appropriate, have offered intensive services first. By inundating the system with false reports and trivial cases, the child savers have made it impossible to provide such assurances.

This is still another reason why protecting those most in need requires narrowing the scope of coercive intervention, not broadening it. The next chapter offers some ideas for doing that.

11

Making Changes

The child savers won't change their orientation from family destruction to family preservation voluntarily. Reducing the amount of coercive intervention in the lives of children will require some coercive intervention into the practices of child savers.

In this chapter, I will outline some of the ways I believe those practices should be changed. These suggestions are intended as guidelines rather than rules, as a place to begin a discussion of reform rather than a place to end it.

I make no claim that these ideas are either exhaustive or original. My major concern is the construction of a legal foundation on which to build a better system (though other areas are touched on as well). The recommendations are drawn from the work of numerous lawyers, social workers, and scholars who have devoted much of their lives to trying to make the child welfare system work better. Occasionally, I have added a modification of my own.

The major influence on this chapter is a model law first proposed by Stanford's Michael Wald in 1976.[1] It served as the basis for a model statute proposed by a committee of the Institute for Judicial Administration and the American Bar Association as part of their Juvenile Justice Standards project. The committee put out a first draft in 1977, then made a number of changes before putting forth a final proposal in 1981. Except as otherwise noted, it is the 1981 version to which I will refer in this chapter.

Of the various proposals I have seen, I believe Wald's model to be the best. It is certainly the most thorough. The law is accompanied by an excellent, detailed commentary, and I recommend the volume, *Standards Relating to Abuse and Neglect* (Cambridge, Mass.: Ballinger Publishing Co., 1981) to anyone interested in a more detailed exploration of the issues raised in this chapter.[2]

As important as any specific clause in this model law is its overall philosophy. First, it is written with the understanding that child abuse, foster care, and adoption are closely interrelated. It attempts to mold the system into a coherent whole with one primary value: that every child is entitled to a permanent and stable home.

The present system makes it easy to put children into foster care and difficult to get them out. Wald's model law attempts to reverse this. It seeks to impose strict limits on when the state can put a child into foster care, and to make it easy for the child to get out—either through return to the natural parents, or, when that isn't possible, through quicker and easier termination of parental rights, which can open the way to adoption.

My first recommendation, however, is not derived from this model law. That's because there is one change that is even more important:

Recommendation 1. Reverse the financial incentives that encourage foster care and discourage permanent homes for children.

At the federal level, foster care is funded through Title IVE of the Social Security Act. As noted previously, this is "an open spigot." States get reimbursed for anywhere from half to more than three quarters of the cost of every foster-care placement for a poor child. Preventive services are funded through another program, called Title IVB. But this title also supports all sorts of other child-welfare services, including child-abuse investigation, adoption, and even some foster care. And the amount available for all Title IVB services is capped. I recommend that the two pots be combined, that the total be increased each year by an amount at least equal to inflation in child-welfare services—preferably more—and most important, that over a period of years the amount of federal funds that can be used for foster care be reduced to zero.

Here's an example. Suppose a state now gets $80 for foster care and $20 for preventive services. Under this plan, the state would get $100 the first year, of which no more than $80 could go to foster care. In subsequent years the total dollars would rise at least as much as inflation but the amount that could go to foster care would gradually be reduced, perhaps to $70 the second year, then $60, then $50 and so on.

Eventually, the federal government would be completely out of the foster-care-reimbursement business. States placing children in foster care would have to pick up the whole tab themselves, even as their allocation for preventive services was increasing. Where local governments split part of the cost of foster care with states, state legislatures should pass similar funding formulas.[3]

These changes would have to include a "maintenance of effort" requirement. States and localities that already spend their own money on preventive services must not be allowed to shift these funds into foster care as more federal money becomes available for prevention.

The incentives for private agencies also must be reversed. At a minimum, reimbursement of foster-care agencies on a per diem basis should be prohibited by state law. Congress should pass legislation barring child-welfare funds from states or localities that use per diem reimbursement.

One possible alternative would be to pay each private agency a specified annual amount regardless of the number of children in care. If they got children back home quickly, they could keep the savings. If they stalled, they'd eat the loss. This would have to be combined with another key change for private agencies: They must be required to take any child referred—no creaming allowed.

If the current financial incentives encourage too much foster care, would reversing them encourage too little? When per diem reimbursement was eliminated in hospitals, for example, they were accused of kicking out patients "quicker and sicker," a charge that I believe had merit in some cases. Would more children be returned too soon, or not be removed at all when removal is essential? I don't think so. There are enormous pressures in addition to financial ones pushing children into foster care, including the background, inclination, and training of the people who staff the system; racial and class prejudice; public demand; media pressure and the defensive social work it engenders. Reversing the financial incentives and imposing limits through the law are essential to provide a counterweight to all these pressures.

Recommendation 2. Reduce the types of maltreatment that professionals are required to report to child-protective authorities.

Under Wald's proposal, the only cases that would be subject to mandatory reporting are cases of "serious physical injury" (a phrase I will define later in this chapter). Wald argues that "neglect" is inherently so vague that reports of neglect may "express only cultural bias and severely harm the children who purportedly are 'rescued.' "

Wald puts even sexual abuse in this category, arguing that "by middle class norms, for example, it would be sexually abusive for children regularly to witness sexual intercourse by their parents, but these norms are regularly disregarded by other groups in this society and there is no substantial reason to believe that these children are thereby harmed." In fact, child savers go further. Recall the National Committee for Prevention of Child Abuse pamphlet that says even hearing an act of sexual intercourse in the next room is sexual abuse.

However, I think Wald's model is too restrictive in this area. Acts of rape and sodomy, for example, are as definable as they are inexcusable. Such acts should be left in the mandatory reporting law.

Eliminating the other categories of maltreatment does not mean they can't be reported; it only means that in these areas professionals would have their professional discretion restored.

Recommendation 3. All mandated reporters should be required to take a course in the mandatory reporting law.

This is already done in some states. The course need be only a couple of hours long, but it should explain both what to report and what *not* to report. It should include advice such as Douglas Besharov's suggestion that behavioral symptoms alone are grounds for a professional to ask questions, but they are not grounds for a report. The same dual emphasis— what to report and what not to report—should be an integral part of all media campaigns about child-abuse reporting. Training also should include education in what other services are available to troubled families, so professionals don't feel a referral to Child Protective Services is the only way to get "help" for a family.

Recommendation 4. Eliminate "educational neglect" from CPS jurisdiction.

In its *Guidelines for a Model System of Protective Services for Abused and Neglected Children and Their Families,* the National Association of Public Child Welfare Administrators states that "failure to attend school is the primary concern of educational authorities. There are other, more effective societal enforcements for compulsory education." The association says the same should apply to controversies over parents educating their children at home.

Recommendation 5. Limit CPS jurisdiction to cases where the alleged maltreatment was the result of actions of the child's parent or guardian, or where that parent or guardian knew the child was being abused by someone else and made no effort to stop it.

All cases involving teachers, day care workers, and anyone else who does not fit the above criterion should be referred to the police and handled by the criminal justice system.

Recommendation 6. Establish a mechanism for screening reports to eliminate cases that are patently false or do not constitute maltreatment under the law.

Typically, there is no official mechanism for screening out a false or trivial complaint when it is made to a child-protective hotline. Often almost any allegation no matter how absurd or how obviously ill-motivated is forwarded to child-protective workers for investigation.

The rationalization for this is that if any cases at all are screened out, a serious case of maltreatment just might be missed. Of course that's true, and the first thing to do in advocating for screening is to acknowledge this. Any system of screening virtually guarantees that some children will be missed, perhaps with fatal consequences.

But when child savers make this argument, they neglect one point: We already have screening. It is stupid, sloppy, de facto screening, but it is screening nonetheless.

—When a worker ends the day without getting to the last cases on the list because the caseload is too high, that's screening.

—When a state bans all visits to check on out-of-state placements, that's screening.

—When more than twenty cases are given to a clerk typist to handle because there is no child-protective worker to handle them—as happened in Massachusetts—that's screening.[4]

—When reports of maltreatment pile up in boxes or are shoved into workers' desk drawers unread—that's screening.

The refusal to institute a system of rational screening guarantees the creation of the present system of irrational screening by overloading the system. "In the short run," Besharov says, screening "will do more to protect children . . . than anything else we could possibly do.[5] . . . The absence of guidelines is not only working to violate parental rights, but it is also costing children's lives."[6]

Child Protective Services is the only major emergency response system that doesn't screen in some way or another.

After false alarms became a major problem in the 1970s, fire departments realized they would have to do some screening, even if that increased the risk of missing a real fire. As a result, many cities replaced boxes where an alarm was sounded by pulling a lever, allowing no screening, with boxes that required the reporter to talk to a dispatcher. In some cases, boxes were removed entirely.[7] Some fire departments also send out less equipment in response to an alarm if it was sounded by an automated system in an office building.[8]

Similarly, to return to Besharov's analogy in Chapter 1, if you call 911 to report littering, or a noisy party, don't expect the police to rush to your doorstep in the order the call was received. They are going to set priorities, and some calls won't be answered at all.

And if you call 911 for an ambulance, the dispatcher is going to ask some questions before sending one out. He or she will want some idea of whether the problem is a heart attack, a sprained ankle, or something in-between. The information taken during this screening process will dictate how soon an ambulance is sent, if at all. This is done even though there have been cases where dispatchers made the wrong decision and a seriously ill patient died. The practice continues because it is understood that if ambulances were sent in response to every call, the seriously ill would have to wait longer and even more people would die. Indeed, in New York City, paramedics have complained that dispatchers don't screen enough and patients died while they were tied up on trivial cases.[9]

The real reason screening is resisted has nothing to do with child protection and everything to do with politics. Besharov calls it "the protect thy tail syndrome. . . . Journalists will zing 'em anytime a case is rejected and the kid is subsequently harmed. They can be sued, they'll be criticized, heads will roll."

Besharov worked on drafting New York's child-abuse law. He says the problem is especially acute in New York because of "the biggest mistake we made" in that process. The mistake was to put the state in charge of taking hotline calls, while counties (and New York City) are in charge of investigating. As long as the state shovels every report down to the county child-protective agency, its hands are clean. The local government gets the blame when the cases pile up in boxes and a child dies. Besharov charges that as a result the state's Social Services Commissioner "is in a terrific position. [He gets to say that] 'mistakes were made—but not by *my* folks.'" At one point, Besharov says, he even offered to study the New York hotline and recommend a screening system—at no charge to the state. He says the current social-services commissioner, Cesar Perales, rejected the offer. Perales says he doesn't remember it.[10]

Although New York remains recalcitrant, child-welfare officials in other states are beginning to endorse screening. The report of their national association concluded that "all states should have the flexibility to screen at the time a report is taken."[11]

Any screening must be done by workers who are specially trained to handle it. These workers must be provided with a series of detailed guidelines and questions to ask that will help them determine two key facts: Would the allegation, if true, constitute maltreatment under state law, and does the reporter have reasonable cause to believe such maltreatment occurred? Establishing these criteria means referring elsewhere cases of less-than-optimal child care that are cause for offering families help on a voluntary basis. It also means that even if the caller alleges serious abuse, the case would be screened out if it was based solely on rumor, gossip, or "a gut feeling." With just this much screening, says Besharov, "you would be surprised how many cases would be screened out."[12]

Michigan has contracted with the National Council on Crime and Delinquency to develop such a model. CPS staff in that state already have put together some preliminary recommendations. Among them are twenty-four specific criteria for rejecting a report, including:

—The allegations were recently reported by a different person and have already been assigned and investigated by CPS staff.

—The complainant is in the midst of a custody dispute and is reporting marginal concerns with a view to prejudicing the court and proving a spouse "unfit."

—Suspicions of the complainant are proven unfounded after contact with a reliable source with more current or accurate first-hand information.

—The concerns of the complainant do not constitute abuse or neglect as defined by CPS policy, or the allegation is too vague to provide a reasonable suspicion of maltreatment. The caller may be directed to a more appropriate resource.

—The complainant is reporting information from second- or third-hand sources and CPS is unable to corroborate information from more reliable sources.

—Similar concerns have been investigated and repeatedly deemed unfounded or the complainant is known to repeatedly make false reports.

—The child is exhibiting normal exploratory sexual behavior.

—The complainant is predicting that harm will come to a child in the future and there is no reason to believe it will really happen.[13]

This is not necessarily the best set of guidelines that can be developed. I offer it as an example of where to start in improving the current hit-or-miss system of irrational screening. It is an attempt at smart screening.

Pennsylvania, on the other hand, offers a case study in dumb screening. The Pennsylvania law limits mandatory reporting to cases where harm has been done to a child and the harm is serious. The first problem is that this law makes no provision for cases where parents attempt to do serious harm to their children but for some reason fail. Obviously, such cases should be included.

Limiting reporting and investigation to cases of serious harm or attempted serious harm would make sense, but the law doesn't do that either. Instead, less serious cases are classified as "General Protective Services." They stay on workers' caseloads, but they get a lower priority. Thus, Pennsylvania gets all the drawbacks of screening and none of the benefits.[14]

Recommendation 7. CPS agencies should refuse to accept anonymous reports.

CPS should still accept reports on a confidential basis—that is, keep the accuser's name secret from the accused, except as described in Recommendation 10—but CPS should not accept a report from anyone who does not leave a verifiable name and address or phone number.

Of all categories of reporters, mandated and non-mandated, the people who refuse to give their names are by far the least reliable. If anonymous reporting were banned but reporters could be assured their names would be kept in confidence (except under circumstances I will describe below), I believe a large portion of anonymous reporters who are sincere and reliable would come forward. But some would not and, therefore, some cases would be missed.

But once again, I believe fewer cases would be missed than are missed now while workers waste their time investigating false tips from anonymous reporters. And obviously, this should cut down a great deal on the use of child-protective hotlines for harassment.

In recommending that anonymous reports be refused, the authors of the study of such reports in the South Bronx note that "the resources of child protective agencies are not limitless. The time and energy spent investigating false reports could be better given to more serious cases, and children may suffer less as a result."[15]

Recommendation 8. Searches of homes and strip-searches of children should be permitted only with the informed consent of the parent or guardian or after obtaining a warrant based on a "probable cause" standard. It should be prohibited to take note of refusal to consent in any case records, or to use it against the parent or guardian in any court proceeding.

Informed consent means that a parent confronted by a CPS worker at the door would get the equivalent of a Miranda warning. Parents would be told they have a right to refuse entry and a right to refuse to answer questions, but that if they exercise that right, and if the worker feels she has enough of a case, she will ask a judge for a search warrant.

This is not a particularly difficult procedure. Warrants can be granted over the phone; if anything, judges will probably issue them too readily.

A very limited exception might be made for exigent circumstances. In cases of dire emergency, a CPS worker or the police should be allowed to enter a home without a warrant, solely for the purpose of alleviating the immediate emergency. They would have to wait for a warrant before proceeding further. Examples of dire emergencies would be cases where the beating of a child could be heard or seen from outside a house or apartment, or where a parent is seen to have pulled a gun or a knife on a child or a gunshot is heard in the house.

The mere act of asserting one's rights should not in itself become grounds for a warrant, nor should it be brought up at any court hearing or included in any written record. (Violation of this standard should result in the dismissal of any pending court action.)

If a parent or guardian consents to a strip-search, or if a warrant allows it, the child should be taken to a doctor or a nurse for the examination, with the parent present to reassure the child. The parent should be allowed to take the child to his or her own pediatrician or nurse practitioner if the child has one.

This kind of strip-search, where the doctor is looking for bruises or welts, is different from an examination for medical evidence of sexual abuse.

That should be done only by court order, with CPS and the parents both having the right to have an examination performed by the doctor of their choice. Judges should be encouraged to get the parties to agree on one doctor—again, to minimize trauma to the child. CPS agencies should not be permitted to keep doctors on their own payroll for this purpose, and courts should regard as suspect any doctor proposed by CPS who relies largely on CPS referrals for his or her income or who finds "evidence" of abuse in almost every case. Conversely, a doctor chosen by a parent who is known never to find such evidence also should be suspect.

Recommendation 9. All interviews conducted in the course of a child-protective investigation must be tape-recorded.

This is particularly important when a child is being interviewed, so that it can be determined whether the child was intimidated or asked leading questions.

Interviews at a CPS or therapist's office and any interview at any location involving the use of anatomically correct dolls, drawings by a child, or any other nonverbal communication should be videotaped. Interviews in the field should be audiotaped. Calls to child-protective hotlines should be routinely recorded, just as calls to "911" emergency-dispatch systems are now.

All tapes should be made available to the accused, except tapes of the person making the accusation if he or she wants anonymity, in which case that interview could not be used as evidence in court. A transcript of such interviews still should be available to the accused, minus identifying information, and the actual tape should be available for review by a judge if the accused suspects the transcript is inaccurate.

In addition to protecting the innocent, tape-recorded interviews can be an enormous help to the child, since if they are done correctly, they reduce the need to question a child over and over again.

This is a very simple requirement to comply with. An easy-to-use camcorder can be purchased for under $800. Microcassette tape recorders that can be easily carried in a pocket or purse can be purchased for less than $50

There should be no exceptions when a tape is "accidentally" erased or there is some other malfunction. When the case goes to court, the rule of thumb must be: if it isn't on tape, it doesn't exist.

Recommendation 10. Deliberate false reports should be subject to civil and criminal penalties.

In Virginia, parents who believe they are the victim of a deliberate false report can ask a judge to look over the file, and if the judge concurs, release the file to them so they can find out who made the report and initiate legal action.[16] (Any records that do not compromise the identity of the reporter should automatically be available to the accused—see Recommendation 12.) The catch is that Virginia still allows anonymous reports. As noted earlier, such reports should be banned, and the Virginia procedure should be the one exception to the rule that reporters can remain confidential.

Recommendation 11. People should be listed in a state central registry only after a court finds them guilty of maltreatment.

Even well-trained workers should not be able to act as judge, jury, and executioner when it comes to stigmatizing parents for life and barring them from some types of employment—and that often is the consequence of a listing in the central registry. And of course, well-trained workers are very rare. On the other hand, if this higher standard is adopted, schools, day-care centers, and other employers who deal extensively with children should be allowed to screen potential employees through the registry, as currently is the case in many states.

A less desirable alternative would be to continue to allow listings by CPS workers but guarantee a right to appeal, at state expense, through an administrative hearing conducted by an independent agency. The burden of proof at these hearings would be on CPS. If this system is adopted, access to the registry should be limited to CPS itself, as well as foster-care and adoption agencies.

Recommendation 12. When a worker decides a case is unfounded, all CPS records on the case should be immediately destroyed.

This includes not only details of the case but any record of who was accused. The only exception should be when the victim of a false allegation suspects malice and asks that records be maintained so he or she can try to get them pursuant to Recommendation 10. In such cases, records that do not disclose the identity of the reporter should be sent to the accused, and the entire file should be sealed. Only the judge and, if the judge allows it, the victim of the false allegation should have access to the entire file.

This recommendation divides child-welfare experts in some surprising ways. Douglas Besharov, who has gained a reputation for seeking limits on coercive intervention, believes records of unfounded cases should be retained. Like the child savers, he argues that just in case the unfounded determination is wrong, keeping the record would provide useful information if a child is reported as maltreated again. On the other hand, the National Association of Public Child Welfare Administrators says that "all documents related to unsubstantiated cases should be destroyed immediately."[17]

In Michigan, the CPS task force called for retaining records of unfounded cases for two years, but commission chairman Steve Murphy disagrees.

There are several reasons to prefer immediate destruction of records in unsubstantiated cases.

—Although in theory these records are confidential, evidence indicates that the child savers can't keep a secret—especially when it involves people they hold in contempt anyway.

—The argument made by Besharov and others cuts both ways. Allowing unfounded reports to remain in the files makes it likely that anyone who is tenacious enough about harassing someone will win out eventually, simply by piling false allegation on false allegation. As Steve Murphy points out: "Does the existence of that information guide you into making it a case? [Do you conclude] they've had two or three reports so there must be some fire there somewhere?"[18]

Recommendation 13. Abolish "voluntary" placement.

One can't stop parents from insisting they want to place their children in foster care. But these placements should be subject to the same safeguards, including immediate review by a court, that should be applied to involuntary placement.

Recommendation 14. Grounds for coercive intervention into families should be significantly narrowed.

This recommendation, along with the recommendations for reversing financial incentives and screening calls, are the most important in this chapter.

The grounds for coercive intervention should be those proposed by Wald in his model law. That law eliminates the terms "abuse" and "neglect" in favor of the term "endangered child." A child is endangered and coercive intervention is authorized when a "child has suffered, or there is a substantial risk that a child will imminently suffer physical harm, inflicted non-accidentally upon him/her by his/her parents, which causes or creates a substantial risk of causing disfigurement, impairment of bodily functioning, or other serious physical injury."

Wald writes that "the intent of the standard is to prevent injuries such as broken bones, burns, internal injuries, loss of hearing, sight, etc. It is not intended to cover cases of minor bruises or black-and-blue marks unless the child was treated in a way that indicates that more serious injury is likely to occur in the future." That does not mean the distant future. The potential injury should be imminent. Wald offers this example: "If a parent throws a child against a wall, but the infant sustains only minor injuries, we should not wait until the child is again injured more seriously before intervening."

Coercive intervention also is authorized when the same type of injury occurs or is equally imminent "as a result of conditions created by [the child's] parents or by the failure of the parents to adequately supervise or protect him/her."

This is Wald's substitute for current neglect laws. Note that those neglect cases child savers are always talking about that are "worse than physical abuse" clearly are covered. Starving a child, for example, or leaving a child alone at too young an age obviously cause or can cause "impairment of bodily functioning" or "serious physical harm."

Wald discusses how the standard would apply in five situations:

—A five-year-old child is regularly left to wander streets late at night. The parent knows of the problem and takes no action. Intervention *is* permissible.

—A child is being physically abused . . . by a person other than the parent or guardian . . . and the parent or guardian is unwilling or unable to protect the child from this third party. Intervention *is* permissible.

—A small child is severely beaten by a baby-sitter. The parent dismisses the sitter and takes steps to insure the adequacy of future caretakers. Intervention is *not* permissible.

—A child is living in a home that is poorly furnished, has some cracks in the plaster, and there is an irregular feeding schedule. The child has not been injured and does not suffer severe malnutrition. Intervention is *not* permissible.

—The home of a three-year-old contains a high-voltage wire which is left exposed despite the fact that the parents have been made aware and given the resources to correct the problem if they are financially unable to do so. Intervention *is* permissible.

It is important to remember, however, that intervention is not synonymous with removing a child.

Another section of the law allows intervention but bars taking a child away "when the child is endangered solely due to environmental conditions beyond the control of the parents, which the parents would be willing to remedy, if they were able to do so." In other words, if a child is in danger because of poor housing, the state can intervene to move the family to a better apartment or to fix the apartment the family already has, but the state may not intervene to remove the child.

This is one of the most important features of Wald's model, but it needs some beefing up. Child savers now sometimes know better than to tell a court they want a child removed solely because of bad housing—even if it's what they really mean. Once under the child saver microscope, some other flaw can be found in any family and some fancy psychological label can be attached to it. I would therefore delete "solely" from Wald's language limiting when a child can be removed, and I would drop the part about parents being "willing" to remedy the problem, since the child savers can make anyone sound "unwilling" if they put their minds to it.

Beyond that, judges simply need to be alert to attempts to place a medical-model label on cases where the real problem is poverty.

Coercive intervention also is authorized "when a child is suffering serious emotional damage, evidenced by severe anxiety, depression, or withdrawal, or untoward aggressive behavior toward self or others, and the child's parents are not willing to provide treatment for him/her."

This is Wald's attempt to replace the current vague laws authorizing intervention for emotional abuse or neglect. Some commentators have argued that alleged emotional maltreatment should never be grounds for coercive intervention because it is so subject to the biases of mental health "professionals" and because the child savers tend to wreak so much emotional havoc themselves when they intervene.[19]

Wald recognizes the pitfalls. He writes: "It is hoped that [testimony of mental health professionals] will take into account developmental and cultural differences in children, as well as the appropriateness of any behavior to the child's environment. For example, a child in an inadequate school or a dangerous neighborhood might be quite appropriately anxious, depressed, or even hostile."

I'm not sure hope is enough. Ultimately, it may be necessary to ban coercive intervention in cases of alleged emotional maltreatment altogether. But Wald's approach at least should be tried, with two possible changes in language: First, because of the concerns Wald cites, coercive intervention should be allowed only where there is serious *and abnormal* emotional damage. Second, the law should guarantee parents the right to choose the therapist and method of treatment they want, subject to applicable state licensing standards.

The proposed standards also would allow coercive intervention where a child is engaging in delinquent acts with parental assistance or approval, where parents refuse to provide medical treatment and that treatment is needed to prevent "death, disfigurement, or substantial impairment of bodily functions," and in cases of sexual abuse.

The model law does not offer its own definition of sexual abuse, suggesting instead that the states rely on definitions of sex crimes contained in their penal laws. This is in order to avoid coercive intervention in cases where "it may be difficult to distinguish between appropriate displays of affection and fondling or other behavior possibly disturbing or damaging to the child." The proposed law also requires that a court find that intervention is necessary to prevent a given behavior from recurring. For example, intervention would not be permitted where a child was unsupervised but, by the time the case goes to court, the parents had arranged for day care.

Recommendation 15. Grounds for taking a child into emergency custody should be strictly limited.

Under Wald's model, emergency custody can be used only when the person taking custody "has probable cause to believe such custody is necessary to prevent the child's imminent death or serious bodily injury" and the parents are unable or unwilling to protect the child. Even then a court order is required unless the risk is "so imminent" that there isn't time to get one. When custody is taken, a petition must be filed on the "next business day" with a hearing no later than the day after.

There is an important exception: When the danger is caused by a child being left unattended, the CPS worker or some other responsible person must stay and wait until the caretaker returns or it is clear the caretaker won't return home; nobody can simply take the child and leave.

The model law proposes two other, excellent provisions. It recognizes the "head start" that the child savers have at the first hearing, when bewildered parents may not even have a lawyer. If a child is kept in temporary custody, it calls for holding a second detention hearing as soon as the parents and their attorney decide they want one.

The law also would require that as long as a child is detained before a full family court trial is held to judge the merits of the case, parents must be allowed to visit their children every day. When necessary, CPS must provide transportation to those visits. This provision recognizes the importance of visits, the presumption of innocence, the trauma of separation to the child, and the child's sense of time. It may be a month before this trial, called an "adjudication hearing," takes place, and often it's a lot longer. For a child, it can seem like forever. The provision has one other benefit. Child savers who know they must provide daily visits for children in "temporary" custody are likely to be deterred from using temporary custody too often and encouraged to move quickly to adjudication when they do use it.

I disagree with the proposed standard, however, concerning the amount of time that can elapse before the first detention hearing. Under the proposal, a child taken into custody on the Friday before a holiday weekend might have to wait five days before the first hearing is held. Remember how much harm was done to Jennifer Humlen in only a few days.

Family courts should be seven-day-a-week, 365-day-a-year operations. Hearings should take place no later than the next day, period.

Even better would be a system in which family courts operated twenty-four hours a day—just like the police. Children would be removed from their homes directly to a nursery at the courthouse if they were too young to be part of the hearings themselves, and hearings would begin immediately upon arrival. Neither side would have a lawyer and the child savers wouldn't have a chance to draw up a petition and give it to the judge ahead of time. For this very first hearing only, it would simply be the worker and the parent, telling their stories to the judge.

Recommendation 16. All decisions made by child-welfare personnel and courts should be based on finding for the child the least detrimental alternative.

This phrase—coined by Goldstein, Freud, and Solnit—should replace the common—and commonly ignored—standard of "the best interests of the child." The change in phrasing is intended to provide all parties with a constant reminder: That the act of intervention is harmful in itself, and the question must always be whether it is less harmful than taking no coercive action. It is an attempt to remind a supremely arrogant system of the need for humility.

Recommendation 17. The burden of proof in all court proceedings must rest with the state. The burden it must meet should be "clear and convincing" proof.

This is the middle standard, lower than "beyond a reasonable doubt" but higher than the "preponderance of the evidence" standard used in many child-welfare proceedings.[20]

Recommendation 18. At all court hearings after the first detention hearing, children and parents should each have the right to an attorney. The attorney should be publicly funded if the parents can't afford it. The attorney for the child always should be publicly funded. At the first detention hearing such attorneys should be appointed immediately if the parents have been unable to make their own arrangements.

The reasons for giving everyone a lawyer are obvious, though not obvious enough to make it standard operating procedure in all states. Less obvious is what the lawyer for the child should do. Should the lawyer do what lawyers traditionally do for adults: try to get the client whatever he or she wants, even if the lawyer thinks it's bad for the client? Or should the lawyer act as "guardian ad litem," setting out to determine the least detrimental alternative for the child and advocating it even if the child disagrees.

My own feeling is that from the age the child can speak, his or her lawyer should do what the child wants done, if it bears any resemblance to reality (as opposed to, say, a child who wants to be placed with Santa Claus). The role of guardian ad litem duplicates what the judge is supposed to do: sort through the competing claims and decide which has the most merit. Unless the child has a lawyer functioning solely as his or her advocate, the child can wind up the only party to a proceeding with no way to speak up for what he or she wants. If a child wants something that is unsafe or unrealistic, then it is up to the lawyers for the state and/or the parents to point that out, and up to the judge to decide.

If a judge feels there is also a need for an objective investigator, he or she should have the option of naming a Court Appointed Special Advocate. These are citizen volunteers trained to act in this role and report on their findings. A CASA should be appointed only *in addition* to a lawyer for a child, not as an alternative.

Recommendation 19. From the moment they take custody of a child, foster parents should be allowed to participate at all court proceedings. They should be allowed legal representation, paid for with public funds when they can't afford to pay. In addition, foster parents should have a right to a court hearing whenever an agency tries to remove a child from them—even when the removal is back to the child's own parents—unless the foster parents are accused of maltreatment, in which case the same procedures that apply to natural parents should apply to them.

This may seem to contradict the thrust of this book, which is to emphasize family preservation and avoid placement. But, as Peter Forsythe likes to say, "I'm not against placement. I'm against *unnecessary* placement." The way you find out if a placement is still necessary is by consulting everyone who might have relevant information.

Will foster parents often be "biased" against natural parents and fight to keep their foster children, even when that is not the least detrimental alternative? Probably. But everybody who comes before a court is biased. Again, it's the job of the judge to sort through all the biases and try to come up with the truth. A child should never be returned to a family because a judge didn't know something he or she should have known.

The other purpose of this recommendation is to allow foster parents to become advocates for the children in their care with less fear of retaliation from agencies who presently can and do shuffle children around if foster parents "make trouble." Just the fact that the agency would have to go through a court hearing to engage in such retaliation should discourage the practice somewhat.

Recommendation 20. In addition to the limits on coercive intervention described in Recommendation 14, additional limits should be placed on when a child can be removed from his or her parents.

One of those additional limits—barring removal when the problem is poverty—has already been discussed. In addition, Wald's proposal would require the court to find that removal from the home is the only way to protect the child from the specific harm that prompted the intervention, and that a safer alternative than the child's home actually is available.

I would make two additions. First, by the time an adjudication hearing takes place, often a month or more after the very first hearing, the child savers should have figured out exactly where they plan to put the child if they obtain custody. They should be required to provide this information to the court. If they don't know, the court can reasonably infer that the child will be placed in a shelter, turned into a "nomad child" or be otherwise shabbily treated. The judge should consider this in deciding whether removal is really the least detrimental alternative.

Second, at any stage in court proceedings, including the initial temporary-custody hearing, when a judge finds a child is endangered because of the actions of a parent, and there is no way to protect the child while the whole family is at home, the judge should give first preference to removing the accused parent—not the child—from the home.

Recommendation 21. After an adjudication, parents should be allowed to visit their children at least once a week for several hours at a time; the visits should take place at the parents' home; and the visits should be unsupervised unless the attorneys for the state or the child can prove to the court that any or all of these provisions would be seriously harmful to the child. Agencies should be required to provide transportation for visits when necessary and to schedule visits at night and on weekends as needed.

Recommendation 22. If parents are receiving Aid to Families With Dependent Children, these payments should continue without reduction while the child is in foster care.

This would help prevent the downward spiral that often occurs when a child is removed when AFDC benefits are cut, the parents lose their apartment, and so on. In addition, being forced to pay for AFDC and for foster care simultaneously is one more fiscal incentive to reduce foster care.

If child-protective workers believe parents are deliberately placing children in foster care in order to keep benefits while having fewer mouths to feed, they can go to court and try to prove it. If they do prove it, this should be grounds for termination of parental rights. An alternative might be to allow the worker to seek a court order allowing the worker to administer that portion of the AFDC grant that would have covered care to the children. Any such order would have to ensure that the worker was required to spend the money on things like food and rent before it was spent on "counseling" and other child saving interventions.

Recommendation 23. The status of every child in care should be reviewed by an outside agency every six months. The state should be required to prove by clear and convincing evidence that foster care is still needed, and it has made reasonable efforts to reunify the family.

Under the Adoption Assistance and Child Welfare Act, some form of review is required every six months. States have used one of three options: court hearings, independent citizen-review boards, or reviews within the state's child saving agency itself.

Obviously, the latter should be unacceptable. If review boards are used, they must have the same decision-making power and must provide families with the same due-process protections as courts.

Recommendation 24. Whenever a child is returned home from foster care, the agency must continue to provide help to the family for at least six months.

This proposal, included in Wald's model, is intended to reduce the number of children who return to foster care because the family was given no help in adjusting to their return.

Recommendation 25. Because the preceding recommendations should make it much more difficult to put children in foster care, and easier to return them home, when reunification is not the least detrimental alternative, termination of parental rights should be made easier, so efforts can be made to place a child in a permanent adoptive home.

Exactly how much easier was the most vexing question for the committee that worked on the ABA Standards and Goals volume. Ultimately, they decided that Wald's original draft made it too easy, and they made some substantial changes. The revised version is discussed here.

Conditions that would allow, but not require, termination include:

—The child has been abandoned for sixty days—meaning the parents voluntarily left the child and made no attempt at contact even though they were able to do so. (I would make it thirty days for children under age two, if the agency with custody of the child can show that it made a "diligent effort" to find the parent.)

—The child was placed in foster care and the parents made no contact for a year, even though the foster-care agency made a "diligent effort" to keep the parents and children in touch. Sending one post card or making one phone call would not be enough to constitute contact under this provision.

—The child was returned home only to be abused again, or the child has now been in foster care a second time for at least six months and it is unlikely that the child can be safely returned again.

—The child was placed in care because he or she was found to be endangered. The child has remained in care for at least two years if under the age of three or at least three years if older. There is "substantial likelihood" that the conditions forcing the child into care won't improve. The agency has done everything it promised to do to keep the family together under a plan approved by the court.

As noted in the previous chapter, I would add to these grounds certain cases in which the maltreatment was so severe that there should be no second chances and other, less severe cases, where there should be no third chances. Also, I would add as a ground for termination cases where intensive services, including Homebuilders-type programs, were tried for six months, followed by six months of foster care with intensive but unsuccessful efforts to make it safe for the child to go home.

Even if one or more of these standards is met, the proposed law states that courts still should not order termination if "because of the closeness of the parent-child relationship it would be detrimental to the child"; the child is with a relative who does not want to adopt; the child is in a residential treatment center, not a substitute family; there is no way to place a child in a permanent home; or the child is over age ten and doesn't want the parents' rights terminated.

There is one other ground for termination in the proposed model law, and it raises some of the most difficult questions in all of child welfare. Termination should be allowed when the child was placed in care for any reason, formally or informally, voluntarily or involuntarily; the placement has continued for three years regardless of the child's age; the foster parents want to adopt the child; the child is at least twelve years old and wants to be adopted; return of the child to the parents "will cause the child to suffer serious, sustained, emotional harm."

What makes this clause so controversial is what it does not say. It does not require that the parents have done anything wrong to have their rights terminated. They might simply have been sick, for example. And it does not require the agency to make diligent efforts—or any efforts at all—to keep the family together. Presumably, an agency could actively thwart efforts by parents to remain close to their children and this standard still would apply.

This clause is rooted in the theories of Goldstein, Freud, and Solnit. They argue that when a child is out of touch with his parents for what is (by the child's standards) a very long time and placed with loving substitute parents, there is an excellent chance that the substitutes will become that child's "psychological parents." As far as the child is concerned, the foster mother is mother and the foster father is father.

It doesn't always happen that way, and the concept of "psychological parent" is another one of those ideas that can be exaggerated and distorted. (This is accounted for in the proposed law, which says that even when other grounds apply, rights should not be terminated where there is a close parent-child relationship.)

Furthermore, carried to its logical extreme this standard could require that a child be kept with a kidnaper if they stayed in hiding long enough and a close bond developed between them. How different is that, in fact, from an agency thwarting reunification for three years? Cases for which this ground would apply are rare—but when they happen, what choice is a judge faced with? Commit and act of unspeakable cruelty against parents by severing all ties with their children when those parents have done nothing wrong, or commit an act of unspeakable cruelty to children by tearing them away from the only parents they know and forcing them to live with people who, to the children, have become strangers. It's the sort of dilemma that would have made King Solomon want to go into another line of work. But the dilemma must be faced and a decision made. And if one truly believes in placing the interests of the child first, in almost all such cases the child must be allowed to stay with the substitute parents.

Agencies, however, must not be allowed to get away with not doing their jobs. A termination clause like this could become an irresistible temptation to child savers to sabotage relationships between impoverished natural parents and their children in middle-class foster homes. Since refusing to terminate parental rights in such circumstances would mean punishing the child for the agency's failure, something else must be done.

I would add to any proposed termination statute a clause stating that if termination were approved where the parents were not at fault, and contact with the child was lost because of agency failure, the judge would be required to levy a stiff fine against the agency. The judge should have the option of shutting down a private agency if such failures occur repeatedly. And in either a private or public agency, a judge should consider throwing the head of an agency in jail, at least for a few days. Few things are likely to move a mayor or governor to improve an agency faster than the sight of one of his or her commissioners being hauled off to jail.

Any new termination provisions should be the last part of a new law to take effect. It should take effect only if the remainder of the law has, in fact, succeeded in reducing placement in foster care.

Recommendation 26. Appeals of court decisions in cases involving foster-care placement or termination of parental rights should be taken to a special Court of Children's Appeals.

Though it is not in his proposed law, this also is a suggestion from Michael Wald. Again, because of the need for permanence and the child's sense of time, cases should not drag on for months or years. In states large enough to have midlevel appellate courts, a panel or panels of judges would be chosen from among these courts and their job would be to hear only cases involving child custody. There would be a ninety-day time limit between a lower court's decision and the time this special court would have to hear and decide appeals. Cases still could be appealed to a state's highest court, but Wald says he doubts many decisions would be overturned, "so you could at least have some feeling of finality."[21]

Recommendation 27. Parents and children must have a means of legal redress when they have been abused by the system.

Many of these recommendations include requiring agencies to do things, either in the normal course of their duties or by order of a judge. But child savers have a long record of ignoring the courts when they don't feel like carrying out such orders.

There are two principal means of redress when child savers break the law. One is to bring a class-action lawsuit against systemwide deficiencies. Several such lawsuits have been discussed in this book. Generally, these suits have been brought in federal courts charging violation of the constitutional rights of children. More recently, suits have been brought charging violations of the federal Adoption Assistance and Child Welfare Act.

There is some difference of opinion emerging in the federal courts over the extent to which rights supposedly guaranteed under that act can be enforced through lawsuits.[22] The issue revolves around what Congress intended. Congress should amend the law to make clear that courts are empowered to enforce all of its provisions.

The second approach is for individual children or parents to sue for damages because of what the system has done to them. At present, the chances of a successful suit against a child saving agency or the people who work for it range from slim to none. In many cases—Elene Humlen's is an example—both the agencies themselves and the people who work for them have absolute immunity for much of what they do, no matter how badly they do it. As a practical matter, for the reasons described in Chapter 4, the protection is greater when workers wrongly remove a child than when they leave a child home and something goes wrong.

This must change. Where it does not already exist, individual workers should be granted what the law refers to as "good faith" immunity rather than absolute immunity. That's still a lot of protection. In layman's terms, "good faith" immunity means that the action or inaction of the individual worker must be the result of outrageous laziness, stupidity, or both, for the worker to be found guilty.[23] This immunity should not extend to agencies, however. Where state laws prohibit suing such agencies, those laws should be repealed, and there should be no form of immunity. Agencies should be liable when they break the law and their lawbreaking hurts people, just like the rest of us. As one attorney put it: "The only language they understand is 'I'll see you in court.' "[24]

While acknowledging the value of class actions to change agency practices, Besharov argues against individual suits against agencies for damages. "If people were serious about using tort law to obtain better child welfare services, they would not sue agencies," he writes. "They would sue state budget officials, governors, state legislatures, the President, and the Congress."[25] This argument assumes that lack of money is at the root of all child-welfare evil. As the comments of Marcia Lowry and others make clear, there is more to it than that. In addition, a few large judgments, payable by the taxpayers, might be just the thing to get the attention of lawmakers and make them pour more money into the system. Besharov argues that such lawsuits have not accomplished this yet, but perhaps that's because they are so difficult to win.

In addition, the lawsuit has a purpose beyond systemic change. Money is poor compensation for a child brutalized by foster care or a parent who has unjustly lost his or her child. But it is the only compensation we have.

If lawsuits are made easier, it must be done in a way that balances incentives. For example, the United States Supreme Court has barred federal lawsuits when a child is left at home unprotected and is seriously injured or killed. But states can still allow such liability and all the other risks cited in Chapter 4, such as criminal prosecution and trial by media, still apply. If states do allow liability for failure to remove a child, they must ensure equal liability for wrongly intervening in a family's life by strip-searching children, for example, or by removing them to foster care unnecessarily.

Workers will complain about being damned if they do and damned if they don't. But they should be given good faith immunity. Furthermore, when a job deals with matters of life and death, that kind of risk goes with the territory. Every time a police officer draws his gun he faces the same dilemma. If he shoots when he didn't need to use deadly force, he faces disciplinary action within the department and maybe a lawsuit as well. If he waits too long to shoot, he could lose his life. Either way, he could endanger innocent bystanders.

The compensation for such risk should be in the form of better pay and working conditions, not absolute immunity for workers—and certainly not immunity for their bosses.

Recommendation 28. All records maintained by any agency in connection with a child protective or foster care case should be public documents, with only the following exceptions:

—Records should remain secret for the limited time period during which a worker determines whether a case is "indicated" or "unfounded." If the determination is "unfounded" the records should be destroyed as provided for in Recommendation 12.

—Records disclosing the name of someone reporting maltreatment should remain secret if the reporter so requests except as provided in Recommendation 10.

—The attorney representing the parents or the attorney representing the child may go to court and request that records be withheld entirely, or that they be released with only the names deleted. The attorney must prove by clear and convincing evidence that this is the least detrimental alternative for the child. Agencies should not be allowed to request confidentiality.

Virtually everything done by the child savers is done in secret. They claim the secrecy is in the child's interest, but the evidence is overwhelming that secrecy protects only child savers from being held accountable for their actions. Justice Brandeis said that "sunshine is the best disinfectant," and there is no cesspool more in need of a good cleaning than the child-welfare system.

For the same reason:

Recommendation 29. All Family Court proceedings should be open to the press and the public, subject only to the same potential restrictions as those applying to records.

Recommendation 30. The minimum qualification for beginning child-welfare workers should be a bachelor's degree in social work. Higher starting salaries should be provided for candidates who also have child-welfare experience or who received training in foster-care or child-protective work in college.

This might encourage social work schools to take on some of the burden of training that child-protective agencies now are forced to try to do themselves. When training is provided at all, the investment often goes to waste because the worker quits soon after the training period ends.

Recommendation 31. Higher qualifications must be accompanied by higher pay, better working conditions, and improved training with an emphasis on family preservation.

Along with the higher pay must come some basics, like adequate secretarial assistance and office supplies and dignified, respectful treatment from supervisors.

Recommendation 32. Duplicative paperwork must be eliminated. Workers often complain about the amount of time they spend filling out forms. On the other hand, with worker turnover so high, a form may be the only way the new worker knows what's going on with a particular child. More important, a lot of paperwork is essential to provide even minimal accountability in a system that operates largely in secret.

What is needed is, first, to sort through all the forms and figure out what one really needs to know in order to help children and ensure accountability. Throw out the rest. Second, put what's left on a computer. The goal of the computer program should be simple: No single piece of information about a child—from the name to the description of family circumstances—should have to be typed more than once. With a few keystrokes, the computer should be able to copy information from form to form as needed.

Recommendation 33. The federal government, perhaps through the National Center on Child Abuse and Neglect, should begin research into the effectiveness and "side effects" of child-abuse-prevention programs for children.

The results of these evaluations should be publicized so parents and school officials can know which of the many available programs to choose. Prevention programs should not be attempted in preschool in light of existing evidence that they don't work for that age group and may have harmful side-effects.

Recommendation 34. The federal law we have now must be enforced.

The first thing the Reagan administration did with the Adoption Assistance and Child Welfare Act was try to repeal it. Failing that, the administration spent eight years trying to sabotage it.

The Department of Health and Human Services is supposed to check up on states to be sure they are following the law. The then-head of HHS's Administration for Children, Youth, and Families acknowledged during a Congressional hearing in 1988 that all the federal auditors do is look at forms to see if the right boxes have been checked. As Marcia Lowry put it: "It is almost impossible to fail an HHS audit."[26]

Among other information to emerge from federal officials at the hearing:

—The federal government doesn't even know how many children are in foster care.

—Regulations issued by the Carter administration in 1980 to implement the law were withdrawn and never replaced.

—Louisiana had actually managed to flunk a federal audit, but the Assistant Secretary then in charge of child welfare programs, Sydney Olson, had no idea what, if anything, her agency had done about it. This prompted an exasperated chairman of the House Select Committee on Children, Youth, and Families, Congressman George Miller (D-California), to ask Olson: "What do you do in this department?"

—Olson didn't know anything about the lawsuit concerning overnighters in New York City, either.

—Another federal official said there were a number of states doing a good job with some child-abuse grant money from the federal government. But he couldn't name any.

But perhaps the best indication of the administration's contempt for children came when Congressman Thomas Downey (D-New York), who was co-chairing the hearings, read aloud from the prepared testimony of Olson's predecessor at hearings held one year earlier. He then compared it to the testimony Olson had just finished giving. The excerpts were identical. Word for word. "This reminds me of one of the book reports I used to do in high school," Downey said. "I recycled them in tenth grade and twelfth grade. . . . My reports didn't change. Remarkably, apparently neither does your testimony from year to year."

"What you are really engaged in," added Miller, "is state-sponsored child abuse."[27]

Recommendation 35. Advocates of family preservation must be aggressive in taking their case to the public.

The child savers learned how to get "good press" more than 100 years ago, and it's time those who disagree learned the same lesson.

Advocates of family preservation cannot confine their writing to scholarly journals and their speeches to professional seminars. They must go public with stories about their successes and the child savers' failures. No attempt to make family preservation the scapegoat for child saver failure should pass unchallenged. When reporters and editors won't listen, they must take to the letters columns and the op-ed pages. Charlotte Booth of Homebuilders lamented not having the time to reply to one article she had seen. From now on, advocates of family preservation have to make the time.

*   *   *

I have not tried to put a price tag on these recommendations. Since no one is sure how much the current system costs, I know of no reliable way to estimate what these recommendations would add or, in some cases, subtract.

But this much is known: though some of these recommendations would add costs, others have the potential for enormous savings. Preventive services more than pay for themselves, because they cost a lot less than foster care. Screening out false reports and limiting coercive intervention also have obvious savings. Furthermore, enacting these recommendations probably would force some increase in funding. That's because foster care is so popular with the public. If the federal government stops funding foster care, the states will have to make up some of the difference with new money.

From these sources a great deal of the needed preventive services, voluntary help, increased court costs, and increased costs for worker salaries and caseload control could be funded.

Maybe it's not enough. If not, then it's up to all the people who ask, "Why didn't somebody do something?" when a child dies. Then they should do something themselves: put their tax money where their mouths are. That means middle-class Americans, who take (publicly financed) highways to their (FHA-mortgaged interest-deductible) homes in the suburbs where they have dinner (that won't poison them, because the food was government-inspected) with grandma (who's on social security) and the kids (just back from the state university they attend with a guaranteed student loan), are going to have to stop claiming that you can't solve problems by throwing money at them.

That money will come only when people know enough to become as indignant over what happened to a foster child like Anne Williamson as they became over what happened to Lisa Steinberg.

The objection that child savers will raise to any limits on coercion is obvious. It is the same as the objection to screening. Put any real definition on what constitutes "abuse" or "neglect" and we might miss another Lisa Steinberg.

The argument is disingenuous.

You don't need a broad, general definition of "neglect" in order to intervene in cases of murder. You don't need it in cases of rape. You don't need it in cases of brutal beatings. There was never any legal question that what happened to Lisa Steinberg and Eli Creekmore was abuse.

The real reason child savers want broad laws is so they can intervene in areas where there is far less societal consensus, but do it secretly so there won't be a massive backlash. For example, you could eliminate a whole lot of ambiguity just by prohibiting all corporal punishment. Bring that hidden agenda into the open, however, and CPS might never recover from the public outcry. So the laws are kept nice and vague.

Attacks on more specific definitions typically are conducted by finding an obscure, exceptional case or constructing a hypothetical case in which a child could be seriously abused, yet not fall under the narrower definition. The temptation is to try to accommodate each of these eventualities as they arise—to say, "All right, let's amend the law to account for this, and this, and this." Before long, however, that would return us to where we are now—all you need to separate children from their parents is a child saver's "gut feeling." The only sensible alternative is to try to find a reasonable model that holds coercive intervention to a minimum while doing as much as possible to protect children who are genuinely maltreated.

Such a model will not reach everybody. Some children will be missed entirely—their cries of pain will be screened out. Other children will suffer when their parents refuse voluntary help, but have not done them enough harm to justify coercive intervention. Some children will be seriously injured. Some children will die.

But that is exactly what's happening now on a much larger scale. Children are dying because investigators are too busy tracking down false reports to get to them on time. Children are dying because there is no time for a thorough investigation. And children are dying in lousy foster homes.

Former juvenile court commissioner Gary Seiser recalls what he was once told by another judge: "I have left children in their own homes and they have died. I have returned children to their own homes and they have died. I have placed children in foster homes and they have died."[28]

The model proposed in this chapter and the preceding chapter is not a model that will protect all children. It is a model that will protect *more* children.

12

Update

The children kept coming. All day and all night. Infants and toddlers and teenagers. They were tired. They were scared. Sometimes they were angry. And no one had any idea what to do with them.

So they were dumped into an office building at 810 W. Montrose Ave. on Chicago's North Side. The building housed Chicago's only emergency shelter for children taken from their parents. But by May 1993, the shelter was full. So the children were shoved into office space in the same building.

First twenty, then thirty, then forty-nine, then sixty children would be crammed into the office space on any given night. Many children were teenagers whose placements had "disrupted"; either they had run away or their foster parents had kicked them out. But at least one-third were entering the system for the first time.

Some of the children truly had been in danger in their homes. But in 10 percent of the cases, they were sent back home within forty-eight hours because everyone—even the Illinois Department of Children and Family Services, which had removed the children in the first place—agreed there had been no need to take them away and throw them into the shelter.

One child wound up at the office because a foster parent who was about to adopt him had died. No one at the office so much as talked to him. He just sat in a chair all night and cried.

"Here they are undergoing perhaps the most traumatic night of their lives and they can't even get a decent place to sleep," says Benjamin Wolf of the Illinois chapter of the ACLU. Two years earlier, Wolf had settled one of the class action lawsuits discussed in chapter 7. Among the provisions: a promise by DCFS never again to house children in offices. Now the promise was being broken.

The children lacked more than a decent place to sleep. They did not get enough food, they had no decent place to bathe, and the living area was dirty. Cribs for the infants reeked of urine. The youngest children were separated from the oldest by only a six foot partition. But that, at least, was an improvement. Before they were separated by age, the older children would sneak the younger ones outside and abuse them sexually, Wolf said. One advocate called the shelter "a time bomb."

One day an eleven-year-old boy at the makeshift shelter got hold of a gun—nobody is sure how—and fired it.

The *Chicago Tribune* described shelter life in this way:

> A surly teenager with a bad attitude struts and shouts swear words a few yards away from the abused and neglected little ones, so young they can barely tell you their names . . . 16-year-old Harry is boasting: "I stole 50 cars this week!" A few yards away is 5-year-old Michael, so very scared and trying with all his might not to cry. "I'm the big brother," Michael explains, gently stroking the hair of Christopher, 4, who gulps heavy, sleepy breaths and sucks his thumb on a cot in a corner. . . . When a visitor tried to shake the little boy's hand, he threw his arms around her, starving for a hug. . . .
>
> "I want my mom," Michael said . . .

The account is as ironic as it is poignant, for as we will see, the *Chicago Tribune* helped create the very conditions it now was exposing.

In December, DCFS "solved" the problem. The office space was officially rechristened a "shelter" and made just habitable enough to comply with the consent decree. It was licensed to house seventy-three children. "We don't want seventy-three children there," declared a DCFS attorney, "we want zero." But just four months later, the *new* shelter was itself at capacity. Now the children were overflowing into a nearby conference room. They slept on chairs and on the floor. There were "wall to wall babies" said a DCFS spokeswoman. "If you're going to have that many babies in a place, how much attention is each baby going to get?"

But that's not what finally motivated DCFS to act. The agency took action only after eight of the conference room "residents" attacked a DCFS worker.

The new solution: Ship the children to all parts of Illinois, hundreds of miles from their families. A mother who had visited her ten-month-old every day since he was placed because of alleged neglect showed up at the office only to find her son had been shipped off to East St. Louis, at the other end of the state.[1]

The cause of all this is no mystery. Chicago was and, as this is written, still is in the midst of a foster care panic. It began the way all foster care panics begin: A child "known to the system" was returned to an abusive parent who killed him. But unlike the other such panics discussed in this book, the panic in Chicago threatens to engulf the entire nation.

"Why won't we take children from bad parents?" asked *Newsweek*.[2] "Young and in Danger: Why Kids Get Sent Back to Abusive Homes" said the headline in *USA Today*.[3] Two television "newsmagazine" programs also piled on. Nearly all of the stories focused almost exclusively on Chicago.

Of course, all of these accounts blamed "the law," but now there was a new twist. The media had a name for anything that ever went wrong. That name was "family preservation."

At the time *Wounded Innocents* first was published, family preservation had a very specific meaning: a systematic determination of those families in which children could remain or be returned safely, and provision of all the services needed to ensure that safety. And intensive family preservation programs meant programs that rigorously followed the Homebuilders model. But by the time the child savers and the media were through, family preservation had a new meaning: all-purpose scapegoat.

Was a child left at home because a worker with fifty cases never got to number fifty-one? That's "family preservation." Was a child returned home and abandoned, with no help for the family and no visits to see how the family was doing? It's because of "family preservation." Did a judge return a child home because no one ever told him the home was dangerous? Blame "family preservation."

Since *Wounded Innocents* first was published in 1990, there have been many new developments concerning the child protective system, foster care, and family preservation. These developments did not occur in a vacuum. The media played a crucial role in determining the fate of children caught in the child savers' net.

Family Preservation Under Attack

If not for the harm done to so many children needlessly removed from their homes, the attacks on family preservation actually could be viewed as good news—maybe even the best news in the four years since *Wounded Innocents* was published. It is good news in this sense: The fact that family preservation is under sustained attack from the child savers means that family preservation has grown big enough and strong enough to be a threat to them.

Just four years ago, family preservation was confined largely to pilot projects. Today, though it is still only a small part of a system dominated by foster care, these programs help thousands of families every year. And further expansion is likely as a result of new federal legislation. The amount of new money is far less than some media accounts have suggested, but the mere passage of legislation signals the potential for a change in funding priorities—which is enough to strike terror into the hearts of child savers and send them scurrying to friendly reporters.

There are other reasons for the attacks:

—President Clinton is in favor of family preservation, so the knee-jerk Clinton-haters have to come out against it.

—The families helped by family preservation are almost always poor, often black, often black single parents, and sometimes black single parents on welfare. That doesn't go over well right now. For much of the public, a series of myths about who gets welfare and why, combined with some old-fashioned racism, has turned the "welfare mother" into the root of all evil. Child savers have played on welfare mother stereotypes as they attacked family preservation.

Even with all this going for the child savers, real family preservation programs are so fundamentally sound that it took an extraordinary combination of factors to set off the current firestorm.

First, somewhere in America there had to be a child welfare agency so dumb, or so beholden to special interests, that it would take every rule about how to run an effective family preservation program and break it. Enter the Illinois Department of Children and Family Services.

With much fanfare, DCFS inaugurated a program called Family First in 1989. Almost everything that made Homebuilders-type programs a success in other states was ignored in Illinois:

—The *median* number of cases per worker in Illinois was five—two and a half times the *maximum* permitted in Homebuilders. In half the Illinois programs, the caseload was even higher. As a result, workers in these so-called intensive programs spent an average of only 32.4 minutes per day with a family. This diluted service was stretched out over 90 days or more, again contradicting the Homebuilders model.

—In the Homebuilders model, the Homebuilders worker helps with even the most mundane tasks, using the time to observe how the family functions, discuss family problems and build trust. In Illinois, these tasks were delegated to homemakers who spent an average of 9.6 minutes per day with the family.

—After a Homebuilders intervention, families are supposed to be linked with less intensive follow-up services. In Illinois, provision of such services was "haphazard and inadequate" according to an independent evaluation of the program.

—Agencies providing the services in Illinois were allowed to downgrade their hiring standards for workers.

—DCFS was in turmoil during the experiment. The agency ran through four directors in four years, and never figured out what it wanted its "family preservation" program to accomplish.

—The program served large numbers of children who were not at imminent risk of placement in the first place. "Control groups," who received only conventional services, also were filled with such children. As a result, Family First did no better than conventional services at preventing placement, because few children in either group were at risk.[4]

Worse, this diluted program could not maintain the safety record of other family preservation programs. Out of 17,000 children who have gone through Family First since its inception, six have died.

Why did DCFS ignore all the lessons about how to run a family preservation program? Both Wolf and Diane Redleaf of the Legal Assistance Foundation of Chicago suspect the problem lies with the the state's politically powerful private agencies. Their support was needed to get Family First through the legislature, Redleaf said. She believes that, in exchange, they got a program tailored to their convenience instead of a program geared to what works.

A poorly designed program was the first problem. Second, there had to be someone around anxious to take advantage of DCFS's failure. Enter Patrick Murphy, Cook County Public Guardian—and born-again child saver. Yes, the same Patrick Murphy who condemned the scope of neglect laws, the same Patrick Murphy who said foster care turns children into "emotional pulp."

Murphy's office serves as "guardian ad litum" for abused and neglected children, which means Murphy can advocate for what he thinks is best for each child, regardless of what the child may think.

Murphy insists that he reversed himself because things are different now than they were when he wrote his book in 1974. Although the neglect law has not changed since he condemned it, he insists that "social agencies," as he called them, suddenly have begun removing only children in real danger.

And at a time when everybody loves a liberal who's "seen the light," Murphy throws in some pandering to the current vogue for welfare-bashing. "Liberals are afraid to come to grips with their failures," he says. "We cannot give people money and services without demanding something in return."[5]

Murphy gleefully embraces the National Committee for Prevention of Child Abuse[6] party line: Child abuse can't have anything to do with poverty because most poor people don't abuse their children. (Of course, this does not explain why it is that the courts in which he practices are filled almost exclusively with poor people).

In fact, Murphy's conversion is more recent than he lets on. He brought his class-action lawsuit against stripsearching in 1984. Does he believe such abuses have disappeared in ten years? He called DCFS "the worst parent in the State of Illinois" in 1988[7] And when Murphy made the comment on page 174, the one in which he talks about teenagers who become prostitutes *"not because of what happened to them in the home,* but because of what happened to them in the system" [emphasis added] it was 1989.

Indeed, Murphy often slips up and says the same sort of thing today. On October 13, 1993 he wrote: "Taking a child, even from a borderline parent, is traumatic. And not infrequently, DCFS is a more abusive parent than the real one."[8] "If you stick [children] with DCFS it gets even worse," he said in 1994. "Will the kid go through 12 foster homes? Get beat up and maybe raped?"[9] And *Newsweek* tells us that "Murphy believes that most families should be reunited."[10]

Yet Murphy has made a national name for himself by trashing the very programs that make such reunification possible. In the *New York Times,* Murphy wrote that the overwhelming majority of poor families struggling to raise their children get nothing, while family preservation services are lavished on those who brutally abuse their children.[11] He describes recipients of family preservation help as "thugs and cowards who beat up, torture, and rape their children"[12] and insists over and over again that helping those who crack under the stresses of poverty is "patronizing" to those who don't.

Although Murphy says, "There haven't been gray cases in years,"[13] he can't even make up his own mind about what kind of parent is good enough to be worthy of having her family preserved. One day he says the only worthy parents are "parents who are very poor and who may have inadvertently neglected their children but who are trying very hard to make life better both for themselves and their children."[14] On another day, Murphy may be more charitable. "Take the depressed parent who wakes up at 25 with four kids," he said in an interview with the *New York Times.* "The crack vials are up to the ceiling. The kids are filthy. There are rats, cats, elephants in the place. Everyone at school makes fun of the kids because they stink. But the kids down deep love that mother."[15]

Asked about this, Murphy said he was misquoted by the *Times.* He denied having included "crack vials up to the ceiling" in the scenerio and says such a mother should "lose her kid immediately."[16]

In February, 1994, Murphy was on national television condemning parents whose children had been living in squalor.[17] A week later he supported return of children to a grandmother who was living in squalor.[18]

"Patrick Murphy is a person who operates without standards," says Redleaf, whose office often opposes Murphy's office in court. "His standards are personal standards. If he likes a person he will fight for them. . . . There is no consistency."[19]

Some of the apparent contradictions might make sense if Murphy were arguing that family preservation should be expanded to the many worthy poor people who now, he says, get nothing. It even might make sense if he were arguing only that services should not go to the highly unrepresentative horror-story cases he cites over and over.

But Murphy has been an equal opportunity destroyer. Though he says that "no one believes in returning kids home as strongly as I do,"[20] he has sought to deprive both the "worthy" poor and the "unworthy" poor of family preservation. The new federal money that the Clinton administration approved for family preservation previously had been vetoed by George Bush, at the strong urging of, among others, Patrick Murphy. In Illinois he sought legislation that even the *Chicago Tribune,* a Murphy ally, said would have "effectively defeated" family preservation in that state.[21] And in a *New York Times* Op Ed piece that helped make him a national media star, he calls for using foster care, with relatives or strangers, as an "alternative" to family preservation.[22]

But Murphy also filed a class action lawsuit alleging that when DCFS used his preferred alternative, the agency "continually placed children in living arrangements where they were sexually assaulted by other children."[23] He charged that thirteen children were raped or sexually attacked in foster care during a single sixteen-day period—and those were only officially reported cases.[24]

In other words, Patrick Murphy repeatedly has advocated policies that would force thousands more children into a system that Patrick Murphy has acknowledged is unsafe.

Some suspect Murphy's behavior is politically motivated. Three times in the 1970s and 1980s he declared and then withdrew his candidacy for public office, and in 1992, Murphy lost a race for District Attorney (called State's Attorney in Illinois). But it's also possible that, like other child savers, Murphy is sincere, but blind to the many contradictions in his approach.

Why did the source of such a muddle of contradictions become a media darling? Partly it's because in a system that hides so much behind the claim of "confidentiality," Murphy will go public, releasing information that supports his point of view. No reporter wants to burn a source. But it's also because, though the things Patrick Murphy says don't make a lot of sense, he says them very, very well.

"One of journalism's dirty little secrets," says *Washington Post* media critic Howard Kurtz, is "its dependence on 'spokesmen' who can supply succinct sound bites on deadline."[25] And no one can do that better than Patrick Murphy. He is Mr. Goodquote; the man-of-a-thousand-sound-bites.

For Murphy, a rent subsidy to prevent a child from losing his parents becomes a way to "bribe them not to abuse their children."[26] Murphy takes the cycle of desperation and despair that begins with the removal of a child—the loss of AFDC benefits, the imposition of impossible conditions, the barriers to visits, the pointless "counseling," the intimidation by workers with the power of God—and boils it down to parents allegedly not wanting to see their children because they don't have carfare. Having set up the straw man, he then knocks it down memorably, declaring: "Most parents would climb over a mountain of glass barefoot to see their kids."[27]

In addition, the things Murphy says have enormous visceral appeal for journalists. When Patrick Murphy bashes bureaucrats, he is saying out loud and on the record what reporters say to each other in the newsroom. While lobbying for his antifamily preservation bill, Murphy called private child welfare agencies "whores" and "vultures feeding on the flesh of dead children." He said the agencies "must be smoking dope" and he used an obscenity when talking to a representative from Catholic Charities. When the agencies made the mistake of filing a formal complaint about this, Murphy called the person he'd insulted "a dopey bureaucrat," thereby making himself that much more of a media hero.[28] Indeed, when a *New York Times* reporter made the mistake of asking only about the obscenity, Murphy bragged: "I also called them whores and vultures."

And the *Times* loved it. Murphy "is so driven by outrage that he dismisses diplomacy as a tactic of those who would sacrifice children's best interests," the *Times* declared. "Consumed by the brutalities he encounters every day, he has no time for niceties."[29]

And he doesn't stop with sound bites. To push his bill to kill family preservation in Illinois, he sent every Illinois legislator autopsy photos of a child who died in Family First. He even used the brother of a dead child as a prop at a news conference, holding the baby while the cameras flashed. The picture made the *Tribune* twice and was reprinted in *Newsweek*.

When Murphy fought the child savers he labored in obscurity outside Chicago. After he underwent his conversion, the national media couldn't get enough of him. In addition to the fawning profiles in the *Times* ("A Defender of Chicago's Children Refuses to be Polite About Abuse") and *Newsweek* ("A One-Man Children's Crusade"), he's been on "NBC Nightly News," CBS's "Eye to Eye," and ABC's "Turning Point." He made "20/ 20" two weeks in a row. And all of this attention came months *after* a special commission accused Murphy of misrepresenting his role in the very case that made him a national figure.

Of course there is nothing wrong with coming up with good quotes.

Had I thought of the "vultures" line I might have used it myself when I wrote about the private agencies in New York City. But Murphy's media savvy allowed him to protect his policies and the workings of his own office from critical scrutiny. No reporter wants to kill the goose that gives the golden quotes.

Of course all the good quotes in the world mean nothing if there's no one to print them—which brings us to the third element in this story.

Enter the *Chicago Tribune*. In October, 1992, a seven-year-old boy was killed by a sniper as he walked to school. The death shocked the *Tribune* staff into concluding that it was time to stop treating the deaths of children as business-as-usual. As Deputy Managing Editor Ann Marie Lipinski obligingly told the ABC News series "Turning Point": "That story was a turning point for us."[30]

Tribune editors resolved that every violent death of a child in 1993 would be front-page news. And they would pour time and effort into explaining why so many children die and what can be done about it. The effort focused on all violent deaths, whether they were gang shootings, murders by strangers, or child abuse deaths. The crusade was begun not to "sell newspapers" or to sensationalize, but for the most noble of purposes: to save young lives and better the community. But it went terribly wrong.

Eventually, the *Tribune* staff would conclude that family preservation is vital for the protection of children. They would conclude that the concept had been unfairly tainted by the failure of Family First. And they would lament a "lingering public misperception" of what family preservation is all about. But it would take almost a year for the *Tribune* to reach those conclusions, and by then it was too late.

With each new death, the *Tribune* would keep count, with the number prominent on the front page. It was number sixteen that made all the difference.

On Feb. 16, 1993, a frustrated juvenile court judge pleaded for more information about the case before him. "Would somebody simply summarize what this case is about for me and give me an idea why you're all agreeing to this before I approve it?" he said. What everyone was agreeing about was Amanda Wallace, mother of three-year-old Joseph Wallace. Amanda's lawyer wanted the family reunited. So did the Department of Children and Family Services. So did the Cook County State's Attorney's office, which prosecutes child-abuse cases. And, perhaps most important, so did Patrick Murphy's Public Guardian's office, which represented Joseph.

So the judge agreed. "It sounds like you're doing o.k.," the judge said. "Good luck." Two months and three days later, Joseph Wallace was dead, allegedly hanged by his mother.[31]

This was not a case where no one could have known what was coming.

Amanda Wallace, herself a former foster child, had a lengthy arrest record and an even longer history of mental illness. She had set herself on fire and tried to disembowel herself. She ate batteries and drank drain cleaner. Yet twice before, once in Chicago and once in another part of the state, judges had returned Joseph Wallace to his mother.

Eventually it would emerge that the people who made the decisions, the judges, didn't know much about Amanda Wallace. What little they were told they had little chance to digest. Chicago's Juvenile Court has eleven times the recommended caseload for such courts—the cases race by in minutes. And in every case except one, the judges were ratifying unanimous recommendations.

But what about DCFS? How in the world could an agency that fiercely resists returning so many children, actually recommend return in this case?

Apparently, for all her craziness, Amanda Wallace had one skill: the ability to con a caseworker. She did the things child savers love to see: She sought out "counseling," kept her apartment clean and, it appears, she knew how to act repentant. As one of Joseph's foster parents put it: "She played the system like a Stradivarius violin."[32]

So what went wrong in the Wallace case was what almost always goes wrong in such cases: Overworked, undertrained workers making bad decisions ratified by judges drowning in cases and kept in the dark.

But Walter Williams, one of the judges who returned Joseph Wallace to his mother, made a reference to the fact that "we try to reunite families." Williams also had been involved in a much more ambiguous case that had brought down upon him the wrath of a *Tribune* columnist in 1991. And, of course there was Patrick Murphy, who had an extra incentive to blame "the law" and "family preservation"—it diverted attention from the failings of his own office.

That was more than enough. The *Chicago Tribune* was on a righteous-indignation high. One front-page story declared that Joseph was doomed by "a system of judges, lawyers, social workers and doctors that all but conspired to kill him"[33]—and no part of the paper was immune. The editorial board crusaded—not for more judges, or more caseworkers or better training or, God forbid, screening to get false reports out of the system to give everyone more time to focus on parents like Amanda Wallace. No, over and over again editorials declared that, as one put it, "the most critical element" was a bill to change "the law" to make "the best interests of the child" more important than family preservation.[34]

The crusade was not confined to the editorial page. "DCFS Asked: What About Kids Rights?" declared a story on April 25. "In Illinois, critics fed up with child abuse cases that end tragically said the system too long has bent over backward to coddle dangerous parents," the story said. Why?

Because of "the law," of course. Story after story repeated that theme. Over and over again, the claim appeared that the law required that children be returned home "whenever possible."[35] In fact, those words never appeared in Illinois' law. The law said only that "reasonable efforts" should be made to prevent placement and that families should be reunified "where appropriate."[36]

The columnists weighed in as well. Bob Greene and Mike Royko wrote column after column reinforcing the child saver line. "DCFS has always been obsessed with the idea of reuniting families, even if the family environment was nothing more than a torture chamber," Royko wrote.[37]

As important as what was written was what was not written.

In the year following Joseph Wallace's death, almost nothing appeared in the *Tribune* about abuse in foster care. Even when Patrick Murphy's lawsuit about sexual abuse in foster care was dismissed (because the issue already was covered in Ben Wolf's lawsuit) the story was buried. And Murphy's claim that thirteen foster children had been raped or sexually assaulted in sixteen days rated only a ten-paragraph story on an inside page.

The omission is particularly glaring since, Wolf says, the Illinois foster care system is like "a laboratory experiment in how to produce sexual abuse of children."

> It's hard to imagine creating a system that could be more dangerous. Older children, some of them victims themselves, get little therapy and help [and are placed with] . . . a lot of young, vulnerable kids. You put them in where they're moved around a lot and have little supervision—the likelihood of the older kids attacking the younger is very high. . . . I have interviewed a significant number of kids in the system. An incredibly high percentage have stories of that kind.

Furthermore, DCFS doesn't even keep track of the "known sexual attackers" as they are moved through the system. And Wolf believes many deaths of foster children attributed to accidents are really suicides.[38] "The kids will tell story after story after story" about abuse in foster care, Wolf says. But it does not appear that the *Tribune* ever asked.

Also absent from the *Tribune* was any serious scrutiny of the role Murphy's office played in the Wallace case.

Initially, according to the *Tribune*, "Murphy said he personally handled Joseph's case the first time it went to court." Again according to the *Tribune*, Murphy "had pleaded with a judge to keep [Joseph and his brother] in a foster home." The *Tribune* goes on to quote Murphy directly: "This was my personal case," Murphy said. "I can't tell you how sick I am now."

And later in the story, Murphy even claims to remember exactly what he said to the judge. "I remember telling Williams: 'This is not family preservation. There is no family to preserve here.'" As for the final return, to which his office agreed, Murphy charged that a DCFS worker may have withheld crucial information and should face criminal prosecution. And, of course, he blamed the law. "The fact is, under law, if Mom does what is required of her, the kid goes back home," Murphy said.[39]

A few days later, and just ten days after Joseph died, Murphy issued a "report" on the death. Though many groups and individuals would issue such reports, Murphy got his out first, making it even easier for him to shape the debate.

Murphy devoted most of the report to slamming family preservation. He also repeated his claim of personal involvement, declaring that "I was personally involved in the Joseph Wallace case and I attempted to convince Judge Williams to change his mind."[40]

According to the *Tribune,* Murphy "castigate[d]" himself.[41] In fact, he took blame only for not appealing the first decision to return Joseph home and for believing DCFS. But a little repentance went a long way. He won praise from the *Tribune,* which declared that everyone else should follow Murphy's enlightened example and engage in similar "critical self-analysis."[42]

In October 1993, a special commission of three lawyers named by Harry Comerford, chief judge of the Cook County Circuit Court, exposed Murphy's real role in the Wallace case. Among the Commission's findings:

—In the first case, when the Public Guardian's office argued against return, that office and the State's Attorney did a lousy job of it. They performed so poorly, the report states, that "they must accept the lion's share of the blame . . ." for the court order returning Joseph. As for Murphy bemoaning his failure to appeal, the report concludes that his office's legal work was so poor that an appeal never could have succeeded.

—In the final case, in which Murphy claims his office did not have enough information, the report lists document after document that was available to Murphy's office. Rather than failing to have the information, the report concludes, Murphy's staff failed to tell the judge about the information they had.

—In addition to the information regularly available, the Assistant Public Guardian who handled the *first* Wallace case prepared a special file for the assistant who handled the final case. Along with the file came a strong recommendation to oppose Joseph's return. Instead, the Assistant Public Guardian on the second case ignored the available information, preferring to believe a caseworker who urged that Joseph be returned.

—Murphy's office didn't just go along with returning Wallace; his office persuaded the State's Attorney's office to support the return. The report concluded: "Joseph died because a DCFS caseworker and an APG [Assistant Public Guardian] became persuaded that Amanda Wallace was a proper caretaker. They imposed that decision on two judges by their silence."

And what about the claim by Murphy, referred to in the report as the "PG," that he personally pleaded with judge Williams not to return Joseph. According to the report: "When confronted with the fact that *the transcripts show that the PG never appeared before Judge Williams,* the PG privately recanted." [emphasis added]

Murphy says that, on the matter of his personal involvement, once again he was misquoted. "I didn't say it was my personal case," Murphy says. "I said I was *personally involved* in the case," by which he meant he had spoken directly to Joseph's foster parents and gave instructions to the Assistant Public Guardian who argued it in court. But in a June 3, 1993 letter to the commission, Murphy acknowledged that "it does appear I erred when I stated that 'I attempted to convince Judge Williams to change his mind.' "[43]

The report also had some things to say about what did *not* cause Joseph's death:

> Ever since Joseph's death, the term "family preservation" has been stigmatized to mean leaving a child in a dangerous home. . . . After a review of the record, we believe that no judge or lawyer in this case agreed to return Joseph to his mother merely because of his or her desire to preserve families.

Indeed, family preservation almost saved Joseph Wallace.

While living out of the Chicago area, the Wallace family was placed in Family First. Because even a poorly designed program like Family First gives a worker more time to observe a family than a DCFS worker has, the Family First worker was able to observe Amanda Wallace's bizarre behavior. While Family First still was working on the case, Amanda Wallace overdosed on a prescription drug. She was hospitalized and her children placed in foster care. At a court hearing two days later, the Family First worker strongly recommended *against* letting Wallace get her children back. The judge followed that recommendation. A few months later, with the children still in foster care, Amanda Wallace moved back to Chicago and her case was transferred to Chicago courts.[44]

The commission found that the facts of the Wallace case were precisely the opposite of what the public had been led to believe. Family First almost saved Joseph Wallace, while the Public Guardian's office helped send him to his death.

When the report came out, it was the lead story in the *Tribune,* bannered across the top of page 1. But none of what you have just read about the report's findings made it into the *Tribune's* story. Instead, Murphy was quoted the next day blasting the report as a "canard" produced by "silk-tie lawyers"[45] and a *Tribune* editorial suggested the report was a "whitewash."[46]

All the news stories and editorials and columns did a great deal of good—for the *Tribune.* The editorials won a Pulitzer Prize and the entire effort was a finalist for the Pulitzer for public service. The series won at least ten other awards, by the *Tribune's* own count, including one from the National Committee for Prevention of Child Abuse.[47]

But while the plaques piled up in the *Tribune* newsroom, the children piled up in the shelters. Between February and June 1993 the number of children coming to the Montrose Avenue shelter doubled. Between June and July it doubled again.[48] Statewide, more children were taken into foster care in the year following Joseph Wallace's death than in any year in the history of DCFS.[49]

But that was only part of the problem. A far bigger problem was the refusal to let children already in care go home. Between June 1993 and June 1994, an estimated 8,592 children were taken from their parents while only 1,300 children were released from DCFS custody.[50] And, although 74 percent of Illinois foster children come from the Chicago area, only one-third of the children returned to their homes in 1993 were from the Chicago area.[51] In other words, two-thirds of the children allowed out of foster care in 1993 lived in parts of Illinois where Patrick Murphy and the *Chicago Tribune* have less influence.

As a result, during the 14 months after the Wallace death, while foster care populations changed little in most big American cities, in Chicago, the foster care population soared by 30 percent. In the rest of Illinois, where Murphy and the *Tribune* were less of a factor, it increased by 17 percent.[52]

Getting children home already was becoming more and more difficult, according to Benjamin Wolf, in part because of the growing role of private agencies, paid on a per diem basis. These agencies are now responsible for 62 percent of the state's foster children, up from 34 percent in 1989— and they're grasping for more.[53] The length of stay for those children is double the length for those under DCFS supervision, Wolf said.

But after the Wallace case "it got much worse," Wolf said. The case "reinforced all the trends against permanency."

Murphy and Gov. Jim Edgar began fighting over which of them could shove the words "best interests of the minor" into more parts of state law. The final bill included at least thirty such references.

Six workers, including three handling the Wallace case, were fired.

"The worker who wants to keep the job gets the message," Wolf said. "You will never have a problem here if you never send a child home."

Calls to the state's child abuse "hotline" increased 10 percent in the year following Joseph's death. A hotline worker described what went through his mind: "You're saying: 'I'm not going to get fired. I'm taking down every damn thing that comes in.' "[54] That went double for judges. Comerford promised to "evaluate the philosophy of judges being considered for the juvenile court."[55] Four judges, including two who dealt with the Wallace case, were transferred. A new supervising judge, William Maddux, was named for abuse and neglect cases. He spent his teenage years in Boys Town. "I wasn't raised in a family after the age of 12," says Maddux. "I didn't miss it."[56] The commission that investigated the Wallace death stated flatly that "Joseph's death has resulted in the unnecessary separation of families."[57]

In fact, in much of Chicago, the role of judge, jury, and family executioner has been assumed by Patrick Murphy. In most courtrooms, "it's just impossible to get kids home" unless Murphy's office approves, Redleaf says.[58] In Chicago today, any mother who "climbs over a mountain of glass barefoot to see [her] kids" is likely to bleed to death before she gets them back.

They are the *Tribune*'s children. They are jammed into shelters, spread across the state and bouncing from foster home to foster home. And it was all done "in the best interests of the child."

Eventually, the *Tribune* came down from its righteous-indignation high. There was a profound change in much of the coverage. It began when the reporters stopped looking at the system through Patrick Murphy's eyes and started looking for themselves. It began the day reporter Andrew Gottesman walked into Juvenile Court to see for himself.

In a two-part series published in December 1993, Gottesman wrote that "while extreme cases like Joseph's receive the bulk of media attention, the great majority are far less clear-cut. Many, experts say, could be resolved quickly if social services were available for parents who aren't directly harming their children but who don't have the means to care for them properly." Recommended solutions include "placing a premium on family preservation."

There was more: "Many experts believe that Cook County judges and attorneys are too quick to remove children, largely as a result of Joseph's death," Gottesman wrote.[59] By the time the *Tribune* concluded a six-part series on DCFS in March 1994, the turnaround was approaching 180 degrees.

First on the *Tribune*'s list of solutions: "keep children safely at home while families get help." For the first time, the *Tribune* drew a distinction between the Illinois Family First program and real family preservation. And the *Tribune* lamented the fact that family preservation efforts may be hampered by federal financial incentives that favor foster care and by a "lingering public misperception." The *Tribune* did not say where this "misperception" came from.[60]

The *Tribune*'s new approach could be seen in its coverage of the other case that caused a national furor, the case known in Chicago simply as "Keystone." Nineteen children and six adults were found crammed into a filthy, rat- and roach-infested two bedroom apartment at 219 N. Keystone Avenue after police raided the house looking for drugs—which they did not find, though one of the mothers gave birth that day to a baby who tested positive for drugs. The case drew comparisons to Calcutta and got Patrick Murphy his two appearances on "20/20."

As the trial reached its conclusion, in April 1994, a *Tribune* news account was headlined "Keystone Kids Neglect Case Unraveling." Reporter Tom Pelton wrote that "the case might not be as clear-cut as first thought."

None of the nineteen children whose parents were tried in April was abused.[61] None was malnourished. The children were not "home alone"; three adults were present. Although police claimed there was no food or other essentials in the house, the defense unfurled a three-foot-long grocery receipt which included milk, toothpaste, and shampoo. A witness said a month's worth of food had been purchased twelve days before the raid. One of the children, a fourteen-year-old boy, testified that the piles of garbage were thrown around by the police during the raid. The police denied it, and the judge didn't believe it. But what was most interesting was how the prosecution sought to discredit this testimony: by alleging that the child loved his mother so much he would lie to get back to her.

That conditions in the home were hideous is undeniable. But how did they get that way? The house on Keystone Avenue was inhabited by five sisters and their children. The sisters had moved in with each other when some were burned out of their own apartments and couldn't find other housing. Some of the mothers may indeed have been neglectful and it may turn out that the least detrimental alternative for their children is to be permanently taken from them. But others may have been overwhelmed by trying to care for their own children and their sisters'.

In Michigan, when child protective workers came upon a strikingly similar case, but with only one family and one child involved, the family was safely kept together thanks to a family preservation program—much to the relief of the child, who, on her fifteenth birthday, said her birthday wish was "to be with my family for the rest of my life."[62]

In finding the sisters guilty of neglect, Judge James B. Linn saw the case the way child savers often do: Just because you're poor doesn't mean you have to live in squalor. But it was a *Tribune* columnist, Mary Schmich, who saw what child savers so often miss. Arguing that "poverty was on trial," Schmich wrote:

> Most anyone who has ever lived in poverty knows how easy it is for lives to spin into chaos. For the refrigerator to go empty. For things to get dirty, really dirty. For people to get dirty too. For all of this to occur in families that are better off together than apart.
>
> We doubters have wondered whether much of the dismay over the Keystone case is rooted in middle-class dread of body odor and a greasy stove.[63]

Even the *Tribune* editorial board concluded that if the sisters can clean up their act and do so quickly, they should get their children back.[64]

The conversion at the *Tribune* is far from complete. The newspaper remains infatuated with orphanages, and it has yet to face up to the issue of abuse in foster care. Worse, the *Tribune*'s new understanding of these issues comes too late. The early, Murphy-driven coverage discredited family preservation in Illinois in a way the later coverage has not repaired.

By the end of 1993, DCFS had replaced Family First in Chicago with a program modeled on Homebuilders. (Inexplicably, it is continuing to use Family First in the rest of the state.) But the new Chicago program is almost certainly doomed. If any harm comes to a child in the program, Murphy will be ready to deal the death blow. But if agencies take only cases where it is 100 percent certain nothing can go wrong, they will be taking cases in which foster care probably could be averted even without the program. Indeed, in the new Chicago program, agencies have been given the right to engage in "creaming." They have turned away half the families DCFS has referred.[65] If the next evaluation shows no improvement in placement prevention, that too will bring condemnation from the child savers.

It will take years to undo the damage. And even then, it will happen only if the *Tribune* and other Chicago media tell stories about the need for family preservation and the harm of foster care in a way which packs the same emotional wallop as the stories about Joseph Wallace. Until that happens, "misperceptions" will continue to linger.

They certainly linger among the national media. Although the reporters writing these stories often used the *Tribune* as their guide, all of the subtlety of the *Tribune*'s later coverage was lost on the national news organizations that swooped down on the story after the Joseph Wallace death and the Keystone case.

ABC's "Turning Point" series devoted a full hour to the *Tribune* and its crusade. Yet "Turning Point" ignored what the *Tribune* learned. Instead, "Turning Point" reported that Joseph Wallace was returned to his mother because "family reunification was the absolute priority."[66]

This sort of approach was not limited to television. On April 25, 1994,

Newsweek weighed in with a five-page story made up largely of horror stories from Chicago. And what caused those horrors? "It's not simply social custom that keeps families together," *Newsweek* declared, "it's the law." *Newsweek* quotes from the report issued after Wallace's death. But the story leaves out the conclusion that family preservation played no role in the death. Also left out is the story of the Family First worker who almost saved Joseph. There is no mention of what the report said about Murphy's office and Murphy's misrepresentation. On the contrary, Murphy gets his own, glowing half-page story.[67]

Like *Newsweek, USA Today* also behaved as though all the family preservation success stories and foster care failures from places other than Illinois did not exist. For two days in April "the nation's newspaper" presented story after story parroting the child-saver line. The main story on April 7 ran 1,478 words—an epic by *USA Today* standards.

Like *Newsweek, USA Today*[68] began with horror stories about children returned to abusive homes, and lumped everything under the heading family preservation.

The heart of the *USA Today* stories is the statement, "In March's last five days, headlines yielded these horrors," followed by four cases of children returned to parents who beat them to or almost to death. But during those same five days, there were other horrors in the headlines, among them:

—The story of China Marie Davis of Phoenix, Arizona. First a babysitter and then China Marie's parents warned authorities that the little girl was being abused in foster care, but no one would listen—possibly because she was always well-dressed in expensive clothes. China Marie was two years old when she died of a perforated bowel. The foster mother has been charged with murder. She is herself a former foster child, and she was abused in two Arizona foster homes.

In the ten months that China Marie Davis lived in foster care she endured the following injuries, many of which were never treated: two broken collarbones, a broken left arm, a broken right rib, two fractures of the left upper arm, a fracture of the right upper arm, a broken left hand, a broken left wrist, a broken left forearm, a broken right wrist, a broken right forearm, fractures of both thigh bones, and a compression fracture of the spine.[69]

Perhaps someone should send the autopsy photos to Patrick Murphy.

—The story of three-year-old Tajuana Davidson, also of Phoenix. While in foster care, she suffered a broken shoulder blade, a black eye, and bruises on her stomach, back, legs, and arms. But it was the "seven crushing blows to the head" that killed her.[70]

—The story of Jerrell Hardiman of La Porte, Ind. Jerrell's foster parents allegedly beat the four-year-old boy with a garden hose. Then they allegedly hosed him down and left him outside on a cold October night wearing only a drenched T-shirt. He died six days later. The foster mother has been convicted of reckless homicide. As this is written, the foster father faces murder charges.[71]

USA Today mentions none of these cases, and the agony of foster children is dismissed in a single sentence: "Foster parents abuse much less often than parents reabuse, studies show." The "studies" are never specified, and by referring to "foster parents" rather than "foster care" *USA Today* does not have to be inconvenienced by evidence of foster children raping each other.

In fact, in the years since *Wounded Innocents* was published more evidence—including two more studies—has emerged documenting widespread abuse in foster care.

In Los Angeles, the state took over the licensing of foster homes from the county after it found rampant abuse in foster care. State auditors found what a review commission termed a "secret room" housing fifteen file cabinets filled with three thousand cases in which foster homes had problems that were never reported to the state.[72] In one case, ten foster children slept on the floor of a garage, with another ten crammed into a bedroom upstairs. Three of the children were abused. One had a fractured skull and two broken limbs. But the home was not closed until five months after the conditions were discovered.[73] Between mid-1989 and mid-1990, the county paid $18 million in damages to children injured in foster care.[74]

A second study from Baltimore (the first is cited in chapter 7) found that substantiated allegations of sexual abuse are four times higher in foster care than in the general population.[75]

But perhaps most alarming is a study of the Casey Family Program in the Pacific Northwest. The program is designed for children who already had gone through multiple placements and so may be harder to handle. But the privately funded program also was designed with all sorts of "extras." Workers' caseloads were kept low so foster families could get extra attention. The workers and the foster parents were carefully recruited. They got special training and higher pay than their counterparts in conventional programs. Generous funding was available to provide additional services to the foster children. This was not ordinary foster care, this was Cadillac foster care. Yet when children who had "aged out" of the program were interviewed, 24 percent of the girls said they were victims of actual or attempted sexual abuse while in Casey foster care.

The authors acknowledge that their study had a relatively low response rate, and those who did not respond were more likely to have been abused than those who did. Furthermore, the survey asked only about the Casey home in which the foster child had resided the longest. This is crucial. It means that any case in which a child was abused in a Casey home and then quickly moved to another would be omitted from the survey results.[76]

The way *USA Today* handled the question of abuse in foster care is typical. The garage full of foster children in Los Angeles was at least as bad as the Keystone case, yet it got no nationwide attention. The deaths of children like China Marie Davis and Jerrell Hardiman get little attention outside their home towns. In life they suffer foster care abuse. In death, they suffer media neglect.

Although the *USA Today* stories did not focus exclusively on Chicago, they had help from that city. The *USA Today* stories had the fingerprints of the Chicago-based National Committee for Prevention of Child Abuse all over them.

NCPCA now does the annual "hotline" survey formerly done by the American Humane Association. In 1994, NCPCA gave this data to *USA Today* before giving it to anyone else. While providing exclusive information does not give an organization control over a news story, it does put the news organization in the giver's debt, making it less likely that NCPCA's underlying assumptions would be questioned.

The minimization of abuse in foster care is a staple of NCPCA literature. The *USA Today* articles also included an explanation of "unfounded" reports that is misleading—and almost identical to NCPCA's.

That NCPCA would become particularly upset about family preservation now is not surprising either. All of a sudden there is money at stake.

Both *Newsweek* and *USA Today* claimed that the federal government will be spending an additional $1 billion on family preservation. That is wrong. First of all, the money will be spread over five years (*USA Today* got that much right, *Newsweek* did not). But more important, contrary to the *Newsweek* and *USA Today* accounts, that money does not have to be spent on *any* kind of family preservation, much less programs like Homebuilders. The money can go either into "family preservation" or "family support" or both, and it's going to be up to state and local governments to divvy it up.

There are five different categories of programs under the law's definition of "family preservation" and only one of these categories includes programs like Homebuilders. Also included are "parent education," adoption services, and even respite care for foster parents. The "family support" category is even broader, including just about anything that would "enhance child development" and defining "families" to include "adoptive, foster, and extended families."[77] The National Center for Youth Law has warned advocates that they will have to fight to make sure the money is not "captured by politically powerful service providers."[78]

The kind of "prevention" NCPCA pushes—lots of "counseling" and "parent education" is more likely to fall under the heading "family support." It's reasonable to believe that that is where NCPCA would like to see most of the federal money go. And NCPCA has reason to worry that this may not happen. In its most recent survey, it asked representatives of child protective agencies themselves to rank five "policy initiatives" in order of importance. "Investigating all reports of abuse and neglect" came in fourth. "Support services to parents of newborns" (an NCPCA priority), came in second. Priority One was: "expanding family preservation services."

The "institutions lobby" also is in an uproar. "Directors of some children's institutions are convinced that 'family preservation' will take money directly out of institutional pockets," frets the *Atlantic Monthly* in a twenty-page paean to the joys of modern-day orphanages.[79] The director of one of the institutions profiled notes that for the first time in anyone's memory, her facility doesn't have a waiting list, and she's mighty upset about it.[80]

And, in a sworn affidavit that is part of a lawsuit in New York City, a social worker testified that she was told by a representative of one of the city's private agencies that the agency had imposed a three-month moratorium on sending children home "because it was not receiving sufficient referrals to fill its beds."[81]

*   *   *

When we put aside the media caricatures of family preservation, what do we find? What have we learned about *real* family preservation over the past four years?

Michigan also has a family preservation program. But the only thing it has in common with Illinois is a similar name: Families First. The Michigan program sticks rigorously to the Homebuilders model.

In Michigan, as in Illinois, children placed in family preservation were compared to a "control group." The result: After one year, among children referred because of abuse or neglect, the control group children were nearly twice as likely to be placed in foster care as the Families First children. Thirty-six percent of the control group children were placed, compared with only 19.4 percent of the Families First children.[82]

Families First is the largest family preservation program in America. It began in September 1988, and became available statewide in 1992. It now serves 3,000 families per year. In its first four years, Families First dramatically slowed the growth of Michigan's foster care population. In the two years since Families First became available statewide, the foster care population has gone *down* by 10 percent.[83]

Families First is not 100 percent safe. In six years, two of the 22,799 children served by Families First died during the intervention.[84] Michigan's Department of Social Services keeps no statistics on deaths in foster care, according to spokesman Chuck Peller.[85]

An experiment in Utah and Washington State also used a comparison group. After one year, 85.2 percent of the children in the comparison group were placed in foster care, compared to only 44.4 percent of the children who received intensive family preservation services.[86]

In Alabama, a lawsuit prompted the state to agree to reform its child welfare system over several years, including a strong emphasis on family preservation. In those counties already operating under the new system, the foster care population dropped by 30 percent in two years and, according to an independent monitor "children were found to be at less risk of harm" than they were before the new system was put into place.[87]

The biggest problem to emerge as family preservation has grown is the "targeting" problem. The programs do tend to include children who wouldn't have been placed anyway. To some extent this is inevitable. All good caseworkers want the best for the children on their caseload, and some are bound to exaggerate the risk to a child to get that child into a family preservation program.

We can and should debate the extent to which family preservation is a proven success. But this much we know: Foster care is a proven failure.

The Devil in San Diego

About a month after Bill and Betty Jones (not their real names) had their three grandchildren taken from them, they wanted to send a birthday card to the youngest, who had just turned nine. The card could not have animals on it, declared caseworker Sue Plante. She explained that such pictures are what devil-worshipers sometimes use to send subliminal signals to the children in their thrall. No clowns either, for the same reason. Earlier, Plante had confiscated all the letters the grandparents had written to their grandchildren, claiming they contained subliminal Satanic messages.

Six weeks after the children were taken, they had their first chance to visit with Bill and Betty. But no hugs were permitted because the grandparents might use the opportunity to whisper to the children. The grandparents also were prohibited from touching their ears or their noses or making references to time. All of these were considered methods of Satanic control.

Several weeks earlier, based on the claims of a mentally unstable relative, caseworkers and police had swooped down on the Jones home and snatched away the children, two girls and a boy, aged twelve, ten, and eight at the time. The aunt had told Plante that, after much therapy, she had come to believe much of her family was part of a Satanic cult that had practiced sexual abuse and human sacrifice. Plante's own suspicions were heightened by a scar on the boy's stomach. Though the family produced medical records showing the scar was the result of surgery, Plante said that Satanic cults sometimes control children by cutting them open and claiming they are placing a bomb or a live rat in the wound.

The oldest child wrote to the judge in the case pleading for help. "I am a 12-year-old and everyone acts like I have no brains," she wrote. "I wish someone would listen to me. Nothing is going on!! My sister doesn't even know what a colt [sic] is!! We all love God very much. I have prayed every day since I got taken away." The girl's therapist said she was in "denial."

It took two months before charges were dropped and the family was reunited.[88]

The Jones family was not alone. The *San Diego Union*[89] found at least five other families that had been investigated on charges of Satanic ritual abuse. Two children were taken from their parents for two months because the parents allegedly were preparing to sacrifice the younger boy to Satan on his third birthday.[90]

Believers in Satanic conspiracies are often found on the fringes of the child saving movement. In San Diego, they held center stage. When Bill Jones first found Sue Plante in his house pulling up his children's shirts looking for scars, he threatened to call the police. He says Plante replied: "Go ahead. You'll find out who I am and what I can do."[91]

Plante was a member of the San Diego County Ritual Abuse Task Force, a group created by the county's Commission on Children and Youth. The Task Force produced a widely circulated booklet called "Ritual Abuse— Treatment, Intervention, and Safety Guidelines." According to the booklet:

> Numerous cults exist which have sophisticated suppliers of sacrificial persons, from kidnappers through "breeders" (women who bear children intended for sexual abuse and sacrifice). . . . Doctors, attorneys, politicians and wealthy individuals often form a powerful shield and are principals in many established abusive cults.[92]

In addition to distributing the booklet, the task force conducted training seminars for caseworkers and mental health professionals.

The San Diego group was patterned after a similar task force in Los

Angeles which once called a news conference to claim that Satanists were poisoning them by pumping a pesticide into their offices, homes, and cars.[93]

But what may be most amazing about the San Diego Satan scare is this: It's over. The task force has no credibility in the community and the booklet no longer is distributed. Indeed, a transformation of the entire child protective system has begun. An intensive family-preservation program has been established, and the number of children in foster care declined by 12 percent between 1991 and 1994.

It happened thanks to some dedicated journalists and a group of concerned citizens. And because of a case in which the injustices were so glaring that all of San Diego was forced to look.

Carol Hopkins remembers the day well. It was the fall of 1991, and she was deputy foreman of the 1991–92 San Diego County Grand Jury. A Member of Congress had asked the Grand Jury to examine the child protective system. The Grand Jury's work already was well underway when the director of the County Department of Social Services asked to meet with them to complain about their work. That same day, a letter had arrived about one particular case. Hopkins asked the director: "If it's true that you do everything right, and we could show you a case where everything has gone wrong, would you fix it?"[94]

At about the same time an editor at the *San Diego Union* asked reporter Jim Okerblom to return a call from an aide to a state legislator in Missouri. The aide told Okerblom a story about a miscarriage of justice involving the son of one of his boss's constituents, a chief petty officer in the Navy stationed in San Diego. The allegations seemed so bizarre that "I felt: this is baloney. I didn't believe it," Okerblom said.[95] But Okerblom investigated the story and the story checked out. Ultimately, he and colleagues John Wilkens and Mark Sauer would write story after story about the injustices of the child welfare system. At the same time, Hopkins led the grand jury through a parallel investigation, producing report after report that reached similar conclusions.

The case that made such an impression was the case of eight-year-old Alicia and her parents, Jim and Denise.[96] It began during the night of May 8, 1989. A man came through Alicia's window, took her from her bed, brutally raped her, then brought her back home. Despite injuries so severe they required surgery, Alicia said nothing the next morning. But when she complained about pain using the bathroom, her parents suspected she had a kidney infection and took her to a Navy clinic. Both parents broke down in sobs when they saw the extent of her injuries.

Child Protective Services was called and a worker arrived two hours later. For the first of what would be more than a hundred times over thirteen months, Alicia told what had happened to her, including a detailed description of her attacker. But this was one more child the child savers refused to believe. Instead, they assumed from the beginning that Alicia was raped by her father and refused to consider any other explanation.

Certainly Alicia's story sounded unlikely and suspicion would have been understandable—except for the fact that for the past month police had been looking for a man who had committed several very similar attacks in Alicia's neighborhood.

Immediately, Jim was ordered to have no contact with his daughter. He would not see or speak to her for two-and-a-half years.

Alicia then was taken to the Center for Child Protection at Children's Hospital—the place where director David Chadwick says they do examinations "in order to prove abuse." Again, Alicia told about her abduction and again she was not believed. In a videotaped interview, a caseworker asked Alicia who she would feel safe with. The caseworker claimed Alicia replied "my mom and my brother." The failure to mention her father repeatedly would be used as "evidence" that he had raped his daughter. It even was cited by Chadwick himself. But what Alicia really said was "my mom, *my dad,* and my brother." The grand jury saw the actual tape. "The best that can be said is that these people heard what they wanted to hear," the grand jury concluded. "The worst is that they committed perjury."

Five minutes before Alicia was taken into surgery, two security guards arrived and kicked Denise out of the hospital. She didn't even have a chance to say good bye.

After the surgery, Alicia asked a nurse to call her father. But Jim was under orders to have no contact with his daughter. He couldn't take the call. "I could hear Alicia there, in the background [saying] 'Let me talk to my daddy, let me talk to my daddy,' " Jim said.

Alicia was placed in foster care. When one foster mother believed Alicia's story and said Alicia was desperate to go home, a child protective worker got the mother's foster-care license revoked and moved Alicia to another home with foster parents eager to adopt her.

Jim was forced into group therapy for sex abusers. When he maintained his innocence, he was forced into the "deniers group."

Alicia was in "therapy" too, with a therapist specially chosen by the child protective worker then handling the case. The worker and therapist frequently worked together. Twice a week for thirteen months Alicia was made to tell her story, and twice a week for thirteen months the therapist told her she was wrong. "I've told [my therapist] I love my parents and want to see them," Alicia said to another caseworker. "She doesn't hear me." In a sworn statement, Jim's lawyer alleges that Alicia said she had been told she could go home if she "told the truth about her dad." Finally, she changed her story. She was sent back to the Center for Child Protection for another videotaped interview. Lying on the floor, almost in the fetal position, Alicia forced herself to accuse her father.

Immediately criminal charges were pressed against Jim and moves were made to terminate Jim and Denise's parental rights. Denise attempted suicide.

All this was happening despite the fact that a full year before—just one month after Alicia was attacked—the police arrested Albert Carder, Jr. for the other similar crimes in the neighborhood. Carder eventually pleaded guilty and is now serving a seventeen-year prison sentence.

The prosecutor on that case was Deputy District Attorney E. Jane Via. In one court document, Via declared that Carder was a suspect in Alicia's rape and that Alicia's description of her attacker matched Carder. Several months later, Via transferred to the office of the County Counsel which prosecutes child-abuse cases. By coincidence she was assigned Alicia's case. But this time, she insisted that Carder could not possibly have raped Alicia. "I was the D.A. on [the Carder] case," Via said during a juvenile court hearing. "There are no similarities to this; it's a waste of time to even consider it."

But what about Via's earlier written statement? Although it was in the District Attorney's file, it was not in the court file and so "not discoverable" by Jim's lawyers.

As part of the preparations for Jim's criminal trial, the clothing Alicia had worn when she was attacked was re-examined. Semen stains that had gone unnoticed in the initial investigation were discovered and DNA tests were performed. The tests proved beyond a shadow of a doubt that Jim could not have raped his daughter. Among the five percent of the population who could have raped Alicia: Albert Carder, Jr.

Having been presumed guilty, Jim had proved his innocence. In the world as we know it, that would have been the end of the story. Alicia immediately would have been returned home and the caseworkers, prosecutors and people at the Center for Child Protection would have lined up to apologize. But this is not the world as we know it; this is the world of the child savers.

The child savers continued to push for the termination of Jim's parental rights. A supervisor in the district attorney's office cited "conflicting evidence"—meaning that there was a conflict between the DNA results and the statement the therapist had dragged out of Alicia.

It was not until Carol Hopkins laid down her challenge to the Director of Social Services that the attempt to take Alicia from her parents forever finally was stopped. And it was not until Okerblom and Wilkens told the story on the front page of the *San Diego Union* that all charges were dropped, the court issued an extremely rare "true finding of innocence," and Alicia finally was freed from the system that had guarded her "best interests" for two-and-a-half years. By then, Alicia was eleven. As the *Union* noted, she had spent three birthdays, three Thanksgivings and three Christmases away from her mother, her father, and her brother.

But the grand jury was amazed to find that even months later, Via, District Attorney Edwin Miller, and members of Miller's staff were coming up with all sorts of bizarre theories to try to link Jim with the crime. "Refutation of each of these theories was in the D.A.'s own file or in the DSS [Department of Social Services] file which was readily available to the D.A," the grand jury found.[97]

"I thought it was going to be a one-time story" about a single aberration in the system, Okerblom says. Then the calls started coming. At least 500 of them, all saying "this is what happened to me." Okerblom had to put a special message on his voice mail asking callers to please be patient as he checked out the stories. "Some were self-serving. Some were trying to take advantage of [the situation]," Okerblom says. "But there were a number of others whose cases were very troubling."[98]

Okerblom and Wilkens kept digging, ultimately producing an exhaustive multi-part series documenting widespread abuses in child protective services. Reporter Rex Dalton exposed problems at Chadwick's Center for Child Protection, where even outside experts who normally testify for the prosecution said doctors were seeing abuse where it did not exist.[99]

The grand jury also was swamped with letters and calls and it too kept digging. A series of scathing reports concluded that families were needlessly destroyed, often because of poverty, so-called "reunification plans" were impossible to comply with, sometimes intentionally so, and "some social workers lie routinely, even when under oath in court." The grand jury concluded that the child protection system in San Diego was "a system out of control, with few checks and little balance."[100]

More than 2,300 copies of the grand jury's reports have been sent to people all over the United States.[101]

The Department of Social Services responded quickly to the attention from the press, the grand jury, and the County Board of Supervisors. Edwin Miller did not. He persuaded the following year's grand jury to exonerate his office. In its very brief review of Alicia's case the grand jury offers no words of sympathy for Alicia, Jim, or Denise. Rather they lament the fact that the publicity about the case hurt E. Jane Via "professionally, socially, and emotionally."[102]

In deciding which grand jury is more credible, it's worth noting whom they relied on for expertise: The grand jury that exonerated the District Attorney's office relied on staff from that very office. The grand jury that condemned the District Attorney used independent staff.

Miller also insisted on prosecuting Dale Akiki in what became San Diego's equivalent of the McMartin case. Akiki babysat for children at a local church while their parents attended services. After one hundred hours of questioning by therapists—most of whom were suggested to the parents by one of the principal authors of the Ritual Abuse Task Force booklet—children began making the kinds of wild allegations typical of so-called "mass molestation cases." When the first deputy district attorney assigned to the case expressed strong reservations about the evidence and decided not to press charges, she was replaced.[103]

In November 1993, after spending two-and-a-half years in jail, Akiki was acquitted of all charges. A third grand jury, which, like the first one, had independent staff, criticized Miller's handling of the Akiki case.

By 1994, Miller, who had been District Attorney for twenty-three years, was in trouble. He tried to salvage his career by taking a page from the Patrick Murphy playbook: He attacked family preservation. But by then, both the press and the public in San Diego had become too sophisticated to buy the snake oil Miller was selling. In June 1994, there was a five-way primary for district attorney. Miller came in fourth.

*   *   *

Why have things turned out so differently in Chicago and San Diego? Why did one newspaper get caught up in child-saving hysteria while another helped to end it? I believe there are three reasons:

The first is what I call the reporter's "entry point." To a much greater extent than we'd like to admit, where we come into a story determines how the story comes out. Our first encounter with an issue determines what we ask and who we ask it of.

The most common entry point into stories about child abuse and foster care is the one the *Chicago Tribune* encountered: A child "known to the system" has died. Such cases become police matters and generally lead to criminal trials. That means an enormous amount of information that normally can be hidden by confidentiality rules becomes public. If the child-welfare system is like the Loch Ness Monster (only real), the failures involved in the death of a child "known to the system" is the one and only part that keeps breaking through the surface of the water. Reporters then confuse this part of the beast with the entire monster. In contrast, as we've seen, Jim Okerblom's entry point was Alicia's case, a case in which a man falsely accused actually could prove his innocence.

The second reason for the differences in coverage involves something reporters hate: ambiguity. In sexual abuse cases the issue is simple: Was there abuse or wasn't there? Or, in a case like Jim's: Did he do it or didn't he?

The families that programs like Homebuilders deal with raise issues that are not so clear cut. Often the parents in these families are flawed, sometimes deeply so. And even when the parents are relatively blameless, they often are neither telegenic nor articulate.

The third and most important reason is related to the second: It is the division in American society we almost never talk about: division by class.

Among my biggest disappointments over the past four years has been the failure of the growing skepticism about allegations of sexual abuse to translate into similar skepticism about the far more pervasive problem of the confusion of poverty with neglect. Just a year before *Newsweek* trashed family preservation, for example, the same magazine ran a seven-page cover story called "Rush to Judgment" which expressed skepticism about high-profile sex abuse cases.[104]

The victims in such cases have tended to come from middle-class families. Almost by definition, the families dealt with in family preservation programs do not. Reporters might be able to identify with a Navy man like Jim, or a day care worker, or the other middle-class families who are often the subjects of stories about false allegations of sexual abuse. They are unlikely to identify with an inner-city welfare mother.

This is especially disturbing now, when the debate over the child-welfare system threatens to be engulfed by the larger debate over welfare and families. That debate has been fueled by a series of myths:

Myth: The growth in the percentage of children born out of wedlock is the primary cause of poverty.

Fact: In the 1990s, when illegitimacy is said to be at the root of all evil, about 20 percent of America's children are poor. In the 1950s, when all was said to be right with the American family and the illegitimacy rate was far, far lower, 30 percent of America's children were poor. It was liberal antipoverty programs that brought the child poverty rate down, and it was Reagan-Bush cutbacks in those programs that sent it soaring again.

Of course a single-parent family is more likely to have a lower income than a two-parent household, because changes in the economy have eliminated so many of the high-paying blue collar jobs that allowed one breadwinner to support a family. As historian Stephanie Coontz has written: "Job and wage structures, not family structures account for most of our country's poverty. . . . The fastest growing poverty group in America since 1979 has been married-couple families with children."[105]

The economic pressures brought on by unemployment often destroy families. Teenage girls who feel they have no hope for a better future turn to having a baby as their only solace. Teenage boys who can't prove their manhood with a job substitute by making babies instead. Illegitimacy does not cause poverty. Poverty causes illegitimacy.

Myth: Welfare causes illegitimacy.

Fact: Contrary to stereotypes, mothers on welfare average 1.9 children. Only 10 percent of welfare mothers have four or more children. Furthermore:

—Women receiving welfare have lower birthrates than women in the general population.

—States that provide the highest welfare benefits have the lowest rates of illegitimacy, and vice versa.

—The longer a woman stays on welfare, the less likely she is to give birth.

—During the past twenty years, as illegitimacy has increased, the real value of welfare has plummeted. Adjusted for inflation the average Aid to Families with Dependent Children check is worth 45 percent less than it was two decades ago.[106]

Myth: Welfare benefits increase with family size.

Fact: Although the total check increases, the amount available per person goes down. For example, suppose a state provides $200 per month for a woman with one child, and an additional $65 per month for each additional child. That means the mother with one child gets $100 per month per person, while the mother with two children gets $88.33 per person.

Myth: Welfare is a "way of life." Welfare families stay on the dole forever, breeding generations of dependency.

Fact: Half of single parents who get AFDC get off welfare within one year. 70 percent are off within two years.[107]

These myths are fueling the most dangerous trend in child welfare during the past four years: the growth in the "back to the orphanage" movement described in chapter 7.

Charles Murray used these myths in a famous "Op Ed" article in the *Wall Street Journal.* (He's now been joined by House Speaker Newt Gingrich.) Based on the false premises that welfare causes illegitimacy and "illegitimacy is the single most important social problem of our time . . . because it drives everything else" Murray called for abolishing welfare altogether. "The child deserves society's support. The parent does not," Murray said of welfare families. Under his plan, Murray says that to support their families poor mothers could enter into shotgun marriages or try to find private charity. If they don't, Murray writes, "there are laws already on the books about the right of the state to take a child from a neglectful parent."

What happens to the children then? Adoption when possible. For the rest: "the government should spend lavishly on orphanages. . . . In 1993, we know a lot about how to provide a warm, nurturing environment for children, and getting rid of the welfare system frees up lots of money to do it. . . . Those who prattle about the importance of keeping children with their biological mothers may wish to spend some time in a patrol car or with a social worker seeing what the reality of life with welfare-dependent biological mothers can be like."[108]

Murray deserves credit for this much: He's brought the hidden agenda of child saving out into the open. He acknowledges that neglect laws are a wonderful way to get children away from people who have committed no crime but to be poor, and he thinks it's a great idea.

But that's all he deserves credit for. His suggestion that people who disagree with him get their impression of families on welfare by accompanying social workers or police is classic deck-stacking. Anyone who did this would see not a random sample of welfare families, but only those in which the adults have been accused of abuse, neglect, or some other crime.

As for spending lavishly on orphanages, a year in an orphanage costs anywhere from $25,000 to $50,000 or more. At the $50,000 figure—and remember, Murray wants to "spend lavishly"—writer Michael Massing has pointed out that even if 75 percent of children now on AFDC were adopted or supported in some other way, orphanage bills for the rest would run to $112 billion per year, five times the present cost of welfare.[109] Even doing it on the cheap would cost $56 billion. How many Americans are willing to spend that kind of money on children who are overwhelmingly poor and disproportionately black?

But the worst part of Murray's proposal is his failure to consider that children generally refuse to despise their parents the way Murray does. How much damage would even a good orphanage have done to a child like Boyd A., for example?

And the odds of the orphanage being good are pretty slim. Even if it is true that "we know a lot about how to provide a warm, nurturing [orphanage] environment for children," there is little evidence that this knowledge has been put into practice. Yet the claim is widely believed. Television news and glossy magazines offer us tours of resortlike model orphanages.[110] And over and over again we are assured that this time it's going to be different.

"I am not recommending Dickensian barracks," says Murray. "No one advocates a return to the warehouse orphanages of the Dickens era," says USA Today. "Advocates insist [orphanages] need not be the impersonal warehouses that recall the bleak images of Charles Dickens's 19th Century England," says the Washington Post. "Gone are the grim, Dickensian conditions long associated with orphanages," says Fortune. "Today's orphanages look nothing like the dormitory-style orphanages of the 1940s," says Gannett News Service. "Orphanages are not what they used to be," says the *Atlantic Monthly*. They're "new and improved" says the *Phoenix Gazette*. One commentator even denied that Dickensian orphanages existed in Dickens' time.[111]

Not surprisingly, the back-to-the-orphanage movement has gained the most ground in Chicago. The governor is for them, a legislative task force is looking into the idea at the urging of a lawmaker who says "the question is no longer if there will be orphanages in Illinois. The question is how and in what manner."[112] And, of course, Patrick Murphy—who first gained local fame in the 1970s by suing to shut down institutions that brutalized children—now thinks orphanages are "a great idea."[113]

This is one area in which the *Chicago Tribune* has learned little. In one story, a *Tribune* reporter states flatly that "today's orphanages . . . bear little resemblance to the hopeless, dank places made infamous by Dickens."[114] Just one month before the reporter made this claim, Murphy was alleging physical and sexual abuse at one of Chicago's new, mini-orphanages—a facility that had opened just three months earlier.[115] And just five months earlier, Murphy filed suit seeking $5.5 million in damages for eleven foster children who had endured "horrifying conditions" in a group home shut down the previous year.[116]

Another *Tribune* story begins with another one of those luxury orphanage tours, this time of a facility that had not yet opened. Although the story says that orphanages are only for children "unlikely to be adopted or returned to their parents," the fact that the facility toured by the *Tribune* is only for children *aged ten and under* apparently aroused no suspicion.[117]

What all this overlooks of course is that no one *advocated* Dickensian orphanages in Dickens' time either—they just kept ending up that way. As for the present, if any of the advocates who prattle about the joys of institutions, or any of the reporters who have declared the Dickensian orphanage dead, actually read the report about the New York City baby warehouses cited in chapter 7, it is not apparent. Since that alone doesn't seem to be enough to make reporters realistic about orphanages, and since orphanage tours seem to be all the rage right now, I have organized a short orphanage tour of my own:

We begin in Watkinsville, Georgia, where, according to the *Atlanta Journal and Constitution,* "it's back to business as usual at the Hampton Boys Home after the February 17 [1994] arrest of a founder and director of the facility for troubled teenagers." The indictment of the man on several charges of sexually abusing former residents "came as a shock." According to the chairman of the group that owns the facility, "he was the one most responsible for creating and running the program," which, the chairman went on to say is "the finest thing of its kind in the state."[118]

On now to the Bethel Children's Home in Lucedale, Mississippi. According to a thirteen-year-old former resident, the children were expected to work twelve or thirteen hours a day six days a week building houses. One youth cut off his finger in an accident with a saw. "The saw he was using didn't have a guard, and he cut his finger off. I saw him run out of the building with blood dripping off of his finger," the boy said.[119]

Next stop: The JDM Residential Treatment Center near St. Louis. The facility was chronically short of food, and, during the winter, the thermostat was set at 55 degrees. "Nobody else there cared about [the children]," a former executive director—one of five who quit in less than a year—told the *St. Louis Post-Dispatch.* "They wouldn't even give them a ball to toss around. There were days when they didn't have any food. The whole thing was just a way to make money off the state." Those sentiments were echoed by a counselor who called the County Sheriff's department because she feared for the children's safety. Between February and October 1993, there were at least three cases of child abuse at the facility, two of them serious.[120]

Our tour continues at Crossroads, a facility in The Bronx that houses one hundred teenagers. An investigation by *New York Newsday* found "evidence of unchecked violence and criminal activity at Crossroads—including reports of residents threatening each other with loaded handguns and knives and committing armed robberies—making the facility unsafe for children and a danger to the community around it." The investigation was begun after a sixteen-year-old resident took a loaded shotgun he had hidden, slipped through a fence, wounded another Crossroads resident, and shot a third at point-blank range, killing him on the spot.[121]

Now it's on to Staten Island, where *New York Newsday* reports, "city officials have begun an internal inquiry into reports of gang sex, beatings, and neglect at the Mission of the Immaculate Virgin . . . where the city places hundreds of its wards each year. Adolescents returning from temporary placements . . . described a pattern of incidents in which longer-term residents raped, robbed, or assaulted newcomers while night-shift staff slept on the job. . . . MIV, as it is called, has become so notorious . . . that some choose to run away from city care and sleep in the subways rather than accept a bed there for even one night."[122]

We go next to Westchester County, New York, home of Linden Hill and Hawthorne Cedar Knolls, two institutions once "considered among the state's best." Again, *New York Newsday* is our guide to institutions "plagued by violence, unchecked sex, and poor supervision." Said one counselor: "They have lost sight that the program is no longer safe to kids. It's outrageous."

In one case, a teenage boy with a history of aggressive sexual behavior allegedly forced a fourteen-year-old girl to have sex with another boy. The director of Linden Hill insisted the sex was consensual. "Do you set up a situation that is locked down or do you allow kids to try their wings?" he said. "[You ask] how could it happen? Well, it's almost inevitable. Love knows no locksmith."[123]

It seems appropriate to end our tour in Illinois, specifically at Mooseheart, about forty miles from Chicago, one of the institutions that expanded as part of the Illinois orphanage boom.[124] Within the past five years four Mooseheart "houseparents" were convicted of sexually abusing the children they were supposed to care for. In the most recent case, a houseparent was convicted of molesting six preteen boys in less than a year. When the *Chicago Tribune* finally put the story on the front page, much of the story was devoted to lamenting how tough it all was—not on the child victims, but on the institution.[125] And columnist Bob Greene declared that "a place devoted to doing good now faces the task of making itself better."[126]

In another of his exercises in deck-stacking, Charles Murray likes to ask: "Imagine that tomorrow you and your wife are going to be run over by a bus and you have two choices: Put your children in a *well funded, well run* orphanage, or turn them over to a name chosen at random from a list of [welfare] recipients in the District of Columbia [emphasis added]."[127] A more realistic question would be: Would you rather put your children in the home of a loving single parent who is on welfare because she can't get a job that pays enough for day care and health insurance, or would you rather put them in Crossroads, Mission of the Immaculate Virgin, or a baby warehouse?

"State institutions never go away," warns Missouri Social Services Commissioner Gary Stangler, an orphanage opponent. "They just get lousy."[128]

*   *   *

There have been other changes over the past four years. These are some of the most significant, in order of the chapter in which the issue is discussed:

Child Saving Now

James Norman, whose struggle with the child savers is chronicled in chapter 3, has left an extraordinary legacy. In January 1990, a federal magistrate ruled that the Illinois Department of Children and Family Services does indeed tear apart families solely because they lack adequate housing. The magistrate called Norman's case and the others like his "conscience-shocking."[129]

After that decision DCFS settled. Thanks to the efforts of Diane Redleaf and Laurene Heybach, who heads the Legal Assistance Foundation of Chicago's Homeless Advocacy Project, every year $1.8 million is set aside to be used whenever lack of adequate food, clothing, or shelter threatens to cause a child to be placed or is preventing a child from being returned home. Such families now are eligible for extra help to find decent housing, partial continuation of AFDC benefits after children are placed, and one-time grants of up to $800, called "Norman money," to pay for security deposits and similar expenses. The court named a monitor to make sure the terms of the decree were followed.

As mentioned at the beginning of this chapter, the Illinois ACLU settled a major suit as well. Their consent decree called for reforming every facet of the system—no longer would foster children have fewer rights than prisoners. An outside team of experts evaluated DCFS and recommended scores of changes. As in the Norman case, a monitor was appointed by the court to push the agency to follow through. As always, progress was slow, but there was progress.

Unfortunately, both consent decrees have been undercut by the Chicago Foster Care Panic. In 1993, resources made available under the Norman consent decree were "underutilized" according to the monitor. Indeed, the rate at which families were certified for such aid fell dramatically, with the biggest decline in the Chicago area. "The shockingly low percentage of children going home in Cook County is alarming," the monitor wrote.[130]

*   *   *

NCPCA has withdrawn the pamphlet about neglect described in chapter 3. The replacement explicitly acknowledges the role of poverty in *causing* neglect. This is progress. But it still fails to acknowledge that poverty often is *confused with* neglect. The pamphlet's tone is almost schizophrenic, as though NCPCA doesn't quite know how to integrate the exotic new notion that poverty plays a role in neglect into its pre-existing belief system.

A little more encouraging is NCPCA's support of efforts to replicate Hawaii's "healthy start" program. Under the program, mothers of newborns are offered the option of being screened for "risk factors" that can lead to abuse. About half of the parents of Hawaii's newborns are screened and ten percent of those are deemed at risk. They are offered the help of a home visitor who comes once a week for at least a year. Like the screening, the visits are strictly voluntary, but 95 percent of parents accept the offer. Most important, as in Homebuilders, the visitors combine parent education with help in obtaining "hard" services like housing and jobs.

A study of two hundred children hospitalized for abuse in Hawaii found that only 3 percent were from parts of the state where Healthy Start is available.[131] And the state's foster care placement rate is probably the nation's lowest.[132]

Attempts to replicate Healthy Start are encouraging, provided:

—The program remains voluntary. Child savers may be tempted to pervert Healthy Start into a mandatory program in which parents who have too many "risk factors" can have their children taken from them.

—The workers who make the visits are exempt from mandatory reporting laws (they would, of course, remain free to report abuse whenever, in their own judgment, there was reasonable cause to suspect it).

—The emphasis on "hard services" is not diminished. This is of concern both because the program is being pushed by NCPCA, which has shown little interest in such services before, and because most states don't have the extensive social safety net available in Hawaii, including generous welfare payments and statewide universal health insurance. Indeed, Hawaii's low rates of child abuse and foster care make clear that liberal social programs are among the best ways to prevent child abuse.

The Numbers

As noted earlier, the annual survey of child protective hotlines, formerly conducted by the American Humane Association, now is done by NCPCA.

In 1993, the most recent year for which data are available, there were an estimated 2,989,000 "reports" alleging some form of child maltreatment, a figure almost identical to 1992. But while total reports have leveled off, false reports continue to soar. In 1993, there were 1,972,740 false reports, up from 1,761,000 the previous year, or an increase of 12 percent. This happened because while the total number of reports stayed about the same, the number of so-called "substantiated" reports plunged from 40 percent in 1992 to 34 percent in 1993.[133]

Of course, this is not how NCPCA reported the results. Their press release declared that the 1993 numbers "are essentially the same as the number of cases reported and confirmed last year."[134] NCPCA reached this conclusion because it regularly asks respondents to recheck figures from previous years. When the 1992 figures were rechecked, it turned out that substantiation rates were much lower than NCPCA had been claiming: only 36 percent rather than 40 percent. By comparing the *revised* 1992 figures to the *first* 1993 figures, NCPCA was able to claim there was little change. When apples are compared to apples, however, the change is substantial.

Nevertheless, there was one significant improvement in the way NCPCA reported the 1993 data. In past years, NCPCA's press release would mention only "reports" of maltreatment. The release would state that journalists could get a more detailed document on request, but it didn't mention that this document dealt with the substantiation issue—or that such an issue even existed. In 1994, for the first time, NCPCA acknowledged the existence of false reports in its press release, giving figures both for reports of maltreatment and cases they described as "confirmed." I believe this happened for two reasons. First, a group of volunteers with which I am involved, the National Coalition for Child Protection Reform, began sending out an annual "counter-press kit," taking issue with NCPCA's interpretation of the data. Second, in 1993, *Time* magazine branded NCPCA's numbers an example of "flagrantly flimsy figures."[135]

The next step is to get NCPCA to stop using terms like "confirmed" for cases that can be no more than a worker's gut feeling and otherwise giving misleading information about what constitutes "substantiation."

In its package of stories slamming family preservation, *USA Today* claimed that "unfounded" child abuse reports "run the gamut from vague suggestions of abuse to strong cases that fall just short of unequivocal proof."[136] As is explained in detail in chapter 4, that statement simply is not true. Furthermore, new evidence of its falsity became public—including a front page story in the *New York Times*—just one month before the *USA Today* stories appeared.

Ruling in a New York case, the United States Court of Appeals for the Second Circuit found that the "some credible evidence" standard is unconstitutional when used as the basis for telling an employer that a job applicant is listed in a central registry as a suspected child abuser.

In a unanimous ruling, the court declared that the standard is unconstitutional because it requires only "the bare minimum of material credible evidence to support the allegations. . . . The 'some credible evidence' standard results in many individuals being placed on the list who do not belong there."[137]

Finally, there is new information about the prevalence of child sexual abuse. Seven Canadian researchers reviewed twenty different studies. They found that the studies with the best methodology consistently found that between 10 and 12 percent of girls under age 14 are sexually abused by anyone, not necessarily a parent or guardian. Diana Russell's study was singled out for criticism.[138]

Innocent Families

On Saturday, Nov. 10, 1990, Mary Seay of Jacksonville, Florida, answered the door and found a child protective worker from the state Department of Health and Rehabilitative Services (HRS) standing there. The worker had received a child abuse report about an eight-month-old in the house named Princess. According to the report, Princess had been grabbed by the scruff of the neck and locked in the bathroom. What's more, she reportedly had two black eyes.

"I demand to see Princess now," the worker said.

So Seay complied and brought out Princess—the family's pet raccoon.

"I want to see the *child*," the worker insisted. Seay suggested calling the family veterinarian to confirm Princess' identity.

"A vet for a child?" the worker replied.

The worker talked to the veterinarian's receptionist, who confirmed Princess' identity. She searched the house. She questioned the neighbors. Finally she left. Seay thought her troubles were over.

But the following Monday another worker called. The worker ordered the Seays to bring Princess in the next day for "counseling." Again, Seay tried to explain, to which the second worker replied: "I'm tired of hearing this denial."

The Seays showed up, but first they obtained a note from the vet attesting to Princess' identity. They also notified the media. This finally persuaded HRS, but the Seays' problems were not quite over. HRS somehow got the impression that Princess had been brought to the office because she had *bitten* a child and would have to be killed and tested for rabies.

This mix-up too was straightened out and Princess was spared. But the Seays were listed in Florida's registry of potential child abusers for thirty days.[139]

I mention the Seays' story to illustrate the fanaticism that damages so many families that really do have children. Families like Denise Perrigo, who lives with her daughter near Syracuse, New York. Shortly before her third birthday, the girl was taken away because her mother was still breastfeeding.[140] One year later, when finally they were reunited, Perrigo recalled what her daughter said: "Oh, mommy, my heart has been so empty of you. Hold me and fill it back up."[141]

This attitude remains common in child protective services offices. But the attitude may be changing.

In the years since *Wounded Innocents* was published there has been a growing realization among the people actually responsible for doing child protective work that the child-saving model does not work and cannot continue. One sign of this is the NCPCA survey which found that representatives of state child protective agencies considered family preservation the most important of five policy initiatives. Other signs include:

—When Florida workers were surveyed about barriers to doing their jobs, 63 percent cited "responding to minor neglect reports" and 64 percent cited "completing reports on obviously unfounded cases."[142]

—In California 42 percent of workers acknowledged removing children from their homes who could have stayed home safely had proper services been available.[143] And the real number probably is higher. A study in El Paso, Texas, compared the reasons workers *think* they remove children to the *real* reasons. Most workers believed that the main reasons they took children from their homes were physical and sexual abuse. But when case records were examined the most common reasons were lack of supervision and physical neglect.[144]

A New York City worker who got fed up and quit summed up his job this way: "Most of the time, I was taking their kids away for no good reason."[145]

Or consider the views of another frontline worker. Keith Richards was a child protective worker on Long Island for eight years. He is now a supervisor. He wrote about his experiences in *Tender Mercies: Inside the World of a Child Abuse Investigator* (Chicago: The Noble Press/Child Welfare League of America, 1992).

Much of the book is devoted to the real abuse and neglect he saw every day. But he doesn't stop there. Richards writes:

> People try to manipulate the CPS system all the time. You know, schools and hospitals calling to protect their behinds when a kid has a hangnail, neighbors harassing neighbors, estranged spouses trying to zap it to their ex. . . . Sometimes it does more damage to a child for their family to have to go through the investigation. . . . At times it still feels like I'm being made to conduct some kind of damned witch-hunt. . . .
>
> Then everybody wonders how a Joel Steinberg is able to do what he did. . . . It's fortunate we haven't lost more kids like Lisa than we have, while we're running around checking out three dozen other referrals concerning dirty households and tiny bruises.

Of course, not everyone has gotten the message. Though Richards' book was copublished by the Child Welfare League of America, it does not appear as though the League's executive director, David Liederman, has read it. When asked about false reports, he replied: "Sure, there are loads of frivolous reports being made into the hotlines, but so what?"[146]

*   *   *

Children won another major court victory thanks to a brave family from Scarsdale, N.Y.

On Oct. 30, 1988, New York State's child protective "hotline" received an anonymous report alleging that three girls had been physically abused while at the beach (in late October) with their parents. The family's name began with the initial A, and they reportedly lived at an address in Scarsdale.

The family actually at that address was the family of David and Jeanne Beck. They have two children, a boy and a girl. The "A" family actually lived in a town that had the same name as the Beck's street.

The worker knew all of this by the time she got to the schools the Becks' children were attending. The worker interrogated and stripsearched both children. First sixteen-year-old Jennifer, then thirteen-year-old David. She told both children they had been abused and lied to David, telling him she had found welts and bruises on Jennifer's body.

"I felt like I had been attacked," Jennifer wrote later. "I felt so alone and afraid and I realized that no one else who was in that room cared to protect me." What upset her most, she wrote, was being unable to protect her brother. David wrote that "I began having dreams that she came to our house and took away Mom and Dad."

The Beck's attorney, Nelson Farber, sued Westchester County. The family refused to accept only monetary damages, demanding systemic reforms and limits on stripsearching. They won those limits in a consent decree. Unfortunately, the decree has to be approved by the state Department of Social Services, and the state has been stalling for almost three years.[147]

Sexual Abuse

The debate over the reliability of children's memories is over, and the child savers have lost.

Over the past four years study after study has documented what the *New York Times* termed "the surprising ease with which children can become convinced that something they only imagined or was suggested to them really happened."[148]

In one experiment, the *Times* reports, children not only came to believe what was suggested, but their false memories were so vivid and elaborate that when tapes were shown to psychologists who specialize in interviewing children about abuse they could not tell the false memories from the real ones. Five more studies with a total of 574 preschool children found that 58 percent of them made up at least one false account of a fictitious event after they were repeatedly told it happened. Twenty-five percent of them made up stories for most of the phony events described. Furthermore, in each study, about 25 percent of the children could not be talked out of believing the phony "memory" even after the researchers tried to explain what they had done. And all this was accomplished without using the kind of fear and intimidation often used by child savers in real situations.

This does not mean that a child can never be a reliable witness. It just reinforces the need to question children with extreme care, and tape record every interview.

The growing sophistication about child witnesses is reflected in what has been happening in the major "mass molestation" cases. The Akiki verdict discussed earlier is part of an encouraging trend. Over the past four years: all remaining charges in the McMartin case were dismissed after the second trial ended in a hung jury, the Bakersfield, California convictions discussed in chapter 6 were overturned on appeal; and in a case much like Akiki's, the conviction of Margaret Kelly Michaels, accused of mass molestation at a day care center in New Jersey, also was overturned on appeal.

Equally significant is the case that didn't happen. In Bucks County, Pennsylvania, the district attorney and the police refused to let McMartin-style allegations against a teacher at the Breezy Point Day School be "investigated" by therapists. "My first reaction was that this was the crime of the century," District Attorney Alan Rubenstein said. But after a careful investigation, he concluded that all he had was "the uncorroborated fantasies of four-year-olds fueled by their parents' hysteria."[149]

As this is written, one major case remains, the "Little Rascals" case in Edenton, North Carolina. There have been two convictions, though several jurors subsequently said they regretted their "guilty" verdicts. If these cases are overturned on appeal, it might mark the beginning of the end of one part of the child-abuse witch hunt.

By 1993, even Roland Summit, guru of the ritual-abuse movement and inventor of the "child sexual abuse accommodation syndrome," was beginning to be more cautious.[150] But by then, he had done more than his share of damage.

In both the Akiki and the Bucks County cases, the number and scope of the allegations exploded in October 1989, right after the broadcast of a made-for-TV movie on CBS called "Do You Know The Muffin Man?"[151] Although it included a brief disclaimer at the end describing the movie as fiction, it was actually McMartin the way the child savers wished McMartin had turned out. People and incidents were thinly disguised versions of their McMartin counterparts—except in this version, the hero bursts in on the villainous day-care-center operators just as a satanic ritual is getting underway.

At the end of the movie, an unnamed study is quoted giving purported numbers of children under age six who are sexually abused. That is followed by the admonition to parents: "Talk and listen to your children." Apparently, in Bucks County and in San Diego, they did.

The producers of "Muffin Man" didn't think all this up by themselves. They had a "technical consultant:" Roland Summit.

Of course, sometimes children *do* lie. The age-old practice of tormenting the substitute teacher took a sinister turn in a Chicago fourth-grade classroom in 1994. When Albert Thompson threatened to report his students' misbehavior, one of them offered $1 bribes to ten classmates if they would claim that Thompson fondled them. Although Thompson was cleared, as this is written he has not gotten another teaching assignment. Said a spokeswoman for the Chicago Teachers Union: "What's so scary—and so sad—is that you've got nine-year-old kids sophisticated enough to know they can get a teacher by saying he fondled them."[152]

The child savers insisted the Thompson case was an aberration. But in New York City, two-thirds of the sex abuse charges made against teachers in 1991 were unfounded.[153] To which Dr. Charol Shakeshaft, a member of a commission studying sexual abuse in city schools replies, in essence: Who cares? "What about it?" she says. "What happened to their character and career? What happened to them? Did they lose their jobs? Did they become alcoholics because they're so torn up over this? Did they lose their wives or husbands?"[154]

And NCPCA's Anne Cohn[155] is confident that Thompson's case will become "old news really fast."[156]

Now that it's become clear how easy it is to plant memories in the minds of children, some child savers have turned to a new "market": persuading adults that they were abused as children but forgot all about it. So-called "recovered memory" cases were almost unknown when *Wounded Innocents* was first published. Now they're the latest fad in child saving.

Like almost everything else the child savers say, the notion that memories can be repressed and suddenly return is not always wrong. Some of the allegations are certainly true. But it is worth noting that the most credible "recovered memory" case is very different from most. In that case, Frank Fitzpatrick recalled being molested more than twenty years before by Father James Porter. More than one hundred other victims also came forward, most of whom had never forgotten.[157] But Fitzpatrick's memory came back spontaneously, without the aid of hypnosis or drugs or any other "help" from a therapist.

Cases are more dubious when they begin in the pop psychology section of a bookstore and end in the office of a therapist who believes almost everyone has been sexually abused.

In the most notorious of the guidebooks, *The Courage to Heal,* authors Ellen Bass and Laura Davis declare: "If you are unable to remember any specific instances . . . but still have a feeling that something abusive happened to you, it probably did. If you think you were abused and your life shows the symptoms, then you were." And what are the symptoms? "You feel bad, dirty, and ashamed; you feel powerless, like a victim, you have trouble feeling motivated; you feel you have to be perfect, etc. etc."[158]

Another author tells us that if you doubt you were abused, minimize the abuse, or think, Maybe it's my imagination, that's "post-incest syndrome."[159]

In a critique of such books, social psychologist Carol Tavris writes that the authors "all rely on one another's work as supporting evidence for their own. . . . If one of them comes up with a concocted statistic—such as 'more than half of all women are survivors of childhood sexual trauma'—the numbers are traded like baseball cards, reprinted in every book and eventually enshrined as fact."[160]

The next stop is the therapist's couch, where according to two therapists, "It may take considerable digging on the part of the therapist to discover incest as the source of the symptoms being experienced by the client."[161]

But these are adults, not children. Can they too be persuaded that something happened when it did not? Yes, and it's not even that hard.

Elizabeth Loftus conducted an experiment in which parents of adult volunteers cooperated to produce a list of events that supposedly occurred during the volunteers' childhoods. Three of the "memories" were true and one, a story about being lost in a shopping mall, was false. Twenty-five percent of the adults came to believe the false memory and about ten percent were able to describe their "memories" in great detail.[162]

And when some therapists "dig" they do more than just suggest a false memory. They encourage patients to mix reality, memory, and imagination, inject patients with sodium amytal and/or use hypnosis. All of these techniques leave patients even more vulnerable to accepting a therapist's suggestion as fact. In one study, twenty-seven people were told while hypnotized that as they slept the night before they had been awakened by the sound of a car backfiring. When questioned a week later, thirteen of the test subjects reported having heard the car backfire, and six of them were so convinced that, like the children in a similar experiment, they couldn't be talked out of it.[163]

Also as with children, when adults are pressed hard enough, their stories can become more and more elaborate, including tales of bizarre satanic rituals like those alleged in San Diego. Jim Okerblom, the *Union-Tribune* reporter, attended a seminar at an annual conference sponsored by the Center for Child Protection. "Survivors" of satanic ritual abuse were giving testimonials. "It was like The Twilight Zone," he said. One "survivor" had recovered memories of being raised in a town full of Satanists, including the mayor and the police chief. "The next woman said: 'I recovered memories of being abused before I was born. Now I have memories of being abused on the day of my birth.' And all the therapists applauded. I seemed to be the only one thinking: This is bizarre."

Later, Okerblom said, he saw the moderator of the seminar again—testifying for the prosecution at a preliminary hearing in the Akiki case.[164]

Among those who believe that "Yes, there is satanic, ritual abuse" is Dr. Bennett Braun of Rush-Presbyterian-St. Luke's Medical Center in Chicago. *Time* magazine reports that Braun is being sued by a former patient who charges that Braun persuaded her that she had three hundred different personalities. She also charges that, while under Braun's care, she "recovered" memories of satanic rituals with her parents and other relatives. These rituals included torture, murder, and cannibalism—about fifty people consumed on an average weekend.[165]

There is still no physical evidence for any allegation of satanic ritual abuse, not even a mass outbreak of indigestion.

But back in 1986, when NCPCA put out the "fact sheet" referred to in chapter 6, the one that effectively convicted the McMartin defendants, that "fact sheet" also noted that "allegations like those at the McMartin School are not limited to day care settings." NCPCA cited an authority who had dealt with over two hundred cases of adults allegedly abused as children. "Their descriptions of the abuse run from fondling to extreme sexual abuse which included ritualistic murder," the fact sheet said. And who was NCPCA's authority? Dr. Bennett Braun.[166]

The woman suing Braun is one of many who once believed they had been abused and now realize that the only abuse was the emotional abuse inflicted by their therapists. Laura Pasley sought help for bulimia only to be persuaded by her therapist that she had been sexually abused by her mother, brother, grandfather, and a neighbor. She won "a significant settlement" after suing the therapist. "These therapists are doing something as evil as evil can be," Ms. Pasley said. "It wasn't just my life they took. I had a six-year-old daughter when I began treatment. When I woke up, she was 12."[167]

But even that is not the greatest evil of the recovered memory movement and the broader hysteria of which it is a part. Two evils are worse.

One is the defensiveness about showing normal affection to children discussed in chapter 6. That seems to have gotten worse. What was once an informal pulling back has been codified into "no touch" policies at some schools and day-care centers. "The notion of telling workers not to touch children is nuts. It's not a good idea," says Cohn, without so much as a suggestion that NCPCA's "fact sheet" about day-care abuse and satanic cults or its pamphlet declaring a man suspect if he says "wait till she grows up" or similar efforts might have contributed to the problem.[168]

Charol Shakeshaft goes further, suggesting that people who say they're afraid to touch children are really mad at them for exposing child abuse. "The response to kids coming forward and saying: 'I've been sexually abused by teachers and I want it to stop' has been almost as if people have said: 'OK, if you're going to make us stop, then we're going to punish you. We're just not going to be nice to you,' " Shakeshaft said.[169]

But the greatest evil is the same evil caused by the entire child-saver mentality: that those who really have been abused *will* not be believed because so many who have gone before have said things that *should* not be believed.

Foster Care

When *Wounded Innocents* first was published, Marcia Robinson Lowry, director of the ACLU Children's Rights Project, said that the only meaningful accomplishment of the Adoption Assistance and Child Welfare Act of 1980 was that it increased the grounds for class-action lawsuits. Many suits were based at least in part on allegations that states were not making "reasonable efforts" to keep children out of foster care. Now, the law isn't even good for that, and a lot of people think America's children have Patrick Murphy to thank for this.

In chapter 11 I noted that lower courts differed over whether children have a right to sue to enforce the "reasonable efforts" requirement in the law, though most courts had been saying yes. On March 25, 1992, in the case of *Suter* v. *Artist M.,*[170] the U.S. Supreme Court said no. Although it had upheld similar language in other cases, the court ruled that the "reasonable efforts" clause was too vague to be enforced by lawsuits.

Immediately, state agencies raced to the courts to, in effect, reassert their newfound "right" to mistreat the children in their care. At least eight such cases were filed within three months of the ruling.[171] Many of these efforts were beaten back, but some were not. In Arkansas, for example, the decision blew a potential settlement out of the water.[172]

The damage didn't end with child welfare. The Supreme Court opinion included language that might be read as suggesting that any law requiring states to have a plan to do something requires only that—a plan, without any requirement that the plan actually be carried out. Says Martha Matthews, a staff attorney for the National Center for Youth Law: "It's the kind of argument you make when you're six years old and you don't want to do something."[173]

But some courts bought it. Bureaucracies began using the decision to their advantage in litigation involving welfare, food stamps, child support, and education for the homeless.[174] More often than not, they still lost, but they have been able to drain the resources of their opponents. "It has given Attorneys General something new to bludgeon poverty lawyers with," says Matthews. "[They'll say:] Oh, you want to file a Medicaid case? We have to fight about Suter first."[175]

Suter v. *Artist M.* was initially brought by the "old" Patrick Murphy.

By the time it reached the Supreme Court, Murphy had undergone his conversion to child saving. Six lawyers involved in the litigation say that Murphy did a poor job of handling a case for which he appeared to have little enthusiasm.

First of all, according to Diane Redleaf and Ben Wolf, the case never should have been allowed to reach a Supreme Court packed with Reagan-Bush appointees. DCFS had settled the two big cases discussed earlier. The settlement in Wolf's case included enforcement of "reasonable efforts" to prevent placement. Yet Murphy did not settle.

Once the case reached the Supreme Court, Murphy turned down the chance to have the case argued by any of several leading national experts with extensive Supreme Court experience, including Prof. Walter Dellinger of Duke University, who after a brilliant oral argument had won a similar case just months earlier. Instead, Murphy assigned the case to Michael Dsida, a member of his staff who had never argued a federal appeal before.

Dsida was up against DCFS, the hired guns at Skadden, Arps, and the attorneys general of thirty-eight states, who filed a brief supporting DCFS. Dsida had potential allies too, national groups, called "amici," that were preparing "friend of the court" briefs in support of his position. But Patrick Murphy allegedly barred Dsida from even speaking to these groups. "Patrick could have been a lot more cooperative with the amici than he chose to be," says Robert Schwartz, executive director of the Juvenile Law Center, which filed a brief in the case. "He seemed remarkably untrusting of people on the same side of the case . . . and it meant the amici wasted an inordinate amount of time."

Lowry says she doesn't know if even the best-prepared lawyer could have won the case, but "I certainly do not think a lot of thought went into how the case was handled. Almost all the advocates were very troubled about how it was handled."

"Here was this guy, not really philosophically committed, litigating it all the way to the Supreme Court and not willing to get help from people who were really committed to it," says Martha Matthews. "I'm not accusing him of losing it on purpose to screw other people, but it worries a lot of advocates that this wasn't something on a gut level that he was committed to."[176]

Murphy says the case wasn't settled because DCFS "didn't offer to settle." He says it would have been bad for morale in his office to let "some Professor Sniffypoo" handle oral argument. Asked if he prohibited Dsida from speaking to the amici, Murphy did not answer directly. "I never told him he couldn't talk to Schwartz or Matthews," Murphy said. "I may have said [he couldn't talk to] Redleaf."[177]

But Dsida confirmed the other lawyers' allegations. He said the case "probably could have been settled" but his office didn't pursue it. When preparations began for the appeal to the Supreme Court, Dsida said, Murphy wanted him to sign "a loyalty oath" promising to discuss the case with no one except three attorneys within the Public Guardian's office. Eventually, Dsida said, Murphy relented, but only to the point of allowing him to talk to attorneys at two private law firms. Dsida said that "without Murphy's blessing," he talked to a third attorney as well.

"He did make it more difficult," Dsida said. "Murphy's limitations . . . made this a much more stressful endeavor."

In general, Dsida said, Murphy is less interested in cases like *Artist M.,* that revolve around interpreting a law, than in Constitutional cases. In addition, Dsida said, "I know [Murphy's] views about the importance of family preservation changed over the life of the case. I don't know if it ever got to the point where he was just as happy losing. I know someone with more enthusiasm for family preservation and reunification would have put more energy and focus on it."

Dsida now works for the city corporation counsel's office. He says he left the Public Guardian's office in part because of Murphy's handling of *Artist M.*[178]

How can the damage be undone? Legislation is pending in Congress that would make clear that when a state comes up with a plan under a "state plan" statute, the plan must be put into effect, and if it isn't, people have a right to sue. That would take care of the spin-off effects of *Artist M.* Making it possible to sue under the "reasonable efforts" clause will require either that Congress or the Department of Health and Human Services pass regulations making the law more specific.

*   *   *

One other development in foster care is worth noting: the growth in "kinship care," the placement of foster children with their own relatives. In some big cities, more than half of all foster children now are placed with relatives. On balance, this is a positive trend. But it also carries with it a risk: Children in kinship care tend to stay in foster care even longer than children placed with strangers. Workers and agencies appear to have the attitude that "at least they're with grandma, so it's not so bad." But even an aunt, uncle, or grandparent is no substitute for a parent. Kinship care cannot be allowed to become an excuse for complacency about keeping families together.

Recommendations

The final recommendation in *Wounded Innocents* is that advocates of family preservation become aggressive about taking their case to the public. That process has begun.

Shortly after *Wounded Innocents* was published, I was contacted by Elizabeth Vorenberg, a former Assistant Commissioner of Public Welfare in Massachusetts and, at the time, a member of the National Board of the ACLU. She asked me to help her organize a group of volunteers to help make the case for family preservation and against child saving.

Vorenberg obtained a grant to hold an organizing conference at Harvard Law School, out of which emerged the National Coalition for Child Protection Reform. There is no paid staff and no multimillion dollar budget: just a small group of volunteers who have encountered the child protective system in their professional capacities and want to change it. The group advocates changes in the system; we do *not* deal with or offer advice concerning individual cases.

*   *   *

In addition to the thirty-five recommendations in chapter 11, I would add one more:

Recommendation 36: Congress or the Department of Health and Human Services should narrow the criteria for the type of programs for which the new federal money discussed in this chapter can be used.

The new federal money is in addition to the current unrestricted funding for foster care. That is regrettable. I continue to believe that foster care funding should be capped and the money gradually transferred into family preservation.

In the absence of such action, however, Congress or HHS should at least make sure that the new money isn't wasted on child-saving. Congress should require that states spend at least 75 percent of their allocations on family preservation, not "family support." And at least two-thirds of that 75 percent should go only to programs that strictly follow the Home-builders model. In other words, Congress *should* do exactly what much of the media wrongly claims it already has done.

*   *   *

Finally, a new edition of *Wounded Innocents* is also an opportunity to reconsider.

I found no issue more difficult to wrestle with than the question of what to do in cases where parents have been separated from their children for many years through no fault of their own—indeed, an agency may well have sabotaged efforts to stay together—and the child has "bonded" with foster parents.

In chapter 11, I said that it was better to be cruel to the parents than to the child so the child should be left with his or her new caretakers, and the agencies should be fined or shut down. I acknowledged that "carried to its logical extreme, this standard could require that a child be kept with a kidnaper if they stayed in hiding long enough and a close bond developed between them."

What I did not count on was how close we would come to just that, and how strongly much of the public would support it. In a New Jersey case, the hypothetical question about kidnaping was put to a psychologist for the state's Division of Youth and Family Services when he testified in favor of termination of parental rights because a child allegedly had "bonded" with a foster parent. The psychologist said that in the hypothetical case, the child should be kept with the kidnaper.[179] A guardian ad litum said the same thing when I put the question to her during a panel discussion in Schenectady, New York, a couple of years ago.

And then came "Baby Jessica."

Cara Clausen gave birth to the baby she called Anna in tiny Blairstown, Iowa, on February 8, 1991. Iowa law says a mother must have three full days to think about the decision before signing away rights to a child. But somehow, Clausen's signature was on the surrender in fewer than two.

On March 1, Anna was placed with Roberta and Jan DeBoer. Just five days later, Cara Clausen changed her mind.[180] Anna's father, Daniel Schmidt, came forward to accept responsibility for his child. Daniel and Cara were married.

Had the DeBoers truly been thinking first and foremost about "the best interests of the child" they could have acted in those interests and given Anna back to her mother. Instead, they went to court. They lost time and time again. But each time they would find a new way to delay the inevitable: a new motion, a new appeal. They stalled and stalled and stalled and stalled. And then, after two-and-a-half years, when all the appeals finally ran out, they said: You can't take the child away from us. We're the only parents she's ever known.

Everything the DeBoers did was legal. But ethically, it was a kidnaping. And yet, overwhelmingly, the press and the public sided with the DeBoers.

The DeBoers were masters of media manipulation, right down to the moment when they finally had to give up the child they had named Jessica. Everyone remembers the pictures of the crying child being driven from the DeBoers' home. Few know that just before that moment, Roberta DeBoer had lunged for her daughter, provoking the tears.[181] The DeBoers even made sure the child's carseat was placed next to the window closest to the television cameras.

And it worked. The Schmidts were reviled everyplace from CNN to the *New York Times*. A *Times* Op Ed piece branded Daniel Schmidt "Jessica's sperm father."[182] When they sold their story for the inevitable made-for-TV movie, the DeBoers, who, as one account put it, "looked as if they just stepped out of a Volvo ad,"[183] were portrayed as loving and sophisticated, the Schmidts as "beer guzzlin' truckers living in a trailer with hubcaps nailed to the side."[184] It's no wonder that when the child finally was returned, hundreds of Americans helped her adjust by sending hate mail to her parents.

"Judging from media support for the DeBoers, here is the right way for adoptive couples to behave when a birth mother changes her mind," wrote one of the few dissenters, freelance journalist Olya Thompson. "Try at all costs to hold the birth parents to the terms of the contract, determined to exact your pound of flesh. Arrogantly ignore court rulings and go before the cameras, never hesitating to teach someone else's child to call you Mommy and Daddy. The longer you keep her, the more wrenching the image of taking her away. And this self-serving campaign is promoted as children's 'rights'?"

At the heart of the media's approach, once again, was the issue of class. Thompson writes:

> Perhaps those media spokespersons, now well into their own careers, relate more readily to trendy issues like infertility or the shortage of adoptable children. . . . than they do to the painful dilemma of a poor parent who finds herself with a child she cannot raise. It boils down to this: They simply could not imagine themselves in Cara Schmidt's situation, but they could easily have been the DeBoers.[185]

Perhaps Anna Schmidt would have been "better off" with the DeBoers. But to have left her there would have encouraged other prospective adoptive parents to behave as the DeBoers did. Worse, it would have encouraged hundreds of child-saving agencies to keep families apart, knowing that if they could just wait long enough, they could get the birth parents out of their children's lives. Someday, it may become possible to prevent this by penalizing agencies, but that hasn't happened yet and it's not likely to happen anytime soon.

This does not mean that parents who really have done something wrong and who have been given help to change should be allowed an unlimited amount of time to clean up their acts. But to allow a child like Anna to stay with her "paper parents" would be to place what might be the interests of the one child we see ahead of the many more children we don't see. And that is exactly what has caused so much pain for so many children.

Epilogue

"I'm sorry, I'm sorry, I'm sorry."

The cries of a three-year-old girl filled the night as a sheriff's deputy wrenched her from her mother, tucked her under his arm, and walked out of the house with her.

Moments earlier, two deputies had arrived at the Carmichael, California, home of Gary and Barbara Smith (not their real names). The deputies announced that Gary was suspected of abusing a niece.

The children, three-year-old Simone, five-year-old Sam, and seven-year-old Tommy, insisted their father had not hurt them. The child savers would not listen. The father produced names of witnesses. The child savers would not listen. The father said: "At least leave the children with relatives." The child savers would not listen. Finally, the father said, "Take *me* instead. Place *me* under arrest." The child savers would not listen.

"I'm sorry, I'm sorry, I'm sorry."

The parents got their children back when the child savers realized that they had confused Gary with the boyfriend of his niece's mother—a man named Carey. It took the child savers twenty-six days to figure this out and clear Gary.

When the parents visited their children, the seven-year-old got angry at his mother for not bringing them home sooner. "To him it had been forever," the mother said. "I had abandoned him." The five-year-old said he had been a good boy so he should be able to go home. That's also what Simone was thinking when she was taken: "If they are taking me away, I must have done something wrong." So she promised, as best she could, that she would never do it again.

"I'm sorry, I'm sorry, I'm sorry."[1]

It's very important to the child savers that everyone else say they're sorry.

Parents who have brutally beaten or molested their children say it—if they're smart enough—because they know it's what the child savers want so badly to hear. If they can put on a good enough act of repentance, like Eli Creekmore's father did, they'll get their child back over and over and over again.

Innocent parents say they're sorry because it's what everyone tells them to say. Admit to something, anything, and you can have your children back. Insist on your innocence and they'll try to keep them forever. "How do you know [my husband] is guilty?" Susan Gabriel asked the caseworker. "We know he's guilty because he says he's innocent," the caseworker replied.

And of course the children say they're sorry because they are so sure they are being punished, so they must have done something wrong.

*   *   *

When I began writing this book, I was determined not to use the term *witchhunt*. It's been overused, for acts of mindless persecution in general, and concerning the actions of the child savers in particular. But I found the parallels in the behavior of the child savers and the circumstances surrounding the "original" witchhunt in Salem, Massachusetts, in 1692 too striking to ignore.

First, of course, unlike any of the figurative witchhunts in between, during the so-called "mass molestation" cases, some of the child savers have literally gone looking for witches.

But there are other parallels.

The Salem outbreak began with children suddenly engaging in fits of hysteria in church. There were people in Salem who did not believe these were anything more than schoolgirl pranks, but they were silenced by a majority who insisted that children would never lie about such a thing. Indeed, anyone who doubted "the afflicted girls" quickly became a suspect. Even a judge on the tribunal hearing the cases who quit because of his doubts was accused as a result. He escaped prosecution, but most did not. Some went to the gallows for expressing doubt.

Initially, the children named no one as the cause of their "affliction." They kept saying they did not know who or what was hurting them. But then the adults of the town began suggesting specific names. The girls quickly picked up on those cues and named anyone the adults suggested. Soon others joined in making accusations. The cry of witchcraft became a potent way for neighbors to settle old scores.

There was no possible defense against an accusation of witchcraft, because the prosecution relied on "spectral evidence." The girls declared they had seen someone's ghost—their "shape"—commit a crime, and that was that. "Let an accuser say: 'Your shape came into my room last midnight' and the accused had no defense at all," writes Marion Starkey in her history of the Salem trials. "No conceivable alibi can be furnished for the whereabouts of a 'shape,' one's airy substance."

The only way out was to repent. Admit guilt and be treated with the solicitude of the court. Proclaim innocence and hang.[2]

Children never lie. Adults tell children whom to name. Doubters become suspects. Only repentance is acceptable. There is even a child saver equivalent of spectral evidence: It's "syndrome evidence." There is no defense against syndrome evidence. Let a child deny being abused or withdraw an accusation and it is simply more proof that the abuse really happened—because the "syndrome" says that's what children always do.

There is one difference between what happened in Salem nearly three hundred years ago, and what is happening all across America today. Witchcraft isn't real. Child abuse is. But that only adds another element to the current tragedy. In Salem, there was no danger that "real witchcraft" was going undetected while the innocent were hanged.

It is the children who have suffered most from the present witchhunt.

In the name of child protection, we invade more than a million homes a year where no one has done anything wrong. We show the children in those homes how vulnerable they are to the larger world outside, and how little their parents can do to protect them. "If it ever happens again," says Gary, "I'm going to fight the deputies—not because I think I can win, but because I never again want to see the look on my children's faces when they were wondering why I don't save them."

In the name of child protection we go to the schools and teach children that their bodies are their own. Then we subject them to strip-searches by strangers based on no more than an anonymous allegation.

In the name of child protection we terrify children into "admitting" maltreatment that never happened. The process guarantees that the innocent will suffer. And when it is discovered, it taints legitimate prosecutions and guarantees the guilty will go free.

In the name of child protection we waste millions of dollars breaking up families where the only "maltreatment" is poverty and something as simple as a security deposit for a new apartment could keep them together. Then we insist everything would be fine if we just do more of the same.

In the name of child protection, we throw thousands of children into the "no attachment zone" of foster care, shoving them from home to home and discharging them years later as "emotional pulp." Foster care is the garbage dump, says Anne Williamson. And the child savers treat children like garbage. Says Marcia Lowry: "We are breeding generations of psychopaths."[3]

In the name of child protection, we overwhelm the child-protection system, making it impossible to reach thousands of children who really need protection. When we find them, they often get the worst of foster care. They are turned into "nomad children" taking their possessions from place to place in plastic garbage bags. Or they are left in hospitals and modern-day orphanages.

In the name of child protection, we make it almost impossible to find new permanent homes for the children who need them. There is no time to find adoptive homes. There is no time to terminate parental rights. And there is no way to persuade many judges to do it, because they know how capriciously the child saving system operates.

There is one other way in which the witchhunt in Salem and the witchhunt today are alike. Though in both cases some took advantage of the times for selfish ends, in both cases the witchhunters were almost always good and decent people.

The witchhunters of Salem *believed* in spectral evidence. They believed they were protecting the community from the work of the devil. They believed they were acting in the best interests of the children. They were not deliberately doing wrong, but they could not see the wrong that they were doing.

The Reverend John Hale came to understand that. He had testified against at least one of the accused witches. He had believed what almost everyone else believed. Until one day, when his own wife was accused.

Starkey writes:

> Hale knew his wife had done nothing of the sort. . . . But he now knew, and the revelation came to him with the force of a physical blow, that just so must . . . a hundred others [have felt] when wife or child or mother was taken. If his present feeling was justified, why not theirs?
>
> He went home to brood among his books and papers; when he had thought the thing through he would not be silent about his conclusions. He was a humble and courageous man. . . .

Five years later, Hale wrote an account of what had caused the witchcraft madness. He wrote: "We walked in clouds and could not see our way. And we have most cause to be humbled for error . . . which cannot be retrieved."

For a great many children it is already too late. But for others, and for generations of children yet unborn, the errors of the child savers *can* be retrieved.

John Hale realized his mistake. Perhaps someday the child savers will, too. And perhaps they will begin the process of change the way John Hale did: By saying they're sorry.

Appendix

Can You Live Up to Child-Saver Standards?

Norman Polansky and his colleagues suggest that child-protective workers use this checklist to determine whether parents are "neglecting" their children. Parents gain one point for each "correct" answer. In some cases the right answer is yes, in others no.

Any score under 63 is considered neglectful. A score of 77 or above is required for "acceptable" child care, and 88 or above is required to be considered "good."

The Childhood Level of Living Scale

	Yes	No
1. Mother plans at least one meal consisting of two courses.	x	
2. Mother uses good judgment about leaving child alone in the house.	x	
3. Mother plans for variety in foods.	x	
4. Mother sometimes leaves child to insufficiently older sibling.		x
5. Mother plans meals with courses that go together.	x	

	Yes	No
6. The child receives at least nine hours of sleep most nights.	x	
7. Child is offered food at fixed time each day.	x	
8. Bedtime for the child is set by the parents for about the same time every night.	x	
9. Mother has evidenced lack of awareness of child's possible dental needs.		x
10. Mother expresses concern about feeding a balanced diet.	x	
11. Mother enforces rules about going into the street.	x	
12. Child has been taught own address.	x	
13. Child has been taught to swim or mother believes child should be taught to swim.	x	
14. Mother will never leave child alone in the house.	x	
15. Mother uses thermometer with child.	x	
16. Storm sashes or equivalent are present.	x	
17. Windows are caulked or sealed against drafts.	x	
18. Doors are weatherproofed.	x	
19. House is dilapidated.		x
20. There are window screens in good repair in most windows.	x	
21. Wood floors are cracked and splintered.		x
22. There are screen doors properly mounted.	x	
23. There is an operating electric sweeper.	x	
24. Floor covering presents tripping hazard.		x
25. Living room doubles as a bedroom.		x
26. There are food scraps on the floor and furniture.		x
27. Child five years or older sleeps in room with parents.		x
28. At least one of the children sleeps in the same bed as parents.		x

	Yes	No
29. Mother plans special meals for special occasions.	x	
30. Windows have been cracked or broken over a month without repair.		x
31. Clothing usually appears to be hand-me-downs.		x
32. Buttons and snaps of child's clothing are frequently missing and not replaced.		x
33. There are dirty dishes and utensils in rooms other than the kitchen.		x
34. There are leaky faucets.		x
35. The roof (or ceiling) leaks.		x
36. The floors of the house appear to be swept each day.	x	
37. Bathroom seems to be cleaned regularly.	x	
38. Mother takes precautions in the storage of medicine.	x	
39. Mattresses are in obviously poor condition.		x
40. Repairs one usually makes oneself are undone.		x
41. Mother has encouraged child to wash hands before meals.	x	
42. Ears are usually clean.	x	
43. Mother mentions she makes effort to get child to eat food not preferred because they [sic] are important to child's nutrition.	x	
44. Poisonous or dangerous sprays and cleaning fluids are stored out of child's reach.	x	
45. Mother has encouraged child to wash hands after using toilet.	x	
46. Mother cautions child to be careful of flaking paint.	x	
47. It is obvious that mother has given attention to child's grooming at home.	x	
48. Planned overnight vacation trip has been taken by family.	x	

	Yes	No
49. Child has been taken by parents to see some well known historical or cultural building.	x	
50. Child has been taken by parents to see a spectator sport.	x	
51. Mother mentions that in the last year she has: taught the child something about nature; told the child a story; read a story to the child.	x	
52. Family has taken child downtown.	x	
53. Child has been taken by parents to see various animals.	x	
54. Child has been taken by parents to a carnival.	x	
55. Mother is tuned into child's indirect emotional signals.	x	
56. Mother mentions that she has played games with child.	x	
57. Mother mentions use of TV to teach child.	x	
58. Child has been taken by parents to a parade.	x	
59. A prayer is said before some meals.	x	
60. Mother comforts the child when he is upset.	x	
61. There are magazines available.	x	
62. The family owns a camera.	x	
63. The child says prayers at bedtime.	x	
64. Child has been taken to a children's movie.	x	
65. Mother mentions that she answers child's questions about the way things work.	x	
66. Child has been taken by parents to the firehouse.	x	
67. Child has been taken fishing.	x	
68. Mother seems not to follow through on rewards.		x
69. Mother mentions that she cannot get child to mind.		x
70. Child is often ignored when he tries to tell mother something.		x

	Yes	No
71. The child is often pushed aside when he shows need for love.		x
72. Mother seems not to follow through on threatened punishments.		x
73. Spanking is sometimes with an object.		x
74. Mother threatens punishment by imagined or real fright object.		x
75. Very frequently no action is taken when discipline is indicated.		x
76. Mother frequently screams at child.		x
77. Mother is made uncomfortable by child's demonstration of affection.		x
78. Mother complains a lot about life.		x
79. Mother mandates child's play according to sex (i.e., girls may only play with dolls).		x
80. Child is never allowed to make a mess.		x
81. Dolls are available to the child for play.	x	
82. Mother expresses to the child her concern for child's safety if there is real danger.	x	
83. There is a designated area for play.	x	
84. Parents guard language in front of children.	x	
85. Child is immediately spanked for running into the street.	x	
86. Mother mentions child asks questions showing curiosity about how things work.	x	
87. Child is taught to be respectful of adults.	x	
88. Mother puts child to bed.	x	
89. Mother mentions that she limits child's TV watching.	x	
90. Child is encouraged to care for own toys.	x	
91. Child is taught to respect property of others.	x	

	Yes	No
92. Mother expresses pride in daughter's femininity or son's masculinity.	x	
93. Mother is able to show physical affection to child comfortably.	x	
94. There are books for adults in the house.	x	
95. An effort is made to provide choices for the child.	x	
96. Crayons are made available to the child.	x	
97. A play shovel is available to the child.	x	
98. Child is sometimes rewarded for good behavior with a treat.	x	
99. The child has a book of his own.	x	

Reprinted by permission from "Assessing Adequacy of Child Caring: An Urban Scale," Norman Polansky, et al. *Child Welfare,* 57, no. 7 (1978): 443–448. Washington, D.C.

Notes

Chapter 1: Overview

1. Conditions at MacLaren Hall around the time Jennifer Humlen was there are described in numerous stories from the *Los Angeles Times,* among them: Marylouise Oates, "Celebrity Day at MacLaren Hall," March 18, 1986, 1; Rich Connell, "Major Reforms at MacLaren Urged," June 22, 1985, 6; Bill Boyarsky, "Back to the Beginning for Children's Services," April 21, 1985, part 4, p. 1; Lois Timnick, "New Director to Take Reins at MacLaren," April 13, 1986, 3. The statement that the place has been refurbished is from the author's interview with the current director, Helen Maxwell. See also: Steven Eames, "Shelter in the Storm for the Smallest Victims," *San Gabriel Valley Tribune,* Oct. 19, 1989, E1.

2. Information for Elene Humlen's story comes from the following sources: interviews with Elene Humlen, Jeannette Humlen, Chris Humlen, Jean Sutorius, Allen McMahon, Norman Kallen, Larry Strid, the attorney handling the Humlens' civil suit, and Dr. Ann Kwun, the Humlens' pediatrician; an essay by Elene Humlen, "For the Love of Baseball"; briefs and supporting documentation filed by both sides in a civil lawsuit brought by Elene Humlen on behalf of her children (*Christopher Humlen and Jennifer Humlen, etc.* v. *County of Los Angeles, et al.,* case #SEC 54871, Superior Court of the State of California for the County of Los Angeles), including reports filed by the school nurse, the investigating officers, and the emergency room physician, as well as depositions of the nurse, the officers, the physician, and Chris's teacher; the court decision dismissing the lawsuit and motion to appeal that decision.

3. Except as otherwise specified, the term *child abuse* is used in this book generically to cover all forms of alleged maltreatment for which child protective services agencies intervene, including neglect.

4. Katie Leishman, "Child Abuse: The Extent of the Harm," *Atlantic Monthly,*

November 1983, p. 22.

5. Interview with the author.

6. Quoted in Douglas Besharov, " 'Doing Something' about Child Abuse: The Need to Narrow the Grounds for State Intervention," *Harvard Journal of Law and Public Policy,* 8, no. 3, Summer 1985, p. 543.

7. Tom Charlier and Shirley Downing, "Justice Abused: A 1980s Witch-Hunt," Memphis, Tenn., *Commercial Appeal,* reprint, p. 15. This article was one of a multi-part series printed by the newspaper in January 1988 and now publicly available in reprint form. Page numbers in citations for "Justice Abused" refer to the reprint page.

8. P. McEnroe and D. Peterson, "Jordan: The Accuser," *Minneapolis Star and Tribune,* Oct. 21, 1984; cited in Hollida Wakefield and Ralph Underwager, *Accusations of Child Sexual Abuse* (Springfield, Ill.: Charles C. Thomas, 1988), p. 123.

9. A copy of such a letter is in the possession of the author. Massachusetts now uses the term "supported" instead of "substantiated."

10. Charlier and Downing (see Note 7), p. 13.

11. Author's interview with Susan Gabriel.

12. Interview with the author.

13. Interview with the author.

14. See Chapter 4.

15. Douglas Besharov, "Unfounded Allegations—A New Child Abuse Problem," *Public Interest,* no. 83, Spring 1986, p. 27.

16. Ohio Statutes, Sec. 2151.04; Illinois Statutes, Chapter 23, Sec. 2053; Mississippi Statutes, Sec. 43-21-105; South Dakota Statutes, Sections 26-8-6 and 26-8-2.

17. Patrick Murphy, *Our Kindly Parent: The State* (New York: Viking, 1975), p. 157.

18. National Charities Information Bureau Report on the National Committee for Prevention of Child Abuse, July 20, 1988, p. 5

19. Leontine Young, *Physical Child Neglect,* pamphlet published by the National Committee for Prevention of Child Abuse (Chicago: 1986), p. 1.

20. Cornelia Spelman, *Talking About Child Sexual Abuse,* pamphlet published by the National Committee for Prevention of Child Abuse (Chicago: 1985), p. 6.

21. Charlier and Downing (see Note 7), p. 18.

22. Interview with the author.

23. "Complaint" and "Plaintiffs' Post-Trial Memorandum," *Fields et al.* v. *Johnson,* No. 89 C 1624 United States District Court for the Northern District of Illinois, Eastern Division.

24. San Francisco data are from *Every Three Hours: A Report to the Technical Advisory Committee, Family and Children's Division, San Francisco Dept. of Social Services,* June 15, 1986, p. 1. Other data are from American Humane Association, *Highlights of Official Child Neglect and Abuse Reporting, 1986* (Denver: 1988), p. 10.

25. *Child Abuse and Neglect in America: The Problem and the Response,* Hearing before the Select Committee on Children, Youth, and Families, U.S. House

of Representatives, March 3, 1987, transcript, p. 43.

26. *Hearing on Child Abuse Reporting Laws and Dependency Statutes,* Select Committee on Children and Youth, California Legislature, Dec. 4, 1986, p. 54.

27. State laws vary concerning when—or if—children can have their own lawyers. In California, an appellate court has ruled that when a child is old enough to make a mature judgment, and the child's wishes differ from those of the people keeping him or her in custody, separate counsel must be appointed for the child. Technically, therefore, the attorney who represented Chris did not also represent Jennifer, since Jennifer was too young to tell anyone she did not want to be in MacLaren Hall.

28. Author's interview with Helen Maxwell. When Jennifer Humlen was at MacLaren Hall there was even less separation by age: children from birth to age three were housed together, according to news accounts.

29. *E.Z.* v. *Coler,* 603 F. Supp. 546 (Northern District of Illinois, 1985).

30. Testimony of Kathy Doellefeld-Clancy, Court Appointed Special Advocates, St. Louis County, before the Missouri House of Representatives Interim Committee on Children, Youth, and Families, Sept. 30, 1985. (Testimony is included in the committee's *Report to the Speaker on: Child Abuse Reporting Law* (December 1985), p. 88.

31. Interview with the author.

32. Remarks of former foster child Joan Graham at the 1989 Annual Convention of the National Association of Foster Care Reviewers.

33. Interview with the author.

34. Defendant's Memorandum in Support of Motion to Dismiss, *B.H.* v. *Johnson,* No. 88 C 5599, United States District Court for the Northern District of Illinois, Eastern Division, Nov. 15, 1988, pp. 13, 38.

35. Suzanne Daley, "Child Dead in Family Welfare Agency Forgot," *New York Times,* Jan. 20, 1989, 1

36. Joseph Shapiro, "Whose Responsibility Is It, Anyway?" *U.S. News and World Report,* Jan. 9, 1989, p. 29.

37. David Whitman, "The Numbers Game: When More Is Less," *U.S. News and World Report,* April 27, 1987, p. 39.

38. State Communities Aid Association, *Caring for Families and Children: The Failure to Create Responsive Child Protective Services,* January 1988, p. 6.

39. Eli Newberger, "The Helping Hand Strikes Again: Unintended Consequences of Child Abuse Reporting," *Journal of Clinical Psychology,* 12, no. 3, Winter 1983, p. 308.

40. David Hechler, *The Battle and the Backlash: The Child Sexual Abuse War* (Lexington, Mass.: Lexington Books, 1988).

41. David Gil, *Violence Against Children: Physical Child Abuse in the United States* (Cambridge, Mass.: Harvard University Press, 1970).

42. Murphy (see Note 17), p. 157.

43. Michael Wald, "State Intervention on Behalf of 'Neglected' Children: A Search for Standards for Placement of Children from Their Homes, Monitoring the Status of Children in Foster Care, and Termination of Parental Rights," *Stanford*

Law Review, 28 (1976), p. 626.

44. Joseph Goldstein, Anna Freud, Albert J. Solnit, *Before the Best Interests of the Child* (New York: Free Press, 1979).

45. Interview with the author.

46. Barbara Nelson, *Making an Issue of Child Abuse: Political Agenda Setting for Social Problems* (Chicago: University of Chicago Press, 1984), pp. 66-67.

47. Child Welfare League of America, *Too Young to Run: The Status of Child Abuse in America* (Washington, D.C.: 1986), p. 7. The dates during which the survey itself was conducted are not given.

48. Anne McGraw (UPI), "Stiffer Penalties Urged for Abuse of Children," *Philadelphia Inquirer,* Feb. 25, 1988, B5.

49. Richard Wexler, "More Calls Strain Child Abuse Hotline," Albany, N.Y., *Times Union,* Dec. 1, 1987.

50. State of New York, *Executive Budget,* fiscal year 1989-1990, p. 365. See also Richard Wexler, "Experts say Cuomo's Priorities in Child Abuse Fight Wrong," Albany, N.Y. *Times Union,* Jan. 20, 1989, 1.

51. Deborah Gesensway, "Effort to Subsidize Families Fails," Albany, N.Y. *Times Union,* August 12, 1989.

52. Ed Penhala, "House OK's Child Abuse Bill Despite Flaws," *Seattle Post-Intelligencer,* April 16, 1987, D1.

53. *Foster Care, Child Welfare and Adoption Reforms,* Joint Hearings before the Subcommittee on Public Assistance and Unemployment Compensation of the Committee on Ways and Means and the Select Committee on Children, Youth and Families, U.S. House of Representatives, April 13 and 28, May 12, 1988, transcript, p. 58

Chapter 2: Child Saving Then

1. This account of the Mary Ellen case is drawn from extensive excerpts from coverage at the time in the *New York Times.* These excerpts are reprinted in Gertrude Williams, ed., *Traumatic Abuse and Neglect of Children at Home* (Baltimore: Johns Hopkins University Press, 1980), pp. 70-74.

2. At her trial, Mary Ellen's foster mother, Mary Connolly, testified that Mary Ellen was the illegitimate daughter of Thomas McCormack and a woman whose surname apparently was Wilson. At birth, Mary Ellen was placed with a woman named Mary Score. When she was eighteen months old the Board of Charities "indentured" Mary Ellen to McCormack and his wife Mary. After McCormack died, Mary married Francis Connolly. Some scholars maintain that Mary Connolly's testimony concerning even a minimal relationship between herself and Mary Ellen was false (Stephen and Joyce Antler, "From Child Rescue to Family Protection: The Evolution of the Child Protective Movement in the United States," *Children and Youth Services Review,* 1, 1979, 178ff.). At a minimum, it is clear that at the time Mary Ellen was abused, she was living with neither of her biological parents and was supposedly under the supervision of the Board of Charities.

3. Although the case was brought to the attention of the court by the president of the New York SPCA, Henry Bergh, he specified that he was acting as a "humane citizen" not in his official capacity. Mary Connolly was convicted of felonious assault, not cruelty to animals. New York City in fact has had a law against child abuse since 1833. (See Mark Testa, *Child Welfare in Sociological and Historical Perspective* [Chicago: Chapin Hall Center for Children, 1985], p. 10.)

4. Jeanne Giovannoni and Rosina Becerra, *Defining Child Abuse* (New York: Free Press, 1979), p. 36

5. Joan Gittens, *The Children of the State: Dependent Children in Illinois, 1818-1980s* (Chicago: Chapin Hall Center for Children, 1986), pp. 9-15.

6. D. J. Rothman, *The Discovery of the Asylum* (Boston: Little, Brown, 1971), quoted in Martha Cox and Roger Cox, eds., *Foster Care: Current Issues, Policies, and Practices* (Norwood, N.J.: Ablex Publishing Corp., 1985), p. 10.

7. Anthony Platt, *The Child Savers: The Invention of Delinquency* (Chicago: University of Chicago Press, 1977), p. 37.

8. Linda Gordon, *Heroes of Their Own Lives* (New York: Viking Penguin, 1988).

9. Ibid., pp. 46, 14, 15.

10. Gittens (see Note 5), p. 16.

11. Charles Loring Brace, *The Dangerous Classes of New York and Twenty Years Work Among Them* (New York: Wynkoop and Hallenbeck, 1872), pp. 154-156.

12. Except as otherwise noted, information about Charles Loring Brace and his work comes from Miriam Langsam, *Children West: A History of the Placing-Out System of the New York Children's Aid Society, 1853-1890* (Madison, Wis.: The State Historical Society of Wisconsin, 1964).

13. Platt (see Note 7), pp. 26-30.

14. Elizabeth Pleck, *Domestic Tyranny: The Making of American Social Policy Against Family Violence from Colonial Times to the Present* (New York: Oxford University Press, 1987), p. 145

15. Platt (see Note 7), p. 31.

16. Cox and Cox (see Note 6), p. 7.

17. Ibid.

18. Gordon (see Note 8), pp. 334ff.

19. Michael Katz, *Poverty and Policy in American History* (New York: Academic Press, 1983), p. 197.

20. Ibid., p. 196.

21. Testa (see Note 3), p. 6.

22. Platt (see Note 7), p. 130.

23. Giovannoni and Becerra (see Note 4), p. 52.

24. *NBC Nightly News,* April 21, 1989.

25. Gittens (see Note 5), pp. 24, 56.

26. Cox and Cox (see Note 12), p. 11.

27. Langsam (see Note 6), p. 2.

28. "The Needy Mother and the Neglected Child," *Outlook,* June 7, 1913,

reprinted in Edna Bullock, ed., *Selected Articles on Mothers' Pensions* (White Plains, N.Y.: H. S. Wilson, 1915), p. 27.

29. *Report of the New York State Commission on Relief for Widowed Mothers,* 1914, reprinted in Bullock (see Note 28), p. 32.

30. Mark Leff, "Consensus for Reform: The Mothers' Pension Movement in the Progressive Era," *Social Service Review,* 47, Sept. 1973, p. 401.

31. Frederic Almy, "Public Pensions to Widows: Experiences and Observations Which Lead Me to Oppose Such a Law," *Child,* July 1912, reprinted in Bullock (see Note 28), p. 155.

32. C. C. Carstens, "Public Pensions to Widows with Children," *Survey,* Jan. 14, 1913, reprinted in Bullock (see Note 28), p. 170.

33. Ibid.

34. Ronald Taylor, *The Kid Business* (Boston: Houghton Mifflin, 1981), p. 80.

35. Gittens (see Note 5), p. 76

36. Bullock (see Note 28), p. 27.

37. Giovannoni and Becerra (see Note 4), p. 63.

38. Leff (see Note 30), pp. 412-413.

39. Pleck (see Note 14), p. 80

40. Katz (see Note 19); Gordon (see Note 8).

41. Gordon (see Note 8), pp. 48, 54

42. Pleck (see Note 14), p. 84.

43. Gordon (see Note 8), p. 38

44. Ibid., pp. 28, 38, 95.

45. Patrick Murphy, *Our Kindly Parent: The State* (New York: Viking, 1975), p. 4.

46. Platt (see Note 7), p. 142.

47. Gittens (see Note 5), p. 49.

48. Catherine Ross, "The Lessons of the Past: Defining and Controlling Child Abuse in the United States," in Gerbner, Ross, and Zigler, eds., *Child Abuse: An Agenda for Action* (New York: Oxford University Press, 1980), p. 78.

49. The Illinois Supreme Court attacked the vagueness of the law and the indeterminate sentences that could be imposed under it:

> "What is the standard to be? What extent of enlightenment, what amount of industry, what degree of virtue, will save from the threatened imprisonment? . . . There is not a child in the land who could not be proved by two or more witnesses to be in this sad condition. . . .
>
> "Such restraint upon natural liberty is tyranny and oppression. If without crime, without the conviction of an offense, the children of the state are to be confined for the 'good of society' then society had better be reduced to its original elements and free government acknowledged a failure. . . . Even criminals cannot be convicted and imprisoned without due process of law."— *People* v. *Turner,* 55 Ill. 280 (1870), cited in Giovannoni and Becerra (see Note 7), p. 54; Murphy (see Note 4), p. 3, and Platt (see Note 45), p. 104.

50. *In re Gault,* 387 U.S. 1 (1967).

51. Allen Carlson of the Rockford Institute, an ultraconservative think tank.

52. Tom Charlier and Shirley Downing, "Justice Abused: A 1980s Witch-Hunt," Memphis, Tenn., *Commercial Appeal,* reprint, p. 12.

53. Defendant's Post-hearing Memorandum in Opposition to Plaintiff's Motion for Preliminary Injunction, *E.Z.* v. *Coler,* #82 C 3976, United States District Court for the Northern District of Illinois, Eastern Division, April 17, 1984, pp. 40, 41

54. Platt (see Note 7), p. 26

Chapter 3: Child Saving Now

1. Information concerning the Norman case comes from the report submitted by the worker who visited the Norman home; from the "Introductory Statement" and the "Plaintiffs' Post-Trial Memorandum" in the case of *Jaqueline Fields, James Norman et al.* v. *Gordon Johnson,* No. 89 C 1624 United States District Court for the Northern District of Illinois, Eastern Division; from "DCFS Neglects Parents, Creates Tragedies," an unpublished essay by Diane Redleaf; and from interviews with Redleaf and William Curtis.

2. Malcolm Bush, *Families in Distress: Public, Private and Civic Responses* (Berkeley: University of California Press, 1988), p. 80.

3. *Study Findings: Study of National Incidence and Prevalence of Child Abuse and Neglect: 1988* (NIS-2) (Washington: U.S. Dept. of Health and Human Services, National Center on Child Abuse and Neglect, 1988), chap. 5, p. 26.

4. Ibid., chap. 5 pp. 26, 31.

5. Murray Straus, Richard Gelles, and Suzanne Steinmetz, *Behind Closed Doors: Violence in the American Family* (New York: Anchor/Doubleday, 1980), p. 148.

6. Interview with the author.

7. Interview with the author.

8. Elizabeth Elmer, "Traumatized Children, Chronic Illness, and Poverty," in Leroy Pelton, ed., *The Social Context of Child Abuse and Neglect* (New York: Human Sciences Press, 1981), p. 213.

9. Ray Nunn (Producer), "Crimes Against Children: The Failure of Foster Care," *ABC-News Closeup,* Aug. 30, 1988, transcript, p. 4.

10. Since most single parents, and most parents accused of neglect, are women, for the sake of simplicity I have used the pronouns "she" and "her" when describing them. I have done the same with child protective caseworkers, for the same reason.

11. Interview with the author.

12. New York State Department of Social Services, *Child Abuse and Maltreatment: Allegations and Determinations,* August, 1983.

13. "Medical Care Spending Found a Major Concern Within City," *New York Times,* Jan. 30, 1983.

14. Mary Ann Jones, *Parental Lack of Supervision: Nature and Consequence of a Major Child Neglect Problem* (Washington: Child Welfare League of America, 1987), p. 2.

15. Illinois Department of Children and Family Services, *Child Abuse and Neglect Statistics: Annual Report, Fiscal Year 1988,* p. 10.

16. Jones (see Note 14), pp. 34, 39.

17. Connecticut Statutes, Title 46b Sec. 466-120.

18. Letter from Mary Case, M.D., to the St. Charles County Commission, April 30, 1987.

19. Complaint, *Jaqueline Fields et al.* v. *Gordon Johnson,* No. 89 C 1624 United States District Court for the Northern District of Illinois, Eastern Division, p. 14.

20. Interview with the author.

21. Juvenile Law Center, *Year End Report,* 1988, pp. 5-6.

22. Verified Complaint of Plaintiffs, *Cosentino* v. *Perales,* Case #43236-85, New York State Supreme Court, New York County, April 27, 1988.

23. Ibid.

24. Michael D'Antonio, "Catch-22: Working Dad Can't Live With His Kids," *Newsday,* Dec. 5, 1988, 5.

25. Decision of Judge Elliott Wilk, *Cosentino* v. *Perales,* 43236-85, New York State Supreme Court, New York County, April 27, 1988. (In New York State, the "Supreme Court" is actually a trial court. The state's highest court is the Court of Appeals.)

26. Complaint, *Fields* v. *Johnson* (see Note 19), p. 11.

27. Memorandum of Points and Authorities in Support of Motion for Preliminary Injunction, *Hansen* v. *McMahon,* Superior Court, State of California, No. CA 000 974, April 22, 1986, p. 1; California Department of Social Services, *All County Letter No. 86-77* ordering an end to the practice; author's interview with Melinda Bird, attorney for plaintiffs.

28. Dan Zegart, "Sterilization: Do Social Workers Pressure Parents?" Newburgh, N.Y., *Evening News,* June 1, 1988, 1.

29. Association for Children of New Jersey, *Splintered Lives: A Report on Decision Making for Children in Foster Care,* June, 1988, pp. ii, 15

30. City of New York Office of the Comptroller, Office of Policy Management, *Whatever Happened to the Boarder Babies?* January 1989, pp. 11-12.

31. Studies cited in Karen Benker and James Rempel, "Inexcusable Harm: The Effect of Institutionalization on Young Foster Children in New York City," *City Health Report,* no. 2, May 1989 (New York: Public Interest Health Consortium for New York City).

32. Suzanne Daley, "Few Are Getting Rent Subsidies to Avoid Foster Care," *New York Times,* Dec. 7, 1989, B1.

33. Sol Wachtler, *The State of the Judiciary, 1989* (Albany, N.Y.: New York State Court of Appeals, December 1989), p. 24.

34. Richard Bourne and Eli Newberger, " 'Family Autonomy' or 'Coercive Intervention'? Ambiguity and Conflict in the Proposed Standards for Child Abuse and Neglect," *Boston University Law Review,* 57, no. 4, July 1977, p. 692.

35. Interview with the author.

36. Interviews with the author.

37. Moira Bailey, "Homeless, With Children; Poverty and Despair Are Forcing Some Parents to Give Up Their Kids," *Orlando Sentinel,* April 14, 1988, E1.

38. Interview with the author.

39. Ray Helfer, "The Litany of the Smoldering Neglect of Children," in Ray Helfer and Ruth Kempe, eds., *The Battered Child,* 4th ed. (Chicago: University of Chicago Press, 1987), p. 309.

40. Barbara Nelson, *Making an Issue of Child Abuse: Political Agenda Setting for Social Problems* (Chicago: University of Chicago Press, 1984), p. 13.

41. C. Henry Kempe et al., "The Battered Child Syndrome," *Journal of the American Medical Association,* 181, no. 1, July 7, 1962, p. 24, cited in Nelson (see Note 40), p. 13.

42. Richard Gelles, "Child Abuse as Psychopathology: A Sociological Critique and Reformulation," *American Journal of Orthopsychiatry,* 43, p. 611.

43. Bush (see Note 2), p. 293.

44. Eileen Anderson, "Therapists and Power: The Unexamined Addiction," *Newsletter,* Minnesota State Chapter, National Association of Social Workers, June 1985.

45. Bush (see Note 2), pp. 117, 287.

46. Nelson (see Note 40), p. 2.

47. "The Homelessness Test: There Is a Right Answer," editorial, *New York Times,* March 11, 1990, 26.

48. David Gil, "The United States vs. Child Abuse," in Leroy Pelton, ed., *The Social Context of Child Abuse and Neglect* (New York: Human Sciences Press, 1981), p. 312.

49. Jonathan Rauch, "We Overestimate Underclass—and Fail to Understand Poor," Albany, N.Y., *Times Union,* July 2, 1989 (excerpted from an article in the *National Journal*).

50. United Press International, "Stereotype of Needy Disputed," Sept. 8, 1989.

51. Nelson (see Note 40), pp. 15,107. See also Gil's account of his experience as lead-off witness during Mondale's hearings, in Pelton (see Note 48), p. 310.

52. Norman Polansky with Mary Ann Chalmers, David P. Williams, and Elizabeth Werthan Buttenwieser, *Damaged Parents: An Anatomy of Child Neglect* (Chicago: University of Chicago Press, 1981).

53. Ibid., p. 24.

54. Cited in Linda Gordon, *Heroes of Their Own Lives* (New York: Viking Penguin, 1988), p. 163.

55. Polansky (see Note 52), p. 70.

56. Vincent Fontana, *Somewhere a Child Is Crying: Maltreatment—Causes and Prevention, Revised and Updated Edition* (New York: Mentor Books, 1983), p. 5.

57. Fontana writes: "Infanticide . . . was almost a popular pastime in the 17th Century when unwanted children were easily and casually disposed of without guilt or recrimination, fear or prosecution. It is less popular today, for reasons which may be no more noble or humane than fear of being caught or prosecuted. . . ." (Fontana [see Note 56], p. 5).

58. Massachusetts Department of Social Services, *Characteristics of Abusive*

Families, undated, probably 1983 or 1984, pp. 3, 4.

59. *What Everyone Should Know About Child Abuse* (South Deerfield, Mass.: Channing L. Bete, 1976), pp. 4, 5. The pamphlet is currently distributed by state child welfare departments in Missouri and New Jersey.

60. Leontine Young, *Physical Child Neglect,* pamphlet published by National Committee for Prevention of Child Abuse (Chicago: 1986).

61. William Raspberry, "Child Spanking: Is It Discipline—or Assault?" syndicated newspaper column, March 31, 1989.

62. Edward Zigler, "Controlling Child Abuse: Do We Have the Knowledge and/or the Will?" in George Gerbner, Catherine Ross, and Edward Zigler, eds., *Child Abuse: An Agenda for Action* (New York: Oxford University Press, 1980), p. 27.

63. Testimony of Frederick Green, M.D., president, National Committee for Prevention of Child Abuse, *Child Abuse and Neglect in America: The Problem and the Response,* Hearing of the Select Committee on Children, Youth and Families, U.S. House of Representatives, March 3, 1987, transcript, p. 26.

64. Deborah Daro, "Reporting About Child Abuse," letter to the editor, *Wall Street Journal,* August 1988.

65. Testimony of Carol Bryant, director, Child Abuse Prevention Council of Contra Costa County, California, *Hearing on Child Abuse Reporting Laws and Dependency Statutes,* California Legislature, Senate Select Committee on Children and Youth, December 3, 4, 1986, transcript, p. 56.

66. Richard Bourne, "Child Abuse and Neglect: An Overview," in Bourne and Newberger, eds., *Critical Perspectives on Child Abuse* (Lexington, Mass.: Lexington Books, 1979), p. 3, cited in Douglas Besharov, *The Vulnerable Social Worker: Liability for Serving Children and Families* (Silver Spring, Md.: National Association of Social Workers, 1985), p. 144.

67. "Parents and Experts Split on Spanking," *New York Times,* June 19, 1985, C9.

68. Besharov (see Note 66), p. 144.

69. Susan Wells, *How We Make Decisions in Child Protective Services Intake and Investigation* (Washington, D.C.: National Legal Resource Center for Child Advocacy and Protection, November 1985), p. 64.

70. Zigler, in Gerbner et al. (see Note 62), p. 9.

71. Interview with the author.

72. Zigler, in Gerbner et al. (see Note 62), p. 14.

73. Ad reprinted in Gerbner et al. (see Note 62), p. 237.

74. Caroline Young, "Foster Care in Chaos: To Spell Out the Solution, It's M-O-N-E-Y," *Seattle Post-Intelligencer,* Oct. 23, 1987, 1.

75. Nick Chiles, "Teacher Alert on Child Abuse," New York, *Newsday,* Sept. 21, 1988.

76. Cynthia Mohr Trainor, *The Dilemma of Child Neglect: Identification and Treatment* (Denver: American Humane Association, 1983), p. 10.

77. Ibid., p. 3

78. Cathy Spatz Widom, "The Intergenerational Transmission of Violence,"

Occasional Papers of the Harry Frank Guggenheim Foundation, no. 4, 1989, pp. 40, 42.

79. Marguerite Rosenthal and James Louis, "The Law's Evolving Role in Child Abuse and Neglect," in Pelton (see Note 48), p. 87.

80. Cornelia Spelman, *Talking About Child Sexual Abuse,* pamphlet published by National Committee for Prevention of Child Abuse (Chicago: 1985), p. 5.

81. Richard Gelles and Murray Straus, *Intimate Violence: The Causes and Consequences of Abuse in the American Family* (New York: Touchstone Books, 1989), p. 49.

82. Leroy Pelton, "Child Abuse and Neglect: The Myth of Classlessness," *American Journal of Orthopsychiatry,* 48, 1978, 608.

83. Fontana (see Note 56), p. 55.

84. *What Everyone Should Know* (see Note 59), p. 2.

85. New York State Federation on Child Abuse and Neglect, *Fact Sheet,* March 1988, p. 1.

86. Richard Gelles, "Family Violence: What We Know and Can Do," in Eli Newberger and Richard Bourne, eds., *Unhappy Families: Clinical and Research Perspectives on Family Violence* (Littleton, Mass.: PSG Publishing, 1985), p. 4.

87. Complaint, *Geraldine Churchwell* v. *Marie Matava,* Supreme Judicial Court, Suffolk County (no case number given). A statement by Churchwell and a letter from Churchwell's allergist is attached to this document. When asked to respond, the Massachusetts Department of Social Services offered no rebuttal to the facts as described in the complaint. Children's Hospital did not return calls for comment on the Churchwell case.

88. Perri Klass, M.D., "Child Abuse: The Interrogation," *New York Times Magazine,* undated clipping, 1989.

89. NIS-2 (see Note 3), chap. 2, pp. 1-4.

90. Pelton (see Note 48), p. 29.

91. E.g., Bernard Horowitz and Isabel Wolock, "Material Deprivation, Child Maltreatment and Agency Interventions Among Poor Families," ibid., p. 138.

92. Bush (see Note 2), pp. 249, 250.

93. Jeanne Giovannoni and Rosina Becerra, *Defining Child Abuse* (New York: Free Press, 1979), pp. 235, 236.

94. Zigler (see Note 62), p. 13.

95. Gelles, "Child Abuse as Psychopathology . . ." (see Note 42), p. 53.

96. American Humane Association, *Highlights of Official Child Neglect and Abuse Reporting, 1982* (Denver: 1984), p. 24.

97. In a letter to the editor of *The Progressive* responding to an article I wrote, Cohn states: "When professionals discuss the 'classlessness' of abuse and neglect, they are saying that 'child abuse occurs in all income groups' *not* that it is occurring equally in all groups." (Emphasis in original.) Anne Cohn, "Readers Respond to 'Invasion of the Child Savers,'" *The Progressive,* November, 1985, p. 5.

98. Gelles, "Child Abuse as Psychopathology . . ." (see Note 42), p. 54.

99. Anne Cohn, *An Approach to Preventing Child Abuse,* pamphlet published

by the National Committee for Prevention of Child Abuse (Chicago: 1983), pp. 25-30.

100. Marvel Comics/National Committee for Prevention of Child Abuse, *Spider-Man,* special issue, 1987.

101. Polansky (see Note 52), p. 170.

102. Gordon (see Note 54), p. 292.

103. Gordon writes: ". . . Before condemning the very enterprise of intervening into the family, one must ask: Whose privacy? Whose liberties? The conception of liberties dominant in the nineteenth century was one of individual rights against the state, which was in fact an attribution of rights to heads of households. . . . Such rights did not protect subordinate members of families against intrafamily oppression or violence. On the contrary, privacy rights have been invoked to remove some individuals from the public guarantees of these liberties" (Gordon [see Note 54], p. 294.)

104. Elizabeth Pleck, *Domestic Tyranny: The Making of American Social Policy Against Family Violence from Colonial Times to the Present* (New York: Oxford University Press, 1987).

105. Interview with the author.

106. Author's interview with Judge Leah Marks.

107. Interview with the author.

108. *Keeping Families Together: The Case for Family Preservation* (New York: Edna McConnell Clark Foundation, 1985), Introduction.

Chapter 4: The Numbers

1. Diana Russell, *The Secret Trauma: Incest in the Lives of Girls and Women* (New York: Basic Books, 1986).

2. Richard Gelles and Murray Straus, *Intimate Violence: The Causes and Consequences of Abuse in the American Family* (New York: Touchstone Books, 1989), p. 249.

3. *Study Findings: Study of National Incidence and Prevalence of Child Abuse and Neglect: 1988* (NIS-2) (Washington: U.S. Dept. of Health and Human Services, National Center of Child Abuse and Neglect, 1988), chap. 3, p. 2.

4. U.S. Bureau of the Census, middle range projection for 1990.

5. American Humane Association, *Highlights of Official Child Neglect and Abuse Reporting, 1986* (Denver: 1988), p. 10.

6. Author's interview with AHA spokeswoman Katie Bond.

7. George Esper, "Reports on Abuse Up 223% from '76 to '86," Associated Press, May 8, 1988.

8. American Humane Association, *Highlights of Official Child Neglect and Abuse Reporting, 1982* (Denver: 1984), p. 18.

9. State of New Jersey, Division of Youth and Family Services, *Child Abuse and Neglect in New Jersey: 1987 Annual Report,* p. 26.

10. Interview with the author.

11. American Humane Association, *Highlights of Official Child Neglect and Abuse Reporting, 1984* (Denver: 1986), p. 12.

12. AHA, *Highlights . . . 1986* (see Note 5), p. 12.

13. Anne Cohn, "Readers Respond to 'Invasion of the Child Savers' " *The Progressive,* November 1985, p. 6.

14. Interview with the author.

15. Thomas Roach, Commissioner of Social Services for Ulster County, New York, made the comment at a conference attended by the author in January 1989.

16. Susan Wells, Theodore Stein, John Fluke, and Jane Dowling, "Screening in Child Protective Services," *Social Work,* January 1989, p. 48.

17. Brenda McGowan et al., *The Continuing Crisis: A Report on New York City's Response to Families Requiring Protective and Preventive Services* (New York: Neighborhood Family Services Coalition, 1987), p. 135.

18. Multi-Disciplinary Team, *Philadelphia Child Protective Services: A Report to the Secretary of Public Welfare,* Nov. 12, 1987, p. 61.

19. Complaint, *Geraldine Churchwell* v. *Marie Matava,* Supreme Judicial Court, Suffolk County (no case number given).

20. Interview with the author.

21. Douglas Besharov, "Protecting Abused and Neglected Children: Can Law Help Social Work?" *Family Law Reporter,* 9, no. 41, August 23, 1983.

22. Interview with the author.

23. Interview with the author.

24. Besharov (see Note 21).

25. Douglas Besharov, "The Tragedy of Child Abuse: We All Share the Blame for the Death of Bradley McGee," *St. Petersburg Times,* Sept. 5, 1989, 1D.

26. Author's interview with John Weeden, Foster Care Program Manager, Washington State Department of Social and Health Services.

27. Governor's Commission on Children, *Final Report,* January 1989, p. 72.

28. Interview with the author.

29. ABC-News *Nightline,* May 19, 1988, transcript, p. 3.

30. Author's interview with Paul Elisha, spokesman, New York State Department of Social Services.

31. Don Yaeger, "HRS Claims Over Child Abuse Stir Concern," Jacksonville, Fla., *Times-Union,* Feb. 5, 1989, 1.

32. Deborah Daro, "Reporting About Child Abuse," letter to the editor, *Wall Street Journal,* August 1988.

33. NIS-2 (see Note 3), chap. 5, p. 5.

34. NCPCA Fact Sheet: "What Do We Know About 'Unsubstantiated' Child Abuse Reports?" (Chicago: National Committee for Prevention of Child Abuse, January 1986).

35. AHA's report covering data from 1982 includes percentages for "substantiated or at risk" and "unsubstantiated" with a straightforward explanation. But in the report covering 1983, this information is totally absent. Every other table from the previous year is included, and several new ones are added. But the reader would have no clue that false reports even exist.

The next year, the data on "indicated" and "unfounded" reports was back, but minus the qualifier about "at-risk" cases. The accompanying text included a strong warning about false negatives, and not one word about false positives. AHA spokeswoman Katie Bond says she does not know why this data disappeared one year and returned the next. (AHA, *Highlights* . . . 1982-1986, and author's interview with Katie Bond.)

36. American Humane Association, *Technical Report #3: Definitions,* pp. 3-35.

37. AHA, *Highlights* . . . *1982* (see Note 8), p. 18.

38. Cited in Jeanne Giovannoni and Rosina Becerra, *Defining Child Abuse* (New York: Free Press, 1979), p. 11.

39. Ibid., p. 89; also Joseph Goldstein, Anna Freud, and Albert J. Solnit, *Before the Best Interests of the Child* (New York: Free Press, 1979), pp. 76, 77.

40. Walter Bally, "Defining Emotional Maltreatment in Child Protective Services" in *Guidelines for a Model System of Protective Services for Abused and Neglected Children and Their Families* (Washington, D.C.: National Association of Public Child Welfare Administrators, 1988), p. 45.

41. AHA, *Highlights* . . . *1986* (see Note 5), p. 22; and AHA, *Definitions* (see Note 36), chap. 3, pp. 32, 33.

42. AHA, *Highlights* . . . *1986* (see Note 5), p. 23.

43. NIS-2 (see Note 3), pp. 1-5

44. "Serious" maltreatment was: "a life-threatening condition, represented [*sic*] a long-term impairment of physical, mental, or emotional capacities, or required professional treatment aimed at preventing such long-term impairment. Moderate injuries/impairments were those which persisted in observable form (including pain or impairment) for at least 48 hours. For example, bruises, depression, or emotional distress (not serious enough to require professional treatment), and the like."

45. Another 127,800 cases are listed as "probable" maltreatment, but they are not broken down between serious and moderate. It seems reasonable to assume that the proportion of serious cases here would be no greater than the proportion of serious cases among those that were confirmed—about 20 percent.

46. There were 297,200 "at risk" cases. NIS-2 uses the term "endangered" to describe these children. NIS-2 (see Note 7), chap 3, pp. 10, 11.

47. David Gil, *Violence Against Children: Physical Child Abuse in the United States* (Cambridge, Mass.: Harvard University Press, 1970), p. 50.

48. Richard Light, "Abused and Neglected Children in America: A Study of Alternative Policies," *Harvard Educational Review,* 43, no. 4, November 1973, p. 567.

49. Edward Zigler, "Controlling Child Abuse: Do We Have the Knowledge and/or the Will?" in George Gerbner, Catherine J. Ross, Edward Zigler, eds., *Child Abuse: An Agenda for Action* (New York: Oxford University Press, 1980), p. 5.

50. Gelles and Straus, *Intimate Violence* (see Note 2), p. 249. The authors define "abusive violence" as kicking, biting, hitting with a fist, beating up, or using a gun or a knife. According to their survey, the rate of such abuse is 1.9 in 100. When children threatened with a gun or a knife are added, the number rises to 2.1 in 100.

The study reported in *Intimate Violence* was the second done by these researchers in ten years. It found a significantly lower rate of violence against children than their first study (which found that 4.7 in 100 children were victims of "abusive violence," for example). child savers generally hailed the first study and refused to believe the second one, but the researchers demonstrate convincingly that their methodology was better the second time (*Intimate Violence* [see Note 2], pp. 109-113).

The statement that respondents took the term "beaten up" to mean "something more than just a single blow" is from an article about the authors' first study. (Richard Gelles, "A Profile of Violence toward Children in the United States," in George Gerbner, Catherine J. Ross, and Edward Zigler, eds., *Child Abuse: An Agenda for Action* (New York: Oxford University Press, 1980), p. 87.

51. Gelles, in Gerbner (see Note 50).

52. All data in this section are from Russell (see Note 1).

53. Cases where siblings—or other relatives—committed the abuse but the parents did nothing about it should be under CPS jurisdiction.

54. Studies cited are from, David Finkelhor, *Sexually Victimized Children* (New York: Free Press, 1979); David Finkelhor, *Child Sexual Abuse: New Theory and Research* (New York: Free Press, 1984); G. Kercher and M. McShane, "The Prevalence of Child Sexual Abuse Victimization in an Adult Sample of Texas Residents," *Child Abuse and Neglect: The International Journal*, 8, 1984, p. 495; A. P. Sapp and D. L. Carter, *Child Abuse in Texas: A Descriptive Study of Texas Residents' Attitudes* (Huntsville, Tex.: University Graphic Arts Dept., 1978); D. G. Kilpatrick and A. E. Amick, *Intrafamilial and Extrafamilial Sexual Assault: Results of a Random Community Survey*, paper presented at the Second National Family Violence Research Conference, Durham, N.H., 1984. All of these studies are cited in Russell (see Note 1), pp. 65-68.

55. Gelles and Straus (see Note 2), p. 66.

56. Jon R. Conte, *A Look at Child Sexual Abuse*, pamphlet published by the National Committee for Prevention of Child Abuse (Chicago: 1986), p. 10.

57. NCPCA *Fact Sheet #5*, November 1986.

58. Jones and McGraw, "Reliable and Fictitious Accounts of Sexual Abuse to Children," *Journal of Interpersonal Violence*, 2, no. 1, March 1987, pp. 27-45.

59. According to the study, there is a little bit of overlap. Some misunderstandings are included in the "fictitious" category as well.

60. Conte (see Note 56), p. 12.

61. Daniel Goleman, "Researcher Is Criticized for Test of Journal Bias," *New York Times*, Sept. 27, 1988.

62. Michael Zeigler, "Missing the Real Story," Rochester, N.Y., *Democrat and Chronicle*, April 6, 1986, 1.

63. David Finkelhor, Gerald Hotaling, and Andrea Sedlak, *Missing, Abducted, Runaway, and Throwaway Children in America: First Report: Numbers and Characteristics, National Incidence Studies* (Washington, D.C.: U.S. Department of Justice and Delinquency Prevention, May 1990), Executive Summary, p. xiv.

64. Zeigler (see Note 62).

65. Jeanne Giovannoni and Rosina Becerra, *Defining Child Abuse* (New York: Free Press, 1979), p. 256.

Chapter 5: Innocent Families

1. Author's interview with Susan and Clark Gabriel.

2. John Cahar, "Child Protection, Parental Rights on Collison Course," Albany, N.Y., *Times Union,* April 30, 1989, 1.

3. Glenn Joyner, "False Accusation of Child Abuse—Could it Happen to You?" *Woman's Day,* May 6, 1986.

4. Joyner (see Note 3); also: Testimony of Robin Johnson, *Hearing on Child Abuse Reporting Laws and Dependency Statutes,* Select Committee on Children and Youth, California Legislature, p. 90; Robin Johnson, letter-to-the-editor, Victorville, Calif., *Daily Press,* March 12, 1989.

5. Terri Langford, "Clay foster mother embittered by now-dismissed abuse charge," Jacksonville, Fla., *Times Union,* Feb. 5, 1989, 1

6. Joyner (see Note 3).

7. *Doe v. Hennepin County, Family Law Reporter,* 10, 1504, July 24, 1984.

8. Testimony of Cathleen Dillon McHugh, *Public Hearing,* New Jersey Legislature, Senate Committee on Children's Services, Sept. 27, 1988, transcript, p. 156; court documents dismissing the case against Dillon McHugh's father are in the posession of the author.

9. Childhelp USA, *Child Abuse and You* (Woodland Hills Calif: Undated).

10. Cornelia Spelman, *Talking About Child Sexual Abuse,* Jon Conte, *A Look at Child Sexual Abuse,* and *Basic Facts About Child Sexual Abuse,* all National Committee for Prevention of Child Abuse; New York State Department of Health, *Say "NO!" Protecting Children Against Sexual Abuse* (Albany, N.Y., Undated); New York State Department of Health, *Child Sexual Abuse: Guidelines for Health Professionals: Recognizing and Handling the Problem* (Albany, N.Y., Undated); Council of Family and Child Caring Agencies, *Child Abuse Alert: A Desk Reference* (New York: 1987).

11. National Association of Social Workers, *Listen to the Children: A Child Protection Guide for Parents* (Silver Spring, Md.: Undated).

12. Council of Family and Child Caring Agencies (see Note 10).

13. *Child Abuse and Neglect in America: The Problem and the Response,* Hearing before the Select Committee on Children, Youth, and Families, U.S. House of Representatives, March 3, 1987, transcript, p. 41.

14. Letter from Wayne I. Munkel, Medical Social Consultant, Cardinal Glennon Children's Hospital, St. Louis, Mo., to State Rep. Kaye Steinmetz, Sept. 11, 1985, reprinted in Interim Committee on Children, Youth, and Families, *Report to the Speaker on: Child Abuse Reporting Law,* December 1985, p. 66.

15. Interview with the author.

16. Interview with the author.

17. *Basic Facts About Child Sexual Abuse,* 3rd ed., pamphlet published by National Committee for Prevention of Child Abuse (Chicago: 1988), p. 5.

18. Perri Klass, M.D., "Child Abuse: The Interrogation," *New York Times Magazine,* undated clipping, 1989, 54.

19. Benjamin Spock, M.D., *Baby and Child Care* (New York: Pocket Books,

1985), p. 640. I partially disagree. Our extremely active two-and-a-half-year-old so far has not been in any serious accidents and my wife and I work very hard to keep it that way. We think her character is just fine, thank you. But in indicating that children do sometimes have real accidents, as opposed to a repeated, suspicious pattern of alleged accidents, Dr. Spock obviously is correct.

20. *Hearing on Child Abuse Reporting Laws and Dependency Statutes,* Select Committee on Children and Youth, California Legislature, Dec. 4, 1986, p. 5.

21. Michigan Department of Social Services, *Children's Protective Services Task Force Report,* March 1988, p. 5.

22. Richard Kindleberger, "Violations Seen in Reporting Child Abuse," *Boston Globe,* April 13, 1988, 26.

23. Legislative Commission on Expenditure Review, *State Child Abuse and Maltreatment Register, Child Abuse Hotline* (Albany, N.Y.: March 23, 1987), p. 25.

24. Interview with the author.

25. Interview with the author.

26. Richard Wexler, "Lessons from the Dumpster Documents: Why Our System for Protecting Children Doesn't Work," Rochester, N.Y., *City Newspaper,* March 6, 1986, p. 7.

27. Bob Hohler, "The Youngest Victims, System Deluged with Child Abuse Cases," *Boston Globe* (New Hampshire Week), March 13, 1988, 1.

28. Information for the Meyer case comes from interviews with Gary, Jean, and Danny Meyer, Danny's elementary school teacher in the year before his run and his school principal the year after, the Meyer family doctor, a spokeswoman for the Webster, N.Y., school district, the adoption agency caseworker with whom the family dealt, Kenneth Herrmann, and David Ambuske. The Meyers also released the record of the co_nplaint against them, which they are entitled to receive by law (minus the accuser's name, if he or she demands anonymity).

29. Information about this case comes from interviews with Kathy and Alan Heath, Jeffrey Heath's principal and teacher, letters from the county child protection agency showing that all three cases were unfounded, and a letter from a caseworker stating that the accuser had given a false address and phone number.

30. First Amended Complaint, *Mary Lou Buckman et al., v. Marie Matava,* Civil Action no. 75505, Superior Court of Suffolk County, April 22, 1986, p. 10.

31. Affidavit of Marie A. Matava, *Buckman et al. v. Matava,* Oct. 31, 1985.

32. Kathleen Haddad, "TV Guidelines Urged to Curb Child Abuse," Albany, N.Y., *Times Union,* Oct. 5, 1988, B1.

33. David Davis (Producer), *The Unquiet Death of Eli Creekmore,* KCTS-TV, Seattle, Washington, 1988, transcript, p. 33.

34. Joseph Goldstein, Anna Freud, and Albert J. Solnit, *Beyond the Best Interests of the Child* (New York: Free Press, 1973), pp. 9, 25.

35. Dan Zegart, "Solomon's Choice," *Ms.,* June 1989, p. 78.

36. Interview with the author.

37. Richard Wexler, "The Dumpster Documents," Rochester, N.Y., *City Newspaper,* February 13, 1986, p. 5.

38. Interview with the author.

39. Pennsylvania Department of Public Welfare, Office of Children, Youth, and Families, *1988 Child Abuse Report* (Harrisburg, Pa.: 1989), p. 5.

40. National Association of Public Child Welfare Administrators, *Guidelines for a Model System of Protective Services for Abused and Neglected Children and Their Families* (Washington, D.C.: 1988), pp. 29, 31.

41. Douglas Besharov, "Contending with Overblown Expectations: CPS Cannot Be All Things to All People," *Public Welfare,* Winter 1987, p. 7.

42. Missouri House of Representatives, Interim Committee on Children, Youth, and Families, *Report to the Speaker on: Child Abuse Reporting Law* (December 1985), p. 7.

43. Children's Protective Services Task Force Report (see Note 21).

44. American Humane Association, *Highlights of Official Child Neglect and Abuse Reporting, 1986* (Denver: 1988).

45. Study cited in Susan J. Zuravin, Brenda Watson, and Mark Ehrenschaft, "Anonymous Reports of Child Physical Abuse: Are They as Serious as Reports from Other Sources?" *Child Abuse and Neglect: The International Journal,* 11, 1987, pp. 521-529.

46. Ibid.

47. William Adams, Neil Barone, and Patrick Tooman, "The Dilemma of Anonymous Reporting in Child Protective Services," *Child Welfare,* 61, no. 1, January 1982, p. 3.

48. *White by White v. Pierce County,* 797 F.2nd 816.

49. Mark Hardin, "Legal Barriers in Child Abuse Investigations: State Powers and Individual Rights," *Washington Law Review,* 63, no. 3, July 1988, pp. 511-516.

50. Information for the case of "Althea Clark" comes from an interview with her attorney Kevin Bosworth, confirmed in "Battle Over Child Leads to Inquiries," *New York Times,* Sept. 18, 1983, NJ-4. A spokeswoman for the New Jersey Department of Youth and Family Services said no one in the department can comment on a specific case.

51. Tom Charlier and Shirley Downing, "Justice Abused: A 1980s Witchhunt," Memphis, Tenn., *Commercial Appeal,* reprint, January 1988, p. 15.

52. Buckman v. Matava (see Note 30), p. 15; and author's interview with Marjorie Heins, attorney, Massachusetts Civil Liberties Union Foundation. The Department of Social Services declined to provide any material rebutting the allegations made in the case.

53. Interview with the author.

54. Information for this section came from: *Darryl H. v. Coler,* 585 F. Supp 383 (district court) April 25, 1984; 801 F.2d 893 (appeal) Sept. 9, 1986; Plaintiffs' Complaint, undated; First Amended Complaint, undated; Memorandum in Support of Plaintiffs' Motion for This Court to Reconsider . . . June 29, 1984; Defendants' Response to Plaintiffs' Motion to Reconsider . . . Aug. 3, 1984; Plaintiffs' Memorandum in Further Support of Their Motion to Reconsider . . . undated; Author's interview with the school principal involved in the case; *E.Z. v. Coler* (the ACLU case), 603 F. Supp 1546 (district court), March 12, 1985; 801 F. 2d 893 (appeal—

renamed *B.D. by C.D. v. Coler*) Sept. 9, 1986; Plaintiffs' Post-Hearing Brief, March 21, 1984; Defendants' Post-Hearing Memorandum, April 17, 1984; Plaintiffs' Post-Hearing Reply Brief, May 9, 1984; author's interview with Dr. Ner Littner.

55. Nanette Dembitz, "What a City Can Do to Save Young Lives," letter to the editor, *New York Times,* Oct. 25, 1983.

56. *Hearing on SB-14—Chapter 978 Statutes of 1982,* Senate Judiciary Subcommittee on Corrections and Law Enforcement Agencies and Assembly Committee on Human Services, California Legislature, Oct. 17-18, 1985, transcript, p. 15.

57. Charlier and Downing (see Note 51), p. 13.

58. Kent Pollock, "The Child Protectors: Flawed Guardian of Young," *Sacramento Bee,* Aug. 4, 1986, 1.

59. Dr. Case's lecture was videotaped by members of Victims of Child Abuse Laws, who made a copy of the tape available to the author.

60. Interview with the author.

61. Wexler, "The Dumpster Documents" (see Note 37), p. 1.

62. Fitzgerald, "Rights of Neglected Children and Attempts by the State to Regulate Family Relationships," *Child Welfare Strategy in the Coming Years* (Washington, D.C.: Department of Health Education and Welfare, 1978), pp. 371, 378, cited in Douglas Besharov, "'Doing Something' about Child Abuse: The Need to Narrow the Grounds for State Intervention," *Harvard Journal of Law and Public Policy,* 8, no. 3, Summer 1985, pp. 570ff.

63. Jeanne Giovannoni and Rosina Becerra, *Defining Child Abuse* (New York: Free Press, 1979), p. 8.

64. Wald, *Hearing on Child Abuse Reporting Laws* (see Note 4), p. 2.

65. Multi-Disciplinary Team, *Philadelphia Child Protective Services: A Report to the Secretary of Public Welfare,* Nov. 12, 1987, p. 8.

66. Interview with the author.

67. Don Yaeger, "HRS Claims Over Child Abuse Stir Concern," Jacksonville, Fla., *Times-Union,* Feb. 5, 1989, p. 2.

68. Interview with the author.

69. Interview with the author.

70. Douglas Besharov, *The Vulnerable Social Worker: Liability for Serving Children and Families* (Silver Spring, Md.: National Association of Social Workers), p. 90.

71. Lucy Alf Younas, *State Child Abuse and Neglect Laws: A Comparative Analysis, 1985* (Washington, D.C.: National Center on Child Abuse and Neglect, 1987), Table 14.

72. Affidavit of Marie Matava, *Churchwell v. Matava,* Sept. 27, 1987, p. 8.

73. Younas (see Note 71), Table 14; the number may be higher. New York is one of the few states that supposedly "expunges" unfounded cases. But after more than 100 cases were discovered in his dumpster, including some that apparently were unfounded, Monroe County District Attorney Howard Relin said his office routinely keeps "unfounded" reports. Relin said the law on expungement doesn't apply to district attorneys. Several other New York State D.A.'s have the same policy, even though the state Department of Social Services says it's illegal.

Also in New York, until the state stopped the practice, some counties sent a written notice to the person who first alleged maltreatment informing that person that his or her accusation was unfounded. The notice went on to request that the reader please destroy the letter!

74. *Report of the Public Child Fatality Review Committee on Fatality Cases for the Year 1985* (Dec. 23, 1986), pp. 63-64, cited in, Law and Public Policy Committee, the LISA Organization to Stop Child Abuse, Inc., *The Lisa Report: A Report on the Prevention and Treatment of Child Abuse in New York State,* March 9, 1989, p. 84.

75. Anne Cohn, "Readers Respond to 'Invasion of the Child Savers,' " *The Progressive,* November 1985, p. 6.

76. Diane Dodson, *The Legal Framework for Ending Foster Care Drift: A Guide to Evaluating and Improving State Laws, Regulations and Court Rules* (Washington D.C.: Foster Care Project, National Legal Resource Center for Child Advocacy and Protection, American Bar Association, August, 1983), chap. 1, p. 1.

77. E.g., *Suzanne R. v. D'Elia,* Order to Show Cause, New York State Supreme Court, Nassau County, October 6, 1988.

78. Dodson (see Note 76), chap. 1, p. 6.

79. Studies cited in Michael Wald and Robert Burt, *Standards Relating to Abuse and Neglect,* Project of the Institute for Judicial Administration and the American Bar Association (Cambridge, Mass.: Ballinger Publishing Co., 1981).

80. Dodson (see Note 76), chap. 1, p. 3.

81. Marcia Slacum Greene, "Sitting on a Time Bomb Waiting for Kids to Die," *Washington Post,* Sept. 12, 1989, 1.

82. Interview with the author.

83. Marion McCarthy, *Report of the Special Subcommittee on Foster Care* (Boston: Massachusetts House of Representatives, May 1989), pp. 76-77.

84. Leroy Pelton, *The Social Context of Child Abuse and Neglect* (New York: Human Sciences Press, 1981), p. 117.

85. Hilary Stout, "Neediest Cases Fund Aids Woman's Fight," *New York Times,* Nov. 26, 1987.

86. Interview with the author.

87. Younes (see Note 71), Table 9.

88. John E. B. Myers and Wendell Peters, *Child Abuse Reporting Legislation in the 80s* (Denver: American Humane Association, 1987).

89. New York State Department of Social Services, *An Assessment of the Operations of the Child Welfare Administration of the Human Resources Administration of New York City,* May 1989, p. 3.

90. Interviews with the author.

91. Besharov, *The Vulnerable Social Worker* (see Note 70), pp. 156-157.

92. Interview with the author.

93. Kirk Johnson, "Social Worker Took Children of Deaf Woman," *New York Times,* Dec. 4, 1987.

94. Interview with the author.

95. Younes (see Note 71), Table 9.

96. Johnson (see Note 93); that was not the end of this family's problems. According to a summary of the case from the ACLU Children's Rights Project: "Because [the city] failed to provide any preventive services [the mother and her children] were forced to return to her husband's home. Weeks after being notified of the dangerous situation [the city] . . . again removed the children without considering preventive services. This time the city placed the children in an institution far away from their mother . . ." The ACLU had to get another court order placing the children with their grandmother.

97. Interview with the author.

98. Interview with the author.

99. Goldstein, Freud, and Solnit, *Beyond* (see Note 34), pp. 40-41.

100. American Humane Association, Children's Division, *Evaluation and Consultation, Cook County CPS Program, Illinois Department of Children and Family Services* (Chicago: 1977), cited in Malcolm Bush, *Families in Distress: Public, Private, and Civic Responses* (Berkeley: University of California Press, 1988), p. 49.

101. J. Lawrence Aber III, "The Involuntary Placement Decision: Solomon's Dilemma Revisited," in George Gerbner, Catherine J. Ross, and Edward Zigler, eds., *Child Abuse: An Agenda for Action* (New York: Oxford University Press, 1980), pp. 158, 166-167

102. Edna McConnell Clark Foundation, *Strategy Statement of Program for Children,* December, 1988, p. 22

103. Henry Goldman, "In Family Court, Children Without a Voice," *Philadelphia Inquirer,* Oct. 30, 1988, B1.

104. Ira M. Schwartz, *In-Justice for Juveniles: Rethinking the Best Interests of the Child* (Lexington, Mass.: Lexington Books, 1989), p. 163.

105. National Council of Juvenile and Family Court Judges, Child Welfare League of America, Youth Law Center, National Center for Youth Law, *Making Reasonable Efforts: Steps for Keeping Families Together* (New York: Edna McConnell Clark Foundation, 1987), p. 8.

106. Information concerning the Gabriel case comes from: interviews with Clark, Susan, and Sara Gabriel, Barbara Midyett, Larry Dickinson, and a juror at the Gabriel trial; letter of J. Gregory Walta to Philip Kleinsmith, Sept. 8, 1986; psychological report of Lawrence Lichstein, June 5, 1986; affidavit of Det. Mark Teasdale, Colorado Springs police, March 24, 1986; stipulated order, *People v. Susan Gabriel, Clark Gabriel, and Larry Dickinson,* May 1, 1987 (settlement agreement in abuse/custody case); letter from Nancy M. Dollar, legal assistant, State of Colorado Office of the Attorney General to Thomas R. Moeller, Administrative Law Judge, stating that the Gabriels' listing in the Central Registry had been expunged, July 27, 1987. The CPS caseworker who initially handled the case has since left CPS and could not be reached for comment.

107. Remarks of Robert VanCleave, Director, El Paso County Department of Social Services to VOCAL of Southern Colorado, July 13, 1989.

108. *Olmstead v. United States,* 277 U.S. 438, 1928 (dissenting opinion), cited in Ray E. Helfer and Ruth S. Kempe, *The Battered Child,* 4th ed. (Chicago: University of Chicago Press, 1987), p. 402.

109. Author's interview with Becky Malinowski, a caseworker in Erie County, Pennsylvania.

110. National Committee for Prevention of Child Abuse, *NCPCA Catalog, 1989/1990,* p. 22.

111. John McAloonan, "Cap'n Hook," *Orlando Sentinel,* May 14, 1988.

112. *Public Hearing,* before Senate Committee on Children's Services (see Note 8), p. 118.

113. Complaint, *Fields et al. v. Johnson* no. 89 C 1624 United States District Court for the Northern District of Illinois, Eastern Division, p. 18.

114. Ruth Hubbell, *Foster Care and Families: Conflicting Values and Policies* (Philadelphia: Temple University Press, 1981), p. 5.

115. *Hearing on SB-14* (see Note 56), p. 45.

116. Helen Harris Perlman, *Social Casework: A Problem Solving Approach* (Chicago: University of Chicago Press, 1957) p. 65., quoted in Bush (see Note 100), p. 288.

117. Davis (see Note 33), p. 19.

118. Information concerning the Dickerson case comes from: interviews with Laura and Dawn Dickerson and Joe Pickard; prehearing report and transcript of hearing, *The People of the State of Colorado in the Interest of Dawn Dickerson, a Child, and Concerning Bill and Laura Dickerson, Respondents,* Detention Hearing, October 18, 1985; bills and letters dated January 23, March 11, April 15, 1986, from Arapahoe County Department of Social Services attempting to bill the Dickersons $177.61 for Dawn's foster care. Lawsuit filed against the Dickersons over this bill April 7, 1987, and the Dickersons demand for a jury trial; deposition of Anne Parks, *Bill Dickerson and Laura Dickerson v. Ann Curtis,* et al., #86-K-778, U.S. District Court for the District of Colorado, March 6, 1987; settlement agreement, *Dickerson v. Curtis,* Nov. 13, 1987. Agreement includes the withdrawal of the county's attempt to collect the $177.61; letter of apology from Ann Curtis, Director, Arapahoe County Department of Social Services to the Dickersons, November 16, 1987; letter from Pam Hinish, Director, Central Registry for Child Protection, to Laura Dickerson stating that their record in the registry has been expunged.

Chapter 6: Sexual Abuse

1. Michael McKeon, "Guilderland Teacher's Secret Sex Saga Ends in Guilty Plea," Albany, N.Y., *Times Union,* July 28, 1989, 1.

2. Ann Landers column, Oct. 30, 1989.

3. Tom Charlier and Shirley Downing, "Justice Abused: A 1980s Witch-Hunt," Memphis, Tenn., *Commercial Appeal,* January 1988, reprint, p. 1.

4. Ibid.

5. Kathleen Coulborn Faller, "Is the Child Victim of Sexual Abuse Telling the Truth?" *Child Abuse and Neglect, The International Journal,* 8, 1984, p. 475.

6. Roland Summit, "The Child Sexual Abuse Accommodation Syndrome,"

Child Abuse and Neglect: The International Journal, 7, 1983, p. 177.

7. Albany County Rape Crisis Center, *You Can Help Protect Your Children from Sexual Abuse* (Albany, N.Y.: 1982). This pamphlet was still being distributed as of June 1990.

8. Cited in: *In Re Christine C.* 236 Cal. Rptr. 631 (Cal. App. 1 Dist., 1987).

9. Bakersfield: Office of the Attorney General Division of Law Enforcement, Bureau of Investigation, *Report on the Kern County Investigation* (Sacramento: September 1986), p. 9; Fort Bragg: Charlier and Downing (see Note 3), p. 20; Airplanes: "The McMartin Tapes," *California Magazine,* January 1987, p. 58; Missouri: Statement made by Charles Bridges, defense attorney in Deposition of James A. Monteleone, M.D., *State of Missouri v. Keith D. Barnhart,* Cause #CR187-345FX, Dec. 28, 1987, p. 79; El Paso: Debbie Nathan, "The Making of a Modern Witch Trial," *Village Voice,* Sept. 29, 1987.

10. Keay Davidson, "Child Molestation Charges Need Scrutiny, Study Says," Albany, N.Y., *Knickerbocker News,* 1986 (reprinted from the *San Francisco Examiner*); also, Alvin Rosenfeld et al., "Determining Incestuous Contact Between Parent and Child: Frequency of Children Touching Parents' Genitals in a Nonclinical Population," *Journal of the American Academy of Child Psychiatry,* 25, no. 4, 1986, pp. 481-484.

11. State of New Jersey, Division of Youth and Family Services, *Child Abuse and Neglect in New Jersey: 1987 Annual Report,* p. 25.

12. *Basic Facts About Child Sexual Abuse,* pamphlet published by National Committee for Prevention of Child Abuse (Chicago: 1988), p. 5. The pamphlet states that "nontouching offenses may include . . . letting down the bars of privacy so that the child watches or hears an act of sexual intercourse."

13. Roy Howson, "Child Sexual Abuse Cases: Dangerous Trends and Possible Solutions," *The Champion,* August 1985, p. 6.

14. Dorothy Rabinowitz, "From the Mouths of Babes to a Jail Cell: Child Abuse and the Abuse of Justice: A Case Study," *Harper's Magazine,* May 1990, p. 63.

15. Interview with the author.

16. Vol. 7, pp. 177-193.

17. For example, in a study to determine how well CPS workers kept up with the most essential literature in the field, a sample of workers were asked if they had read any of 11 key "scholarly" articles. Summit's was one of them (George Freyer, Jenny Poland, Donald Bross, Richard Krugman, "The Child Protective Service Worker: A Profile of Needs, Attitudes, and Utilization of Professional Resources," *Child Abuse and Neglect: The International Journal,* 12, 1988, p. 483).

18. David Hechler, *The Battle and the Backlash: The Child Sexual Abuse War* (Lexington, Mass.: Lexington Books, 1988), p. 160.

19. *Report on the Kern County Child Abuse Investigation* (see Note 9); Charlier and Downing (see Note 3), p. 14.

20. Office of the Attorney General, State of Minnesota, *Report on Scott County Investigations* (St. Paul: Feb. 12, 1985); Charlier and Downing (see Note 3), p.

10; Debra Cassens Moss, "Are the Children Lying?" *ABA Journal,* May 1, 1987, p. 59.

21. Information concerning the McMartin case comes from: Charlier and Downing (see Note 3), pp. 3, 17; "The McMartin Tapes . . ." (see Note 9); Hollida Wakefield and Ralph Underwager, *Accusations of Child Sexual Abuse* (Springfield, Ill.: Charles C. Thomas, 1988); ABC-News *Nightline,* April 24, 1984, transcript; all network nightly news programs, Jan. 18, 1990; and David Shaw, "Where Was Skepticism in Media?" *Los Angeles Times,* Jan. 19, 1990, reprint, p. 1; "Reporter's Early Exclusives Triggered a Media Frenzy," Jan. 20, 1990, reprint, p. 7; "*Times* McMartin Coverage was Biased, Critics Charge," Jan. 22, 1990, reprint, pp. 16, 18.

22. Charlier and Downing (see Note 3), p. 13.

23. Kent Pollock, "The Child Protectors: Innocent Suffer in War to Protect," *Sacramento Bee,* Aug. 3, 1986, 1.

24. Debbie Nathan, "The Making of a Modern Witch Trial," *Village Voice,* Sept. 29, 1987.

25. Ibid., p. 30.

26. *Hearing on Child Abuse Reporting Laws and Dependency Statutes,* Select Committee on Children and Youth, California Legislature, Dec. 4, 1986, p. 82.

27. Charlier and Downing (see Note 3), p. 18.

28. John Crewdson, *By Silence Betrayed, Sexual Abuse of Children in America* (Boston: Little Brown, 1988), p. 150.

29. *Hearing on Child Abuse Reporting Laws* (see Note 26), p. 83.

30. Elizabeth Loftus, "Mind Games: China's Rulers Changing Memories," Albany, N.Y., *Times Union,* Oct. 15, 1989, D1.

31. Debbie Nathan, "Child Abuse Evidence Debated," *Ms.,* March 1989, p. 81.

32. Lucy Berliner, "Deciding Whether a Child Has Been Sexually Abused," in E. Bruce Nicholson, ed., *Sexual Abuse Allegations in Custody and Visitation Cases* (Washington, D.C.: American Bar Association, National Legal Resource Center for Child Advocacy and Protection, February 1988), p. 49.

33. "The Youngest Witnesses," *Newsweek,* Feb. 18, 1985, p. 73.

34. Marguerite Rosenthal and James Louis, "The Law's Evolving Role in Child Abuse and Neglect," in Leroy Pelton, *The Social Context of Child Abuse and Neglect* (New York: Human Sciences Press, 1985), p. 85.

35. Bruce Ennis and Thomas Litwack, "Psychiatry and the Presumption of Expertise: Flipping Coins in the Courtroom," *California Law Review,* 62, 1974, pp. 693-752.

36. David Faust and Jay Ziskin, "The Expert Witness in Psychology and Psychiatry," *Science,* July 1, 1988, p. 30. Interviewed by Associated Press, "Study Says Experts Unreliable," undated clipping, 1988.

37. Andrew Cohen, "The Unreliability of Expert Testimony on the Typical Characteristics of Sexual Abuse Victims," *Georgetown Law Journal,* 74, 1985, p. 429.

38. "The McMartin Tapes" (see Note 9).

39. Hechler (see Note 18), p. 254.

40. Debbie Nathan, "Victimizer or Victim? Was Kelly Michaels Unjustly Convicted?" *Village Voice,* Aug. 2, 1988, 38; Charlier and Downing (see Note 3).

41. Deposition of James A. Monteleone, M.D. *State of Missouri v. Keith D. Barnhart,* Cause #CR187-345FX, Dec. 28, 1987.

42. Crewdson (see Note 28), p. 140.

43. "Justice Abused . . ." (see Note 3), p. 18.

44. NCPCA *Fact Sheet,* "Handling Child Sexual Abuse Cases," November 1986.

45. Federation on Child Abuse and Neglect, *Issues and Answers, Issue: Sexual Abuse,* undated. The interview is with Margaret McHugh, M.D., director of Adolescent Ambulatory Services and Chairwoman of the Child Abuse Team at Bellevue Hospital, New York City.

46. Charlier and Downing (see Note 3), p. 7.

47. Lucy Berliner, "Deciding Whether a Child Has Been Sexually Abused," in E. Bruce Nicholson. ed., *Sexual Abuse Allegations in Custody and Visitation Cases* (Washington D.C.: American Bar Association, National Legal Resource Center for Child Advocacy and Protection, 1988), p. 49.

48. Anne Cohn, "Our National Priorities for Prevention," in Ray Helfer and Ruth Kempe, *The Battered Child,* 4th ed. (Chicago: University of Chicago Press, 1987), p. 449.

49. Robert Daviau, "Trial by Ordeal, Ordeal by Trial," *Maine Voice of VOCAL,* June 1989.

50. Charlier and Downing (see Note 3), p. 15.

51. Ibid., p. 25.

52. Ibid., p. 11.

53. Crewdson (see Note 28), p. 150

54. Shaw (see Note 21), p. 18.

55. *Annual Report of the American Bar Association,* vol. 63 (Chicago: ABA, 1938) p. 588, cited in Elizabeth Pleck, *Domestic Tyranny: The Making of American Social Policy against Family Violence from Colonial Times to the Present* (New York: Oxford University Press, 1987), p. 156

56. Nicholson (see Note 32), pp. 282-289.

57. Richard Wexler, "Lessons from The Dumpster Documents," Rochester, N.Y., *City Newspaper,* March 6, 1986, p. 1.

58. McKeon (see Note 1), 1.

59. Daniel Goleman, "Perils Seen in Warnings About Abuse," *New York Times,* November 21, 1989, C1.

60. Toni Toczylowski, "Teacher Is Cleared of Abuse Allegations Traced to Film Pupils Saw," Albany, N.Y., *Times Union,* April 28, 1989, B2.

61. Interview with the author.

62. Debbie Nathan, "The Making of a Modern Witch Trial" (see Note 9).

63. Jill Duerr-Berrick, "Sexual Abuse Prevention Education: Is It Appropriate for the Preschool Child?" *Children and Youth Services Review,* Spring 1989; author's interview with Jill Duerr-Berrick.

64. Steve Bogira, "Be Careful!" *Reader,* Chicago, Ill., June 20, 1986, p. 29.

65. National Committee for Prevention of Child Abuse/Marvel Comics, *The Amazing Spider-Man,* April 1990.

66. C. Anderson, "A History of the Touch Continuum," in M. Nelson and K. Clark, eds., *The Educators Guide to Preventing Child Sexual Abuse,* pp. 175–177, cited in Bonnie Trudell and Marianne Whatley, "School Sexual Abuse Prevention: Unintended Consequences and Dilemmas," *Child Abuse and Neglect: The International Journal,* 12, 1988, p. 103.

67. David Finkelhor and Nancy Strapko, "Sexual Abuse Prevention Education: A Review of Evaluation Studies," in Diane Willis, E. Wayne Holder, and Mindy Rosenberg, eds., *Child Abuse Prevention* (in press).

68. Sherryll Kerns Kraizer, "Rethinking Prevention," *Child Abuse and Neglect: The International Journal,* 10, 1986, p. 259.

69. Bogira (see Note 64), p. 1.

70. Interview with the author.

71. Interview with the author.

72. Bogira (see Note 64), p. 32.

73. Caryle Murphy, "Child Abuse in Custody Cases: Charges Increasingly Made, Experts Say," *Washington Post,* March 9, 1987, 1.

74. Nicholson (see Note 32), p. 4.

75. Murphy (see Note 73), p. 1.

76. *Hearing on Child Abuse Reporting Laws* (see Note 26), p. 40.

77. Missouri House of Representatives, Interim Committee on Children, Youth, and Families, *Report to the Speaker on: Child Abuse Reporting Law,* December 1985, p. 67.

78. David P. H. Jones and Ann Seig, "Child Sexual Abuse Allegations in Custody or Visitation Disputes," in Nicholson (see Note 32), p. 22; Arthur Green, "True and False Allegations of Sexual Abuse in Child Custody Disputes," *Journal of the American Academy of Child Psychiatry,* 25, no. 4, 1986, p. 449; M. Dwyer, *Guilty as Charged—Or Are They?* (University of Minnesota Program in Human Sexuality, unpublished paper, 1986), cited in Wakefield and Underwager (see Note 21).

79. *Report on Scott County Investigations* (see Note 20), p. 3.

Chapter 7: Foster Care I

1. Information for Angela's story comes from interviews with Angela's parents; tape recordings of conversations between Angela and her mother; Angela's school essay about foster care; a letter Angela wrote to a state legislator describing what happened to her; a lengthy handwritten narrative of their case written by Angela's parents; numerous court documents; and a letter from a therapist who treated the entire family in which he concludes that Angela's parents have "excellent parenting skills" and blames Angela's problems on circumstances beyond her parents' control, including "abuse while in foster care." To spare the children involved any further trauma, all names in this account have been changed.

2. Information for the Huot case comes from: Henry Goldman and Robert J. Terry, "Boy Dies in Foster Care; Was on DHS Caseload," *Philadelphia Inquirer,*

Jan. 28, 1988; "Murder Case, Foster Care, Violent Past," *Philadelphia Inquirer,* March 10, 1988; Linda Loyd, "Two Convicted in Death of Foster Child," *Philadelphia Inquirer,* Nov. 23, 1989.

3. Kent Pollock, "The Child Protectors: Innocent Suffer in War to Protect," *Sacramento Bee,* Aug. 3, 1986, 1.

4. J. Lawrence Aber III, "The Involuntary Placement Decision: Solomon's Dilemma Revisited," in George Gerbner, Catherine J. Ross, and Edward Zigler, eds., *Child Abuse: An Agenda for Action* (New York: Oxford University Press, 1980).

5. Kiley Armstrong, Associated Press, Dec. 5, 1989. Story appeared in the Schenectady, N.Y. *Daily Gazette* under the headline, "Abused Kids Need Love says NYC Foster Mother."

6. U.S. Department of Health and Human Services, Administration for Children, Youth, and Families, Office of Human Development Services, *Child Welfare Statistical Fact Book, 1985: Substitute Care,* Exhibit IV-9a, chap. 4, p. 71. In addition to being out of date, the data are based on a reporting system that leaves states with considerable leeway to leave out some placements; see text, chap. 8.

7. Ruth Hubbell, *Foster Care and Families* (Philadelphia: Temple University Press), p. 5.

8. Interview with the Author.

9. Supervisorial Staff, Family and Children's Division, *Every Three Hours: A Report to the Technical Advisory Committee, Family and Children's Division, San Francisco Department of Social Services,* June 18, 1986, p. 8.

10. "The Numbers Game, When More Is Less," *U.S. News and World Report,* April 27, 1987, p. 40; Caryle Murphy, "Child Abuse in Custody Cases: Charges Increasingly Made, Experts Say," *Washington Post,* March 9, 1987, 1.

11. Jane Meredith Adams, "Review Is Ordered in Foster Son Deaths," *Boston Globe,* April 6, 1988; "Foster Care Agency Had Expired License," *Boston Globe,* May 5, 1988; Richard Kindleberger, "Report of Confession Spurs Foster Deaths Probe," *Boston Globe,* May 3, 1989; Marion McCarthy, *Report of the Special Subcommittee on Foster Care,* Massachusetts House of Representatives, May 1989.

12. Henry Goldman and Dan Meyers, "Pernsley Is Defended on Council," *Philadelphia Inquirer,* Jan. 11, 1989; Henry Goldman and Martha Woodall, "Children With No Place to Go," *Philadelphia Inquirer,* Dec. 27, 1989, 1.

13. Cheryl Sullivan, "America's Troubled Children: 9 years old, 19 lbs, and a Foster Child," *Christian Science Monitor,* September, 1988, reprint, p. 12; Leslie Ellis, "Boy Suffered Severe Neglect in Foster Home, Lawsuit Claims," Louisville, Ky., *Courier-Journal,* Oct. 18, 1984, B1; Testimony of April Kerr, Assistant Executive Director, Council for Retarded Citizens, Louisville, Ky., *Children in State Care: Ensuring Their Protection and Support,* Hearing before the Select Committee on Children, Youth, and Families, U.S. House of Representatives, Sept. 25, 1986, transcript, p. 210.

14. Diana Smith, "Foster Baby's Death Spurs Corrective Action by State," Associated Press, Dec. 8, 1985; "Race Issue Raised in Baby's Death," United Press International, Oct. 22, 1986; "Woman Faces 7 Years in Foster Child's Death" Associated Press, June 13, 1988.

15. Decision of Justice Elliott Wilk, Supreme Court of New York County, *Martin A. v. George Gross,* April 27, 1987.

16. *Martin A. v. George Gross,* First Amended Complaint of plaintiffs.

17. Author's interview with James Trumm, attorney for Lisa Gallop.

18. Hubbell (see Note 7), p. 3.

19. Interview with the author.

20. Interview with the author.

21. James Robertson, *Young Children in Hospitals* (New York: Basic Books, 1971), pp. 17ff; cited in Karen Benker and James Rempel, "Inexcusable Harm: The Effect of Institutionalization on Young Foster Children in New York City," *City Health Report* (New York: Public Interest Health Consortium for New York City), May 1989, pp. 8-9.

22. Hubbell (see Note 7), p. 89.

23. Interview with the author.

24. Dan Zegart, "Child Removal: Without Any Sensitivity?" Newburgh, N.Y., *Evening News,* June 2, 1988, 1.

25. *Child Welfare Statistical Fact Book, 1985* (see Note 6), chap. 4, p. 78.

26. Maryland Citizen Board for Review of Foster Care of Children, *Foster Care Review Board: 1988 Annual Report,* p. 4.

27. Joseph Goldstein, Anna Freud, and Albert J. Solnit, *Beyond the Best Interests of the Child* (New York: Free Press, 1973).

28. Interview with the author.

29. Caroline Young, "A Bitter Cry: The System Was A Flop," *Seattle Post-Intelligencer,* Oct. 22, 1987.

30. Interview with the author.

31. Interview with the author.

32. Michelle Gillen, "Florida: State of Neglect," WPLG-TV, Miami, 1987.

33. Ibid.; see also discussion of *B.H. v. Johnson* infra.

34. Benker and Rempel (see Note 21), p. 9

35. Testimony of Michael W. Weber, Director, Hennepin County Community Services Dept., *Foster Care, Child Welfare, and Adoption Reforms,* Joint Hearings before the Subcommittee on Public Assistance and Unemployment Compensation of the Committee on Ways and Means and the Select Committee on Children, Youth, and Families, U.S. House of Representatives, April 13 and 28, May 12, 1988, p. 196.

36. Michael Oreskes, "A System Overloaded: The Foster Care Crisis," *New York Times,* March 15, 1987.

37. Testimony of Boyd A., Joint Hearings (see Note 35); Ray Nunn (producer), "Crimes Against Children: The Failure of Foster Care," *ABC-News Closeup,* Aug. 30, 1988, transcript, p. 11; Sara Rimer, "A Foster Child's Nightmare: Moving Ten Times in Five Years," *New York Times,* March 19, 1987, 1.

38. Joint Hearings (see Note 35), p. 43.

39. David Wagner: Michael D'Antonio, "Foster Care Failings," *Newsday,* Dec. 4, 1988; Maria: Young (see Note 29), p. 1; Linda P.: Michael D'Antonio, "Amid Heartbreak, Family Love," *Newsday,* Dec. 4, 1988; Jamal: Michael D'Antonio,

"A Life In Limbo," *Newsday,* Dec. 5, 1988; Joseph: Gillen (see Note 32)—the name is a pseudonym of my invention, no name is given on the videotape; Kathy: Nunn (see Note 37), p. 6.

40. State of Florida Office of the Auditor General, *Performance Audit of the Foster Care Program Administered by the Department of Health and Rehabilitative Services,* Jan. 3, 1989, p. 23.

41. Marcia Slacum Greene, "Sitting on a Time Bomb Waiting for Kids to Die," *Washington Post,* Sept. 12, 1989, 1.

42. McCarthy (see Note 11), pp. 62-63.

43. *Doe v. New York City Department of Social Servives,* 670 F. Supp. 1145 (S.D.N.Y. 1987).

44. Ibid.

45. Dennis Hevesi, "Child Abuse Cases Overwhelm Agency," *New York Times,* undated clipping, 1988, B1.

46. Information for this section from Ronald Garnett, *Report of the Special Master, Doe vs. New York City Department of Social Services,* 86 Civ. 4077, August 1988 and from Judge Lowe's decision in the same case.

47. Ellen Tumposky, "Foster Care Collapsing, Dozens of Children Spend Nights in Office," New York, N.Y., *Daily News,* June 18, 1989, 5.

48. Author's interview with attorney Rose Firestein.

49. State of Florida Office of the Auditor General, *Performance Audit of the Foster Care Program Administered by the Department of Health and Rehabilitative Services,* Jan. 3, 1989, p. 23.

50. Gillen (see Note 32).

51. Jenni Bergal, " 'It's a Crisis' Advocate Says of Foster Home Crowding," Fort Lauderdale, Fla., *News and Sun-Sentinel,* March 6, 1986, B1.

52. Martha Brannigan, "In a State Aid Agency, Overwhelmed Staffers Fight a Losing Battle," *Wall Street Journal,* Aug. 15, 1988, 1.

53. Foster Care Review Board (see Note 26), p. 9.

54. Testimony of Diane Weinroth, *Children in State Care Ensuring Their Protection and Support,* Hearing before the Select Committee on Children, Youth, and Families, U.S. House of Representatives, Sept. 25, 1986, transcript, p. 86.

55. Greene (see Note 41), p. 1.

56. Testimony of Karen Tefelski, *Hearing on SB-14 Chapter 978 Statutes of 1982,* Senate Judiciary Subcommittee on Corrections and Law Enforcement Agencies and Assembly Committee on Human Services, California Legislature, Oct. 17-18, 1985, transcript, p. 215.

57. Multi-Disciplinary Team, *Philadelphia Child Protective Services: A Report to the Secretary of Public Welfare,* p. 26; Goldman and Woodall (see Note 12), p. 1.

58. Interviews with the author.

59. Joseph Shapiro, "Whose Responsibility Is It Anyway?" *U.S. News and World Report,* Jan. 9, 1989, p. 29.

60. Testimony of Marcia Robinson Lowry, Joint Hearings (see Note 35).

61. Terry Demchak, "Abused and Neglected Children," *Youth Law News,*

9, no. 1 (National Center for Youth Law, 1988), p. 24; author's interview with Dennis Lepak, probation officer, Contra Costa County, California; Select Committee on Children, Youth, and Families, U.S. House of Representatives, *No Place to Call Home: Discarded Children in America* (Washington, D.C.: Jan. 12, 1990), p. 50.

62. Ira Schwartz, *In-Justice for Juveniles: Rethinking the Best Interests of the Child* (Lexington, Mass.: Lexington Books, 1989), p. 12.

63. Information about Clifford Masse's case and others like it from: Suzanne Daley, "Disabled Foster Care Youths Kept in New York Hospitals," *New York Times,* April 11, 1989, 1; author's interview with Susan Wiviott, staff of New York City Council President Andrew Stein.

64. The city's child savers keep changing the name of this agency. Child Welfare Administration is the most recent. In the interest of clarity, when quoting from reports that used the most recent previous name, Special Services for Children, I have substituted CWA.

65. City of New York, Office of the Comptroller, *Whatever Happened to the Boarder Babies?* January 1989, pp. 29, 35; City of New York, Office of the Comptroller, *Now We Are Four, Boarder Babies Growing Up in Foster Care: A Follow-up Study,* December 1989.

66. Lois Forer, "For Abused Children, An Answer from the Past," *Philadelphia Inquirer,* April 11, 1988, 11.

67. Suzanne Daley, "At Group Foster Home the Hunger is for Love," *New York Times,* Sept. 30, 1988.

68. *Whatever Happened* (see Note 65), p. 47.

69. Benker and Rempel (see Note 21), pp. 8-9.

70. Glenn Hester and Bruce Nygren, *Child of Rage* (Nashville: Thomas Nelson, 1981), pp. 17-18, cited in Benker and Rempel (see Note 21), p. 11.

71. Marcia Slocum Greene, "States, Cities Begin to Tackle Problem," *Washington Post,* Sept. 12, 1989, 15.

72. Interview with the author.

73. Suzanne Daley, "20 Retarded Children Shunted to Squalid Foster Care Home," *New York Times,* March 29, 1989, 1.

74. Interview with the author.

75. Interview with the author.

76. Hubbell (see Note 7), p. 90.

77. Interview with the author.

78. Interview with the author.

79. *Failed Promises: Report of the Manhattan Borough President's Advisory Council on Child Welfare,* 1989, p. 39.

80. Ibid.

81. *Children in State Care* (see Note 13), p. 88.

82. Hubbell (see Note 7), pp. 122-125

83. Michael Wald, J. M. Carlsmith, P. H. Leiderman, *Protecting Abused and Neglected Children* (Stanford, Calif.: Stanford University Press, 1988), p. 86.

84. Diane Dodson, *The Legal Framework for Ending Foster Care Drift: A*

Guide to Evaluating and Improving State Laws, Regulations and Court Rules (Washington, D.C.: Foster Care Project, National Legal Resource Center for Child Advocacy and Protection, American Bar Association, August, 1983), chap. 3, p. 4.

85. Complaint, Introductory Statement, *Bates v. Johnson,* No. 84 C 10054 United States District Court for the Northern District of Illinois, Eastern Division, Nov. 20, 1984, pp. 9, 10. William Curtis, chief counsel for the Illinois DCFS said he could not respond to the specifics in the Saunders case, but he acknowledged that his agency had failed to abide by a consent decree that would have reformed its visitation policies.

86. Association for Children of New Jersey, *Splintered Lives: A Report on Decision Making for Children in Foster Care,* June 1988, p. vii.

87. D'Antonio, *Foster Care Failings* (see Note 39), p. 5.

88. Florida: Gina Thomas, "HRS Pulls Out All Stops for Foster Homes," *Orlando Sentinel,* July 10, 1986, 1; San Francisco: *Every Three Hours . . .* (see Note 9), p. 11; Philadelphia: *Philadelphia Child Protective Services* (see Note 57), p. 20.

89. Joint Hearings (see Note 35), p. 61.

90. Interview with the author.

91. Interview with the author.

92. Interview with the author.

93. Joint Hearings (see Note 35).

94. *No Place to Call Home* (see Note 61), pp. 197-204.

95. E.g., a suit brought by Lowry against racial discrimination by private child saving agencies, *Wilder v. Sugarman.* As this is written settlement negotiations are under way in the suit concerning New York's "overnighters" as well.

96. Kansas City: *G.L. v. Zumwalt,* 564 F. Supp. 1030; Baltimore: *L.J. By and Through Darr v. Massinga,* 699 F. Supp. 518; New Mexico: *Joseph and Josephine A. et al. v. New Mexico Dept. of Human Services,* 575 F. Supp. 346; Georgia: *J.J. v. Ledbetter,* Civil Action #CV180- 94; Massachusetts: *Lynch v. King,* 550 F. Supp. 325.

97. *L. J. By and Through Darr v. Massinga* (see Note 96).

98. "Massachusetts Is Warned to Improve Its Foster Care," *New York Times,* Sept. 23, 1982.

99. Amended Complaint, *B.H. v. Johnson,* No. 88 C 5599, United States District Court for the Northern District of Illinois, Eastern Division, undated, 1988, pp. 13-17.

100. Plaintiffs' Memorandum in Response to Defendant's Motion to Dismiss, *B.H. v. Johnson,* Undated, 1989, p. 3.

101. Defendant's Memorandum in Support of Motion to Dismiss, *B.H. v. Johnson,* Nov. 15, 1988, p. 3: "Defendant does not dispute that children who are placed in state-operated facilities have a constitutional right to bodily integrity. . . . However, . . . [p]laintiffs' effort in this case to extend the protections . . . to children in foster care—children who are in the state's legal custody but not its physical custody—should be rejected by this court," p. 38; ". . . where the state is not responsible for providing the daily care of children in its legal custody, it

should not be held liable for the conditions of such care," pp. 8ff; "Defendant does not read the amended complaint to include a claim that plaintiffs have a constitutional right to be free from damage to mental health and development, a right, if asserted, defendant would argue also does not exist under the Constitution." Also, *Memorandum Opinion* of Judge John F. Grady, May 30, 1989, p. 13: "Defendant argues that . . . he is not responsible for [plaintiff's] emotional well-being."

102. Defendants' Memorandum (see Note 101), p. 15.

103. Ibid., p. 34.

104. Author's interview with Susan Getzendanner, the Skadden, Arps attorney defending the DCFS.

105. Diane Redleaf, *DCFS Neglects Parents, Creates Tragedies,* unpublished essay, November 1989.

106. Interview with the author.

107. Author's interview with attorney Mitchell Mirviss, Legal Aid Bureau of Baltimore.

108. Hon. Paul E. Plunkett, Memorandum Opinion and Order, *Bates v. Johnson,* No. 84 C 10054, United States District Court for the Northern District of Illinois, Eastern Division, June 29, 1989, pp. 6, 7.

109. Interview with the author.

110. Interview with the author.

111. Hubbell (see Note 7), p. 43.

112. Malcolm Bush, "The Public and Private Purposes of Case Records," *Children and Youth Services Review,* 6, 1984, pp. 7, 8, 9.

113. Complaint, *T.M. v. City of Philadelphia,* no. 5087, Philadelphia County Court of Common Pleas, May 23, 1989, pp. 6, 7.

114. New Jersey Legislature, Senate Committee on Children's Services, *Public Hearing,* Sept. 27, 1988, transcript, p. 202.

115. Interview with the author.

116. Joint Hearings (see Note 35), p. 505.

117. Hearing on SB-14 (see Note 56), p. 43.

118. Interview with the author.

119. Interview with the author.

120. Interview with the author.

121. David Kaplovitz and Louis Genevie, *Foster Children in Jackson County, Missouri: A Statistical Analysis of Files Maintained by the Division of Family Services* (1981).

122. Testimony of Marcia Robinson Lowry, Joint Hearings (see Note 35).

123. Theodore J. Stein, *Del A. v. Edwin Edwards, Casereading* (1988).

124. Memorandum and Order of Judge Joseph G. Howard, *L.J. v. Massinga,* Civil No. JH-84-4409, United States District Court for the District of Maryland, July 27, 1987.

125. Interview with the author.

126. *Hearing on SB-14* (see Note 56), p. 61.

127. Joint Hearings (see Note 35), p. 505.

128. Goldman and Woodall (see Note 12), p. 1.

129. Senate Committee on Children's Services (see Note 114), p. 121.

130. Interview with the author.

131. Chrystyna Obushkevich, *A Study of the Handling of Child Abuse and Maltreatment of Foster Children in New York City* (New York: City of New York Department of Investigation report #1918/79 MR-D, April 1982).

132. Gillen (see Note 32).

133. Joint Hearings (see Note 35), p. 61.

134. Interview with the author.

135. *Every Three Hours* (see Note 9), p. 9.

136. Robert Hanley, "Changes Ordered at Children's Center," *New York Times,* Jan. 21, 1989.

137. Harvey Lipman, "Abuse Rate High In State Facilities," Albany, N.Y., *Times Union,* Dec. 1, 1987.

138. Michael Oreskes, "A System Overloaded: The Foster Care Crisis," *New York Times,* March 15, 1987, 32.

139. Information about Montrose from testimony of Patricia Hanges and Judy Guttridge, *Children in State Care* (see Note 13), pp. 96-115.

140. Formerly a division of the State Health Department, this agency is now the Department of Juvenile Services.

141. *Children in State Care* (see Note 13), p. 11.

142. For example, 71 percent of the child care workers in New York City group homes and institutions have only a high school degree. (*Failed Promises: Report of the Manhattan Borough President's Advisory Committee on Child Welfare,* 1989, p. 70.)

143. *Children in State Care* (see Note 13), p. 120.

144. Council of Family and Child Caring Agencies, *Who Will Care for the Children? A Report on the Work Force Crisis in Child Welfare,* March 1989, pp. 11, 15.

145. "Study: Foster Care Too Silent on Abuse," New York, N.Y., *Daily News,* Sept. 23, 1983.

Chapter 8: Foster Care II

1. U.S. Dept. of Health and Human Services, Administration for Children, Youth, and Families, Office of Human Development Services, *Child Welfare Statistical Fact Book, 1985;* author's interview with Charles Gershensohn; author's interview with Peter Forsythe, Director, Program for Children, Edna McConnell Clark Foundation.

2. Douglas Besharov, *Crack Children in Foster Care: Moral and Administrative Challenges,* testimony prepared for the U.S. Senate Subcommittee on Children, Families, Drugs, and Alcoholism, Nov. 13, 1989.

3. For foster care costs: The federal government spent an estimated $1.022 billion on foster care under Title IVE of the Social Security Act in 1989. Title IVE covers about 40 percent of all children. It pays, on average, 53 percent of

the cost of care for that 40 percent. Thus, Title IVE money covers roughly one-fifth of the cost of foster care. (Data from Select Committee on Children, Youth, and Families, U.S. House of Representatives, *No Place to Call Home: Discarded Children in America* (Washington, D.C.: Jan. 12, 1990), pp. 11, 69, 168). For total costs: According to Jane Henderson, a staffer in the California Legislature, that state spends $1.2 billion a year on its child welfare system. New York City alone spends another $1.2 billion, according to a December 1989 report from the city Comptroller's office. Thus, it costs $2.4 billion to pay for child welfare systems that cover a little less than one-third of the nation's foster care population. My guess simply multiplies that number by three.

4. Children can be placed even if "reasonable efforts" have not been made, but in such cases the federal government isn't supposed to help pay for it.

5. National Child Welfare Resouce Center for Management and Administration, University of Southern Maine, *Pilot Early Review Project, Preliminary Data Analysis,* March, 1989.

6. *No Place to Call Home* (see Note 3), p. 82.

7. *Foster Care, Child Welfare and Adoption Reforms,* Joint Hearings before the Subcommittee on Public Assistance and Unemployment Compensation of the Committee on Ways and Means and the Select Committee on Children, Youth, and Families, U.S. House of Representatives, April 13 and 28, May 12, 1988, transcript, p. 97.

8. Ibid.

9. Interview with the author.

10. Interview with the author.

11. Mary Ann Jones, *Parental Lack of Supervision: Nature and Consequence of a Major Child Neglect Problem* (Washington, D.C.: Child Welfare League of America, 1987), pp. 34, 39.

12. Interview with the author.

13. Data supplied by Joyce Lewis and Gregory Sanders, California Department of Social Services.

14. For example, data compiled by the Neighborhood Family Services Coalition in New York City found that anywhere from 82 to 97 percent of families received "counseling" as a preventive service. No other single service was offered to more than 21 percent of the families. (Neighborhood Family Services Coalition, *Continuing Crisis: A Report on New York City's Response to Families Requiring Protective and Preventive Services,* 1987, pp. 84, 85.)

15. Joint Hearings (see Note 7).

16. Interview with the author.

17. Interview with the author.

18. Interviews with the author.

19. All estimates from interviews with the author.

20. The Albany, N.Y., *Times Union* put this headline over a *Los Angeles Times* News Service story, Jan. 7, 1990, 1.

21. E.g., *ABC-News Primetime,* Feb. 1, 1990.

22. Douglas Besharov, "The Children of Crack, Will We Protect Them?" *Public*

Welfare, Fall 1989, p. 7. The survey that produced the 375,000 figure was conducted by Ira Chasnoff, Director of the Perinatal Center for Chemical Dependence at Northwestern University Medical School in Chicago.

23. "The No-Parent Child," editorial, *New York Times,* Dec. 24, 1989, 10.

24. *Failed Promises: Report of the Manhattan Borough President's Advisory Council on Child Welfare,* 1989, p. 23.

25. Welfare Research Inc., *New York State Children in Foster Care,* October, 1977, p. 11.

26. *Children in Foster Care, 1975-1990,* chart prepared by New York State Department of Social Services.

27. Glenn Collins, "Courts, the Congress and Citizens Are Redefining the Concept of Foster Care," *New York Times,* July 22, 1981, B4.

28. *Failed Promises* (see Note 24), p. 15; *Children in Foster Care* (see Note 26).

29. Interview with the author.

30. *No Place to Call Home* (see Note 3), p. 6.

31. The data directly from Washington State are a little different from the National Survey and probably a lot more reliable. But even this data leave Washington State with a placement rate of 80 per 10,000 children in 1985, high enough to maintain its unenviable number one ranking.

32. Interview with the author.

33. This view is not unanimous, but the vast majority of those I spoke to who had close-up views of their child welfare systems said that the drug cases were in addition to, not instead of, less serious cases.

34. Cheryl Sullivan, "America's Troubled Children," *Christian Science Monitor,* September 1988, reprint, p. 14.

35. Information about Theresa's case comes from: Brief for Defendant Appellant, and Brief of Petitioner-Respondent, *Nassau County Department of Social Services v. Theresa,* and author's interviews with Matthew Muraskin, attorney for Theresa, and Patricia Carroll, attorney for the county.

The county's version of events states that Theresa tested positive for marijuana use during her pregnancy. But Theresa's doctor testified that the tests produce a lot of false positives, and that marijuana stays in a person's system for such a long time that the very low amounts found in the tests easily could have been from before Theresa knew she was pregnant. According to the brief filed by Muraskin, the doctor "testified that in his medical opinion [Theresa] was not using drugs during her pregnancy."

The county's brief also refers to Theresa using cocaine. But testimony from the court hearing, included with Muraskin's brief, shows that this occurred more than a year before Theresa became pregnant.

36. Daniel Goleman, "Lasting Costs Are Found from a Few Early Drinks," *New York Times,* February, 1989.

37. Ray Helfer, "The Perinatal Period: A Window of Opportunity for Enhancing Parent-Infant Communication: An Approach to Prevention," *Child Abuse and Neglect: The International Journal,* 11, 1987, p. 566.

38. Marshall Klaus and John Kennell, "Mothers Separated from their Newborn Infants," *Pediatric Clinics of North America,* 17, 1970, pp. 1015-1037.

39. He also got his facts wrong, stating that any child whose test result comes back positive must have an addict for a mother. He writes: ". . . Does *Newsday* really want vulnerable infants left with drug addicted mothers for the sake of 'bonding'?" (Joseph D'Elia, "Nassau Acts to Protect Newborns," *Newsday,* Sept. 29, 1988, 97.)

40. Michael D'Antonio, "Foster Care Failings," and "A Life in Limbo," *Newsday,* Dec. 4 and 5, 1988, 5.

41. *No Place to Call Home* (see Note 3), p. 212.

42. Massachusetts Department of Social Services, *Guidelines for Social Workers When Working With Families Where There Are Issues of Neglect and Substance Abuse,* undated draft, 1989.

43. Author's interview with Lorraine Carli, spokeswoman for the Massachusetts Department of Social Services.

44. Letter from Robert Moro to Massachusetts Civil Liberties Union, July 18, 1989.

45. Preventive services are funded through Title IVB of the Social Security Act. An estimated $246.7 billion will be spent on Title IVB in the 1989-90 federal fiscal year. But Title IVB funds all sorts of child welfare services and it is estimated that "a majority of the child welfare funds [under Title IVB] (federal and state combined) is spent on foster care services." (*No Place to Call Home* [see Note 3], p. 163.)

46. Malcolm Bush, *Families in Distress: Public, Private, and Civic Responses* (Berkeley: University of California Press, 1988), p. 248; Martha J. Cox and Roger D. Cox, *Foster Care: Current Issues, Policies, and Practices* (Norwood, N.J.: Ablex Publishing Corp, 1985), p. x. The alert reader will notice that these data don't entirely reconcile with the state-by-state examples given earlier. That's because the data used in each case measure slightly different phenomena. The data concerning state-by-state variation measure the number of children who came into care during the year 1985. Children already in care since 1984 or earlier are not included. The historical data, in contrast, are from surveys that measure the total number of children in foster care at any given moment—no matter when they came into care. These totals always will be larger.

47. Author's interviews with Joyce Lewis, California Department of Social Services, and Yoshie Fujiwara, a principal program budget analyst, California Department of Finance.

48. There is a small block grant available for juvenile justice prevention programs, but this money can be used for all sorts of different purposes, not just preventive services, according to Martin Ewing, a principal program budget analyst for the California Department of Finance.

49. Dennis Lepak, "Probation Placement in California," *California Probation News,* 6, no. 3, March 1989, p. 1.

50. Joint Hearings (see Note 7), p. 62.

51. David Young and Brandt Allen, *Cost Barriers in Adoption: An Analysis*

of the Economics of Adoption Reimbursement (New York: Edwin Gould Foundation for Children, 1974), pp. 2, 4, 11.

52. Interview with the author.

53. Eileen Tumposky, "City Adoptions Drop," New York, N.Y., *Daily News,* Oct. 23, 1988, 5.

54. Interview with the author.

55. Interview with the author. At the time the organization was called the Council of Voluntary Child Caring Agencies.

56. Deposition of Sister Marian Cecilia Schneider, Administrator, New York Foundling Hospital, *Wilder v. Sugarman,* July 16, 1976.

57. Author's interview with Marcia Robinson Lowry.

58. Deposition of Harriet Dronska, a private agency worker who conducted these inspections, *Wilder v. Sugarman,* April 7, 1976.

59. Theodore Stein, *An Investigation into the Practices of New York City's Child Welfare Administration and Their Effect on the Implementation of the Wilder Settlement,* Jan. 16, 1990, p. 35.

60. Ari Goldman, "New York Foster Care: A Public-Private Battleground," *New York Times,* April 9, 1987.

61. Bush (see Note 46), pp. 40, 150, 152.

62. Ellen Tumposky, "Foster Care Collapsing, Dozens of Children Spend Nights in Office," New York, N.Y., *Daily News,* June 18, 1989, 5.

63. Stein (see Note 59), pp. 34, 42.

64. Multi-Disciplinary Team, *Philadelphia Child Protective Services: A Report to the Secretary of Public Welfare,* Nov. 12, 1987, p. 20.

65. State of Florida, Office of the Auditor General, *Performance Audit of the Foster Care Program Administered by the Department of Health and Rehabilitative Services,* Jan. 3, 1989, p. 35.

66. Interview with the author.

67. Bush (see Note 46), p. 177. The survey was conducted by the Illinois Children's Home and Aid Society in 1974.

68. Bush (see Note 46), p. 177.

69. Malcolm Bush, "The Public and Private Purposes of Case Records," *Children and Youth Services Review,* 6, 1984, pp. 12, 13.

70. Bush (see Note 46), p. 181.

71. Bush, "The Public and Private Purposes of Case Records" (see Note 69), p. 13.

72. Bush (see Note 46), p. 185.

73. Bush (see Note 46), p. 34.

74. Interview with the author.

75. City of New York, Office of the Comptroller, Office of Policy Management, *Now We Are Four: Boarder Babies Growing Up in Foster Care, a Follow-up Study,* December, 1989, p. 5.

76. Henry Goldman and Martha Woodall, "Child Advocates Urge City to Speed Adoption Process," *Philadelphia Inquirer,* Dec. 28, 1989, A8.

77. Governor's Commission on Children, *Final Report,* January 1989, p. 75.

78. Information for this section from: Caroline Young, *Seattle Post-Intelligencer:* "Caseworkers for State Face a Nightmare," Oct. 20, 1987; "Children Up for Adoption Left in Limbo," Nov. 19, 1987; "Child Protective System to Be Overhauled" Dec. 9, 1987; "State Cuts Foster Pay as It Tries to Find More Homes" June 14, 1988.

Chapter 9: System Failure

1. Interview with the author.
2. Douglas Besharov, "Unfounded Allegations—A New Child Abuse Problem," *Public Interest,* no. 83, Spring 1986, p. 25.
3. Celia Dugger, "Agency's Bungling Allowed Tot to Die of 'Bizarre' Abuse, Report Finds," Knight-Ridder News Service, August 14, 1989.
4. Michael Winerip, "The Denouement Is Never-Ending in Baby Tragedy," *New York Times,* March, 1989, B1.
5. Timothy Egan, *New York Times,* Jan. 1, 1988. Article reprinted in *Seattle Post-Intelligencer* under the headline "Eli's Death May Help Kids Across Nation."
6. Douglas Besharov, " 'Doing Something' about Child Abuse: The Need to Narrow the Grounds for State Intervention," *Harvard Journal of Law and Public Policy,* 8, no. 3, Summer 1985, p. 540; and Besharov, "Unfounded Allegations" (see Note 2), p. 25.
7. Letter from Edward J. Malloy to Jean Petralia, Director of Personnel, Massachusetts Dept. of Social Services, August 1, 1989.
8. Interview with the author.
9. Interview with the author.
10. National Child Welfare Resource Center for Management and Administration, *National Study of Public Child Welfare Salaries* (University of Southern Maine: 1988).
11. Council of Family and Child Caring Agencies, *Who Will Care for the Children?: A Report on the Work Force Crisis in Child Welfare,* March, 1989, p. 9
12. National Child Welfare Resource Center for Management and Administration, *1987 National Study of Public Child Welfare Job Requirements* (University of Southern Maine: 1987)
13. Kenneth Herrmann, *Protecting Abused and Neglected Children: Standards of Service to Children and Families,* unpublished paper, 1985.
14. Interview with the author.
15. *1987 National Study* (see Note 12).
16. Interview with the author.
17. Maryland Citizen Board for Review of Foster Care of Children, *Foster Care Review Board: 1988 Annual Report,* p. 5.
18. Michigan Department of Social Services, *Children's Protective Services Task Force Report,* March 1988, p. 28.
19. Multi-Disciplinary Team, *Philadelphia Child Protective Services: A Report*

to the Secretary of Public Welfare, Nov. 12, 1987, pp. 46-51.

20. *Hearing on SB-14 Chapter 978 Statutes of 1982,* Senate Judiciary Sub-committee on Corrections and Law Enforcement Agencies and Assembly Committee on Human Services, California Legislature, Oct. 17-18, 1985, transcript, p. 356.

21. Wisconsin Department of Health and Social Services, Division of Policy and Budget, Bureau of Evaluation, *Evaluation of the Implementation of the Child Abuse and Neglect Act,* June 1981, p. 31.

22. Neighborhood Family Services Coalition, *The Continuing Crisis: A Report on New York City's Response to Families Requiring Protective and Preventive Services,* 1987, pp. 115-116.

23. Larry Brown, "Seeking a National Consensus," *Public Welfare,* Winter 1987, p. 17.

24. Interview with the author.

25. Quoted in Douglas Besharov, *The Vulnerable Social Worker: Liability for Serving Children and Families* (Silver Spring, Md.: National Association of Social Workers, 1985), p. 156.

26. Interview with the author.

27. Commission on California State Government Organization and Economy, *The Children's Services Delivery System in California: Final Report,* October 1987, p. 98.

28. Dr. Case's presentation was videotaped by members of Victims of Child Abuse Laws. A copy of the tape was made available to the author.

29. Author's interview with Charlotte Booth, Training Director, Homebuilders.

30. Caroline Young, "Foster Care in Chaos: For Many Kids, It's a No-Win Situation," *Seattle Post-Intelligencer,* Oct. 19, 1987, 1.

31. *Failed Promises: Report of the Manhattan Borough President's Advisory Council on Child Welfare,* 1989, p. 63.

32. Martha Brannigan, "In a State Aid Agency, Overwhelmed Staffers Fight a Losing Battle," *Wall Street Journal,* Aug. 15, 1988, 1.

33. *Foster Care Review Board: 1988 Annual Report* (see Note 17), p. 8.

34. Jeanne Giovannoni and Rosina Becerra, *Defining Child Abuse* (New York: Free Press, 1979), p. 144.

35. Shirley Zimmerman, Paul Mattessich, and Robert Leik, "Legislators' Attitudes toward Family Policy," *Journal of Marriage and the Family,* August 1979, pp. 507-517.

36. Brannigan (see Note 32), p. 1.

37. "Jobs Loaded with Stress and Danger," *Milwaukee Journal,* Sept. 2, 1988, B4.

38. Sydney H. Schanberg, "Adult Abuse," *New York Times,* April 28, 1984, 23; a copy of the Inspector General's report, which is untitled and undated, was made available to the author.

39. Michelle Gillen, "Florida: State of Neglect," WPLG-TV, Miami, 1987.

40. Testimony of Irwin Levin before unspecified legislative committee, July 13, 1989. (Levin sent a copy of his testimony to the author.)

41. Henry Goldman and Dan Meyers, "The Failures of a Child Welfare

Agency," *Philadelphia Inquirer,* June 7, 1988, 1.

42. City of New York, Office of the Comptroller, *Now We Are Four: Boarder Babies Growing Up in Foster Care, A Follow Up Study,* December 1989, p. 18.

43. Testimony of Danny Ramos, quoted in Select Committee on Children, Youth, and Families, U.S. House of Representatives, *No Place to Call Home: Discarded Children in America* (Washington, D.C.: Jan. 12, 1990), p. 58.

44. Interview with the author.

45. Interview with the author.

46. Interview with the author.

47. Don Yaeger, "HRS Claims Over Child Abuse Stir Concern," Jacksonville, Fla., *Times-Union,* Feb. 5, 1989, 1.

48. The convicted murderer was classified a "caretaker" rather than a foster parent and, under the regulations in effect at the time, that meant no one had to check his background before Lillie was placed with him. Seven months later, she was removed from the home after complaining that the "caretaker" had made sexual advances toward her.

As of 1988, Ferebee was 21 years old and falling behind on payments for a house she had bought with $50,000 she had received from the city of Philadelphia to settle a lawsuit she had brought against the city's foster care system. She had two children of her own—and both had been placed in foster care. (Dan Goldman and Henry Meyers, "The Failures of a Child Welfare Agency," *Philadelphia Inquirer,* June 7, 1988, 1.)

49. Ibid.

50. Governor's Child Protective Services Review Team, *Crisis in Children's Services,* March 1987.

51. Author's interview with Gary Moore, Executive Director, Washington Federation of State Employees and International Vice President, American Federation of State, County, and Municipal Employees.

52. *Philadelphia Child Protective Services* (see Note 19).

53. Marcia Slacum Greene, "Sitting on a Time Bomb Waiting for Kids to Die," *Washington Post,* Sept. 12, 1989, 1.

54. Gillen (see Note 39).

55. Brannigan (see Note 32), p. 1.

56. Testimony of Maureen Strelich, Children's Services investigator, Los Angeles County, *Hearing on SB-14* (see Note 20), p. 236.

57. Suzanne Daley, "Child Dead in Family Welfare Agency Forgot," *New York Times,* Jan. 20, 1989, 1, and "Child-Protection System Falls Victim to a Paper Maneuver," *New York Times,* Jan. 21, 1989, B1.

58. Nat Hentoff, "It's Time, Commissioner Grinker, It's Time," *Village Voice,* Feb. 7, 1989, 39.

59. Interview with the author.

60. *The Continuing Crisis* (see Note 22).

61. Interview with the author.

62. Joseph Goldstein, Anna Freud, and Albert J. Solnit, *Before the Best Interests of the Child* (New York: Free Press, 1979), p. 18.

63. Kent Pollock, "The Child Protectors: Innocent Suffer in War to Protect," *Sacramento Bee,* Aug. 3, 1986, 1.

64. *The Continuing Crisis* (see Note 22), pp. 27, 67, 70.

65. *Foster Care, Child Welfare and Adoption Reforms,* Joint Hearings before the Subcommittee on Public Assistance and Unemployment Compensation of the Committee on Ways and Means and the Select Committee on Children, Youth, and Families, U.S. House of Representatives, April 13 and 28, May 12, 1988, pp. 21-22, 41.

66. *The Children's Services Delivery System* (see Note 27), p. 83

67. *The Continuing Crisis* (see Note 22), p. 95

68. State Communities Aid Association, *Caring for Families and Children: The Failure to Create Responsive Child Protective Services,* January 1988, p. 6.

69. Jane Gross, "Family Court: Stage for Suffering and Crises," *New York Times,* Dec. 15, 1987, B10

70. Bob Hohler, "The Youngest Victims: System Deluged with Child Abuse Cases," *Boston Globe* (New Hampshire Week), March 13, 1988, 1.

71. Christina Robb, "The Impossible Job," *Boston Globe Magazine,* Feb. 5, 1989.

72. Michigan Department of Social Services, *Children's Protective Services Task Force Report,* March, 1988, pp. 4, 5

73. Author's interview with Steve Murphy, Co-chair, Michigan Children's Protective Services Task Force.

74. Governor's Child Protective Services Review Team, *Crisis in Children's Services,* March, 1987, p. 21.

75. Mary Lee Anderson, Program Manager of Child Protective Services, State of North Carolina, in a response to a survey from the U.S. House of Representatives, Select Committee on Children, Youth, and Families, quoted in the transcript of the committee's hearing, March 3, 1987, p. 4.

76. *Hearing on Child Abuse Reporting Laws and Dependency Statutes,* Select Committee on Children and Youth, California Legislature, Dec. 4, 1986, p. 36.

77. Ibid., p. 42.

78. *Hearing on SB-14* (see Note 20), p. 219.

79. Calaifornia Legislature, Senate Select Committee on Children and Youth, SB1195 Task Force, *Child Abuse Reporting Laws, Juvenile Court Dependency Statutes and Child Welfare Services,* January 1988.

80. Brown (see Note 23), p. 17.

81. Lizbeth Schorr, *Within Our Reach: Breaking the Cycle of Disadvantage* (New York: Anchor/Doubleday, 1988), p. 155.

Chapter 10: Family Preservation

1. Malcolm Bush, *Families in Distress: Public, Private, and Civic Responses* (Berkeley: University of California Press, 1988), p. 309.

2. Barbara Nelson, *Making an Issue of Child Abuse: Political Agenda Setting*

for Social Problems (Chicago: University of Chicago Press, 1984), p. 10. The conference specified, however, that family preservation should be reserved for children who had "reasonably efficient and deserving mothers" and "parents of worthy character."

3. Lizbeth Schorr, *Within Our Reach: Breaking the Cycle of Disadvantage* (New York: Anchor Press/Doubleday, 1988).

4. Ibid., p. 258.

5. Bush (see Note 1), p. 303.

6. *Hearing on SB-14, Chapter 978, Statutes of 1982,* Senate Judiciary Subcommittee on Corrections and Law Enforcement Agencies and Assembly Committee on Human Services, California Legislature, Oct. 17-18, 1985, transcript, p. 80.

7. Interview with the author.

8. Jill Kinney, Barbara Madsen, Thomas Fleming, David A. Happala, "Homebuilders: Keeping Families Together," *Journal of Consulting and Clinical Psychology,* 45, no. 4, 1977, p. 672.

9. Mark Fraser and David Happala, "Home-based Family Treatment: A Quantitative-Qualitative Assessment," *Journal of Applied Social Sciences,* 12, no. 1, Fall/Winter 1987-88.

10. Jill Kinney, *Questions Commonly Asked About the Homebuilders Program* (Federal Way, Wash.: Behavioral Sciences Institute, Homebuilders Division, undated).

11. Ibid., p. 15; author's interview with Charlotte Booth.

12. Christina Mitchell, Patricia Tovar, and Jane Knitzer, *The Bronx Homebuilders Program: An Evaluation of the First 45 Families* (New York: Bank Street College of Education, Division of Research, Demonstration, and Policy, December 1989), p. 12.

13. Kinney (see Note 10), p. 15; author's interview with Charlotte Booth.

14. Christina Mitchell, Patricia Tovar, Jane Knitzer, *The Bronx Homebuilders Program: The First 30 Families,* an Interim Report Prepared for HRA (New York: Bank Street College of Education, Division of Research, Demonstration, and Policy, May 1988), p. 14.

15. Caroline Young, "A Program Killed Her Death Wish," *Seattle Post-Intelligencer, Oct.* 23, 1987, 11.

16. Testimony of Martha, *Preventing Out of Home Placement: Programs That Work,* Hearing before the Select Committee on Children, Youth and Families, U.S. House of Representatives, June 9, 1987, transcript, p. 17

17. Young, "A Program Killed" (see Note 15).

18. National Resource Center on Family Based Services, *Family Based Services: Factors Contributing to Success and Failure in Family Based Child Welfare Services: Final Report* (Iowa City, Ia.: University of Iowa School of Social Work, April, 1988).

19. Interview with the author.

20. The pamphlet was originally published in 1981, seven years after Homebuilders began, but a "second edition" was published in 1983. It was routinely mailed out on request (for $4.00) as of 1989.

21. Leontine Young, *Physical Child Neglect,* pamphlet published by National

Committee for Prevention of Child Abuse (Chicago: 1986), p. 9.

22. Daniel Goleman, "Family Therapist Takes on Agencies," *New York Times,* May 19, 1987, C3.

23. Author's interview with Charlotte Booth.

24. Nanette Dembitz, "A Conflict of Values Behind Child Abuse," letter to the editor, *New York Times,* June 26, 1985.

25. David Davis (Producer), *The Unquiet Death of Eli Creekmore,* KCTS-TV, Seattle, Wash., 1988.

26. National Council of Juvenile and Family Court Judges et al., *Making Reasonable Efforts: Steps for Keeping Families Together* (New York: Edna McConnell Clark Foundation, 1985), p. 62.

27. Interviews with the author.

28. Maryland Citizen Board for Review of Foster Care of Children, *Foster Care Review Board: 1988 Annual Report.*

29. *Foster Care, Child Welfare and Adoption Reforms,* Joint Hearings before the Subcommittee on Public Assistance and Unemployment Compensation of the Committee on Ways and Means and the Select Committee on Children, Youth, and Families, U.S. House of Representatives, April 13 and 28, May 12, 1988, pp. 51, 52

30. Davis (see Note 25), pp. 21, 26

31. Ibid., p. 32.

32. Author's interviews with Charlotte Booth and Peter Forsythe.

33. Davis (see Note 25), p. 20.

34. Abigail Norman, *Keeping Families Together: The Case for Family Preservation* (New York: Edna McConnell Clark Foundation, 1985), pp. 38, 39.

35. J. Lawrence Aber III, "The Involuntary Placement Decision: Solomon's Dilemma Revisited," in George Gerbner, Catherine J. Ross, and Edward Zigler, eds., *Child Abuse: An Agenda for Action* (New York: Oxford University Press, 1980.)

36. Michael Wald, "Family Preservation: Are We Moving Too Fast?" *Public Welfare,* Summer 1988, p. 37.

37. Interview with the author.

38. Davis (see Note 25), p. 26.

39. David Hechler, *The Battle and the Backlash: The Child Sexual Abuse War* (Lexington, Mass.: Lexington Books, 1988), p. 218.

40. Ellen Goodman, "Concern Over Babies Leaves Mothers Forgotten," syndicated newspaper column, Dec. 18, 1989.

41. Interview with the author.

42. Joint Hearings (see Note 29), p. 97.

43. U.S. House of Representatives, Select Committee on Children, Youth, and Families, *No Place to Call Home: Discarded Children in America* (Washington, D.C.: Jan. 12, 1990), p. 212; *Failed Promises: Report of the Manhattan Borough President's Advisory Council on Child Welfare,* 1989, p. 35.

Chapter 11: Making Changes

1. Michael Wald, "State Intervention on Behalf of 'Neglected' Children: Standards for Removal of Children from Their Homes, Monitoring the Status of Children in Foster Care and Termination of Parental Rights," *Stanford Law Review,* 28, p. 623, April 1976.

2. My own enthusiasm for this volume apparently was not shared by the ABA's House of Delegates. Out of 22 volumes in the Juvenile Justice Standards project, the Abuse and Neglect volume was one of only two that was never put to a vote. Now that we have had nearly a decade of additional experience with what the child savers have done to children, the climate might be more receptive.

3. There are often enormous disparities in wealth among local governments. In some cases, it may be too much of a burden to require them to pay 100 percent of foster care costs, but, at a minimum, foster care should be made a significantly greater financial burden for localities than preventive services.

4. Plaintiffs Appellate Brief, *Lynch v. King.*

5. Testimony of Douglas Besharov, *Child Abuse and Neglect in America: The Problem and the Response,* Hearing before the Select Committee on Children, Youth, and Families, U.S. House of Representatives, March 3, 1987, p. 86.

6. Interview with the author.

7. National Fire Protection Association, "Malicious Alarms or Nuisance Alarms: Which Is the Larger Problem?" *Fire Journal,* January/February 1989, p. 54.

8. Richard Wexler, "Albany Considers Cuts in Night Alarm Response," Albany, N.Y., *Times Union,* Nov. 8, 1986, 1.

9. Gale Scott, "Paramedics, EMS at Odds over Errors," New York, N.Y., *Newsday,* Sept. 2, 1988, 3.

10. Author's interviews with Besharov and Perales.

11. National Association of Public Child Welfare Administrators, *Guildelines for a Model System of Protective Services for Abused and Neglected Children* (Washington, D.C.: 1988), p. 30.

12. Interview with the author.

13. Michigan Department of Social Services, *Children's Protective Services Task Force Report,* March 1988, pp. 8, 9.

14. Pennsylvania keeps statewide statistics only on cases that meet the stricter Child Protective Services definition. This gives the misleading impression that people in Pennsylvania report far fewer cases of maltreatment than people in any other state, and therefore that large numbers of children in need are never reported at all. Data from Philadelphia show, however, that CPS cases are, on average, only about 40 percent of a worker's caseload. The other 60 percent are General Protective Services cases. When these cases are combined, they suggest a reporting rate that is still below average, but not nearly so far out of line. (Philadelphia data from author's interview with Patrick Kutzler, program analyst, Philadelphia Division of Children and Youth; data on child abuse reporting rates from American Humane Association, *Highlights of Official Child Neglect and Abuse Reporting,* 1986 (Denver:

1988), p. 10.

15. William Adams, Neil Barone, and Patrick Tooman, "The Dilemma of Anonymous Reporting in Child Protective Services," *Child Welfare,* 61, no. 1, January 1982, p. 12.

16. Author's interview with Delegate Vance Wilkins, sponsor of the Virginia law.

17. *Guidelines for a Model System* (see Note 11), p. 31.

18. Interview with the author.

19. See, for example, Joseph Goldstein, Anna Freud, and Albert J. Solnit, *Before the Best Interests of the Child* (New York: Free Press, 1979), pp. 75-85.

20. Wald's model would allow the use of the "preponderance of the evidence" standard under some circumstances. I disagree.

21. Interview with the author.

22. See for example Judge Grady's ruling in *B.H. v. Johnson* discussed in chap. 8, which concludes that some parts of the law are enforceable through lawsuits, while other parts, including the "reasonable efforts" requirement, are not.

23. The United States Supreme Court has ruled that "good faith" immunity protects "all but the plainly incompetent or those who knowingly violate the law," *Malley v. Briggs,* 106 S.Ct. at 1096 (1986), cited in *Czikalla v. Malloy* 649 F. Supp. 1212 (D. Colo, 1986). This is an especially difficult standard for plaintiffs to meet when suing child protective workers, since it is almost impossible to prove someone "knowingly" violated laws that are as vague and open to interpretation as child abuse statutes.

24. Quoted in Douglas Besharov, *The Vulnerable Social Worker: Liability for Serving Children and Families* (Silver Spring, Md.: National Association of Social Workers, 1985), p. 132.

25. Ibid., p. 159.

26. *Foster Care, Child Welfare and Adoption Reforms,* Joint Hearings before the Subcommittee on Public Assistance and Unemployment Compensation of the Committee on Ways and Means, and the Select Committee on Children, Youth, and Families, U.S. House of Representatives, transcript, p. 24.

27. All quotations in this section are from Joint Hearings (see Note 26), pp. 327-354.

28. Interview with the author.

Chapter 12: Update

1. Information concerning conditions in the Chicago shelters comes from the following sources: author's interview with Benjamin Wolf; Ray Long, "Officials to Inspect Center for Abused Kids," *Chicago Sun-Times,* March 25, 1994; "DCFS to Reveal Names of Children," United Press International, April 5, 1994; and the following stories from the *Chicago Tribune*: Rob Karwath, "Abused Kids Sleep in DCFS Offices," June 29, 1993; Ellen Warren, "Toddlers, Troubled Teens All Wait Together at DCFS," July 21, 1993, p. 1; Douglas Holt, "Boy Finds Gun at DCFS, Injured," Sept. 3, 1993, p. 1; Rob Karwath, "Child Welfare Specialist

Hired to Coordinate Overhaul of DCFS Site," Sept. 10, 1993; Rob Karwath, "DCFS Center Receives OK to House Kids," Dec. 17, 1993; Susan Kuczka, "DCFS Places 40 Local Kids All Over State," March 30, 1994.

2. Michele Ingrassia and John McCormick, "Why Leave Children With Bad Parents?" *Newsweek,* April 25, 1994, p. 53.

3. April 7, 1994, p. 1.

4. John R. Schuerman, et al., *Evaluation of the Illinois Family First Placement Prevention Program: Final Report* (Chicago: Chapin Hall Center for Children, June 1993).

5. Susan Chira, "A Defender of Chicago's Children Refuses to be Silent About Abuse," *The New York Times,* Jan. 30, 1994, Sec. 4, p. 7.

6. The group recently changed its name to National Committee to Prevent Child Abuse. To avoid confusion for readers coming to this volume for the first time, I have continued to use the former name in this chapter.

7. Connie Lauerman, "Designated Street Fighter," *Chicago Tribune Sunday Magazine,* June 5, 1988, p. 10.

8. Patrick Murphy, "Six Dead Children Should Mean Reform of Family First," *Chicago Tribune,* Oct. 13, 1993, p. 23.

9. Chira (see Note 5).

10. John McCormick, "A One-Man Children's Crusade," *Newsweek,* April 25, 1994, p. 56.

11. Patrick Murphy, "Family Preservation and its Victims," *The New York Times,* June 19, 1993, p. 21.

12. "Six Dead Children. . . ." (see Note 8).

13. Ingrassia and McCormick (see Note 2).

14. "Six Dead Children. . . ." (see Note 8).

15. Chira (see Note 5).

16. Interview with the author.

17. The "Keystone" case discussed later in this chapter.

18. Steve Rhodes, "Woman Wins Custody of Five Grandkids," *Chicago Tribune,* Feb. 16, 1994, Sec. 2, p. 5.

19. Interview with the author.

20. Interview with the author.

21. Editorial, "Find Common Ground On Family First," *Chicago Tribune,* Oct. 17, 1993, Sec. 4, p. 2.

22. "Family Preservation. . . ." (see Note 11).

23. Andrew Fegelman, "Ruling Kills Public Guardian Suit Against DCFS on Sexual Abuse," *Chicago Tribune,* Sept. 15, 1993, Sec. 2, p. 4. The lawsuit was dismissed on grounds that the issue already was covered by one of the many other suits against DCFS.

24. Susan Kuczka, "Sex Attacks By Wards of DCFS Climb," *Chicago Tribune,* April 22, 1994, Sec. 2, p. 2.

25. Howard Kurtz, *Media Circus: The Trouble With America's Newspapers* (New York: Times Books, 1993), p. 87.

26. Patrick Murphy, letter to former President George Bush Oct. 16, 1992.

27. Chira (see Note 5), and Ingrassia and McCormick (see Note 2).

28. Rob Karwath, "Murphy Accused of Abusive Words," *Chicago Tribune,* Oct. 13, 1993, p. 3.

29. Chira (see Note 5).

30. Howie Masters (producer), "Front Page Crusade," "Turning Point," ABC News, April 13, 1994.

31. Cameron McWhirter and Andrew Gottesman, "Amanda Wallace's Story: 'Good Luck to you, Mother,' " *Chicago Tribune,* May 9, 1993, Sec. 2, p. 1.

32. Ibid.

33. Julie Irwin and R. C. Longworth, "A Heritage of Tragedy," *Chicago Tribune,* Dec. 19, 1993, p. 1.

34. Editorial, "Take a Stand, Gov. Edgar," *Chicago Tribune,* April 28, 1993, p. 20.

35. See, for example, Rob Karwath, "DCFS Asked: What About Children's Rights," *Chicago Tribune,* April 25, 1993. Karwath writes: "Why does the agency seem biased toward the rights of the birth parents over the best interests of children? . . . [In part because] the law has said that courts should try to reunify families torn by abuse and neglect 'whenever possible.' " The quotation marks around "whenever possible" are unattributed, leaving the impression that this language comes from the statute itself.

36. "Reasonable efforts," Illinois Juvenile Court Act, Sec. 2-10 (2); "where appropriate," Illinois Juvenile Court Act, Sec. 2-14 (a).

37. Mike Royko, "DCFS' Reasoning is Truly Torture," *Chicago Tribune,* April 14, 1994, p. 3.

38. Interview with the author.

39. Andrew Gottesman and Cameron McWhirter, "In The End, Everyone Failed Joseph," *Chicago Tribune,* April 20, 1993, p. 1; Andrew Herrmann, "Murphy Blames DCFS Worker in Boy's Death," *Chicago Sun-Times,* April 21, 1993, p. 4.

40. *Report of Public Guardian Patrick T. Murphy on the Death of Joseph Wallace,* April 29, 1993.

41. Cameron McWhirter and Andrew Gottesman, "A Call for Children's Rights," *Chicago Tribune,* April 30, 1993, p. 1.

42. Editorial, "What Went Wrong in the Courtroom," *Chicago Tribune,* May 2, 1993, Sec. 4, p. 2.

43. Letter from Patrick Murphy to John J. Casey, Joel J. Bellows and Roy E. Hofer, June 3, 1993, p. 1. Casey, Bellows and Hofer were the lawyers appointed by Comerford to investigate the handling of the Wallace case.

44. Joel J. Bellows, John J. Casey, and Roy E. Hofer, *The Report of the Independent Committee to Inquire into the Practices, Processes, and Proceedings in the Juvenile Court as they Relate to the Joseph Wallace Cases,* Oct. 1, 1993.

45. Cameron McWhirter and Andrew Gottesman, "Comerford Clears Four Judges in Joseph's Slaying," *Chicago Tribune,* Oct. 28, 1993, p. 1.

46. Editorial, "The System is The Scapegoat," *Chicago Tribune,* Oct. 29, 1993, p. 20.

47. Steve Johnson, "Tribune Series Wins Top RFK Honors," *Chicago Tribune,*

April 25, 1994, p. 4.

48. Editorial, "Time to Bring Back the Orphanage?" *Chicago Tribune,* July 31, 1993, p. 18.

49. Rob Karwath, "DCFS On Way to Heartbreaking Record," *Chicago Tribune,* June 8, 1994, p. 1.

50. Ibid. The estimates are projections for the twelve-month period based on eleven months of data.

51. Jeanine Smith, *Norman v. Ryder Fifth Monitoring Report,* Dec. 31, 1993, p. 7; Joseph Schneider, *B. H. v. Ryder Monitor's Report* from January 1, 1993, to December 31, 1993, p. 16.

52. Author's canvass of child protective service agencies serving New York City; Los Angeles and San Diego, California; Chicago, Illinois; Philadelphia, Pennsylvania; Detroit, Michigan; Phoenix, Arizona; and Dallas, Houston, and San Antonio, Texas.

53. Ray Long, "Groups Urge Private Care for Abused Kids," *Chicago Sun-Times,* Feb. 18, 1994, p. 20.

54. Rob Karwath, Louise Kiernan, and John W. Fountain, "In Search of Remedies: Each Call May Be A Child's Last Hope," *Chicago Tribune,* March 6, 1994, p. 1.

55. "What Went Wrong. . . ." (see Note 42).

56. Ingrassia and McCormick (see Note 2), p. 58.

57. Bellows (See note 44), pp. 2-3.

58. Interview with the author.

59. Andrew Gottesman, "System Overload: Juvenile Court Can Rarely Spare the Time to Care," *Chicago Tribune,* Dec. 21, 1993, p. 1; and "Two Cities Can Teach Chicago Juvenile Court Lessons," *Chicago Tribune,* Dec. 22, 1993, p. 1.

60. Rob Karwath, Louise Kiernan, and John W. Fountain, "Fixing DCFS Mess Begins With Basic Steps," *Chicago Tribune,* March 11, 1994, p. 1.

61. One child of another relative may have been abused.

62. "Family Preservation an Alternative to Foster Care that Puts Parents on the Right Path," *The Miami Herald,* March 26, 1990, reprint.

63. Mary Schmich, "Poverty's On Trial and it's Guilty as Sin," *Chicago Tribune,* April 22, 1994, Sec. 2, p. 1.

64. Editorial, "Sorting Out the Keystone Saga," *Chicago Tribune,* April 25, 1994, p. 14.

65. "Fixing DCFS. . . ." (see Note 60).

66. Masters (see Note 30).

67. All excerpts are from Ingrassia and McCormick (see Note 2).

68. The excerpts that follow are from Patricia Edmonds, "One Million Young Victims and Counting" and "Young and in Danger: Why Kids Get Sent Back to Abusive Homes," *USA Today,* April 7, 1994, pp. 1, 2.

69. Clint Williams and Norm Parish, "Few Grown-ups Wanted to Bother With China Marie Davis," *The Arizona Republic,* April 9, 1994, p. 1. Although this story ran after the five-day period referenced in *USA Today,* the Davis case was discussed in at least one article published during that period.

70. Ben Winton, "Files Hint of Cover-Up in Foster Child's Death," *The Phoenix Gazette,* March 30, 1994, p. 1.

71. "Foster Mother Gets 5½ Years in Death," *Chicago Tribune,* March 31, 1994, p. 3.

72. Jeanine L. English and Michael R. Tritz, "In Support of the Family: Family Preservation as an Alternative to Foster Care," *Stanford Law & Policy Review,* Winter 1992-93, p. 184. See also, Little Hoover Commission, *Mending Our Broken Children: Restructuring Foster Care in California,* April 1992, p. 73.

73. Little Hoover Commission (see Note 72), pp. 72-73.

74. Sheryl Stolberg, "State May Seize County's Abused Children Agency," *Los Angeles Times,* July 2, 1990, p. 1.

75. Mary I. Benedict and Susan Zuravin, *Factors Associated With Child Maltreatment By Family Foster Care Providers* (Baltimore: Johns Hopkins University School of Hygiene and Public Health, June 30, 1992), charts, pp. 28, 30.

76. David Fanshel et al., *Foster Children in a Life Course Perspective* (New York: Columbia University Press, 1990).

77. Marc Katz, "New Legislation Pours $1 Billion into Family Preservation," *Youth Law News* 14, no. 5 (September-October 1993), p. 8. The definition of "family support services" is: "Community-based services to promote well-being of children and families designed to increase the strength and stability of families (including adoptive, foster, and extended families), to increase parents' confidence and competence in their parenting abilities, to afford children a stable and supportive family environment, and to otherwise enhance child development."

78. Martha Matthews, "HHS Issues Family Preservation & Support Program Instruction," *Youth Law News* 15, no. 2 (March-April 1994), p. 3.

79. Mary-Lou Weisman, "When Parents Are Not in the Best Interests of the Child," *The Atlantic Monthly,* July 1994, p. 60.

80. Ibid, p. 62.

81. Affidavit of Barbara Winter, M.S.W., C.S.W., *Hauser v. Grinker,* Supreme Court, State of New York, Index No. 16409/89, June 6, 1990, p. 20.

82. Carol Berquist, Debra Szwejda, Gavin Pope, *Evaluation of Michigan's Families First Program* (Lansing, Mich.: University Associates, March 1993).

83. Chart with memo from Gerald H. Miller, director, Michigan Department of Social Services, May 23, 1994.

84. Author's interview with Susan Kelly, director of family preservation services, Michigan Dept. of Social Services.

85. One case came to light through a news account. A foster mother with a long record of alleged abuse adopted three of the foster children in her care and allegedly killed one of them. Jack Kresnak, "A History of Abuse Ends With Child Dead," *Detroit Free Press,* Oct. 23, 1993, p. 3.

86. Mark W. Fraser, Peter J. Pecora, and David A. Haapala, *Families in Crisis: The Impact of Intensive Family Preservation Services* (New York: Aldine De Gruyter, 1991), p. 168.

87. Ivor D. Groves, *R.C. v. Hornsby Consent Decree: Performance and Outcome Review,* Jan. 31, 1994.

88. Jim Okerblom and John Wilkens, "Kids Taken From Grandparents on Unchecked, Dubious Cult Claim," *The San Diego Union,* Nov. 8, 1991, p. 1.

89. Now the *Union-Tribune.*

90. Jim Okerblom, "Children Lose Out in Zeal to Protect," *The San Diego Union,* Jan. 10, 1992, p. 1.

91. "Kids Taken. . . ." (see Note 88).

92. Ibid.

93. Alexander Cockburn, "Janet Reno's Coerced Confession," *The Nation,* March 8, 1993, p. 297.

94. Interview with the author.

95. Interview with the author.

96. The family's last name often has appeared in news accounts. I am not using it because a book is a more permanent record, and the family eventually may want to reclaim their privacy.

97. Information about Alicia's case comes from, San Diego County Grand Jury, Report No. 6, *The Case of Alicia W.,* June 23, 1992; San Diego County Grand Jury, Report No. 8, *Child Sexual Abuse, Assault, and Molest Issues,* June 29, 1992; Jim Okerblom and John Wilkens, "Tragedy, Errors Shatter A Family," and "Would A Call to 911 Have Avoided the Nightmare?" *The San Diego Union,* Oct. 20, 1991, pp. 1, 12.

98. Interview with the author.

99. Rex Dalton, "Critics Say Crusader Sees Abuse Where There Isn't Any," *The San Diego Union,* Dec. 11, 1991, p. 1.

100. San Diego County Grand Jury, Report No. 2, *Families in Crisis,* February 6, 1992.

101. San Diego County Grand Jury, Report No. 13, *Protect the Child, Preserve the Family,* June 29, 1993, p. 1. All reports are available at no charge from the Grand Jury office, 1420 Kettner Blvd., Suite 310, San Diego, Calif., 92101-2432.

102. Ibid., p. 11

103. Jim Okerblom and Mark Sauer, "Tales of Terror at Church Nursery Raise Urgent, Troubling Questions," "Detective, Prosecutor Had Doubts About Case," and "Do Therapists Plant Memories of Abuse?" *The San Diego Union-Tribune,* Dec. 27, 1992, pp. 1, 11.

104. Laura Shapiro, "Rush to Judgment" *Newsweek,* April 19, 1993, p. 54.

105. Stephanie Coontz, "It's Hardly as Simple as Two-Parent Families," Albany, N.Y., *Times Union,* May 16, 1993, p. E1.

106. Mark Robert Rank, "AFDC Is No Breeding Factory," *New York Newsday,* April 5, 1994, p. 32.

107. Mark Greenberg, Executive Summary, *Beyond Stereotypes: What State AFDC Studies on Length of Stay Tell Us About Welfare as a "Way of Life"* (Washington DC: Center for Law and Social Policy, 1993), reprinted in *Youth Law News* 14, no. 5 (September-October 1993), pp. 15-18.

108. Charles Murray, "The Coming White Underclass," *The Wall Street Journal,* Oct. 29, 1993, p. 14.

109. Michael Massing, "The Welfare Blues," *New York Review of Books,*

March 24, 1994, p. 48.

110. E.g., "NBC Nightly News" ("America Close-Up" report), Feb. 14, 1994; "Society's Orphans," Fortune Aug. 10, 1992, pp. 70-76; Weisman (see Note 80).

111. Murray (See Note 108); *USA Today*: editorial, "Protect Abused Kids First," April 7, 1994, p. 12; *Washington Post*: "As At-Risk Children Overwhelm Foster Care, Illinois Considers Orphanages," March 1, 1994, p. 9; *Fortune* (see Note 110), p. 71. Gannett News Service: "Boys Town Head: Nationwide Orphanage System Might Work," April 14, 1994; *Atlantic Monthly*: Weisman (see Note 80), p. 43; *Phoenix Gazette*: "Foster Care Problems Raising New Interest in Orphanages," April 8, 1994, p. 1; "One commentator . . ." Abigail McCarthy, "Orphans Need Homes," *Commonweal*, Jan. 26, 1990, p. 38. McCarthy writes: "Some orphanages were huge, cold institutions, improperly staffed by inadequate personnel. But even those were hardly the Dickensian horrors of our imagination."

112. *Washington Post* (see Note 111).

113. Laurie Goering, "Orphanages: Has Their Time Come Again?" *Chicago Tribune*, Feb. 10, 1994, p. 1.

114. Ibid.

115. Maudlyne Ihejirika and Ray Long, "Group Home Faces Evaluation," *Chicago Sun-Times*, Jan. 8, 1994, p. 6.

116. "Murphy Sues DCFS Over Shelter Home," *Chicago Tribune*, Aug. 4, 1993, p. 3.

117. "Fixing DCFS" (see Note 60).

118. Kent Kimes, "Hampton Boys Home 'Going on' After Allegations Against a Founder," *Atlanta Journal/Constitution* March 3, 1994, p. H7.

119. "Hard Labor Reported at Children's Home," Associated Press account in *New Orleans Times-Picayune*, Jan. 6, 1990.

120. Martha Shirk, "As Troubles Come to Light, Home Surrenders License," *St. Louis Post-Dispatch*, Oct. 3, 1993, p. 1.

121. Peg Tyre, "Violent Lives at the Crossroads," *New York Newsday*, Jan. 29, 1992, p. 8.

122. Nina Bernstein, "Probe of Foster Care Nightmares," *New York Newsday*, May 2, 1990, p. 16.

123. Michael Powell, "Violence Rife at Two Homes for Troubled Teens," *New York Newsday*, Nov. 14, 1990, p. 6.

124. Leah Eskin, "Bid to Revive Orphanages is Gaining Ground," *Chicago Tribune*, Oct. 6, 1991, Sec. 2, p. 1.

125. "Ex-Mooseheart Staffer Guilty of Molesting Boys," *Chicago Tribune*, Nov. 5, 1993, Sec. 2, p. 7; Linda Young, "Mooseheart Aches After Sex Abuses," *Chicago Tribune*, Feb. 8, 1994, p. 1.

126. Bob Greene, "Time to Think Hard About Orphanage," *Chicago Tribune*, Feb. 14, 1994, Sec. 5, p. 1.

127. Gannett News Service (see Note 111).

128. Martha Shirk, "Orphanages Won't Solve Foster Care Woes, State Official Believes," *St. Louis Post-Dispatch*, June 4, 1990, p. B1.

129. Rob Karwath, "DCFS Hit on Family Separation," *Chicago Tribune*, Jan.

19, 1990, Sec. 2, p. 2.

130. Smith (see Note 51).

131. Tino Ramirez, "In Hawaii, Healthy Start for At-Risk Infants," *USA Today,* April 11, 1994, p. 3.

132. U.S. House of Representatives, Committee on Ways and Means, *1993 Green Book,* July 7, 1993, chart, p. 945. These data are only for foster children whose foster care placement is aided with federal funds, about half the total foster care population. The only data for the entire population are the data cited in Chapter 8 that are now a decade old.

133. Karen McCurdy, Deborah Daro, *Current Trends in Child Abuse Reporting and Fatalities: The Results of the 1993 Annual 50 State Survey* (Chicago: National Committee to Prevent Child Abuse, April 1994,) and the same document for NCPCA's 1992 survey.

134. National Committee to Prevent *Child Abuse, Child Abuse Rates Remain High,* Press Release, April 7, 1994.

135. Anastasia Toufexis, "Damned Lies and Statistics," *Time,* April 26, 1993.

136. "One Million Young Victims. . . ." (see Note 68).

137. United States Court of Appeals for the Second Circuit, *Decision,* Anna Valmonte v. Mary Jo Bane, Docket No. 93-7183, March 3, 1994, pp. 2242, 2244.

138. William Feldman, et al., "Is Childhood Sexual Abuse Really Increasing in Prevalence? An Analysis of the Evidence," *Pediatrics* 88, no. 1 (July 1991), pp. 29-33.

139. Information about the Seay case is from Gary Karasik, "The Abusers," *Miami Herald Tropic Magazine,* June 16, 1991; Jim Schoettler, "Raccoon's Tale Not Over Yet," *Florida Times-Union,* Nov. 14, 1990.

140. Associated Press, "Nursing Mother Who Lost Custody of Child Vows to Sue," Jan. 17, 1992.

141. NBC News, *A Closer Look,* March 3, 1992.

142. State of Florida, Study Commission on Child Welfare, *A Survey of Florida's Child Protective Investigators,* April, 1991, pp. 10, 28.

143. Office of the Legislative Analyst, *Child Abuse and Neglect in California: A Review of the Child Welfare Services Program,* Jan. 1991, p. 36, cited in Little Hoover Commission (see Note 72), p. 28.

144. Council of Judges Policy Advisory Group on Foster Care, *A Study of the Foster Care System in El Paso County, Texas, February 1989-November 1991,* p. 19.

145. Amy Pagnozzi, "HRA Insider: I Took Kids From Parents For No Good Reason," *New York Post,* Feb. 4, 1991, p. 7.

146. Elena Neuman, "Child Welfare or Family Trauma?" *Insight,* May 9, 1994, p. 6.

147. Information concerning the Beck case is from: Second Amended Verified Complaint, Affidavit of David A. Beck and Affidavit of Jennifer Beck, *Beck v. County of Westchester,* No. 89 Civ. 1131, United States District Court, Southern District of New York; author's interview with Nelson Farber.

148. Daniel Goleman, "Miscoding is Seen as the Root of False Memories,"

The New York Times, May 31, 1994, p. C1.

149. Mark Sauer and Jim Okerblom, "Trial By Therapy," *National Review,* Sept. 6, 1993, p. 34.

150. Ibid., p. 39. Summit now says that "with ten years of intense scrutiny without material evidence, the first alarms must yield to greater caution. At the same time, the glib presumption that all such reports are [caused by therapy] is even further from observable fact."

151. "Tales of Terror . . ." (see Note 103); Theresa Conroy, "The Devil in Bucks County," *Philadelphia,* April 1991, p. 136-137.

152. Debra Hale, "A Not-so-Childish Prank," Associated Press story appearing in *The Boston Globe,* May 18, 1994.

153. Anthony M. DeStafano, "Kids Who Lie," *New York Newsday,* May 25, 1994, p. 5. That figure appears to have remained constant at least through the end of 1993. According to *The New York Teacher* (Feb. 21, 1994) out of 549 allegations from 1991 through 1993, 99 were substantiated.

154. "Sex Abuse Prevention Panelist Counsels Calm," *The New York Teacher,* Feb. 21, 1994, p. 7A.

155. Now Anne Cohn Donnelly, again I am using her former name to avoid confusion.

156. Amanda Vogt, "Can You Believe These Kids?" *Chicago Tribune,* May 24, 1994, sec. 7, p. 3.

157. Miriam Horn, "Memories Lost And Found," *U.S. News and World Report,* Nov. 29, 1993, p. 54.

158. Cited in Carol Tavris, "Beware the Incest Survivor Syndrome," *The New York Times Book Review,* Jan. 3, 1993, p. 1.

159. Ibid., p. 16.

160. Ibid., p. 17.

161. Ibid.

162. Goleman (see Note 148).

163. Ibid.

164. Interview with the author.

165. Leon Jaroff, "Lies of the Mind," *Time,* Nov. 29, 1993, p. 59.

166. *NCPCA Fact Sheet: Handling Child Sexual Abuse Cases* (Chicago: National Committee for Prevention of Child Abuse, November 1986), p. 2.

167. Jane Gross, "Suit Asks, Does 'Memory Therapy' Heal or Harm?" *The New York Times,* April 8, 1994, p. 1.

168. Bettijane Levine, "The Forbidden Touch," *Los Angeles Times,* Nov. 18, 1993, p. E1.

169. "Sex Abuse Prevention Panelist . . ." (See note 154).

170. 112 S.Ct. 1360, 1992.

171. Martha Matthews, "Litigation Strategies in the Wake of *Artist M.,*" *Youth Law News* 13, no. 3 (May-June 1992), p. 8.

172. Author's interview with Martha Matthews, Staff Attorney, National Center for Youth Law.

173. Interview with the author.

174. Matthews (see Note 171).

175. Interview with the author.

176. Information concerning Murphy's handling of Artist M. from author's interviews with Marcia Robinson Lowry, Martha Matthews, Diane Redleaf, Robert Schwartz, Benjamin Wolf.

177. Interview with the author.

178. Interview with the author.

179. Paul D'Ambrosio, "DYFS Faulted in 'System Abuse,' " *Asbury Park Press,* Jan. 5, 1992, p. 1.

180. Alice Bussiere, " 'Baby Jessica' Case Highlights Old Conflict: Parents' Rights vs. Permanence for Children," *Youth Law News* 14, no. 4 (July-August 1993), p. 15.

181. Olya Thompson, "Motherhood Myopia: Blowing the DeBoer Story" *New York Newsday,* Aug. 11, 1993, p. 85.

182. Elizabeth Bartholet, "Blood Parents vs. Real Parents," *The New York Times,* July 13, 1993, p. 19.

183. Michele Ingrassia and Karen Springen, "She's Not Baby Jessica Anymore," *Newsweek,* March 21, 1994, p. 64.

184. Ibid. See also, "Baby Anna," "Prime Time Live," March 12, 1994.

185. Thompson (see Note 181).

Epilogue

1. Information for this account is from Kent Pollock, "The Child Protectors: Flawed Guardian of Young," *Sacramento Bee,* Aug. 4, 1986, 1.

2. Information concerning the Salem trials is from Marion Starkey, *The Devil in Massachusetts* (New York: Anchor Books, 1969).

3. *Foster Care, Child Welfare and Adoption Reforms,* Joint Hearings before the Subcommittee on Public Assistance and Unemployment Compensation of the Committee on Ways and Means, and the Select Committee on Children, Youth, and Families, U.S. House of Representatives, transcript, p. 21.

Index